ORCHESTRATING THE INSTRUMENTS OF POWER

Orchestrating the Instruments of Power

A Critical Examination of the U.S. National Security System

D. ROBERT WORLEY

POTOMAC BOOKS
An imprint of the University of Nebraska Press

Library of Congress Cataloging-in-Publication Data
Worley, D. Robert (Duane Robert), 1949–
Orchestrating the instruments of power: a critical
examination of the U.S. national security system /
D. Robert Worley.
pages   cm
Includes bibliographical references and index.
ISBN 978-1-61234-720-2 (paperback: alk. paper)
ISBN 978-1-61234-752-3 (epub)
ISBN 978-1-61234-753-0 (mobi)
ISBN 978-1-61234-754-7 (pdf)
1. National security—United States.   2. Strategic
planning—United States.   3. Strategic forces—
United States.   4. United States—Defenses.
5. United States—Military policy.   6. United
States—Strategic aspects.   I. Title.
UA23.W7766 2015
355'.033073—dc23   2015001108

Set in Minion by Westchester Book Group.

To Andrew J. Goodpaster
and Brent Scowcroft

CONTENTS

List of Illustrations   ix

List of Abbreviations   xi

Preface   xv

Acknowledgments   xvii

Introduction   xix

PART 1. FOUNDATIONAL CONCEPTS AND PRINCIPLES

1. A Primer on Security Concepts   3

2. War and American Democracy   31

3. War Powers   58

PART 2. NATIONAL SECURITY STRATEGIES

4. Grand Strategy   89

5. Cold War Strategies   109

6. Post–Cold War Strategies   178

PART 3. NATIONAL SECURITY APPARATUS

7. Instruments of Power   225

8. Mechanisms of Power   245

9. National Security Council   296

PART 4. NATIONAL SECURITY REFORM

10. Major Reform Proposals   327

11. Strategy First   363

Notes   373

Bibliography   391

Index   405

ILLUSTRATIONS

1. Political orientation   41

2. Movement on the political spectra   42

3. The myth of a polarized electorate   55

4. Nominal cabinet department management hierarchy   247

5. Department of State organization   258

6. Pre–World War II national security organizational relationships   267

7. Defense Department organization   268

8. Military departments   269

9. Office of the Secretary of Defense   270

10. Joint Chiefs of Staff and Joint Staff   275

11. Notional National Security Council system organization   306

12. NSC staff organization 2000   312

13. Departmental hierarchy versus mission management   346

ABBREVIATIONS

ACDA	Arms Control and Disarmament Agency
AFRICOM	U.S. Africa Command
AIDS	acquired immune deficiency syndrome
AOR	area of responsibility
AQAM	al-Qaeda and Associated Movements
ARVN	Army of the Republic of Viet Nam
ASD	assistant secretary of defense
ATF	Bureau of Alcohol, Tobacco, Firearms, and Explosives
BCE	before common era
BRIC	Brazil, Russia, India, China
CENTCOM	U.S. Central Command
CENTO	Central Treaty Organization
CJCS	Chairman, Joint Chiefs of Staff
CNA	Center for Naval Analyses
CONUS	continental United States
CRS	Congressional Research Service
CRS	Coordinator for Reconstruction and Stabilization
CSIS	Center for Strategic and International Studies
DAE	Defense Acquisition Executive
DCI	Director of Central Intelligence
DEA	Drug Enforcement Administration
DEPORD	deployment order
DHS	Department of Homeland Security
DIA	Defense Intelligence Agency
DIME	diplomatic, informational, military, economic
DINO	Democrat in name only
DOD	Department of Defense
DPG	Defense Planning Guidance
DSAA	Defense Security Assistance Agency

DSCA	Defense Security Cooperation Agency
DTRA	Defense Threat Reduction Agency
EUCOM	U.S. European Command
FAA	Federal Aviation Administration
FNLA	National Liberation Front of Angola
FFRDC	Federally Funded Research and Development Center
FINCEN	Financial Crimes Enforcement Network
FRY	Federal Republic of Yugoslavia
GDP	gross domestic product
GEOINT	geospatial intelligence
GPO	Government Printing Office
HIC	high-intensity conflict
HIV	human immunodeficiency virus
HSC	Homeland Security Council
HUMINT	human intelligence
IC	Intelligence Community
ICA	International Communications Agency
IDF	Israel Defense Forces
IMINT	image intelligence
IPA	Intergovernmental Personnel Act
JCS	Joint Chiefs of Staff
JFCOM	U.S. Joint Forces Command
JSCP	joint strategic capabilities plan
LIC	low-intensity conflict
MASINT	measurement and signature intelligence
METO	Middle East Treaty Organization
MIC	mid-intensity conflict
MIDLIFE	military, informational, diplomatic, law enforcement, intelligence, financial, economic
MPLA	Popular Movement for the Liberation of Angola
NATO	North Atlantic Treaty Organization
NCTC	National Counterterrorism Center
NEC	National Economic Council
NGA	National Geospatial-Intelligence Agency
NIC	National Intelligence Council
NIE	national intelligence estimate
NIMA	National Imaging and Mapping Agency
NIO	national intelligence officer
NLF	National Liberation Front
NOC	non-official cover

NORAD	North American Aerospace Defense Command
NORTHCOM	U.S. Northern Command
NPIC	National Photographic Interpretation Center
NRO	National Reconnaissance Office
NSC	national security council policy paper
NSC	National Security Council
NSDD	national security decision directive
NSPG	National Security Planning Guidance
NSR	national security review
NSSG	National Security Study Group
NVA	North Vietnamese Army
OPLAN	operational plan
OPORD	operational order
OSD	Office of the Secretary of Defense
PACOM	U.S. Pacific Command
PDD	presidential decision directive
PLO	Palestinian Liberation Organization
PNSR	Project on National Security Reform
PRC	Peoples Republic of China (Mainland)
PRT	provincial reconstruction team
QDDR	Quadrennial Diplomacy and Development Review
RINO	Republican in name only
RMA	revolution in military affairs
ROC	Republic of China (Taiwan)
SACEUR	NATO Supreme Allied Commander, Europe
SAD	Special Activities Division
SAE	Service Acquisition Executive
SALT	strategic arms limitations talks
SEATO	South East Asia Treaty Organization
SIGINT	signals intelligence
SIOP	single integrated operational plan
SOCOM	U.S. Special Operations Command
SOUTHCOM	U.S. Southern Command
SO/LIC	special operations and low-intensity conflict
SPACECOM	U.S. Space Command
STRATCOM	U.S. Strategic Command
TRANSCOM	U.S. Transportation Command
UCP	unified command plan
UNITA	National Union for the Total Independence of Angola
USAID	United States Agency for International Development

USD	under secretary of defense
USIA	United States Information Agency
VC	Viet Cong
VOA	Voice of America
WMD	weapons of mass destruction
WPR	War Powers Resolution

PREFACE

National security is a topic discussed by a small number of insiders and specialists, many of whom believe that the necessary specialized knowledge puts the topic beyond the reach of the general public. I think they're wrong. The goal of this book is to reach a wider public audience, to prepare them to participate in an informed debate, and to help them understand what they are choosing when they vote for representatives, senators, and presidents. An informed electorate is required for democracy to succeed.

Some very serious and thorough studies have been conducted by national security professionals since the end of the Cold War. There appears to be a consensus that the U.S. national security system, designed after World War II and that served during the Cold War, is inadequate for the needs of the twenty-first century. There is even a broad consensus on many of the reforms needed.

But meaningful reform of the national security system must be conducted amid a great deal of instability. Following four decades of relative stability in a national security strategy to counter the Soviet Union and the spread of Communism, there is nothing approaching a consensus on U.S. national security strategy or the U.S. role on the world stage today. We still refer to the present as the post–Cold War era or post-9/11 era, naming the present for what it isn't rather than what it is. There is instability on the very meaning of national security and what constitutes a national security issue. And finally, there is a great deal of partisan instability, and it will take bipartisan agreement to undertake meaningful reforms.

No attempt is made to tell readers what conclusions to draw. Presentation of competing schools of thought is prominent throughout. Nor is there any attempt to be creative. The attempt is to collect and communicate an existing body of knowledge to the interested reader. To that end, this book is a collection and synthesis of knowledge from those who have passed the scholarly test, including research and analysis, submission of work to peer review, and surviving the test of time. From that very large pool of knowledge, representative work was chosen primarily because it was useful for the reader.

Orchestrating the Instruments of Power grew from the need to engage graduate students at Johns Hopkins University on the issues of national security in the twenty-first century, and portions have been used at the National Defense University, where uniformed military and civil servants come to study. Until recently national security was seen largely as a military problem with a military solution. But assuring national security, and international security, today requires orchestration of all instruments of national power and not just the percussion provided by the military instrument.

The book is suited to that portion of the general public with an interest in how government provides for the common defense. It is equally suited to graduate students seeking a foundation upon which to conduct research and those looking for thesis topics. A book previously written on military transformation for a defense policy course, *Shaping U.S. Military Forces*, found utility with senior military and civilian officials in the Defense Department who wanted a better understanding of the defense establishment beyond their own service or office. Similarly, this book may be of use to the broader community spanning the State Department, Defense Department, and Intelligence Community who want a broader understanding of the national security system beyond their own department or agency. No prerequisite knowledge is assumed in the field of national security, international relations, or the military arts and sciences; only a keen interest in American national security is required.

A great deal of supplementary material is provided at www.orchstrat ingpower.org, including text boxes providing additional detail from earlier versions of the book as well as hard-to-find official policy statements.

Experts will certainly find errors both of omission and commission for which I am alone responsible. Reports of errors, small or large, will be received appreciatively at drworley@jhu.edu.

D. Robert Worley

ACKNOWLEDGMENTS

The Johns Hopkins University Center for Advanced Governmental Studies has contributed richly to this work. Special thanks are owed to my students who have been exposed to various versions of the text. Many are young congressional staffers working long hours for modest pay. Many come from the executive branch departments of State, Defense, and Justice. Some come from across the Intelligence Community. A few are journalists. All somehow find the time and energy for graduate study to improve their ability to serve the nation. All have taught me something about the workings, good and bad, of our government.

The Project on National Security Reform provided a valuable opportunity. The many meetings brought together working practitioners who experienced firsthand the difficulties of implementing U.S. policies in Iraq, Afghanistan, the Horn of Africa, and in Washington. My thanks to Jim Locher, president and CEO of the Project, and to all those who came together to solve problems.

In the midst of hyperpartisanship, the Congressional Research Service somehow continues to do quality research and analysis. My respect to Louis Fisher and his associates for their work on presidential war power and to Richard Best for his work on the National Security Council.

Special appreciation is owed to the IBM Center for the Business of Government for its generous grant that produced the material on the National Security Council.

I also want to acknowledge a handful of currently serving national security professionals who offered encouragement late in the process when a morale boost was needed. From the Mission Command Battle Lab at Fort Leavenworth, Kansas, are Richard Pedersen and Thomas Bryant;

from the Joint Special Operations University at Tampa, Florida, William Knarr; John Hanley from the Office of the Director of National Intelligence; and from the National Defense University in Washington DC, Michael Mazarr, professor at the National War College, and Frank Hoffman, director of NDU Press.

INTRODUCTION

There is increasing evidence that the U.S. national security apparatus, designed for a decades-long great-power conflict, is ill-suited to the needs of the twenty-first century and that the burden has largely fallen to a military designed for other purposes. Military forces for the Cold War were designed to deter, and if necessary defeat, the military forces of an opposing great-power alliance. Rather than the clash of titans—the militaries of major-power alliances colliding on the field of battle—today's forces are tasked to conduct what the Bush administration called capacity building, the Clinton administration called nation building, the British called operations in support of civil authorities, and the Marine Corps called small wars. This class of intervention requires a deft employment of all instruments of power, not the military instrument in isolation.

Prior to World War II, the Department of War and the Department of the Navy were distinct institutions in parallel with the Department of State. To execute the constitutional responsibilities to conduct foreign affairs, the president, through the State and Navy Departments, could employ gunboats and marines for operations below the threshold of declared war—coercive diplomacy and small wars. The War Department stood by with plans to mobilize for war, to raise an army, should Congress declare war.

Today's national security apparatus is defined in the National Security Act of 1947. The act was the product of an extensive examination of shortcomings identified in World War II—a war between great-power alliances. The Navy and War Departments were unified under the new Defense Department. Amendments to the act were made throughout the Cold War—another conflict between great-power alliances. At the end of the

Cold War great-power competition, there is little reason to believe that the security system is aligned with the needs of the twenty-first century.

An era of great-power conflict ended when the Berlin Wall came down, but great-power conflict will come again. A period between major wars—wars between major powers—is an interwar period. Interwar periods are not peaceful, but they are not characterized by wars between major powers; they are characterized by conflict between major and small powers—small wars.

Official Washington failed to recognize the change in the geostrategic environment for what it was, the end of a period of great-power conflict and the beginning of an ugly interwar period. Instead, the system designed for great-power conflict replaced the Soviet Union with China as the threat and continued churning unabated. But commanders in the field immediately were drawn into small wars with a military force ill-suited to the task. More important than the military force structure, major-war thinking was imposed onto small-war problems with less than optimal results.

The evidence piled up. Studies from inside the Washington Beltway and beyond drew the same conclusions. Political scientists and practitioners have a name for the condition when disparate interests from within and without government come to the same conclusion at the same time—policy ripeness. The time is ripe to reconsider the design of the country's national security system.

What is the nature of the geostrategic environment, not just the terrorist threat? What strategy best assures the nation's security in that environment? What instruments of power must be brought to bear? Which agencies of government house those instruments? Are the capabilities resident in government sufficient in mix and scale? And are we able to orchestrate the instruments of power to assure our nation's security? Formulating national security strategy is the process of answering these questions.

Instability in Organizing Principle

The difference between major wars and small wars is not measured by the number of forces committed, the number of casualties, or the war's duration. The Marine Corps' *Small Wars Manual* of 1940 provides a definition:

Small wars are operations undertaken under executive authority, wherein military force is combined with diplomatic pressure in the internal or external affairs of another state whose government is unstable, inadequate, or unsatisfactory for the preservation of life and of such interests as are determined by the foreign policy of our Nation.[1]

The manual further identifies characteristic differences between major wars and small wars:

Major wars are conducted between "first rate" powers. Small wars are the interventions of a major power into the affairs of a lesser power, typically failed or failing states.

"In a major war, diplomatic relations are summarily severed at the beginning of the struggle. [In small wars,] diplomacy does not relax its grip on the situation."

"In a major war, the mission assigned to the armed forces is usually unequivocal—the defeat and destruction of the hostile forces." "The motive in small wars is not material destruction. It is usually a project dealing with the social, economic, and political development of the people." "[In small wars] the mission will be to establish and maintain law and order by supporting or replacing civil government."

In major wars, the organized forces of peer states seek decisive battle. In small wars, the forces of a major power often clash with irregular forces, and the conflict typically degenerates into guerrilla warfare. "Irregular troops may disregard, in part or entirely, International Law and the Rules of Land Warfare in their conduct of hostilities."

"In major warfare, hatred of the enemy is developed among troops to arouse courage. In small wars, tolerance, sympathy, and kindness should be the keynote of our relationship with the mass of the population."[2]

Neither of these conceptions is an exact fit to the current conflict environment, but a small-wars conception is a far better starting point for discussion. An orientation on major war accommodates, and even encourages, a military instrument isolated from the other instruments of power. An orientation on small wars demands the orchestration of all instruments of national power. But who shall orchestrate?

The shift from major war to small wars did, in fact, take place, but it may not survive. A shift may be taking place from small wars interventionism to seeking economic advantage, a shift from employing military power to building economic power.

Instability in Grand Strategy

Throughout the Cold War, the national security strategy of the United States was associated with the word *containment*. And for four decades a political consensus held to maintain a standing army for the only time in American history. War plans for major war in Europe, Korea, the Pacific, and the Atlantic, and plans for strategic nuclear warfare, drove military force structure design—what professionals call *force development policy.*

The East-West debate—the ideological struggle between the East and West—dominated while the North-South debate—the gap between the haves and the have-nots—was submerged. Conflicts in the Third World were assumed to be *lesser included cases*, that is, a military force designed for major war is capable of prosecuting small wars. A demonstrably false assumption, lesser-included-case thinking allowed force developers— primarily the uniformed services—to concentrate their efforts on the less likely but more dangerous threats to America's vital interests, indeed, its survival.

Since the Cold War ended, presidents have pursued radically different strategies. But their use of force has been consistently high despite the fact that their guiding strategies and reasons for using military force have differed greatly. All made heavy use of force without replenishment, leaving a heavy bill to be paid in the future. There is no reason to believe that strategic stability is on the horizon.

Nothing has replaced the strategy of containment and the political consensus underlying it. The policy elite engaged in a spirited debate following the end of the Cold War that put forward a spectrum of possible strategies. The public was not engaged. The post–Cold War strategic debate ranged from global hegemony to homeland defense, but no stable political consensus has formed around any of the strategic alternatives. Regardless, in this environment described either as strategic vacuum or strategic vacillation, dramatic change is demanded.

Adherents of the various strategies differ on the source of the threat to the United States and, therefore, differ on how to counter the threat. The more restrictive strategies might be inclined to leave the military as an isolated instrument held in reserve for conventional use when vital interests are at stake. The more aggressive strategies require a powerful conventional force for major war, but they also require a force for multiple small wars. All strategies agree on a second-strike nuclear force for deterrence.

Those subscribing to *homeland defense* and *selective engagement* tend to see U.S. interventionism as the source of the problem and recommend various degrees of disengagement and a high threshold for the use of military force. Adherents to a homeland defense strategy narrowly define America's vital interests to be the "security, liberty, and property of the American people." They see the principal threat as porous borders and unsecured ports of entry; and they see a threat to international commerce as of secondary importance. Those favoring selective engagement tend to see war between great powers as the principal threat to the United States, and reserve the use of force to prevent major power conflict, most likely over resource competition.

The *collective-security* strategy is based on the premise that national and international security is a shared responsibility of all states working through international institutions. A threat to one state is a threat to all. *Cooperative security* is a recent variant retaining much of collective security but focusing on the proliferation of weapons of mass destruction as the principal threat to international and national security.

Adherents to American *hegemony* or a *primacy* strategy believe that America's position is bolstered by using force to advance its wide-ranging interests abroad. The challenge is to be seen as a *benign* hegemon rather than as a threat to be countered.

The U.S. government capabilities to be built depend on the strategy chosen. There is no strategic stability on the horizon, and the strategic pendulum may swing faster than the agencies of government can adapt.

Instruments and Mechanisms

Means—the specific resources that the nation is willing and able to commit to achieve its security—are finite. Some reduce means to dollars, which is not unreasonable depending on their position and role in government. For our purposes here, means are described at two levels of abstraction: instruments and mechanisms. The instruments of power are spread across the agencies of government that provide the mechanisms necessary to implement the policies chosen by elected and appointed officials.

Instruments are stable over time. Mechanisms are a slowly shifting mix. Assuring the nation's security is the complex matter of orchestrating the instruments of power by investing in and activating the mechanisms spread across government. National security strategy guides both the production and use of power. Strategies can be changed overnight. Significant changes to mechanisms may take a decade or more. Mechanisms, therefore, must be sized and shaped to support a reasonable range of strategies.

For decades, the acronym DIME has been used as shorthand for the diplomatic, informational, military, and economic instruments of national power. In the 1960s, there was a direct correspondence between agencies and instruments. The Departments of State and Defense housed the mechanisms supporting the diplomatic and military instruments, respectively. The U.S. Agency for International Development represented the economic instrument abroad, and the U.S. Information Agency communicated America's message abroad through a variety of mechanisms. The Kennedy administration had a specific policy statement detailing how those instruments would be wielded to counter Communist-inspired insurgencies. The State Department was designated lead agency.

A more recent acronym, MIDLIFE (military, informational, diplomatic, law enforcement, intelligence, financial, and economic) has gained some currency reflecting the greater complexity in the ways and means of pursuing national security. Others speak of soft power, referring to U.S. influence abroad exerted through private commerce and society rather than through deliberate government effort. But the instruments of power are no longer neatly divided between the agencies. The information agency, when it is clearly needed, has been disestablished. There is no clear policy statement describing how the instruments are orchestrated. No cabinet official has authority beyond his or her department. Only the president has authorities above all departments and agencies, and the office of the president becomes a bottleneck.

Instability in Partisan Politics

There is also evidence that there is instability within the two political parties. Much is made of political polarization within the electorate. It is clear that the two parties are polarized, but neither party accurately represents the public. Increasing percentages of the voting public are renouncing longtime party affiliations and identifying themselves as independents. Many of those who continue to claim party affiliation do not feel that their party accurately represents their values and interests. Dominant parties have broken before, and it is possible that the process is under way again.

The two parties tend to find some common ground with regard to humanitarian assistance and disaster relief abroad. The post–Cold War Democratic Party, as represented by the Clinton administration, had a tendency to engage in peacemaking and peacekeeping operations through the UN where U.S. vital interests were not at risk and public support was generally lacking. The post–Cold War Republican Party, as represented by the second Bush administration, engaged in discretionary war that the public increasingly found to be reckless and counterproductive. Splits over domestic issues are beyond the scope of this book.

The growing perception is that neither party reflects mainstream America's policy preferences. A swinging partisan pendulum is one possibility; the fracturing of a party followed by a new alignment is another. Reorganizing the nation's security apparatus under either of these conditions is problematic at best, perhaps even unwise.

Instability in Economic Thought

One of the most authoritative formal studies in the area examines congressional voting throughout the country's history and identifies a single variable—economic liberalism—that persistently explains partisan movement. A second variable—race—periodically rises to prominence.[3]

There are two prominent and competing families of macroeconomic theories contributing to partisan gridlock. The Keynesian family promotes government intervention in the economy with both monetary and fiscal policy. The Chicago school stands on minimum government intervention. It favors deregulation, opposes fiscal policy interventions, but promotes a gradualist monetary policy.

Keynesian theories—derived from volumes of twentieth-century empirical data—propose active government intervention in monetary policy and the marketplace to assure economic stability and growth. Under conditions of depression or recession, fiscal policy and deficit spending constitute the appropriate and necessary government intervention (previously accepted in practice). Expenditures should be an investment in the future by developing shared infrastructure and should provide jobs during the recovery. During a strong economy, taxes are raised to pay back what was borrowed, and stimulating expenditures are reduced (rejected in practice). Keynesian economics do not argue for long-term borrow-and-spend policies that lead to massive government debt. Keynesian theories reached their peak acceptance in the 1950s but failed to explain the stagflation—simultaneously rising rates of inflation and unemployment—of the early 1970s, generally attributed to oil fluctuations associated with the 1973 Arab-Israeli War.

The alternative family of theories is represented by Milton Friedman, once a Keynesian himself, and the University of Chicago. Rather than build on hard-earned economic knowledge since World War I, Chicago hoped to replace it with libertarian thought favoring the free market and the mechanisms of the private sector reminiscent of nineteenth-century governments. Prior to 1973, the Chicago school was considered outside the mainstream. It prescribes minimum government intervention and favors deregulation of industry. Its anti-interventionism derives from two compelling premises. The first premise is that government intervention is certain to be too slow: "There is likely to be a lag between the need for action and government recognition of the need; a further lag between recognition of the need for action and the taking of action; and a still further lag between the action and its effects."[4] The best government policy is to do nothing and allow the market to correct itself. The second premise is that the regulated industry will *capture* the regulatory government body for its own gain. Having gained considerable prominence during the 1980s, the Chicago school suffered after the effects of deregulation became apparent in the financial crisis of 2007 to 2010 and as it offered no solution to the deep recession.

At the end of the Bush administration, the United States was confronted with the simultaneous problems of massive debt and deep recession. The

United States and European countries that adopted austerity and budget cuts had sluggish recoveries. The empirical evidence favored Keynesian economics, but the partisan divide was ideological rather than empirical. Partisan gridlock prohibited decisive action.

Navigating the Instability

In the post–Cold War period, presidents Clinton and Bush relied on a relatively isolated military instrument for nation building, missions for which the military is poorly suited. For quite different reasons, both parties became heavy interventionists. And those interventions are small wars. A bipartisan consensus grew that to assure U.S. national security, a small-wars capability is required. There is no consensus yet apparent on what an implementation of the capability might be, but there is a clear sense that the country is unprepared.

Unpreparedness for the twenty-first century is apparent in those who authorize the use of force—Congress; presidents use force at will. Those responsible for shaping military force—congressional authorizing and appropriating committees, the secretaries of defense and of the military departments, and the service chiefs—demonstrated their unpreparedness. And finally, the president's National Security Council demonstrated its unpreparedness to orchestrate all the instruments of power in further-ance of American interests. Each agency acts in relative isolation.

That brings us back to the original questions about the suitability of our national security system and the role the military plays in that system. The agencies of government, of which the military is but one, provide the mechanisms through which America's elected officials pursue the country's policies. Policies might change suddenly due to an election or an external shock. The bureaucracies that provide the mechanisms can change only slowly. Perhaps the most critical component of security policy is the national security strategy declared and pursued by the president.

The various strategic alternatives represent the range of policies that the mechanisms of government must support. Mechanisms optimized to support one strategy likely will fail catastrophically when applied to a significantly different strategy. With no persistent strategy in sight, sub-optimal solutions are the only prudent choice. The mechanisms cannot be redesigned and rebuilt with each incoming administration. A collection of mechanisms representing the instruments of power must be in place, and special attention must be paid to the ability to orchestrate the instruments.

The post–Cold War system is designed for major war, with its most apparent manifestation a superb military instrument isolated from the other instruments of power. Should the U.S. military, principally the Army and the Marine Corps, be redesigned to contain all the instruments of power, or should it be designed to represent a more narrowly defined military instrument, leaving to others the orchestration of the instruments of power? Whatever the answer to this question, the mechanisms provided must support the range of strategic policies that presidents are likely to pursue in the twenty-first century.

Post–Cold War administrations have applied dramatically different strategies. There appears to be no consensus developing on a stable strategy, that is, a linkage of ends, ways, and means. The Clinton and Bush administrations, however, developed an apparent consensus relying on military intervention and nation building as a central way of strategy. And it is the nation-building mission carried out primarily by the military that imposed the greatest stresses on the existing system. The Obama administration appears to have reversed course, replacing large-scale military intervention with strikes and raids as a primary way of strategy.

Organization of the Book

The book does not assume any specific academic background, only a keen interest in American national security. Part 1 reviews the concepts of international relations, including realism and idealism and the just war theory, for example. It also includes concepts peculiar to the American tradition. Part 2 is about national security strategy and includes a review of the Cold War strategies and the strategies debated and employed in the post–Cold War era. Part 3 focuses on the instruments of national power, the agencies that house them, and the mechanisms for orchestrating their actions. And Part 4 collects the issues and reform proposals identified.

Considerable supplemental material is available at www.Orchestrating Power.org.

Part 1

Foundational Concepts
and Principles

1   A Primer on Security Concepts

This chapter provides a brief introduction to the concepts underlying international relations and the use of force. International relations theory may seem too abstract for many readers, but it is derived from centuries of empirical evidence and is the necessary and proper intellectual foundation for thinking about twenty-first-century national security. Understanding the two major schools of thought on international relations—*realism* and *idealism*—provides the indispensable starting point.

After seemingly continual war, European Enlightenment thinkers collected the wisdom of the ages and posited a form of self-governance and a system of states that could eventually lead to a *democratic peace.* Enlightenment thinking is readily apparent in the U.S. Constitution, but America has its own history and its own spin on international relations. Ironically, the elements of the Constitution designed to promote the democratic peace have been subverted, largely since the end of the Second World War.

The concepts and lexicon introduced in this chapter are used throughout the text. You will be introduced to the *root causes of war, just war, uses of force,* and the rationale for the timing of *war initiation.* In the context of realism and idealism, we discuss the *security dilemma* and the principles of *self-determination, territorial sovereignty, noninterference, universalism,* and the *indivisibility of peace.* Next to realism and idealism, democratic peace is the most important idea presented in this chapter. In the next chapter, we'll discuss some concepts peculiar to the American view.

Root Causes of War

Through an examination of historical thinking on the origins of war, Ken Waltz found three dominant schools of thought on the matter that he delineates in his 1954 classic *Man, the State and War*. The first school posits that the root cause of war lies in man himself. Some speak of all mankind, while others point more specifically to the male of the species, and still others to the young male. A second school places blame in the structure of the state (government and economy). Those favoring democracy claim it to be more pacific than other forms of government because the public who bears the burden of war has a voice in the decision to war. Marxists, not surprisingly, claim the obverse; to them, capitalism, with its inherent avarice, boom-and-bust cycles, and the inevitable competition over resources and markets, is the source of the problem. The third school observes that states are sovereign with no higher authority and that, therefore, anarchy characterizes the system of states. War is a necessary resort to survive in a "self-help" system of sovereign states.[1]

As can be imagined, where one places the cause of war has a lot to do with the remedies proposed. Those who see the cause of war in man propose measures to meet basic human needs as well as education, religion, and other "civilizing" approaches. Those who see the structure of the state as the problem tout their preferred form of government and apply varying degrees of effort to persuade others to adopt the correct form. Those who see the problem as the anarchic system of states propose international or even supranational institutions to rectify the condition while others who accept the condition rely on military power and alliances.

Given that there is general agreement on the inevitability or at least the existence of war, there should be rules for initiating, waging, and terminating war. Wars should be just.

Just War

Just war theory is debated by ethicists and philosophers and is subject to a variety of interpretations. The just war tradition, in contrast, is a matter of historical record and is codified in ever-evolving international law. The just war tradition "is a set of mutually agreed rules of combat . . . between two culturally similar enemies."[2] If one will do business after the war, these rules must be followed. The rules applied within early European Christendom. Islamic law, *Shari'a*, contains a prohibition against warring between Muslims. But Christians and Muslims could wage war without rules against infidels. At its height, Rome maintained different rules for war between states, *bellum*, and wars against barbarians, *guerra*. The modern majority view is that the rules must apply universally; there should be only one morality. Increasingly, one hears calls to abandon agreed-upon rules and standards in the global war on terrorism.[3]

The just war theory is often associated with the Roman Catholic Church, but the theory's sources are broader and deeper. Elements of it appear in the Hebrew Scriptures, the writings of the ancient Greeks, Islamic law, and Japanese Bushido. It is not a uniquely Western notion. Saint Augustine made the Catholic Church's case in the fifth century, but the Dominican friar St. Thomas Aquinas is credited with bringing these thoughts together in *Summa Theologica*, written between 1265 and 1274.[4]

According to Sir Michael Howard, Aquinas's formulation was a necessary accommodation for the Church to make as it slowly ceded power to the secular state.[5] Michael Walzer goes further to say that some conditions made war the better alternative and that there needed to be a way to justify war to Christian pacifists, who refused war, and to simultaneously restrain Christian crusaders, who were all too willing to war.[6]

The tenets of just war (*justum bellum*) theory include guidance on when to go to war (*jus ad bellum*) and on how to conduct war (*jus in bello*). Hugo Grotius, the seventeenth-century Dutch lawyer, brought the Catholic Church's tradition into secular international law, arguing that righting wrongs and preserving justice were justification for war.[7] In the eighteenth century, Emer de Vattel[8] added legal focus to how war was conducted so as to improve the possibility of a stable peace following war.

Justum Bellum. There should be rules governing war, the majority believes, because if war is fought according to rules, then war can terminate rather than foster a perpetual cycle of retribution. A minority view is that war is immoral and cannot be justified, so any restrictions will only prolong the immorality. If no morality can exist in war, then all means should be employed to minimize the period of war.

Jus ad Bellum. A just war is one having a just cause, being declared by a proper authority, possessing right intention, having a reasonable chance of success, and the end being proportional to the means employed. But there is disagreement on the detailed definition of these criteria.

A *just cause* is a response against aggression, including self-defense, retaliation, or preemption of an imminent attack. But what constitutes an act of aggression is open to interpretation and can range from violation of territory to the less noble, including a slight to national honor or an action taken in support of economic activity and prosperity. As Michael Walzer writes, "The legalistic paradigm rules out . . . preventive wars, commercial wars, wars of expansion and conquest, religious crusades, revolutionary wars, [and] military interventions."[9]

Proper authority was once the Catholic Church, but since the 1648 Treaty of Westphalia it has been the sovereign, secular state. Some argue further that for a state to be a proper authority, it must be representative of its people. Within Islam, the legitimate authority remains religious, but Islam is a religion without a central authority.

More recently, an international body is the proper authority when a military intervention is proposed into the affairs of a sovereign state when that state has not committed a threatening act against another. For example, to intervene in a civil war, to oppose repressive acts of a government against its people, or to restore order would be authorized by the United Nations or an international institution with regional scope.

Right intention includes righting a wrong, restoring or maintaining the peace, but not aggrandizement. Specifically, war should not be waged to acquire dominion over land, people, or resources. This principle is codified in international law.

Peace as the end. The purpose of just war must always be to achieve peace.

Reasonable chance of success. Waging war without chance of success, while possibly appealing to the heroic, is no more than suicide. But it is easy to understand how difficult it is to assess one's chance of success in war. Hubris overpowers reason. More subtle but equally common is the gross overestimation of what can be accomplished with military power.

Proportionality of good to evil. There must also be a reasonable chance of success without resort to disproportionate means. A nuclear power, for example, might assume a reasonable chance of success against a nonnuclear power. But the overall damage to be inflicted must not outweigh the wrong being righted or the good to be gained.

Last resort. All other peaceful alternatives must have been explored before resort to war. But the unsophisticated militant state runs out of options quickly.

Jus in Bello, the law of war. Having entered into a just war, it must be fought in just ways. Proportionality and discrimination are the final two elements of the just war theory. Uniformed combatants are protected by proportionality but not by discrimination.

The principle of *proportionality* allows the war to continue until there is an assurance of no more attack, but it rules out slaughter of the vanquished. Battles, too, must not end in slaughter. Limitations on weapons (poisons and gases, for example) are often included under proportionality.

Discrimination specifies who constitutes legitimate targets in war. Noncombatants include civilians and uniformed military not engaged in hostilities. Specifically, chaplains and medical personnel are noncombatants. In general, targeting noncombatants is forbidden. Civilian casualties, however, are expected from attacks on legitimate military targets like seaports. Under the concept of *total war*, targeting civilians is allowed under the premise that civilians maintain the war machine and are thus legitimate targets. In guerrilla war, discrimination is impossible, as soldiers and civilians are indistinguishable. Within Islam, wars must be conducted within the ethical precepts of the religion, including the sparing of women, children, and the elderly.

While the just war theory provides important guidance on the use of force between states, there remains ambiguity and room for majority and minority interpretations. During the Cold War, the just war theory enjoyed a resurgence and played a significant, although not decisive, role in the debate in the shadow of nuclear conflagration and by the conflict in Vietnam.

More recently, according to Jim Wallis, an evangelical preacher, "virtually every world church body in the United States and the world that spoke out on the prospect of war with Iraq (with the notable exception of the American Southern Baptists) concluded this was not a 'just war.'"[10] But the near-unanimity was not sufficient to carry the day.

Rather than soul searching before declaring war, the language of just war theory is, more often than not, used rhetorically to lay false claim to the moral high ground.

Uses of Force

The alternative strategies of the Cold War and post–Cold War eras vary on the uses of force, but they all are based on a small number of concepts. For example, defense, retaliation, deterrence, coercion, and compellence are well-understood concepts concerning the use of power. As useful as these concepts are to relations between states, they are largely irrelevant when applied against the threat posed by transnational, stateless actors employing terrorist means. And many of those concepts that remain relevant beyond interstate conflict are exhaustive of resources in the context of the "war on terror."

Thomas Schelling's *Arms and Influence* well represents the best modern thinking on the use of force between states.[11] He identifies deterrence, compellence, and coercion as the three principal uses of force. His definitions of each term appear below.

> *Deterrence*: To prevent from action through fear of consequences. . . . Deterrence involves setting the stage—by announcement, by rigging the trip-wire, by incurring the obligation—and by waiting. The overt act is up to the opponent.
>
> *Compellence*: Usually involves initiating an action (or an irrevocable commitment to action) that can cease, or become harmless, only if the opponent responds.
>
> *Coercion*: Coercion requires finding a bargain, arranging for him to be better off doing what we want—worse off not doing what we want—when he takes the threatened penalty into account.[12]

Underlying deterrence, compellence, and coercion is the idea that a state has people and resources that it values and that the state itself seeks to survive. If nothing else, those in power wish to stay in power. During the Cold War, *counterforce* and *countervalue* options were part of nuclear deterrence. Counterforce attacks were aimed at military forces, while countervalue attacks were aimed at civilian populations. Both target sets were valued by states and heads of states.

The militant al-Qaeda is without place and property. While the violent al-Qaeda leadership might wish to survive, it does so by stealth without the trappings of state. Moreover, as with all insurgencies, the movement invites and hopes for a response that appears to be retaliation against the general Islamic public.

A variety of passive and active *defense* mechanisms have been employed in the past. Passive defense measures—like physical security and hardening—mitigate the effect of an attack, thereby raising the cost to the attacker. Active defense measures—like mines, coastal artillery, and interdiction aircraft—on the other hand, raise the cost of the aggressor's attack by attriting the force attempting the attack.

Denying access to the United States, either along its perimeter or at its ports of entry, is exhaustive of resources. Denying the enemy access to potential targets is also exhaustive. Even if it is possible to secure airports, the aggressor will move to attacks at sea, on the highways, at sports complexes, at shopping malls, or at any public place. The aggressor has an infinite set of targets, and defending them all demands infinite resources.

Acts of retaliation and defensive measures are properly seen as elements of a deterrence strategy. One retaliates with brute force to inflict pain for a real or perceived wrong. It is easy to interpret the use of military force in those terms. For example, a terrorist act committed in a Berlin nightclub led to an air attack on Libya.[13] But seen in the larger picture of an ongoing U.S. effort to deter Libya from future terrorist activity, the air attack is seen as an act of deterrence. We should not forget, however, the viscerally guided retaliatory use of brute force. Publics may demand it of a president. Retaliation may feel good, and increased defensive measures may look good, but they cannot be the basis of a sustainable or an effective strategy against committed terrorists.

War Initiation

The words "preemption" and "prevention" are used to describe a variety of phenomena. Preemptive war and preventive war, however, are terms of art with specific meaning concerning the reasons for war initiation. They are about timing. Preemptive strike is a use of force short of war and is often used as the strongest component of coercive diplomacy. And the word "prevention" has been used in a unique way in the post–Cold War era to characterize a use of force short of war to prevent the proliferation of weapons of mass destruction.

Preemptive and preventive wars are not types of wars. Instead, the terms describe motives for war initiation.[14] Both preventive and preemptive wars derive from the better-now-than-later logic but differ in important ways: "Whereas prevention involves fighting a winnable war now in order to avoid the risk of war later under less favorable circumstances, preemption involves the initiation of military action because it is perceived that an adversary's attack is imminent and that there are advantages in striking first, or at least in preventing the adversary from doing so."[15]

> *Preemptive war*: Initiation of war because an adversary's attack—using existing capability—is believed to be imminent.

The former U.S. secretary of state Daniel Webster provides an often-quoted, and perhaps the most restrictive, justification for preemptive war. There must be "a necessity of self-defense, instant, overwhelming, leaving no choice of means, and no moment for deliberation."[16]

The 1967 Arab-Israeli War is often cited as a classic example of preemptive war. With Arab armies poised on the border, Israel initiated the war with air strikes to eliminate the enemy air force on the ground before it could be brought to bear. Nothing in international law requires a country to sustain the first blow before defending itself. There is disagreement, however, about whether Egyptian intentions were defensive or offensive.

While preemption is a tactical response to an imminent threat, prevention is a more strategic response to a long-term, developing, potential threat. "The preventive motivation for war arises from the perception that one's military power and potential are declining relative to that of a rising adversary, and from the fear of the consequences of that decline," writes Jack Levy.[17] Uneven economic development, uneven population growth, or technological development favoring the offense may create the perception of shifting balance.[18] History and international law frown upon preventive war, and it generally is seen as a disguise for naked aggression.[19]

> *Preventive war*: Fighting a winnable war now to avoid risk of war later under less favorable conditions.

The Truman administration debated preventive war and rejected it. As the United States was losing its nuclear monopoly, President

Eisenhower was offered a preventive war option to initiate nuclear war before the Soviet Union and China were capable of mounting a serious threat. Eisenhower explicitly rejected, by name, preventive war.

Preemptive strike should not be confused with preventive or preemptive war. Preemptive strike is a limited and focused attack to destroy a capability. The threat and reality of preemptive strike can be a complement to ongoing diplomatic and economic efforts—coercive diplomacy.

> *Preemptive strike*: An attack tightly circumscribed—in space, time, and effect—to destroy a threatening capability.

The classic modern example of preemptive strike was conducted in 1981 by Israel against Iraq's Osiraq nuclear facility before Iraq could pose a nuclear threat.[20] There was no imminent threat to Israel. If we were consistent with the use of words, this type of operation would be called *preventive strike* rather than preemptive, but preemptive strike is the common usage.

Recently, some ascribe special meaning to the word "prevention."

> *Prevention*: Preventing war by preventing states from assembling the means to aggress against others.

Treaties, arms control agreements, and military force can be employed in the name of prevention, separately or in combination. Arms sanctions against Iran and North Korea may retard but not prevent the acquisition of weapons of mass destruction. The threat of a strike against the capability can be a complement to coercive diplomatic and economic efforts. Punitive or destructive strike is the penultimate step, and the overthrow of a government is the ultimate.

Preventive strike, as typified by Israel's raid on Osiraq in 1981 and by the Clinton administration's actions in 1998 against Iraqi weapons of mass destruction development facilities, inarguably took away Iraqi capability and set back its development.[21] There is a significant strategic difference between preventive strike to destroy Iraqi capability and a preventive war to overthrow the Iraqi government. One difference is the level of U.S. and international commitment required afterward, and the difference is great.

The definition of prevention easily generalizes from states to nonstates. But to date, the nonstate aggressor has shown a preference for readily available weapons rather than for extensive research and development or capital investment in sophisticated weapons. Accordingly, sophisticated weapon systems—launch sites and manufacturing facilities—are not available targets. But preventive strike has clear utility against nonstate actors, for example, by attacking training facilities and assembly areas.

The more traditional reasons for war initiation include response to an attack, as when the United States declared war against Imperial Japan in response to the attack on Pearl Harbor—a *defensive war*. The Japanese initiation of war, on the other hand, was a matter of choice. Such a war is called a *war of choice, war of discretion*, or *war of aggression*. Signatories to the UN Charter have renounced wars of aggression.

Realism and Idealism

Cold War and post–Cold War strategies vary considerably, but both draw heavily from two well-established theories. *Realism* and *idealism* are explanations and predictions (and not necessarily prescriptions) for international relations. Realism is evident throughout history, and it continued to gain strength along with the rise of the European nation-state. The strength of idealism—the intellectual product of the Enlightenment associated with liberalism and the rise of liberal democracy—emanates from the tragedy of the First World War. Both idealism and realism are actually broad families of related theories. For true scholars, the differences within families are significant. Activity in political science is robust, but only the theories with observable effect in Washington practice are presented here.

The formal study of international relations was born of the events surrounding the First World War. Prior to the war, (1) international politics was left to professional diplomats, and warfare was left to professional soldiers; (2) foreign policy was beyond the scope of political parties; and (3) the representative bodies (legislatures) sensed a lack of expertise in the area and deferred to the executive. Secret treaties, rightly or wrongly, were popularly blamed for the fact that an isolated assassination attempt spiraled out of control into a world at war. Such treaty arrangements should be exposed to the light of day. Popularization led to the scientific study of international relations. Edward Carr was one of the early students of the new field and is credited with making the distinction between *realism* and *utopian idealism*. According to Carr, "political science is the science not only of what is, but what ought to be." Realism is of the former and idealism of the latter.[22]

Realism places its emphasis on the acceptance of historical fact and on analysis to determine the causes and consequences that link those facts. For the realist, "morality is only relative, not universal."[23] There is no good other than acceptance and understanding of reality. "Consistent realism breaks down because it fails to provide any ground for purposive or meaningful action," according to Carr.[24]

Idealism places wishing over thinking and places unverified generalizations claiming universal appeal over observation of reality.[25] Idealism is aspirational. The field of international relations was initially dominated by the aspiration to avoid another devastating world war. Idealists attempted to distance themselves from an ugly reality and to project a utopian ideal worthy of pursuit. Consistent idealism breaks down when confronted with reality, says Carr.

Carr insisted that both utopianism and realism are needed. "But there is a stage," he notes, "where realism is the necessary corrective to the exuberance of utopianism, just as in other periods utopianism must be invoked to counteract the barrenness of realism":

> Immature thought is predominantly purposive and utopian. Thought which rejects purpose altogether is the thought of old age. Mature thought combines purpose with observation and analysis. Utopia and reality are thus the two facets of political science. Sound political thought and sound political life will be found only where both have their place.[26]

The long-running realist-idealist debate remains active,[27] but it lacks the granularity necessary for strategy formulation. To say that realists describe what is and that idealists prescribe what should be provides a useful starting point.[28] In addition to their origins, failures, and successes, realism and idealism can be characterized by their respective approaches to the security dilemma and by the positions they take with respect to a small number of principles—universalism, self-determination, territorial sovereignty, noninterference, and the indivisibility of peace.

The reader should keep in mind that Carr uses the terms realism and idealism to describe ways of thinking. Realism is the product of conservative thought applied to international relations. Idealism can produce a range of pursuits, and liberalism is but one of those. In what follows, and in the literature generally, idealism and liberalism are often used interchangeably.

Principles and Positions

The *security dilemma* can be stated simply as follows: failing to maintain the force necessary to guarantee one's own security invites aggression, while maintaining an adequate security force may be perceived by others as threatening, again inviting aggression or an arms race. To complicate the situation, systems acquired for their defensive characteristics often have an offensive application. Realists and idealists rely on different mechanisms to address the security dilemma: balance of power and international institutions, respectively.

The principle of *self-determination* rests on the idea that no single set of rules can be acceptable to all. A *nation*—a people with common language, history, and culture—can and should agree to its own rules. A nation's ability to determine its own rules requires a *state*—a political entity with institutions and borders. Bertrand Russell predicted that there will be no peace until the borders of states are aligned with nations. John Stuart Mill drew a similar conclusion in 1861.[29] If they are correct, then the many artificial borders dating from the colonial era and the world wars do not portend peace. Following from this principle, nations have an absolute right to determine their own rules, and to do so, nations must have the institutions of state to formulate and enforce domestic policies and to defend against foreign influence.

Having entered the First World War to make the world safe for democracy, Woodrow Wilson made self-determination one of his Fourteen Points after the war. He advocated self-determination to prevent the reestablishment of colonialism. But colonialism reappeared thinly disguised as League of Nations mandates over significant parts of the Middle East. Apparently not seeing the contradiction, Wilson, a strict Presbyterian, supported a national Jewish homeland in Palestine, where Jewish residents constituted only 10 percent of the population.

The principal alternative to self-determination is *universalism*. Universalism is the idea that one set of rules can and should govern the behavior of all nations. Two of the world's great religions—Christianity and Islam—posit universalism. Marxists posit a secular universalism, and others believe that democracy and free-market capitalism represent universal values. Today, the United Nations identifies a narrow set of universal human rights, but the UN falls short of being a supranational body that establishes and enforces all rules to be followed by all nations in all states.

The modern system of states formally rests on self-determination rather than on universalism. Globalization increases the trend toward universalism and is threatening to many who fear change and challenges to their sense of national superiority.

The principle of *territorial sovereignty* and the principle of *noninterference* follow directly from the absence of a set of universal rules. Territorial sovereignty relies on a state that establishes and enforces the rules of the nation within the confines of a known border. Intervention by one state into the internal affairs of another produces negative results. Kant argued that it is better to let a neighboring state destroy itself than to intervene in its internal affairs. It is better to allow the troubled state to find its own way, to resist the temptation to intervene in a neighbor's internecine troubles. Eventually, they will see the light. Today, the major powers reserve the right to intervene in the affairs of other sovereign states in the name of universal human rights and the responsibility to protect, either unilaterally or through international institutions, and thus tacitly endorse the doctrine of limited sovereignty for not-so-major powers.

Another principle, the *indivisibility of peace*, also distinguishes realists and idealists. This principle addresses the degree to which wars can be contained to the original belligerents or, conversely, the degree to which local conflicts will grow to global proportions. The First World War provides a case where an initially localized conflict—an assassination in the Balkans while the Ottoman and Austro-Hungarian Empires were collapsing—turned global, but the lesson was generalized well beyond that specific conflict.

Realists and idealists also differ on the role *morality* plays in international relations. Morality is about right and wrong. It is a matter of common, normative practice. Law is a codification of that practice. Law often lags practice but may sometimes lead normative behavior. But the gap can never be too great without rendering law irrelevant. Law is a convention binding only so long as others abide.[30] Carr adds, "Realists hold that relations between states are governed solely by power and that morality plays no part." International relations are amoral. "Utopians [believe] the same code of morality is applicable to individuals and states."[31] President Woodrow Wilson said in his 1917 address to Congress requesting a declaration of war: "We are at the beginning of an age in which it will be insisted that the same standards of conduct and of responsibility for wrong shall be observed among nations and their governments that are observed among the individual citizens of civilized states."[32]

The idealists' optimistic assumptions about the nature of humankind lead to a vision of a better future. Idealism is progressive. The realists' pessimistic assumptions of human and state behavior are permanent. Realism is nonprogressive.

Realism

The Greek historian Thucydides is credited with formulating the logic of realism in his analysis of the Peloponnesian War (431–404 BCE).[33] The logic, however, can be found in the writing of the Chinese strategist Sun Tzu (circa 500 BCE)[34] and Kautilya (circa 300 BCE) of India.[35] Other prominent realists include the Florentine philosopher Niccolò Machiavelli (1469–1527);[36] the British philosopher Thomas Hobbes (1588–1679);[37] the Prussian theorist Carl von Clausewitz (1780–1831);[38] and the Prussian practitioner Otto von Bismarck (1815–1898). Hans Morgenthau is considered by many to be the twentieth century's most prominent realist.[39] According to Morgenthau:

> Political realism believes in the possibility of distinguishing in politics between truth and opinion—supported by evidence and reason, and what is subjective judgment divorced from fact and informed by wishful thinking. Political realism is the concept of interest defined in terms of power and rational order. It is aware of a moral significance, but refuses to identify with moral aspirations.[40]

Realist thinking rests on a pessimistic view of mankind. Man is guided by self-interest, is acquisitive and competitive. Therefore, conflict is inevitable, and the condition is permanent. States, too, are guided by self-interest. The state is the primary actor, and other actors are less important in explaining and predicting events on the world stage. State interactions are *zero-sum games*: for one to gain, another must lose. Survival of the state is *amoral*, and state leaders seek power regardless of religious or ethical considerations. The focus is on state capabilities rather than on uncertain state intentions. Because the system of states is anarchic, states must acquire power sufficient to deter attack and to assure their own survival. War is inevitable. Peace can be obtained only when states acquire independent power or form alliances that balance against each other, e.g., the North Atlantic Treaty Organization and the Warsaw Pact during the Cold War.

Realism survived the progression from city-state to feudal-state to nation-state. The paradigm—the dominant theory—for much of recorded history, realism has been seriously contested by liberalism only after the trauma of World War I. Realists saw as vindication the failure of liberalism's League of Nations to prevent World War II. Modern realists include George Kennan, the originator of the Cold War containment strategy, and Henry Kissinger, Nixon's principal strategist.

According to Mearsheimer, the realist view is premised on five assumptions: (1) that the international system of states is anarchic, (2) the basic motive of the state is survival, (3) states have some offensive capability, (4) there is uncertainty concerning other states' intentions, and (5) that states behave rationally in a world of imperfect information.[41]

The realist school accepts the Westphalian system of states that prescribes rules governing the external, or international, behavior of states and leaves internal, or domestic, behavior to the states themselves. Realism is based on the principles of territorial sovereignty and the corollary principle of noninterference. Realism is premised on the belief that no single set of rules can be agreed to by all peoples. Because there can be no universal set of rules, there can be no government above the sovereign state, and, therefore, the international system is one of self-help. Hedley Bull called *anarchy* this condition of the international system.[42]

Realists since Thucydides have asserted "that states expand in the absence of countervailing power; unbalanced power will act without moderation, and states not subject to external restraint tend to observe few limits on their behavior."[43] Unchecked, states will violate neighbors' territorial sovereignty, imposing *hegemony* or *universal monarchy*. How can a state assure its security under such an assumption?

Realists address the security dilemma through a balance of power, "by which is meant an arrangement of affairs so that no state shall be in a position to have absolute mastery and dominate over the others."[44] Balance of power is the antidote to hegemony. The balance can be upset by many things, including uneven economic development, shifting alliances, or technological advancement favoring the offense.[45] Preserving the balance of power is worth fighting for.

The Napoleonic Wars brought the power of nationalism and mass armies to bear in an attempt to establish French hegemony over Europe. *Levée en mass* versus small, professional armies brought an imbalance to the existing system of European states. The system of states eventually balanced against France to restore the balance of power. The French were victims of imperial overstretch, a pattern in the behavior of great powers.[46]

Great Britain has been the quintessential modern balancer. David Hume recalls the ancients' behavior and contemporary British nature, and he prescribes an appropriate balancing behavior for Britain in his time. Athenians "threw themselves into the lighter scale," and the appropriate response for England, Hume argued, was to balance, to "support the weaker side in every contest." England balanced with Germany against Napoleonic France and balanced with France against Germany in the world wars. Periodic minor wars to preserve the balance of power were preferable to the injustice and major war that would ineluctably follow from attempted hegemony. The imposition of one nation's ways on another would be intolerable.

Hume further argued against permanent alliances, saying that too consistent an opposition to French purposes caused other states to assume too much English support and demand too much of the French in the way of concessions, increasing the likelihood and duration of conflict. He further argued for withdrawing from a coalition when Britain's objectives were met, saying, "Once engaged in a fight where we were accessories, we fight on and mortgage ourselves."[47] The British fought longer than any other nation in World War II, entering early and fighting on in the Pacific long after victory in Europe was realized.

Realism can be further distinguished as either defensive or offensive.[48] Mearsheimer identifies the two poles, but there is an observable middle position. According to *offensive realism*, states are power maximizers. Great powers are in perpetual pursuit of power over their rivals. The ultimate goal of a great power is regional hegemony and even the more lofty global hegemony. Security is pursued through *preponderant power*. According to *defensive realism*, states are security maximizers. The state should acquire enough defensive capability to deter, and if necessary defeat, an attacker. Any greater acquisition of power constitutes an excessive drain on the underlying economy. Moreover, the surplus power will be interpreted as threatening to other states and will lead to costly and dangerous arms races. Security is pursued through *defensive power*. In between is what might be called *balancing realism*, according to which the state should acquire enough defensive capability to deter, and if necessary defeat, an attacker and some additional offensive power—for power projection—that can be combined with the power of other states against common enemies or in pursuit of common interests. Security is pursued through *balancing power*.

Idealism and Liberalism

According to Carr, (utopian) idealism is a way of thinking that is aspirational and purposive, but not necessarily grounded in reality. In fact, idealist thinking attempts to replace an unacceptable reality with something better. Plato's *Republic* is an early expression of utopian idealism. Liberalism, just one example of idealism, is the product of Enlightenment thinking and was influential at the founding of American democracy. It was a broad concept centered on the relationship between individuals and their government. Liberalism included the idea of self-governance—governance by the people rather than by a monarch—and a form of government that best assured individual liberties. Liberalism was largely a matter of domestic politics, but the devastating reality of World War I begged for a better reality in the future, and liberalism became a matter of international politics in hopes of sparing future generations the scourge of a world at war. The labels idealism and liberalism are often, and unfortunately, used interchangeably. Liberalism was the product of idealist thinking when initially put forward in the eighteenth century, but liberalism is no longer without empirical evidence.

Democratic peace is the utopian ideal pursued by liberalists internationally through collective security; individual liberty is the utopian ideal pursued domestically. And by spreading liberal democracy, democratic peace will follow. According to Michael Doyle:

> Liberalism has been identified with an essential principle—the importance of the freedom of the individual. Above all, this is a belief in the importance of moral freedom, of the right to be treated and duty to treat others as ethical subjects, and not as objects or means only. . . . Liberalism also calls for those rights necessary to protect and promote the capacity and opportunity for freedom.[49]

According to Mearsheimer, idealists call for all states (1) to reject the use of force to change the status quo, (2) to act not out of a state's narrow self-interest but for all of mankind, and (3) to trust each other to renounce aggression. Idealists believe that harmony is rational, that change by force is inadmissible, and that democracies would not choose war.[50]

Rather than the realist's pessimistic view of human nature, idealists have an optimistic view. Idealists place tremendous value on humankind's ability to reason (rationality), cooperate, and live peaceably if only the proper conditions can be established.

The idealist school, in contrast to realism, is premised on universality, the belief that one set of laws can and should eventually govern the behavior of all nations and states. And in contrast to realists, idealists believe that war need not be inevitable. In idealist thinking, state preferences (intentions) are more important than state capabilities (acquired power). They believe in the theory of democratic peace, positing that states with democratic institutions promote peace, while states without them promote war. Idealists are likely to promote democratic institutions at home and abroad. More generally, they are inclined to make their internal political philosophy the goal of their foreign policy. Modern idealists argue to reduce arms to the minimum required for self-defense and to subordinate military forces to international cooperative ventures.

For idealists, there is more to international relations than states and the anarchic system of states; there are many opportunities for cooperation. Individuals, while capable of self-interest and competition, will be inclined toward benevolence when the conditions are created for cooperation. Humankind's concern for the welfare of others makes cooperation possible. All states are interconnected and interdependent. Their interdependence promotes communications and understanding, thus reducing the likelihood of war. Rather than zero-sum games, idealists believe that interactions between states are *mutual-benefit games* that can produce settlements with positive outcomes for all participants, thus further promoting cooperation. Idealists work to establish and promote international organizations and laws and to establish cooperative links through international trade and cooperation.

Idealism gained adherents after World War I. Wilson was one convert, and *Wilsonianism* is a name often associated with this line of reason. The failure of the League of Nations to prevent World War II cast doubt on idealism's validity. Idealism gained strength again after the war as a round of international institution creation ensued; the words *institutionalism* and *internationalism* also apply to this school.

Frank Ninkovich provides an interpretation of events surrounding World War I that helps explain the emergence of idealist thinking.[51] The overlapping emergence of the phenomena of liberal democracy and the Industrial Revolution brought unprecedented wealth, more lethal weapons of war, and unimagined social problems. Recent wars had been largely fought by small, professional armies in the name of monarchs; wars were limited. World War I introduced the notion of *total war* and convinced many observers that war was no longer a reliable or useful instrument in international relations. Total war could poison the world for liberal democracy. The European balance of power was "permanently unhinged" and needed a replacement. America's entrance into the war meant that modern politics and war were global. The interconnectedness of the world plus the obsolescence of the balance of power meant that any conflict could escalate into world war; thus, the belief that peace is indivisible was forged.

Liberal idealists address the security dilemma through interlocking and mutually reinforcing international institutions and, moreover, through the institutionalization of international cooperation. They believe that international economic and environmental cooperation lowers the probability of war. Idealists promote democracy at home and abroad. They act to expand and deepen international organizations and law, to link states through trade, and to institutionalize international cooperation. States should reduce arms levels to the minimum necessary for self-defense.

A more refined view of idealism, or liberalism, includes the distinction between sociological, interdependence, institutional, and republican liberalism. Each of these schools shares the fundamental tenets of liberalism but differs in the variable that provides the greatest explanatory value.

Sociological liberalism emphasizes the many global communities with which individuals identify and the understanding, compassion, and cooperation that follow. States are geographically discrete, membership is exclusive, and states collide. But individuals may identify with other individuals beyond their borders who share their religion, gender, language, social class, ethnicity, or position on specific issues. States foster nationalism while the transnational linkages of individuals dampen the state's tendency to conflict.

Interdependence liberalism emphasizes the interdependence of states deriving from free-market capitalist economies. David Ricardo (1772–1823) spoke of the comparative advantage of each state (e.g., access to raw resources, arable land, and skilled labor). If each state did what it did best and markets were free of government interference (e.g., tariffs), then benefit would derive for all. The result of free trade would be economic interdependence between states and fewer tendencies to war.[52]

Institutional liberalism focuses on the role of international institutions and the opportunity they provide for cooperation. International institutions create and increase the opportunities for cooperation rather than conflict. Arms-control regimes, the International Atomic Energy Agency, and nonproliferation treaties are examples of institutions for international cooperation. The European Union provides an example of building and relying on international institutions as a means to cooperate.

Republican liberalism puts great stock in the form of government. Specifically, republican democracies will form a pacific union. This might also be called Kantian liberalism.[53]

Conclusions

International institutions have a place in both realism and liberalism. Idealists believe that strengthening international institutions directly leads to a reduction in the likelihood of war. Realists believe, instead, that balance of power reduces the likelihood of war and that states choose to act indirectly through institutions to increase their power. Realists do not oppose international institutions but instead believe that these institutions reflect the distribution of power between states and, therefore, are based on the self-interest of great powers. For example, the permanent members of the UN Security Council are the five major powers allied during World War II.

Modern American realists—realism is highly correlated with conservatism—hold more dearly to economic liberalism than do idealists and liberals. *Laissez-faire* continues to be popular with conservatives and big-business interests. American liberals accept the need for government intervention in the economy and will adjust the type and degree of intervention according to contemporary demands, but always favoring the individual (populism) over the interest of the powerful few (elitism).

Many scholars of international law—who tend toward institutionalism, internationalism, and universalism—believe that balance of power is a necessary precondition of international law and not something in opposition to it. An unopposed power enforces international law selectively at best. In this sense, they accept important positions of both realism and liberalism.

Realism and idealism tend to be the subject of timeless debate of great interest to the scholarly community, each side declaring the other's theory to be disproved. The debate informs strategy formulation, but no consensus has formed around either view, and the debate is not addressed to the public.

Economic Explanations

For realists, power is the variable with the greatest explanatory value. Idealists place a great deal of emphasis on international relations, including those in the economic sphere. For both, the economy is an important instrument of national power. Economic power defines war potential. Over the years, idealists and realists have adjusted their positions on the relationship between state and economy.

Mercantilism. Wars from the Renaissance to the mid-eighteenth century were trade wars. Autarky—economic self-sufficiency—was an ideal to be pursued. One policy preference was against importation. If there must be imports, then import raw materials and process internally. Another policy preference was for exportation, but export finished products rather than raw materials. Tariffs were an effective tool to encourage these policy objectives at the expense of neighbors. According to Carr:

> Throughout this period, it was universally held that, since wealth is a source of political power, the state should seek to actively promote the acquisition of wealth; and it was believed that the right way to make a country powerful was to stimulate production at home, to buy as little as possible from abroad, and to accumulate wealth in the convenient form of precious metals. Those who argued in this way afterwards came to be known as *mercantilists*. Mercantilism was a system of economic policy based on the hitherto unquestioned assumption that to promote the acquisition of wealth was part of the normal function of the state.[54]

The more modern version of mercantilism continues the belief that the accumulation of economic power is a legitimate function of state, but government encourages the private sector to pursue activities abroad that align with national policy objectives.

Economic liberalism and free-market capitalism. *Laissez-faire* is another product of utopian idealism. Popular thinking in the nineteenth century attempted to separate politics from economics. Law and order was a matter for the public sector, and the economy was the domain of the private sector. Government intervention in domestic business (regulation) and foreign trade (protective tariffs and subsidies) was to be precluded in most cases. According to Adam Smith (1720–1790), general society would benefit if all acted according to self-interest.[55] In this *harmony of interests*, the *invisible hand* would best allocate resources and result in the most good for the most numbers. The logic was applicable to the eighteenth-century economy with its low skill specialization and low levels of capital investment. John Stuart Mill (1806–1883) argued that *laissez-faire* should be the general rule, and every government intervention in the economy constitutes an evil.[56]

The onset of the Industrial Revolution overturned the set of assumptions underlying Smith's thinking. But as the eighteenth century gave way to the nineteenth, Mazinni and Ricardo (1772–1823) generalized *laissez-faire* from national to international economics.[57] Charles Darwin's theory of evolution—competition and survival of the fittest—was generalized from biology to economics and kept *laissez-faire* alive. And generalization to larger society—social Darwinism—equated progress to the elimination of unfit individuals and unfit nations.[58] Thus enabled, the late nineteenth century brought imperialism and colonialism, and economics and politics were reunited.[59]

Laissez-faire was a hallowed principle of those possessing dominant power. As a matter of social class, that meant the *bourgeoisie*, as a matter of commercial interests, it meant the company with dominant market position; and as an international matter, it meant the state that dominated the global economy—Great Britain at the time.

The *centrally planned economy*, the *command economy*, was a concept born of mobilization of national economies for World War I—total war in the industrial age. When it came to national survival, faith in the free market evaporated, and all major powers adopted the centrally planned economy.

Marxism and command economies. Rather than seeking explanations for American foreign policy in exogenous conditions or events, some find explanation in domestic economics. Karl Marx rejected the harmony of interests between capital and labor. Horrid social conditions followed from the Industrial Revolution and *laissez-faire* capitalism. State intervention in, indeed control of, the economy was necessary. Capitalism's boom-and-bust cycles and competition for raw resources and labor would inevitably lead to exploitation and war, according to Marx. Marx and Engels thought Communism would eventually lead to a desirable anarchic condition with maximum individual liberties, but in practice the concentration of power in a central government led instead to totalitarianism.

The more recent *Open Door* school explains American foreign policy as the consequence of a search for markets and the desire to establish a global economic system based on free trade.[60] To deal with underemployment, overproduction of goods, and boom-and-bust cycles—the inevitable byproducts of a capitalist economy—business and political elites seek expanding markets, access to cheap resources and labor, and investment opportunities. The result, according to this line of reasoning, is a foreign policy of empire.

Democratic Peace

The Prussian Enlightenment thinker Immanuel Kant published *Perpetual Peace: A Philosophical Essay* in 1795, which was derivative of an earlier work from 1784.[61] Already the topic of the European salons, and well-known at the time the U.S. Constitution was drafted in 1787, Kant's work is considered the seminal statement of the democratic peace theory. He distinguishes between defensive, preventive, and offensive wars.

In the essay's first section, Kant identifies the contemporary practices that contributed to the natural state of war—including both open hostilities and the unceasing threat of hostilities. The common practices that favored war must be curtailed and replaced with practices more conducive to peace. These new practices, presented in the first section, establish the enabling conditions, and the essay's second section puts forward three definitive articles leading to perpetual peace. First, a review of the preliminary articles.

Statecraft and the Use of Power. Kant defines statecraft as the perpetual maneuvering and acquisition of power common to the monarchies of his era. He asserts that of armies, alliances, and money, the power of money may be the most dependable. All three are seen as threats by other states. The perpetual maneuvering on the chessboard produces instability that creates the conditions for war.

Kant argues against standing armies because they lead to offensive and preventive war. Maintaining an army at a high level of readiness invites an arms race with neighboring states. Kant distinguishes offensive war by standing armies from defensive war as the "voluntary periodical military exercise on the part of citizens of the state, who thereby seek to secure themselves and their country against attack from without."[62]

In addition to a standing army, the accumulation of treasure would be seen as threatening by other states and lead them to preventive war. He further argues that an unrestrained credit system leads to debt that constitutes a dangerous money power. The debt incurred constitutes a war treasure that will either be used or bring down innocent states in the inevitable bankruptcy. Kant distinguishes between incurring debt for the purpose of leveraging the behavior of other states from the debt incurred for the benefit of the domestic economy, e.g., "improvement of roads, new settlements, establishment of stores against unfruitful years."[63]

A shifting alliance structure that aggregates the power of armies and the power of money would produce an imbalance of power that would lead to preventive and offensive wars.

War Initiation, Conduct, and Termination. There must be rules that govern the initiation, conduct, and termination of war so that true peace can follow. Wars should be fought in such ways that the belligerents can return to normal relations after the war. A true peace must be the end state of war. Moreover, adhering to these rules reduces the number of justifications to engage in war. Kant argues against the practice of hiring-out state troops to fight another state's wars. Kant asserts the principle of *noninterference*. Although it may be inviting to forcefully intervene in the internal affairs of a neighboring state experiencing political turmoil, Kant argues against it, instead requiring the troubled state to resolve its own problems. He allows, however, intervention when conditions have degenerated into civil war and asserts the acceptability of intervention and of taking sides. One can see the difficulty in unambiguously distinguishing a civil war from lesser degrees of conflict.

As progress is made on the preliminary articles and the impediments to peace removed, Kant proposes three definitive articles that will lead ultimately to peace.

Republican Government. In Kant's time, Enlightenment thinkers were pursuing the radical idea of self-governance that would best assure freedom and liberty of the individual. According to Kant, government is either republican or despotic. Republicanism separates executive power from legislative power, and the legislature is *representative* of the general will. But in despotism, executive and legislative powers are combined and carry out the will of the ruler(s).

Without a representative form and republican mode, "government is despotic and arbitrary, whatever the constitution may be." Kant takes pains to distinguish between republican and democratic constitutions to avoid the confusion "as is commonly done." He argues that "democracy is . . . necessarily a despotism" that implements the tyranny of the majority over minorities. But how does this republican form of government contribute to peace? According to Kant:

> If . . . the consent of the subjects is required to determine whether there shall be war or not, nothing is more natural than that they should weigh the matter well, before undertaking such a bad business. For in decreeing war, they would, of necessity, be resolving to bring down the miseries of war upon their country. This implies: they must fight themselves; they must hand over the costs of the war out of their own property; they must do their poor best to make good the devastation which it leaves behind; and finally, as a crowning ill, they have to accept a burden of debt which will embitter even peace itself, and which they can never pay off on account of the new wars which are always impending.
>
> [When not republican], the plunging into war is the least serious thing in the world. For the ruler is not a citizen but the owner of the state, and does not lose a whit by the war, while he goes on enjoying the delights of his table or sport, or of his pleasure palaces and gala days. He can therefore decide on war for the most trifling reasons, as if it were a kind of pleasure party. Any justification of it that is necessary for the sake of decency he can leave without concern to the diplomatic corps who are always only too ready with their services.[64]

The word "democracy" does not appear in the U.S. Constitution, written in the same period. It does, however, guarantee every citizen a "republican form of government"; stipulate distinct legislative, executive, and judicial branches of government; and place the decision to war clearly with the legislative branch.

A Pacific Union. As for external relations between states, Kant proposes a league or confederation of nations, a pacific union. The league has as its objective the end of all wars. But the league is not a supranational body. Each nation, through the mechanisms of state, establishes its own civil order through law; there is no universal set of laws to which all nations would subject themselves.

Cosmopolitism. Finally, Kant argues for a new universal social norm asserting hospitality over hostility. He cites three examples of the opposite. To some nomadic desert peoples, contact with another people conferred the right of plunder and enslavement. Similarly, some coastal peoples practiced piracy toward foreign vessels traversing adjacent waters and against stranded travelers. And, third, he spoke of "the inhospitable actions of the civilized and especially of the commercial states" who, upon arrival in foreign lands, "counted the inhabitants as nothing." Travelers should neither plunder and enslave people encountered nor be subjected to similar treatment. Adhering to the *cosmopolitan law* would eventually lead to commerce and peace born of interdependence.

Democratic Peace in the Twentieth Century. Kant's eighteenth-century democratic peace theory argued that in a republic an enlightened public will approach war cautiously whereas an uncontested executive will war at will. But today, Kant's theory of cause and effect has been replaced by an oft-cited correlation—that democracies do not war against each other. The seminal 1976 article by Melvin Small and J. David Singer concludes that democracies are not immune to unnecessary and aggressive wars, but that democracies are not prone to war against each other. Looking deeper, the study further observes that during the study period (1816–65), democracies were not geographic neighbors and that their separation may be the explanation for the lack of wars.[65] Spreading democracy is now the justification for war. Gore Vidal's sardonic title, *Perpetual War for Perpetual Peace: How We Got to Be So Hated*, concisely captures the counterargument.

For Consideration

It is possible to productively view the current geostrategic environment as one in which the system of states, nominally beginning with the 1648 Treaty of Westphalia, is under attack by nonstate actors like al-Qaeda and by the more subtle but deeper phenomenon of globalization. Certainly the state can no longer claim a monopoly on the use of force. The idealist argument that there are strong international linkages beyond and above the system of states is gaining strength. The realist claim that the state is the principal actor on the world stage may be weakening, but it is far from being refuted, and a reassertion of nationalism over globalism may again elevate the state.

National security strategies, the subject of part 2, are informed by both realist and idealist thought. The principles of universalism, territorial sovereignty, and nonintervention remain relevant, and national security strategies take different positions. The belief in the indivisibility of peace and the responsibility to protect encourages intervention in distant internal wars. The belief in mutual-benefit games encourages international cooperation and negotiation; a belief in zero-sum games does not. The misalignment of nation and state boundaries has and is producing conflict. Holding to boundaries that made sense as administrative districts for the colonial powers—in Central Asia, the Indian subcontinent, the Middle East, and Africa—inhibits attempts to create states that represent nations.

Is there only one morality that governs all (universalism, moral absolutism), or are there different moralities for different actors in different situations (moral relativism)? Are there two moralities: one for war between states and another for wars against stateless barbarians? Is a state obligated to behave morally on the international stage as would be the case for an individual acting in a local community, or is the state's international behavior amoral?

2   War and American Democracy

Building on the general theories of international relations, this chapter is oriented on the American system. The system is complex and the approach taken here is to view the system through multiple facets, none complete, but each contributing useful insight. The presentation begins with American traditions and political tendencies with respect to war and the use of force. Specifically, we discuss exceptionalism, exemplarism, vindicationism, and exemptionalism and then turn to the traditions of Alexander Hamilton, John Quincy Adams, Andrew Jackson, and Woodrow Wilson. Considerable effort is devoted to deconstructing American conservative and liberal thought followed by identification of several influential political factions that divide the electorate and coalesce under the political parties. The chapter concludes with issues for further consideration.

Exceptionalism, Exemplarism, Vindicationism, and Exemptionalism

Three ideas run through classic American thinking—exceptionalism, exemplarism, and vindicationism—and they are as apparent today as they were in the nation's early history.[1] A fourth ism has been added recently—exemptionalism.[2]

Exemplarism is the principle that the United States could best serve the spread of liberal democracy by being an enviable example to the world—the shining light on the hill, the beacon.[3] Being a good example requires strengthening the institutions that assure individual liberties, the rule of law, and the prosperity born of industry and commerce. Exemplarists find themselves in agreement with Kant's principle of noninterference into the affairs of other nations.

An opposing principle, *vindicationism*, asserts that America can best serve the world by spreading democracy, not merely by example, but by forceful action. Adherents believe that liberal democracy provides a universal set of rules. Vindicationists, then, reject territorial sovereignty and the principle of self-determination. More accurately, they believe that if the shackles of old world governments were removed, everyone would adopt liberal democracy. America's crusading spirit springs from vindicationism. Jonathan Monten speculates that the Bush administration firmly believed that once Saddam Hussein was overthrown, democracy would quickly blossom in Iraq because democracy is universal and that Iraqis would rush to embrace it.[4]

Exemplarism and vindicationism are principles, not strategies or policies. They help guide and explain U.S. behavior on the world scene. No period of history is driven purely by one or the other. People of principle strongly tend toward one or the other. As a nation, exemplarism dominated until the 1890s, and vindicationism has been on the rise since, reaching a peak with the 2003 invasion of Iraq.

Thucydides observed that states unchecked by external forces expand, and realist thinking includes the belief that a state's interests expand in proportion to its relative power. Realist thinking—because there is no universal set of rules that all nations will accept—tells us that attempts to impose universal monarchy will be opposed. States will resist individually and form alliances to balance against the imposing power.

How, then, can the United States practice vindicationism and honestly not expect strong opposition? The answer, *exceptionalism*, is the third thread that runs through American thinking. Alexis de Tocqueville identified this belief in his 1835 observations.[5] America believed that it was the exception to the rule. Its heart is pure and its intentions benign because it does not seek empire through territorial acquisition. Accordingly, American interventions abroad would be accepted, even welcomed. The United States intervened abroad with positive results in both world wars. The reconstruction efforts after World War II were extraordinary, and the United States left Germany and Japan without claim on territory. As major powers competed for colonial empire in the Middle East, the United States was seen as a force for fairness. Interventions for humanitarian assistance and disaster relief today are well received abroad and supported at home. The invasion of Iraq is seen in stark contrast, as were the frequent earlier interventions in Latin America.

America is bounded east and west by protective oceans, and north and south by non-threatening neighbors. Because of these facts, the United States did not need to maintain a standing army to defend itself, and that fact made America exceptional and made exemplarism a realistic option. Vindicationism, on the other hand, requires the ability to project power beyond the homeland.

And there lies the dilemma. The institutions to project power abroad have a strong tendency to concentrate power in central government and they threaten liberal institutions. Their costs tax the public and divert resources from domestic prosperity. And it is prosperity, liberty, and the rule of law that stem from liberal institutions. By improving domestic order, we improve our image abroad. Weakening the domestic order degrades the image abroad.

To the early Puritans arriving in New England, removing themselves from the problems of the Old World was virtuous. The New World was a place where humankind could possess the liberties that God intended. What later would be called isolationism was God's will according to these early Americans.

One hundred and fifty years later, the framers agreed on the goodness of spreading democracy. They disagreed, however, on the method. Exemplarism was strong with only weak expressions of vindicationism apparent. None other than George Washington doubted the idea of exceptionalism and said in a letter to Madison that no state, including the United States, could be "trusted farther than it is bound by its interest."[6] But even then vindicationism was not entirely silent.

Exemplarism dominated America's international relations until the 1890s. But vindicationism found expression in westward expansion, and Manifest Destiny carried the country to the Pacific coast. By the end of the nineteenth century, the Army was oriented on domestic constabulary duties and defense of the homeland. Navalists, in contrast, were expansionist and looked across the oceans. The Spanish-American War of 1898 was a tipping point in American history. Admiral Dewey defeated the

Spanish Fleet in Manila Bay in short order, and the Army was caught unprepared. The resulting acquisitions in the Pacific and the Caribbean required an imperial army to police them. Rudyard Kipling called for America to "take up the white man's burden," the European version of vindicationism; Europeans had, through foreign empire, the sacred obligation to bring civilization to nonwhite nations.

Coincident with a peak in the recurring cycle of Christian missionary zeal, vindicationism burst onto the scene. Woodrow Wilson would be satisfied by exemplarism until he could no longer resist entering World War I. American military force would be used abroad to remake the world in America's image. Vindicationism would dominate henceforth.

Exceptionalism, as a powerful and persistent component of American identity, can lead to *exemptionalism*. The United States has been successful in building international institutions and law through treaty and, on occasion, the United States has attempted to exempt itself from treaty provisions. Congress has been the strongest proponent of exemptionalism. To assure ratification of the UN treaty, Southern Democratic senators insisted on language that would exempt Jim Crow laws. Post Cold War, the executive branch has claimed a special preordained U.S. role in the world and has exempted itself from international norms. The Senate rejected the Comprehensive Test Ban Treaty and made clear that the same fate awaited the Kyoto Protocol on the environment. President Clinton signed the treaty on the International Criminal Court, but he did not submit it to the Senate. Bush withdrew presidential approval and the U.S. remains outside the court's jurisdiction that allows international prosecution of individuals accused of genocide, crimes against humanity, and war crimes if the individuals' state fails to act.

American choices today remain to promote democracy through example, encouragement, assistance, coercion, or compellence. Some argue that exemplarism was the logical choice of a weak state in its early years and that vindicationism is the appropriate choice for the sole superpower. Many in the world, particularly the downtrodden, accepted exceptionalism and saw the United States as an actor for fair play. The perception of American exceptionalism has been eroding recently, and exemptionalism appears to be on the rise.

American Traditions

Henry Kissinger offers a discriminating and uniquely American view of international relations based on the traditions of Alexander Hamilton, John Quincy Adams, Andrew Jackson, and Woodrow Wilson.[7] These traditions explain and predict the aggressiveness of American foreign policy and the tendency toward or against military intervention.

At the birth of the nation, Alexander Hamilton preferred to distance nascent America from Old World struggles. Hamilton advocated engaging with Britain and France, managing the balance of power in accordance with America's self-interest but without permanent commitment to either European power. Not surprisingly, Hamilton adopted Great Britain's behavior—both the United States and England were separated from the continent by protective seas—and was entirely consistent with Hume's prescriptions.[8]

Andrew Jackson also preferred to distance America from European struggles. Jackson belonged to the era of American continental expansion to the west and general disinterest in Europe's problems to the east across a protective ocean. Jacksonians are isolationist (with respect to Europe) until America's direct interests are challenged and then are prone to a bellicose response. The idea that any war could potentially draw the United States into global war is not part of the Jacksonian tradition: peace is not indivisible. Nor is the use of military force in foreign affairs when America's interests are directly challenged. But Jacksonians were vindicationists with respect to expanding American empire across the North American continent.[9]

John Quincy Adams believed in the benefits of democracy and the desirability of spreading it to the rest of the world. Adams, leaning strongly toward isolationism, believed America could best serve the world by being a shining example of democracy's benefits rather than by imposing its ways on others through aggressive foreign policy and the use of military force abroad.[10]

Woodrow Wilson also believed in spreading democracy to the world but took a far more aggressive stance than Adams. Wilson's original response to the burgeoning European conflict was isolationist. But on the eve of America's entry, Wilson rejected a new balance of power as the desired outcome. Instead, Wilson believed, "the only valid purpose for

America's entry into the war was to remake the world in its own image," to make the world safe for democracy.[11] Wilson rejected realist principles in favor of those of idealists. Rather than pursuing selfish national interests (realism), doing what is right and just in the interest of mankind (idealism) would guide America's foreign policy. Democratic principles, according to Wilson, are universal principles.[12]

In times of relative peace, those with the isolationist tendencies of Adams and Jackson find political coincidence with Hamiltonian balancing at arm's length. But when a direct challenge is made to American interests, Jacksonians are energized and find common cause with those harboring Wilsonian tendencies. During the Cold War, the common perception of an existential threat formed a powerful consensus across these communities. That threat and consensus no longer exists.

Adams and Hamilton belonged to the American meritocracy who had acquired position as landholders and as lawyers in contrast to the European aristocracy who held position by virtue of their ancestors' military acumen. The framers rejected the *ancien régime*. According to Michael Howard:

> The ruling philosophy of the generation that established the independence of the United States was the very quintessence of the Enlightenment, with its belief in the rights and perfectibility of man and his capacity for peaceful self-government once the artificial barriers to his freedom—monarchy, aristocracy and established church—had been destroyed.[13]

But members of the founding meritocracy were concentrated in the Northeast. And later, during the era of expansion, those in the South and in the West developed a warring culture more suited to "the violent conditions of a frontier society." Jackson was the first president to come from this new base.

Jackson was populist and rural. He defied Congress and the Court throughout his administration. Anti-monarchist detractors in his own party referred to Jackson as King Andrew and split from the Democratic Party to establish the Whig Party, which quickly split over slavery. Republicans formed in 1854 from the Whigs' demise. In 1860, the remaining Democrats split between the abolitionist northern democrats and the pro-slavery southern democrats. Although Andrew Jackson is commonly identified as the father of the modern Democratic Party, he is more accurately seen as the father of the vindicationist southern democratic party currently exercising strong influence in the Republican Party.

But not everyone agrees that the Constitution was the product of Enlightenment reason. Some believe it was the result of divine inspiration.

Conservatism and Liberalism

Conservative and liberal are both rich and complex schools of thought, each well beyond the scope of this short section. Too often they are used as dismissive labels applied to political opponents. But because the words are so frequently employed, some attempt at definition must be made.

This section (*a*) defines the permanent components of liberal and conservative thought, (*b*) identifies the initial positions in the late 1770s, and (*c*) provides a short version of the story of positions changing based on changing conditions. In other words it shows that while there is something permanent about the schools of thought, the positions each school takes are situationally dependent—that is, positions taken depend on time and circumstances. The persistent components might be considered *philosophical* liberalism and conservatism, and the transient positions taken might be considered *political* liberalism and conservatism. The observant reader may notice a strong and recent divergence between the philosophical and political.

Persistent Thought

The root axiom upon which *conservative* thought rests is a preference for what is known through experience and a rejection of utopian, idealistic solutions based on pure reason—reason without empirical evidence. Conservatism includes a belief in the *law of unintended consequences*—that the best-intentioned departures from the status quo will result in unintended and undesired outcomes. That does not mean that conservative thought precludes change. Instead, change should be pursued one small step at a time, gathering evidence along the way—*incrementalism*. And conservative thought includes a belief in hierarchy, that is, that there is a hierarchy across and within societies. Not all states are equal in power; not all men are equal in power. Power confers influence.

Conservatism accepts *limits*. There are limits to what can be known, and conservative thought includes a healthy *skepticism* of bold new ideas. There are limits on resources—both financial and human—that can be devoted to any enterprise. There are limits on what can be accomplished through application of resources, including the application of military resources to achieve political goals and the application of financial resources to improve social welfare.

Liberalism, from the pure reason of the Enlightenment, was based on faith in the individual over the monarch and faith in *reason* to solve problems to the benefit of society—*rationality*. People could govern themselves if only they were freed from the coercive institutions represented by monarchy, aristocracy, and established church. The *democracy theory* is that the public can govern itself, and the grand experiment of the United States is a test of that theory. Liberalism has as its objective individual liberty and a rejection of hierarchy; it is inherently *egalitarian*.

Liberalism was not born entirely without empirical evidence. Religious wars, many conducted in the context of the Protestant Reformation, gave conclusive evidence that imposing a specific religion on a population would lead to horribly destructive wars. The Thirty Years' War (1618–48) took nearly one-quarter of the population. No religion was universally acceptable and any attempt to impose a religion would be violently rejected. Separation of church and state was found as a means to an end. Separation of church and state allowed *freedom of religion* (freedom of conscience), a necessary condition for peace.

The astute reader will notice the connection between realism and conservatism. Conservatism is the more general predilection, and realism is the expression of conservative thought in international relations. The reader may also recognize liberalism as one of many possible products of idealistic thinking as defined by Carr. But liberalism is no longer without significant empirical evidence. It has compiled an impressive list of accomplishments; today's liberals and conservatives tout the democratic peace theory and advocate the spread of liberal democracy as the path to security.

Initial Conditions

At the time of ratification of the U.S. Constitution, the privileges and protections of liberalism were narrowly constrained. White male property holders possessed the full range of benefits. But in some states, the white male property owner was required to belong to the state-approved church (always Protestant).

True democracy, it was believed, would give too great a power to the lower classes. The *tyranny of the majority* was something to fear. Limiting full rights to a select few was preferred. And adopting a republican form of democracy that allowed election of representatives was preferred to democracy. As John Jay said, "Those who own the country ought to govern it."[14] The Constitution guarantees a republican form of government, not a democracy.

Recall the several versions of liberalism and realism presented in chapter 1. Those are meaningful distinctions to be made when discussing international relations and foreign policy. But when discussing domestic policy, it is customary to make a distinction between Liberalism and Conservatism.

In the American political realm, both Liberalism and Conservatism are forms of the larger liberalism. They share the common foundation of liberal democracy. According to Doyle, this common foundation has three distinct sets of rights. Rights of the first set are often called *negative freedoms*, which are premised on the need to protect the individual from the coercive powers of government. They include "freedom of conscience, a free press and free speech, equality under the law, and the right to hold, and therefore to exchange, property without fear of arbitrary seizure." Rights of the second set are called *positive freedoms*, that is, rights that expand the opportunity for freedom premised on the need for government to assure a level playing field and to protect individuals from the coercive powers outside of government, for example, the coercive power of big business. They include equality of opportunity through equal access to education, equal access to health care, and equal access to employment. These are judged necessary elements to the conduct of liberal democracy. And the third is the *right of participation* in representative government— the right to vote—the right that guarantees the others. Restricting voting rights is a frequently used technique to protect the few from the many.[15]

There are meaningful tensions between these rights. Emphasizing the positive freedoms leads to the version of liberalism referred to as the social welfare tradition, or the liberal tradition. Adherents are liberal liberals, or just *liberals*. Emphasizing the negative freedoms leads to what can be called the laissez-faire tradition, or the classical liberal tradition. Adherents are conservative liberals, or just *conservatives*.

In Carr's view of international relations, realism and idealism are different but complementary. Both are necessary. Each is valued. Together, in balance, they represent mature thought. In American political theory, liberalism and conservatism have a common foundation and are properly seen as variations on a theme. In political practice, however, conservatism and liberalism appear to be mutually exclusive positions in direct opposition to each other.

Positions Are Situationally Dependent

Today, the terms *Conservative* and *Liberal* are shorthand for positions on a set of issues. Issues rise and fall in prominence over time, and conservatives and liberals differ on which issues are most pressing. And they certainly differ on the positions they take on issues.

Conservatives in the eighteenth century held to monarchy and resisted the untested idea of liberal democracy. A conservative of the nineteenth century held to protective tariffs as government's way to promote prosperity and resisted the untested idea of free markets. A conservative of the late nineteenth century held to free market capitalism and resisted the untested idea of government regulation of industry. Conservatives in the South, where the economic system rested on cheap slave labor, held to slavery over emancipation of slaves and its unintended consequences.

Liberals' positions, too, are relative to the times. To achieve equality of opportunity for all, liberals promoted *laissez-faire* government, that is, minimum government intervention in the private sector. But when the Industrial Revolution created horrible social conditions and inequities, liberals shifted to government intervention and regulation of industry to protect individuals from the coercive power of the business aristocracy. The ends remained fixed on individual liberties, and the ways to achieve those ends shifted on demand. One history of the United States can be told as the continual expansion of the communities granted the full privileges and protections of liberal democracy, to include the propertyless, African slaves, women, and homosexuals—the progressive push of liberals.

Political Orientation

Snow offers a useful extension to the left-right dimension.[16] He defines each of five political orientations based on two issues—position on

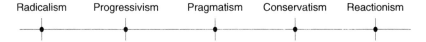

FIG. 1. Political orientation

changing political relationships and the proper role of government with respect to change (see figure 1).

On the far left, *radicals* believe in the need for change, perhaps discarding rather than modifying the current system, and they are often willing to use violence to promote a new, imagined, and untried system. The government is often the system requiring change.

Progressives are generally accepting of political change and generally have a positive attitude toward government involvement in achieving that change. During the Progressive Era (1890s–1920s), unifying goals were purging government of corruption and the influence of party bosses and increasing the efficiency of government by bringing modern, scientific methods to economics, industry, and education. Progressives included both Democratic and Republican presidents. Government would be activist.

On the far right, *reactionaries* advocate change to some past system. That system is often a romanticized version of a system of political relationships that never truly existed. They are often absolutist and intolerant of diversity of view. The labels *retrogressive* or *regressive* might also be used productively.

Moving back toward the center, *conservatives* are suspicious of political change, preferring the status quo or small incremental steps from it. They are skeptical of government activity and prefer a minimal role for government.

Pragmatists take no specific position on change or the role of government. Rather than taking ideological positions, they tend to take positions based on the merits of the individual issue. Change may be advantageous or it may not. Government may have a role to play or it may not. Ideologues of left and right criticize pragmatists for standing for nothing and having no principles. Pragmatists have no political party and they lack entertainment value on political talk shows.

This five-point exposition adds some much needed discrimination to the two-valued, liberal-conservative model, but more understanding can

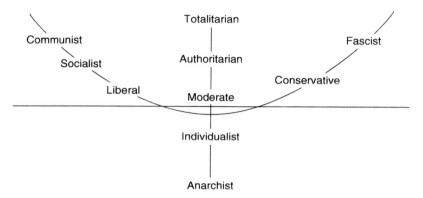

FIG. 2. Movement on the political spectra

be added through a second, independent dimension. The new dimension spans anarchy, individualism, authoritarianism, and totalitarianism (see figure 2). The vertical dimension is different from the traditional small-versus-large government dimension. The size of government is not the issue, nor is the relative power of federal and state governments. This dimension measures how invasive government is in the lives of the citizenry. Both the extreme left and the extreme right of the spectrum are authoritarian.

On the left, radicals can either advocate for anarchism or totalitarianism and the distinction cannot be plotted on the single dimension shown in figure 1. It should be noted that Communism in theory would produce a system that would be plotted in the lower-left quadrant, but Communism in practice would be plotted in the upper left.

The same contradiction exists on the right. *Social conservatives* disavow some important conservative beliefs. Rather than the conservative's preference for empirical evidence, the Religious Right relies on faith that is not supported by, or even contradicted by, empirical evidence. And they favor a strong government that imposes their values on all. They favor a government that aggressively promotes and enforces change in society, and some favor change to an imagined past system. Their intolerance of other religious beliefs and political reversion put them more in the reactionary camp, but their preference for coercive government enforcement cannot be expressed on the single dimension shown in figure 1. These distinctions are more easily plotted on the two-dimensional representation of figure 2. Social conservatives would be plotted in the upper right quadrant, and individualists in the lower right. Movement on the vertical axis appears to have more explanatory value than movement on the horizontal in recent years.

One way to contrast authoritarian with democratic governments is by an asymmetry of information access. In an authoritarian system, the government has considerable access to information about its citizens' activities at the same time that it imposes severe restrictions on its citizens' access to information about government. The reverse is true in a democratic system; most actions of government are *transparent* and the citizen enjoys *privacy*.[17]

Others distinguish authoritarian from totalitarian governments by the limits of their authority to regulate citizens' behavior. In an authoritarian system, the authority extends throughout the public square; in a totalitarian system, authority extends into the home.

For psychologists, authoritarianism is not only a characteristic of those who seek to exert authority from the top, *authoritarian dominators*, but also those individuals who desire authorities to defer to, *authoritarian followers*. Authoritarians of both types respond with "agree" or "strongly agree" to survey questions like, "What this country needs most, more than laws and political programs, is a few courageous, tireless, devoted leaders in whom the people can put their faith."[18] The "rugged individualist," in contrast, is not looking for higher authorities to follow.

Social psychologists observe a tendency toward authoritarianism in *cliques*—groups of people who exhibit a high degree of interactivity between likeminded people within the group and a low degree of interactivity outside the group.[19] In *Authoritarianism and Group Identification*, Duckitt defines *individualism* as "the belief that the requirements of group cohesion should be subordinated as completely as possible to the autonomy and self-regulation of the individual member." And at the opposite extreme, he defines *authoritarianism* as "the belief that the purely personal needs, inclinations, and values of group members should be subordinated as completely as possible to the cohesion of the group and its requirements."[20] Where authoritarianism is prevalent, members conform to the norms of the group, submit to the group's authorities, and exhibit punishment and condemnation toward non-conforming members of the group (*ingroup*) and to non-members (*outgroup*).

The social psychologists' view may shed some light on some current issues in American politics. Terrorist groups clearly have the characteristics of cliques. Fundamentalist groups (whether Christian, Islamic, Hebrew, or secular) prefer isolation from cosmopolitanism in religion, education, and other elements of social life.

The once-dominant three television networks sought broad appeal and contributed to the "shared experience" of America. The proliferation of television channels led to programming targeted to narrow audiences and might be contributing to Balkanization of American thought. One can easily choose a news channel and listen to what the ingroup has to say while being safely insulated from the heresy of the outgroup.

A New Crusading, Hawkish Coalition

Political forces can easily overpower presidential and congressional decision making and prevent strategic response. Some of these political forces are rooted in religion. Only a few years ago, it would have been considered impolitic to broach the subject of religion in a text on American government. Today, however, it would be irresponsible not to do so. Independent of official policy, many in the developing world see a three-pronged American effort to spread democracy, market capitalism, and Christianity, including the use of force.

A modern phenomenon has emerged as a political force promoting the application of military power abroad. Two religious blocs have found common interest with a secular bloc. There are no precise boundaries for these ideological groupings. Rather than sweeping generalizations, the approach taken here is to attempt an abbreviated articulation of the beliefs of the respective thought leaders. The advantage of this approach is that thought leaders tend toward some purity of thought and have taken the time to put their arguments on paper. Their thinking tends to be anchored in a formative period and galvanized by powerful events, like the Great Depression, the carnage of the world wars, the Holocaust, and the political and social foment surrounding the Vietnam War. Accordingly, there is often a generational component that fades over time. The weakness of the approach is that only a few actually subscribe to, or are even aware of, the full range of beliefs championed by the thought leader, and thought leaders often have more extreme views than their followers. Larger numbers—in concentric circles of increasing distance from the center—selectively adopt elements of the belief system and even reject the more extreme aspects. In the outer rings, individuals espouse some of the beliefs without knowing their source. Certainly others may arrive independently at the same beliefs.

Secular Neoconservatives

Neoconservative thought leaders are largely secular Jews who, once liberal urban Democrats, moved far to the right. Leo Strauss provides substantial theoretical support. His thinking includes the belief that truth is the province of an elite group in government and that the elite must tell "noble lies" to the masses who are energized by religion and nationalism. And nationalism is fueled by a real or imagined external threat. Borrowing heavily from Straussian thought, Irving Kristol is considered to be the founder of neoconservatism. His son, William Kristol, and Charles Krauthammer, Robert Kagan, and Norman Podhoretz are more contemporary banner carriers.

The neocon thought leaders are from the World War II generation and their formative experiences center in the Holocaust when Jews, Gypsies, Communists, homosexuals, and the handicapped were victim of atrocities. There are two deeply engrained beliefs deriving from that experience. First, civil rights, the privileges and protections of liberal society, must be assured for *all*. And second, Chamberlin's appeasement at Munich after Germany's capture of the Sudetenland provides the enduring lesson that tyrants must be fought at the outset before they gain war-winning power (preventive war). The first lesson explains why American Jews bonded with the Democratic Party and have been strong activists for civil rights for all. Neocons had favored FDR's New Deal and LBJ's Great Society but became disillusioned with the social welfare and antiwar positions of the Democratic Party.

Some neocon activists were energized to move toward the Republican Party in response to the antiwar movement that developed in the Democratic Party late in the Vietnam War. More left the party during the Carter administration. Many of the best-known neocons coalesced on Senator

"Scoop" Jackson's staff. Jackson, a Democrat from Washington, was often called the Senator from Boeing for his advocacy for spending on weapon systems. Beyond spending on defense, Jackson was pro-union and labor and pursued a liberal domestic agenda. It was a perfect fit for the neocons, but the Democratic Party continued to divide between the traditional promilitary and the burgeoning antiwar wings of the party. These same individuals soon migrated to the Republican Party and received political appointments in the Reagan administration.

For neocons, pursuing American interests is an amoral issue, but religion and the religious can be useful tools in pursuit of their political objectives. They believe that the use of force abroad strengthens America's position and power rather than depleting it. Their beliefs include a sense of inherent national supremacy. The *Weekly Standard*, established and edited by the Kristols, and *Commentary*, edited by Podhoretz, are neocon outlets for advocacy journalism. The American Enterprise Institute is a Washington establishment for policy formulation as is the Project for the New American Century.[21] The elder Kristol's *Neo-conservatism: The Autobiography of an Idea* serves as foundational text.[22]

Theocons

Thought leaders of the *theoconservative* school are Catholic and are sometimes referred to as Catholic neocons. Richard John Neuhaus, Michael Novak, and George Weigel are the principals. Neuhaus, once a Democrat from the radical left and an antigovernment protestor during the Vietnam War, railed against totalitarian "Amerika." A Lutheran minister, he declared a Catholic Moment for America in 1987,[23] converted to Catholicism in 1990 and was ordained a priest in 1991. Michael Novak similarly established himself as a radical during the 1960s. Neuhaus remains subject to periodic outbursts advocating revolt,[24] once causing a temporary rift with neocons.

In the theocon belief system, democracy and free market capitalism are the will of God, thus aligning politics, economics, and religion into one; theocons explicitly advocate the use of force to spread democracy (and implicitly to spread capitalism and their interpretation of Christianity).[25] Theocons used the just war theory to advocate for the invasion of Iraq. The Vatican and the Jesuits, noticeably, did not.

First Things and *Crisis* magazine are theocon advocacy journalism outlets, Neuhaus's *The Naked Public Square* serves as a foundational text,
with Novak's *The Spirit of Democratic Capitalism* and *Toward a Theology
of the Corporation*, and Weigel's *Catholicism and the Renewal of American
Democracy* in support. The Center on Religion and Society and the Institute
on Religion and Democracy serve for policy formulation.[26]

William Bennett and Phyllis Schlafly are two of the better-known contemporary theocons. The *New York Times* called Bennett, who changed
parties in 1986, the leading spokesman for the Traditional Values wing
of the Republican Party.[27] Best known for her anti-feminist position,
Schlafly has also taken anti-abortion, prosegregation, anti-arms control,
anti-immigration, anti-UN, and antiglobalization positions.[28] And like
Neuhaus, she links Americanism and Catholicism.

Social Conservatives

Social conservative thought leaders are fundamentalist Protestants, while
many followers may be fundamentalist, evangelical, or Pentecostal. This
group is often referred to as the Religious Right. Seen as part of the cyclical
rise and fall that includes movements in the Victorian and Progressive
periods, the phenomenon also has been called *neo-Puritanism*. According
to one scholar, American puritanical thought includes an "exaggerated
faith in government's ability to regulate every aspect of private life and
by a strong ethnocentric belief in the correctness of white, Protestant,
middle-class social norms."[29] Thought leaders of this group hope to use
the power of government to impose their religious views on others; this
is big-government authoritarianism rather than small-government
conservatism.

The label "movement conservative" was used to identify a particular
faction in the Republican Party that believed their religious values were
not represented in government action. During the Reagan administration, the modifier was dropped, and the faction was referred to simply
as "conservative," representing a shift in the definition of conservative
and a shift in *the base* of the party. It became a prominent component of
the *New Right*, which displaced *Establishment Republicans*.

Rousas Rushdoony provides a comprehensive basis for sociocons under
the labels of *Christian Reconstructionism* and *Christian Revisionism*.[30]

Not widely known by the laity, Rushdoony's work is credited with providing a compelling rationale that has emboldened the policy elite of the movement. According to Rushdoony, the framers intended to establish a Christian nation rather than a liberal democracy based on Enlightenment reason. The prohibition of an established church was binding on the federal government, not on state and local governments.

For Enlightenment thinkers, there is a natural law that can be reasoned from direct observation of nature. For Reconstructionists, right and wrong are inerrantly expressed in the Bible, and they reject the democratic notion that law is what the majority says it is, calling democracy "mob rule." Man-made law is relativistic and constitutes a secular humanism—a false religion. Reconstructionists believe in *dominionism*, the belief that properly thinking Christians have both the right and obligation to dominion over others.

The Westphalian secular state is a false god claiming sovereignty. Humanism is the established religion of state and is imposed through public education. Taxation, man-made law and courts, and public education are instruments of state control. Democracy is a new religion to serve man, not God. The UN epitomizes the globalization of secular humanism.

In Reconstructionist *theonomy*, the family has primary responsibility for health, education, and welfare; the church is responsible in the larger community funded by biblical tithe; and the state is left with responsibility for defense of church and family through armed force funded by non-biblical tax. Federal government encroachment into health, education, and welfare is totalitarianism and equated with the end of God.

Marvin Olasky, author of *Compassionate Conservatism*,[31] born a Russian Jew, was a militant Trotskyite who joined the Communist Party in 1972. Later disillusioned, he and his wife explicitly sought a belief system at the opposite extreme, found and joined a conservative Southern Baptist congregation.[32] Government should withdraw from its role in social welfare.

The televangelists Marion G. "Pat" Robertson and the late Jerry Falwell are the most recognized contemporary sociocons. Each distanced himself from some of Rushdoony's more extreme positions. Originally brought together in opposition to school integration, sociocons favor states' rights and oppose public education in favor of home schooling. Rushdoony was instrumental in establishing the home-schooling movement and the anti-abortion activist organization Operation Rescue. Falwell held together a political coalition built on a small number of positions, including anti-abortion, antihomosexual, and anti-evolutionary science positions. He declared environmentalism to be the work of Satan rather than allow it to diffuse the focus of the coalition. Rather than rejecting environmentalism under the principle that God rather than man is the prime mover, the new generation of Evangelicals is embracing environmentalism under the principle of good stewardship.

Like theocons, sociocons conflate Christianity with business and politics. And they favor the offensive use of force to spread democracy (and free enterprise and their interpretation of Christianity). This group reemerged as a political force in the Reagan era under the Falwellian banner of the "Moral Majority" and Robertson's Christian Coalition.[33] The Johnson and Nixon administrations severely damaged the public's confidence in authorities; a counterculture rejecting authorities grew in response. Sociocons were in turn energized by the excesses of the counterculture.

Neoconservative Coalition

This hawkish coalition combines the bellicose Jacksonian nature and imperialism (with respect to North America) and the Wilsonian desire to spread democracy abroad with military force. The coalition, however, has none of the isolationist tendencies of the early Puritan settlers in New England or of Jackson (with respect to Europe).

There are important differences within this political coalition. Neocons are pragmatists. That is, they believe that the use of force abroad will produce desirable policy outcomes. Theocons and sociocons use the word "pragmatist" as a pejorative. They prefer adherence to selected principles to guide action rather than the pursuit of objectives in the secular, material, temporal world.

Neocons, theocons, and sociocons share a belief in the offensive and unilateral use of force to spread democracy. All share a belief in the use of force to defend Israel; theocons and sociocons consider it to be the religious obligation of a "Christian America." All share a sense of supremacy reminiscent of the nineteenth century's "white man's burden." These groups share a belief that they are authorized and obligated to dominion over others. All advocated the invasion of Iraq. They are well organized and vocal.

The three groups found common cause in the post–Cold War era and collectively achieved political power beyond their numbers (about 17 percent).[34] Mainstream Jews, Catholics, Protestants, and secularists—the large majority—have yet to establish such a common organizational response. A countermovement from mainstream Protestants appears to be awakening; for example, Jim Wallis, a social justice evangelical and founder of Sojourners, is a name often associated with the growing alternative movement.[35]

The neoconservative label is often used to refer to the collective including secular Jewish neocons, Catholic neocons, and Protestant neocons to distinguish them from conservatives who were more prominent in the past. Conservatives of the past were disinclined to wage war citing the heavy demands on resources and the unintended consequences that would certainly follow. Many religious conservatives of the past cited the immorality of war unless as last resort.

Centrist Democrats

The *centrist Democrat* brings additional political weight to the hawkish coalition. Centrists are fiscally conservative, socially liberal, and highly interventionist. Centrists believe in maintaining a strong military and using it liberally in what is pejoratively referred to as the global police mission. They are represented by the Democratic Leadership Council rather than the Democratic National Committee. The antiwar wing of the party remains strong, and more traditional Democrats sometimes refer to centrists as the Republican wing of the Democratic Party or as Democrats in name only (DINOs). The centrist wing was formed the year after Ronald Reagan won reelection against Walter Mondale. The Public Policy Institute serves as a source for policy formulation. Prominent centrists include Sam Nunn, Bill Clinton, Al Gore, John Kerry, Joe Lieberman, and Hillary Clinton. Centrist Democrats strongly endorsed the 2003 invasion of Iraq. Centrists are motivated by the belief in democratic peace, the use of force in its pursuit, and the use of force through international institutions to preserve peace globally.

Paleoconservatives

Another conservative group, the *paleoconservatives*, lies outside the hawkish coalition. Pat Buchanan is the most visible representative of the paleocons. His book, *A Republic, Not an Empire*, serves as this group's formal statement, along with *Suicide of a Superpower*, which includes such chapter titles as "The Death of Christian America" and "The End of White America." The Rockford Institute in Rockford, Illinois, is perhaps its central organization for policy formulation and advocacy. *Chronicles: A Magazine of American Culture* and the *American Conservative* are advocacy journalism outlets.

Simply put, paleocons believe that "tradition is a better guide than reason." They are more inclined to see the threat to national security as Third World immigration diluting American culture and are more inclined to see the application of military force abroad as increasing the threat from Islamic terrorists. They do not believe that the institutions of Western culture can be imposed on non-Western societies with their own traditions. Paleocons share the belief in cultural supremacy with the hawkish coalition, but they are anti-intervention and antiglobalization, and more neo-isolationist than neoconservative.

Libertarians of the Left and Right

Liberal thought—not shared by all who self-identify as liberal and shared by some who self-identify as conservative—fears concentrated power. Individualist libertarians on the right and civil libertarians on the left share a fear of concentrated power whether in big government, big business, or the church. Corporate libertarians, in contrast, fear concentrated power in big government and prefer power concentrated in big business rather than in government. Moreover, strong national security institutions concentrate power in Washington, and that concentration poses the greatest threat to civil liberties.

Think Tanks

Beyond the partisan and ideologically aligned organizations established to formulate policy, there are organizations established to produce independent and objective analysis. In 1916, a group of business leaders and academics established the forerunner to the Brookings Institution. Its purpose was to bring the best methods of scientific management to American government without partisan or ideological agenda—pragmatism. Other organizations took root in the shadow of the original "think tank" during World War II.

Later, Congress authorized Federally Funded Research and Development Centers (FFRDC) to conduct studies and analyses. The centers are not part of government, and their employees are not civil servants. All are not-for-profit. The Rand Corporation, Institute for Defense Analyses, and the Center for Naval Analyses houses Defense Department FFRDCs. The Homeland Security Studies and Analyses Institute is the new FFRDC for the Homeland Security Department.

During the Cold War, there was a political consensus on the threat and on a strategy of containment. Associated with that was a demand for independent and objective analyses. National security and national defense were mostly bipartisan—"politics end at the water's edge." But the end of the Cold War marked the end of that as well. The Center for Strategic and International Studies, then at Georgetown University, found itself in a financial drought after the defense industry stopped sending funds. Brookings, too, had to reorient on its financial support. And the FFRDCs became more "responsive." They less aggressively offered ideas to fuel the public debate, instead leaning toward the agenda of their sponsoring agencies and current administration.

At the same time, ideologically aligned think tanks amassed enviable endowments. The best-known and most influential serve the various wings of the Republican Party. The American Enterprise Institute was established in 1943 by New York business interests. It has experienced ups and downs coincident with changes in conservatism. It has housed centrist, establishment conservative, neoconservative, and nonideological analysts. The Heritage Foundation was established in 1973 by Paul Weyrich, Edwin Feulner, and Joseph Coors. Energized in opposition to Nixon's perceived liberalism, it pursues a conservative agenda as understood by the New Right. The Cato Institute serves the same purpose for the probusiness libertarian wing (corporate libertarians). It was founded by Edward Crane and funded by Charles Koch in 1977. They are more lobbying or advocacy organizations formulating policy options for use by like-minded politicians. It is hard to find a well-known or influential think tank chartered to pursue a liberal or progressive agenda. The Center for American Progress was established in 2003 as a late entry in the competition, but it has yet to achieve the influence or name recognition of the conservative institutions.

These parallel trends have consequences. Conservatives, of all stripes, have built a distinct advantage. Their think tanks are real and influential. The Democratic Party and its funding sources have not invested in the competition. The FFRDCs have moved away from fierce independence and objectivity toward being responsive to their executive branch sponsors and whichever party occupies the White House. The country is not well served.

Party Traditions

The Democratic and Republican Parties are powerful actors in formulating policy—including national security policy—perhaps the most powerful. With no basis in the Constitution, the parties provide the electorate with its choices. Over the long term, the parties stand for nothing permanent, while political factions have a degree of persistence. In the short term, parties are coalitions of factions formed around a few principles, or better said, around positions on a few issues. Parties prioritize issues differently, and they take different positions on the issues. Over time, the significance of issues rises and falls, and the parties adapt or collapse.[36] The evidence today indicates that the parties are polarized around a small number of issues and that neither polar position represents mainstream Americans.

David Von Drehle retraces the realignments of American political parties—the fracturing of parties and the birth of new parties formed from the remnants—up to the present time and leaves open the possibility that another realignment is in the offing.[37]

George Washington stated flatly that the parties are the "truly worst enemy" of popular government.[38] John Adams added, "There is nothing I dread so much as a division of the Republic into two great parties, each arranged under its leader and converting measures into opposition to each other. This, in my humble opinion, is to be feared as the greatest political evil under our Constitution."[39] Madison, in *Federalist* No. 10, predicted the formation of parties of self-interest separating those with property and those without, and between debtors and creditors.[40] And as one partisan realignment was taking place, Theodore Roosevelt said, "The old parties are husks . . . with no real soul within either, divided on artificial lines, boss-ridden and privilege-controlled, each a jumble of incongruous elements, and neither daring to speak out wisely and fearlessly on what should be said on the vital issues of the day."[41] When Congress convened to consider needed improvements to the Articles of Confederation, Hamilton and his followers favored a stronger role for the federal government relative to the states. Hamilton's Federalist Party was northern, big government, high taxes, and big business. Jefferson's Republicans (who would soon call themselves the Democratic-Republican Party and finally just the Democratic Party) preferred a looser confederation of states with a relatively weak central government. They were southern, small government, low taxes, rural, and populist.

> Once upon a time in America, there was a political party that believed in a strong central government, high taxes and bold public works projects. This party was popular on the college campuses of New England and was the overwhelming choice of African American voters. It was the Republican Party.
>
> The Republicans got started as a counterweight to the other party: the party of low taxes and limited government, the party suspicious of Eastern elites, the party that thought Washington should butt out of the affairs of private property owners. The Democrats.[42]

The Constitution's framers were unable to resolve the issue of slavery and chose compromise over no union. Slavery continued to haunt the country and the parties. When the Democratic Party made school desegregation a plank in the party platform, the States' Rights Democratic Party split from the party and ran its own presidential candidate, Senator Strom Thurman. George Wallace ran as a Democrat and as a third-party candidate during the 1960s. Regionally successful in the Southeast, they could not succeed nationally. The southern Democrats increasingly migrated to the Republican Party. Riffs are apparent in both parties today.

The Myth of Red and Blue States

Morris Fiorina offers evidence of present-day partisan instability in *Culture War? The Myth of a Polarized America*. Partisans who see the world in

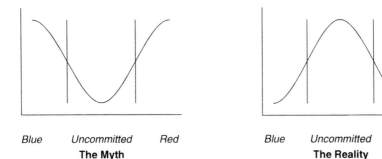

Blue   Uncommitted   Red   Blue   Uncommitted   Red
     The Myth   **The Reality**

FIG. 3. The myth of a polarized electorate

terms of a single two-valued variable depict the contest by painting states in red and blue. Republicans assert the dominance of their party by pointing to a very red map as if the Constitution contained a one-acre-one-vote clause. Some large red states have smaller populations than many large blue cities. The red-and-blue map conveys nothing meaningful except the maldistribution of power represented by Senate seats and the winner-take-all rules of the Electoral College. In most cases, elections are won by small margins, making most states a shade of purple.[43] Elements of the media dutifully pass the red-and-blue image to the public, promoting the myth of a polarized electorate.

The myth and reality of the public's polarization are depicted in figure 3. The myth is that large segments of the population are closely aligned with the positions of either the Democratic or Republican Party. The myth also includes the notion that there is a swing vote represented by the undecided, who are committed to no clear principles. The reality is quite different. When asked, few respondents claim that either party represents their principles. The majority of the electorate (about two-thirds) is not accurately represented by either party. The parties are polarized; the American public is not. The public is centrist or moderate.

According to Fiorina, many Americans imagine their electoral choice to be:

> Between a Republican Party that dreams of dismantling the federal safety net and a Democratic Party that sees tax increases as the only tool for reforming it.

Between a Republican Party that has abandoned fiscal responsibility for "borrow-and-spend" and a Democratic Party that has never credibly renounced its historic commitment to "tax and spend."

Between a Republican Party that equates crony capitalism with free enterprise and a Democratic Party in thrall to public sector unions with vested interests in preserving the status quo and raising government spending.

Between a Republican Party whose appointees subjugate empirical evidence to religion and ideology and a Democratic Party whose activists hold mainstream religion and values in contempt.

And between a Republican Party whose neoconservative ideologues advocate foreign policies they fear are recklessly antagonistic and a Democratic Party whose Michael Moore wing they suspect does not truly believe that the United States is the best country that ever existed.[44]

Discussing the public's attitudes on abortion, Fiorina notes "a significant number of people who believe that abortion is wrong [but] nevertheless support the principle of a woman's right to choose."[45] He deals with this apparent inconsistency by saying that "many people may simply decline to impose their personal views on the rest of society." This simple and plausible explanation leads one to consider movement, not along the horizontal left-right axis, but along the vertical anarchist-totalitarian axis of figure 2.

For Consideration

It is reasonable to conclude that the United States is in a period of deep instability both politically and strategically. The political parties, even collectively, do not represent mainstream America. The public is becoming restless. The next political alignment can be only temporary. The wars in Iraq and Afghanistan held dominance in the national security debate, but even as they draw down, the United States still needs to define its place in the new world more broadly. The era continues to be called the post–Cold War or post-9/11 era, having no name that captures the current and foreseeable geostrategic environment.

The U.S. role in the international system of states dictates, and is expressed in, its grand strategy. Part 2 is devoted to national security strategy, including four decades of relative stability in Cold War grand strategy followed by wild jumps in post–Cold War grand strategy with no stability in sight. Reforming the country's national security apparatus must take place in this morass of partisan and strategic instability.

3   War Powers

The Constitution divides war powers between Congress and the president. The president is chief executive, chief diplomat, and commander in chief of the armed forces. Congress alone can declare war and authorize the use of force, Congress alone can appropriate funds, and Congress alone can raise and supply armies for war. The Constitution's framers thought it should be difficult to take the country into war, and, therefore, the power to commence war was put in the hands of those who would bear the costs. Congress also has the power of oversight and investigation to ensure that the executive branch faithfully implements the will of the people as expressed in legislation. When officials abuse their power, the Constitution grants Congress the authority to impeach.

From George Washington forward, presidents have been consolidating their power over foreign affairs and the use of military force.[1] The general pattern has been for Congress to cede powers to the president in times of war and to reclaim some of them after war. Following foreign policy blunders, Congress has an even stronger hand in reducing presidential war powers. But in the long-term give-and-take, the presidency has gained more than it has lost. Even with the more egregious excesses, presidents suffered setbacks, but the presidency overcame and continued to accumulate power.[2]

That there has been a shift in war powers from Congress to the president is uncontested. There is some agreement that the shift undermines republican democracy. There is serious disagreement on how much power a president needs in the twenty-first century. There are those who assert the continued applicability of the Constitution and those who assert power far beyond the Constitution.

Several explanations exist for why the shift has taken place. The framers recognized that some qualities gave the executive advantage over representative bodies. Some arguments highlight the need for speed. Others argue that the principal explanation for the shift is Congress's desire to avoid risk and accountability. Many attribute the shift from congressional to presidential government to the weakened parties that cannot discipline Congress against a unitary president. To explain more recent behavior, still others point to the lack of widely agreed-to post–Cold War policy objectives.

The nature of the shift is broad and deep. Authorization has shifted from Congress to the president, as presidents since Truman have commenced military operations virtually at will or have claimed authority flowing from the UN or NATO. The existence of a standing military since Truman removed Congress's relevance in raising an army for war. Appropriation has shifted from Congress to the president, as the executive captured the budget process in 1921, reprograms appropriated funds, and even finances operations with funds from foreign sources. And the all-volunteer military reduced the president's need to consider public support. Once the president has deployed forces, Congress is left to "support the troops but not the policy."

This chapter begins with a review of war powers as specified in the Constitution, in case law, and as elaborated in statute. It then summarizes specific uses of force with or without authority. Next, the post–Vietnam War Powers Resolution is summarized and is accompanied by a summary of presidential compliance. The chapter concludes with items for consideration.

Shifting War-Making Authorities

The people, through their Constitution, grant specific war-making powers to Congress and the president. The preponderance of war-making powers is vested in the people's branch. Anticipating the demands of crises, Congress has seen fit to craft additional authorities that can be granted temporarily to the president. After covering the constitutional and statutory authorities, this section briefly retraces the shift from congressional to presidential war making.

Constitutional Authorities

Congress has sole authority to declare war. In war, the president is commander in chief of the armed forces. Presidents are expected to use force to repel invasions without first asking for authority. Congress and the people expect nothing less. These things are inarguably true. But there is much to argue about concerning the use of armed force.

The authority to take the nation to war was a significant subject of debate in 1787 at the Philadelphia convention. Pierce Butler of South Carolina recommended that the president should have that authority because he "will have all the requisite qualities and will not make war but when the nation will support it." Elbridge Gerry of Massachusetts countered that he "never expected to hear in a republic a motion to empower the executive alone to declare war." Charles Pinckney, also of South Carolina, thought the number of representatives in the House was too high for such deliberations and would be too slow; he recommended that the Senate, with its greater understanding of foreign affairs, would be better suited.[3]

As the debate settled, the draft constitutional language gave Congress the power to "make war," but those words were quickly amended. Madison and Gerry "moved to insert 'declare,' striking out 'make' war; leaving to the Executive the power to repel sudden attacks." Common use at the time equated "declare" and "commence."[4] If an enemy commenced war by attacking, the president had the authority and obligation to respond. But absent an enemy attack, the president was obliged to seek congressional authorization to commence hostilities.

Among the framers, Madison favored Congress as policy maker, and in opposition Hamilton championed a strong executive. According to Madison, "it was Congress's constitutional role to determine the substance and direction of American foreign policy, while the task of the president was limited to implementing the will of the legislature."[5] But even Hamilton proposed that the Senate "have the sole power of declaring war" and that the executive "have the direction of war when authorized or begun."[6] "With the war-making propensities of absolute monarchs in mind, the framers of the Constitution took care to assign the vital foreign policy powers exclusively to Congress."[7]

The preponderance of war-making powers resides in Congress.

Article I, § 8. The Congress shall have Power To . . . provide for the common Defense and general Welfare of the United States . . . To regulate Commerce with foreign Nations . . . To define and punish Piracies and Felonies committed on the high Seas, and Offenses against the Law of Nations; To declare War, grant Letters of Marque and Reprisal, and make Rules concerning Captures on Land and Water; To raise and support Armies, but no Appropriation of Money to that Use shall be for a longer Term than two Years; To provide and maintain a Navy; To make Rules for the Government and Regulation of the land and naval Forces; To provide for calling forth the Militia to execute the Laws of the Union, suppress Insurrections and repel Invasions; To provide for organizing, arming, and disciplining the Militia, and for governing such Part of them as may be employed in the Service of the United States, reserving to the States respectively, the Appointment of the Officers, and the Authority of training the Militia according to the discipline prescribed by Congress; . . . To make all Laws which shall be necessary and proper for carrying into Execution the foregoing Powers . . .

Article I, § 9. No Money shall be drawn from the Treasury, but in Consequence of Appropriations made by Law;

The remaining war-making powers reside with the president as chief executive, chief diplomat, and commander in chief of the armed forces.

Article II, § 1. The executive Power shall be vested in a President of the United States of America.

The framers believed that the executive uniquely possessed qualities— "unity, decision, secrecy, dispatch, stability of purpose, special sources of information"—that were desirable in the conduct of diplomacy.[8] The framers also understood that representative institutions, on the other hand, "drew their strength from a mobilized public."[9]

Article II, § 2. He shall have the Power, by and with the Advice and Consent of the Senate, to make Treaties, provided two thirds of the Senators present concur; . . .

Article II, § 3. He shall receive Ambassadors . . .

Foreign policy has both commercial and political aspects. Washington's Farewell Address characterizes a popular sentiment of the founders: "The great rule of conduct for us in regard to foreign nations is, in extending our commercial relations to have with them as little political connection as possible."[10] In accordance with that sentiment, the Constitution gives Congress the more important power to regulate commerce with foreign nations. To the president went the power over what Washington wanted to minimize, political relations with foreign nations. The president may make treaties, but only if two-thirds of the Senate approves.

Hamilton thought differently. The president has the initiative in foreign policy and if necessary takes independent action. In the extreme, he may deliver Congress a fait accompli. Presidents have behaved more as monarchist Hamilton prescribed.

> Article II, § 2. The President shall be Commander in Chief of the Army and Navy of the United States, and of the Militia of the several States, when called into the actual Service of the United States.

The framers were well aware that command of military and naval forces must be guided by one. The principle of unity of command was well understood.

> The President of the United States is to be "commander-in-chief of the army and navy of the United States . . ." The propriety of this provision is so evident in itself. . . . Of all the cares or concerns of government, the direction of war most peculiarly demands those qualities which distinguish the exercise of power in a single hand. The direction of war implies the direction of the common strength; and the power of directing and employing the common strength forms a usual and essential part of the definition of the executive authority.[11]

A strong executive was necessary, not just to command the armed forces in war, but to provide the energy necessary to overcome the inertia of the other branches.[12] But that initiative was not to go unchecked.

The framers were well aware of the problem of too much power residing in the hands of one man or one department. War making was to be one of the most important powers that must be divided. The quotations below make clear the framers' understanding and their intentions.

The Constitution supposes what the history of all governments demonstrates, that the Executive is the branch of power most interested in war, and most prone to it. It has accordingly with studied care, vested the question of war in the Legislature.[13]

The President is to be commander-in-chief of the army and navy of the United States. In this respect his authority would be nominally the same with that of the king of Great Britain, but in substance much inferior to it. It would amount to nothing more than the supreme command and direction of the military and naval forces, as first general and admiral of the Confederacy; while that of the British king extends to the *declaring* of war and to the *raising* and *regulating* of fleets and armies—all which, by the Constitution under consideration, would appertain to the legislature.[14]

To what expedient, then, shall we finally resort, for maintaining in practice the necessary partition of power among the several departments laid down in the Constitution? . . . [T]he great security against a gradual concentration of the several powers in the same department consists in giving to those who administer each department the necessary constitutional means and personal motives to resist encroachments of the others. . . . Ambition must be made to counteract ambition.[15]

In the language contemporary to the constitutional debate, *general war* and *perfect war* were expressions used to describe the condition when two states were mobilized for war. But there was also common language used to describe *limited war* or *imperfect war* when states used military force to pursue limited objectives. Declarations of war were associated with the former, and authorizations for the use of force were for the latter. Both were the domain of Congress.

The logic was quickly confirmed and clarified in Supreme Court rulings. In 1800, the Supreme Court ruled in *Bas v. Tingy* that only Congress could authorize war whether perfect or imperfect: "Congress is impowered to declare a general war, or congress may wage a limited war; limited in place, in objects, and in time." In the 1801 *Talbot v. Seeman* case, Chief Justice Marshall wrote, "The whole powers of war being, by the

Constitution of the United States, vested in congress . . . the congress may authorize general hostilities . . . or partial war."[16]

Congress can place limits on its grants of authority as well. In the 1804 *Little v. Barreme* case, the Court ruled that the commander in chief cannot go beyond Congress's explicit instructions.[17] Limits have included, for example, use of forces limited to naval rather than all armed forces. In *Little v. Barreme*, the limit at issue was the authority to seize ships going *to* French ports rather than *to and from* French ports.

The granting of "Letters of Marque and Reprisal" authorizes an anachronistic form of commerce warfare governed by *Prize Rules*. Such letters authorize privateers to conduct piracy by seizing enemy ships and sharing the booty with the granting government. The United States hasn't authorized this form of warfare since 1815. The Treaty of Paris (1856) outlawed the practice, and although the United States is not a signatory, it has explicitly agreed to honor the international norm. But this clause makes clear that the power to authorize even limited acts of war was granted to Congress.[18]

Standby Statutory Authorities

Congress has crafted extensive standby authorities for the president during a state of war or state of national emergency. By international law, a declaration of war establishes a state of war whether or not armed conflict is ongoing. If there is open armed conflict, whether or not war is declared, then a state of war exists. Under a state of war, declared or not, the international laws of war are in effect. Only Congress can declare war, but the president can declare a national emergency.

In excess of 250 laws are triggered automatically upon congressional declaration of war. The standby authorities are largely enumerated in the Alien Enemies Act (1798), the Trading with the Enemy Act (1917), the National Emergencies Act (1976), and the International Emergency Economic Powers Act (1977).[19] In the aftermath of the Vietnam War, a 1976 Senate investigation found four declared emergencies were still in effect, including a banking crisis (1933), the Korean Conflict (1950), a postal workers strike (1970), and economic inflation (1971). The National Emergencies Act terminated those declarations and withdrew certain authorities. Congress then enacted the International Emergency Powers Act to establish more restrictive presidential emergency powers and stronger congressional oversight.

Collectively, these statutes give the president expansive powers over the military, foreign trade, transportation, communications, manufacturing, alien enemies, and more. For example, President Carter declared a national emergency with respect to Iran in 1973 and imposed economic sanctions, including asset freezing, trade embargos, and travel bans. The resulting actions are typically initiated by presidential executive order.

Many authorities are expedients that give executive branch secretaries authority to act and then notify Congress rather than require advance authorization. Although expansive, they are what a reasonable person would expect in a country mobilized for war. The same reasonable person might find these powers excessive during an easily declared national emergency.

Absent a formal declaration, the existence of a state of war triggers some of the standby authorities. None is automatically triggered by a congressional authorization for the use of force. A presidential declaration of a national emergency may trigger some. Upon declaration of an emergency, the president is subject to consultation and review and is required to report actions taken to Congress. The president must specify which statutory authorities he or she intends to use prior to use. The declaration automatically expires in one year unless the president renews the declaration, and Congress can terminate a declared emergency at any time by joint resolution.

Whether Imperial or Constitutional Presidency

George Washington, Abraham Lincoln, and Franklin Roosevelt wielded extraordinary powers during times of national crisis, but they made no claims to authorities beyond those enumerated in the Constitution.[20] The president took the initiative, engaged Congress, and in extreme cases asked permission after the fact and risked rebuke.

The classic explanation for extraconstitutional powers wielded by the chief magistrate is what John Locke referred to as the prerogative of the crown. The *Lockean prerogative* is "the power to act according to discretion for the public good, without the prescription of the law and sometimes even against it."[21]

Truman was the first to claim extraconstitutional war powers. Eisenhower saw Congress as a full partner but inadvertently contributed to the growth of presidential war powers by establishing the precedent of asking for and receiving preauthorization to use force to deal with a crisis that appeared to be developing off China. Presidential powers grew during the Kennedy-Johnson years and peaked under Nixon. Following Nixon's excesses, Congress's scrambling to reclaim powers greatly contributed to the weakness of the Carter administration. Following Carter, the Reagan administration set out to reclaim imagined powers and presidential dominance. Congress bowed to a popular president and, in Schlesinger's words, showed that even a president "with only a misty understanding of issues" could dominate Congress.[22] The end of the Cold War appeared to usher in a return to constitutional democracy, but only temporarily. Post–Cold War presidents have continued amassing presidential powers.

Presidential historians and scholars converged on the idea of an imperial presidency toward the end of the Nixon-Agnew administration as each was forced from office in disgrace. As the Nixon era came to an end, Arthur Schlesinger published the 1973 classic *The Imperial Presidency*. In 1998, as the House impeached Clinton, the same scholars announced the end of the imperial presidency. But by 1999 a new imperial presidency was emergent. The imperial presidency is very much alive.[23]

By imperial, Schlesinger does not mean that the United States is attempting to acquire empire in the sense of conquest or colonialism; instead, he means an unchecked president. The Constitution favored a strong presidency and an equally "strong system of accountability." "When the constitutional balance shifts to the presidency," Schlesinger writes, "the presidency can be said to become imperial." Schlesinger goes on to argue that the domain of foreign policy is the "perennial threat to the constitutional balance." At this point, the obligatory reference must be made to Edward S. Corwin and his conclusion that the Constitution is "an invitation to struggle for the privilege of directing American foreign policy."[24]

Two modern-day schools of thought are apparent. One school favors a conservative interpretation of the Constitution with congressional dominance in war powers. The other school favors a liberal extrapolation granting extraconstitutional authorities to the president.

The *doctrine of original intent* forces interpreters of the constitutional text to seek meaning from the intentions of the framers, including the debates during the summer of 1787 captured in Madison's notes and the *Federalist* and *Anti-Federalist Papers* that accompanied the ratification process. Some opponents doubt the underlying assumption that the fifty-plus men who attended the convention ever arrived at unified intent. *Textualists* reject the doctrine of original intent, instead following the text that is written rather than the rationale that produced it. Conservatives tend to either textualist or intentionalist interpretations. Leonard Levy provides the mainstream intentionalist view that "the imperial presidency has no support in the Framer's understanding."[25] It is exceedingly difficult to understand how presidential war derives from a textualist or intentionalist interpretation of the Constitution. Such claims are made nonetheless; John Yoo presents both congressionalist and presidentialist perspectives under intentionalism.[26]

Still others believe that the framers could not have anticipated the technological advances of two centuries and that the text must be open to interpretation in the current context. They subscribe to the *living document* school. For some of them, therefore, the constitutional text and the authors' original intentions are anachronisms and are of interest only to academics. Liberals tend to the living document interpretation. The living document school is typified by David Mervin's response to an article criticizing the Clinton administration's unauthorized use of military force:

> The framers sought to make Congress preeminent in war making, an understandable and plausible intention at the end of the eighteenth century. More than two hundred years later, the situation has changed profoundly. Prodigious technological development, the expiration of U.S. isolation, and the massive information advantages that now accrue to the executive have combined to undermine the reasoning that lay behind the fashioning of the War Clause. These realities have gained credence among members of Congress, judges, and the public at large, but have yet to be widely accepted in the academic community.[27]

Honest people may disagree on what powers a president needs in the twenty-first century. The dominant parties have not taken permanent positions on the issue of presidential war. As with many principles, the parties have traded places over time. Today, both parties exhibit a strong-presidency preference, especially when their president is in power. As Gary Hess writes:

> The "strong presidency" advocates—who have shifted from "liberal internationalists" during the early Cold War to "conservative unilateralists" in recent decades—have considered such [congressional] resolutions [authorizing force] a political annoyance, not a constitutional necessity. Supporters of preserving congressional power to declare war—whose core political constituency has shifted from conservative to liberal—have resented the resolutions as preemptive presidential "blank checks."[28]

Immediately upon inauguration in 1933, FDR began expanding the executive branch in the face of worldwide depression, and he initiated the practice of conducting foreign policy through *executive agreement* rather than through the constitutional treaty provision.

The landmark Supreme Court ruling, *U.S. v. Curtiss-Wright Corporation et al.*, was delivered in 1936.[29] Justice George Sutherland reaffirmed the requirement for narrow delegation from Congress to the president in domestic affairs but insisted that different rules applied in foreign affairs. He asserted "the very delicate, plenary and exclusive power of the President as the sole organ of the federal government in the field of international relations."[30]

Sutherland's opinion quoted a speech given in the House of Representatives in 1799 by Representative John Marshall (later to become Justice Marshall). Marshall referred to the president as "the sole organ of the nation in its external relations." Given the full context, Corwin concludes that Marshall was referring to "the President's role as instrument of communication with other governments."[31] The president was the sole organ for communicating foreign policy but not for formulating foreign policy.

Furthermore, the case was about foreign commerce, not war powers. For those reasons, Justice Robert H. Jackson subsequently dismissed these statements as *dicta*—comments made by a judge with only incidental bearing on the point to be decided and therefore nonbinding.[32]

Regardless, in the 1937 *U.S. v. Belmont* case and again in the 1941 *U.S. v. Pink* case, Sutherland reaffirmed the position he took in *Curtiss-Wright*. The president had adopted the practice of using *executive agreements* rather than treaties in dealing with foreign powers. The Senate is not required to vote on executive agreements, and the Court ruled that executive agreement has the same effect as treaty. The Senate became irrelevant in the process. *Curtiss-Wright* represents a pronounced shift of foreign relations authorities away from Congress and to the president. *Belmont* is "without doubt . . . one of the most extreme extensions which could be accorded to the power of the President."[33]

With legislation from the world wars repealed and wartime Supreme Court support for executive preeminence withdrawn, Truman ran into trouble. After he took over the steel industry under his claimed authority as commander in chief, the Supreme Court ruled against Truman in *Youngstown Sheet & Tube Co. v. Sawyer*. In *Youngstown*, Justice Hugo Black wrote that had Truman based his action on other of the available statutes, he may have prevailed. Instead, Truman based his actions on his constitutional commander-in-chief authorities, and Black concluded that those authorities did not extend to the domestic manufacturing sector. The president is commander in chief of the armed forces, not of the nation. Also in *Youngtown*, Justice Robert H. Jackson added what would later be cited frequently as the three-part test:

1. The president's power is "at its maximum . . . when the president acted pursuant to an express or implied authorization of Congress";
2. the president's power is "at its lowest ebb" when the president took action incompatible with the express or implied will of Congress; and
3. "there is a zone of twilight" when the president relied on his independent power in the absence of congressional grant or denial of authority.[34]

Impeachment and Censure

The Constitution provides for the removal of the highest officials of the land, including the president.[35] Thomas Jefferson proclaimed "a party of revolution against the royal prerogatives—the divine right of kings and the corruptions of empire associated with an essentially unfettered monarch."[36] We would be a nation of laws, not men. Nixon's statement, "When the president does it, that means that it is not illegal," captures the rule-of-man over rule-of-law attitude and Locke's prerogative of the crown.[37] But presidents have arrogated to themselves extraconstitutional powers reminiscent of the era of divine right monarchy. They have shown contempt for the people's branch and contempt for the Constitution. And these are exactly the fears that prompted the framers to include impeachment in the Constitution. Responding to Nixon's excesses, "rule-of-law Republicans" moved toward impeachment, saying, "The power of impeachment is the Constitution's paramount power of self-preservation."[38]

Our impeachment process is borrowed from the British. It is an integral part of the development of the rule of law over the rule of man, as parliamentary democracy slowly supplanted divine right monarchy.[39] The first impeachment was in 1376, when the first speaker of the House of Commons impeached two noblemen for raiding the public treasury. The next impeachment was in 1386 and introduced the catchall phrase of *high crimes and misdemeanors* while charging officials with "squandering away the public treasury" and "procuring offices for persons who were unfit, and unworthy of them."

Another phrase was introduced early in the evolution of divided government: Parliament's *power of the purse*. King Charles was in the habit of employing public resources in support of his royal relatives waging wars on the European continent. In 1620, Parliament limited grants of public funds for those wars. When so challenged, Charles repeatedly dissolved Parliament, acts that led to what became known as the Eleven Year Tyranny under claims of divine right monarchy. To the category of high misdemeanor was added "attempting to subvert the fundamental laws of the kingdom." Charles was eventually overthrown and executed.

As the distribution of power between government branches grew clearer, impeachment was called many things, including the "primary instrument of parliamentary resistance to the crown," "the chief institution for the preservation of government," the tool through which we have "broken the grip of monarchy and embraced the rule of law," and the "key weapon in the long struggle of parliament against the abuse of executive power."[40] Impeachment was well known to the founding fathers.

During the American constitutional convention, impeachable offenses included terms both broad and narrow. They included "treachery, corrupting electors, and incapacity," "malpractice and neglect of duty," "treason and bribery," "attempts to subvert the Constitution," and "maladministration."[41] In the final document, the wording was reduced to "Treason, Bribery, or other high Crimes and Misdemeanors." We would not elect an unfettered king for four years.

Articles of impeachment brought against modern-day presidents are diverse but resonate with the charges of earlier centuries. The second article brought against Nixon was for abusing the power of office to attack his critics.[42] Articles brought against Reagan concerned the shipment of arms from Israel to Iran, funding the Nicaraguan Contras, failing to notify Congress, and "his disregard for the laws of the United States and pattern of assault and irresponsible decisionmaking." The fourth article brought against the elder Bush concerned "committing the United States to acts of war without congressional consent and contrary to the UN Charter and international law."[43]

Censure is not specified in the Constitution, but it is an established part of congressional traditions. Andrew Jackson was censured by the Senate in 1834 for assuming unconstitutional powers by defunding the Bank of the United States. The House censured John Tyler in 1842 for a veto and the tone of his veto message. James Polk provoked "an armed skirmish between American and Mexican forces" and then asked Congress for a declaration of war. Congress granted the declaration in 1848, but first it voted to censure Polk for instigating an unconstitutional and unnecessary war. Censure provides a formal method short of impeachment for publicly holding the president accountable.[44]

Uses of Force

Not all uses of military force are equal. To put the nation on a war footing, Congress may *declare war*. To achieve more limited objectives, Congress may *authorize the use of force*. Presidents may request authorization anticipating future need, and presidents increasingly use force without authorization. The Constitution does not require a declaration of war. It does, however, require that Congress initiate the use of force.

Congressional Declarations of War

In earlier centuries, declarations of war were part of formal international relations. Declarations specified the grievances of one state against another, specified what the offending state must do to redress those grievances, and specified what would be done if those grievances were not redressed. But the formal declaration of war was falling out of favor in the sixteenth century.

A formal declaration of war creates a *state of war* under international law. Generally, a declaration of war terminates diplomatic and commercial relations between the two states and abrogates their treaties. Independent of congressional declarations of war and authorizations for the use of force, the *international laws of war*—for example, the Geneva and Hague Conventions—are in effect whenever a state of war exists.

Hallett makes the distinction between *reasoned* and *unreasoned* declarations of war.[45] He cites the Declaration of Independence as a clear example of a reasoned declaration. By reasoned, he means that the grievances leading to war and the political objectives sought are specified. Those political objectives set the highest level military objectives to be achieved and, simultaneously, set the conditions for war termination. Specifying political objectives is an initial step in strategy formulation. Coincidentally or not, the Declaration of Independence also meets the requirements of just war deliberations.

There have been eleven formal declarations of war spanning five wars: the War of 1812, the Mexican-American War in 1846, the Spanish-American War in 1898, and the two world wars.[46] All were at the request of the president.

The Spanish-American War stands alone among U.S. declarations of war. Rather than a response to an attack on the United States, war was declared to drive Spain out of the Western Hemisphere, specifically out of Cuba. The result was the removal of Spain as a world power and what has been called "empire by default" for the United States as it acquired colonial responsibilities in the Pacific and Caribbean.

None of the eleven congressional declarations of war meets the standards of a reasoned declaration or presents the basis of a just war. The presidential requests, however, typically contain elements of both. This is just one more thing that Congress has passively ceded to the president. By its action and inaction, Congress has retained for itself the authority to state the obvious.

Short of declared war, Congress has authorized the use of force for a variety of purposes.

Congressional Authorizations for the Use of Force

With advisory forces already committed to Vietnam, Congress granted President Lyndon Baines Johnson (1963–69) broad and open-ended authorization in what is commonly known as the Gulf of Tonkin Resolution. On 2 August 1964, the USS *Maddox* destroyer in international waters off North Vietnam reported a possible attack. *Maddox* was conducting intelligence gathering simultaneously and in close proximity to ongoing U.S.-sponsored commando raids conducted by the South Vietnamese against the North. On 4 August, with tensions high, another incident occurred, but it appears that no attack by the North actually took place. Johnson ordered retaliatory air strikes the same day. Johnson, looking to escalate, seized the opportunity of the apparent attack and met with congressional leaders to request support on 5 August. Congress passed a joint resolution on 10 August authorizing the use of force as necessary to assure peace and security in Southeast Asia and to assist any member state of the Southeast Asia Treaty Organization. The eventual employment of more than five hundred thousand troops to Vietnam was conducted under this open-ended authorization, and Congress acquiesced.

President Richard Milhous Nixon (1969–74) campaigned against and inherited an increasingly unpopular war in Vietnam. Nixon very soon approved a secret bombing campaign in Cambodia conducted between March 1969 and May 1970. In March 1970, Nixon authorized a ground incursion into Cambodia; he publicly announced the incursion the night of 30 April, and the operation was conducted from 1 May to 30 June 1970.

In late December 1970, congressional appropriations legislation sought to constrain the president and the war by prohibiting the use of funds for the introduction of ground forces or advisors into Cambodia. Congress repealed the Gulf of Tonkin Resolution on 12 January 1971. In late June 1973, appropriations language included a prohibition on the expenditure of funds after 15 August 1973 to support "combat activities in or over North

Vietnam, South Vietnam, Laos or Cambodia."[47] December 1974 legislation limited presence in Vietnam to four thousand troops within six months and to three thousand within a year.

Presidential dominance over Congress, which was established largely through claims of supposed commander-in-chief authorities and virtually uncontested from 1945 to 1965, underwent a temporary reversal after Vietnam.

Presidential Uses of Force without Congressional Authorization

Throughout American history, presidents have had the responsibility and authority to repel invasion. During the Cold War, this manifested in the authority to launch a massive nuclear counterattack against the Soviet Union. That the president had this immediate authority, without the need to confer with Congress, was a critically important component of deterrence. It could be no other way.

Presidents have ordered military force to extract embassy personnel and citizens from abroad when the local situation is threatening. Those evacuations are too numerous to list. No one contests the president's authority and responsibility for those uses of force to protect American lives. But there are debatable uses of force without authorization. Presidents have employed air strikes without congressional authorization. Truman bypassed Congress to initiate war in Korea, Eisenhower requested preauthorization for possible contingencies, and Clinton waged an air war in Kosovo after Congress denied authorization.

Presidents have conducted a variety of air strikes without congressional authority. Air strikes were conducted against Libya (1986), Iraq (1993), Bosnia (1993), the Sudan and Afghanistan (1998), and Yugoslavia (1999). One can argue that these air strikes are part of a larger coercive diplomacy effort rather than acts of war and, thus, are within the president's purview to conduct foreign policy under the Constitution. Previously allowed under international law, the UN Charter made illegal the reprisal—an act that follows a previous illegal act of another state. Reprisals continue, however, and are usually rationalized as acts of self-defense. The legality of modern reprisals—for example, Reagan's air strike against Libya and Clinton's air strike against Iraq—are questionable at best.

But the war in Korea cannot be so rationalized. President Truman bypassed Congress completely. He asked for neither a declaration of war nor an authorization for the use of force. Instead, he cited as his authority a UN resolution.[48] It should be noted that Article 43 of the UN Charter stipulates that providing military forces "shall be subject to ratification by the signatory states in accordance with their respective constitutional processes." In the UN Participation Act of 1945, Congress demanded that Article 43 be satisfied, providing forces "shall be subject to the approval of the Congress by appropriate Act or joint resolution." Similarly, the North Atlantic Treaty says that a country's military forces will be committed "in accordance with their respective constitutional processes."

On Saturday afternoon, 24 June 1950, Secretary of State Dean Acheson informed President Truman, who was visiting his home in Missouri, of the North Korean invasion of the South. Acheson also notified the UN Security Council, which by Sunday afternoon produced a U.S.-drafted resolution against North Korea.

Upon Truman's return to Washington, rather than convene the National Security Council, he sought the advice of his principal military advisors after dinner Sunday evening. After deliberations, Truman instructed his advisors not to discuss the issue during meetings with congressional committees scheduled for the following day, Monday, 26 June.

Truman met first with congressional leaders to discuss Korea on 27 June. When asked if the United States would defend South Korea, he answered yes and further offered that the response would be under the UN resolution. On this, day three of the conflict, Truman ordered air and sea forces to support the South. On the seventh day of the conflict, as North Korea routed South Korean forces, Truman belatedly committed ground forces. Only afterward did Truman meet again with members of Congress to formally notify them of his actions.

Acheson recommended that the president address a joint session of Congress to report, not to request authorization. Truman declined even that. The president had general support on the substance of his decision but not on his legal authority. There is every reason to believe that Congress would have granted the authority had it been requested.

As an immediate result, bipartisan support in Congress on foreign and national security policy, most notably led by Republican Senator Arthur H. Vandenberg, was damaged. Bipartisanship prior to the Korean Conflict produced both the North Atlantic Treaty and the European Recovery Act (the Marshall Plan).[49]

Truman's so-called "police action" in Korea was the "first full-scale United States war without a Congressional declaration."[50] Truman later deployed forces permanently to Europe in support of NATO without congressional authorization. His third act involved the declaration of a state of emergency and the seizure of steel mills in 1950 to support the Korean Conflict. Only Congress has that authority. Thus, Truman's third act was rebuked by the courts and declared unconstitutional in *Youngstown.*

Eisenhower campaigned on the promise to end Truman's war. Unlike Truman, Eisenhower considered Congress to be a full partner. Anticipating the need to defend Formosa and the Pescadores against Chinese encroachment, Eisenhower requested congressional authorization to use force in advance.[51] He received it, but conditions did not require its use. To institute the Eisenhower Doctrine, he asked Congress in advance to agree to military action in support of the territorial integrity and political independence of states in the Middle East against "aggression from any nation controlled by International Communism." In a closed-door session of the Senate Foreign Relations Committee, Secretary of State John Foster Dulles said that Eisenhower "takes a more conservative view than some other Presidents have taken" referring to Roosevelt and Truman. By "conservative," he meant conserving the constitutional roles of Congress and the presidency. The Doctrine was debated and authorized. Democratic Senator Hubert Humphrey called it a "predated declaration of war."[52] In 1958, Ike sent marines to Lebanon under the statutory authority granted in 1957. Subsequent presidents requested and abused preauthorizations as open-ended blank checks.

Congress held war power dominance from 1919 to 1939. Franklin Delano Roosevelt, remaking government to overcome the Great Depression, continued to build presidential power as the war in Europe intensified. Presidents continued to consolidate presidential dominance until it peaked under Vietnam-era presidents. The 1973 War Powers Resolution (WPR) was a legislative attempt to regain congressional dominance in war making.

Presidents continued to dominate, but the next serious assertion of extra-constitutional authority came from the Clinton administration.

The breakup of Yugoslavia produced the Federal Republic of Yugoslavia from the former republics of Serbia and Montenegro. The new republic's southern province of Kosovo was almost entirely Muslim Albanians, who agitated for independence. Serbs deployed forces to quell the uprising in the spring of 1998.

In support of the ethnic Albanians, Clinton threatened air strikes against Serbia. That course of action was opposed by Russia and China and likely would have produced a veto in the UN. Without UN sanction, and without congressional authorization, Clinton ordered air strikes. NATO began a massive air campaign on 24 March 1999. On 26 March, the administration reported to Congress as required by the War Powers Resolution.

Congress attempted throughout April and May to constrain the president's use of force and to prevent deployment of ground forces. Eighteen members of Congress, led by Representative Tom Campbell, filed suit in federal district court to force the president to get authorization for the air war. The House passed a bill to prohibit funds for ground forces without prior authorization. Additional measures were considered to limit the expenditure of funds. A proposal in the House to declare a state of war was almost unanimously defeated. In the Senate, McCain's proposal to authorize all uses of force was defeated. Still, on 20 May, Congress submitted for presidential signature an emergency supplemental with billions for operations in Kosovo.

On 25 May, the sixtieth day had passed since commencement of the air war and no thirty-day extension had been requested as required by the WPR. The president cited the alleged constitutional defects of the War Powers Resolution. Both the House and Senate considered authorizing air and missile strikes.[53] The Senate leaned toward air operations. The House was split. No prohibitive or authorizing legislation was passed.

The constitutional process had worked its way to completion and denied the authorization to use force. Clinton continued air operations regardless. It was the "first time in our history that a president has waged war in the face of a direct congressional refusal to authorize the war."[54]

The president waged without authority the most "intensive and sustained" air campaign since Vietnam. Congress chose to "support the troops" through appropriations, but "not the policy" through authorization. Members of Congress filed suit. The Supreme Court refused to hear the case.

Congressional Take-Back Attempts

The conflicts in Korea and Vietnam were long and costly undeclared wars. Both were wars of limited objectives conducted in the context of the Cold War. Truman bypassed Congress to use force in Korea. Johnson built on a contrived incident to request and receive broad authority to use force in Southeast Asia. The War Powers Resolution was written in anger at the end of the Nixon administration. Its legitimacy and effectiveness remain controversial.[55] Among other things, the legislative veto and redelegation of authority are at issue. Congress made a second attempt to reclaim its constitutional war-making authorities at the end of the Cold War and again when Clinton employed military force in Kosovo after Congress refused authorization.

War Powers Resolution of 1973

Congress sensed too great a shift of authorities from the people's branch to the executive and, over the veto of President Richard Nixon, passed the War Powers Resolution on 7 November 1973. With his 24 October veto, Nixon claimed the Resolution to be "both unconstitutional and dangerous to the best interests of our nation."[56] The perceived encroachment on presidential prerogatives has met with continuous rejection by administrations since.

The *purpose* of the Resolution is, as stated in section 2, consistent with the "intent of the framers of the Constitution," to

> insure that the collective judgment of both the Congress and the President will apply to the introduction of United States Armed Forces into hostilities, or into situations where imminent involvement in hostilities is clearly indicated by the circumstances, and to the continued use of such forces in hostilities or in such situations.

The key phrase, "into hostilities or into situations where imminent involvement in hostilities is clearly indicated by the circumstances," is repeated several times in the text, but most importantly in section 4(a)(1).

Section 2 of the Resolution further specifies the *limits* of the president's authority to introduce forces: "The constitutional powers of the President as Commander-in-Chief to introduce United States Armed Forces into hostilities, or into situations where imminent involvement in hostilities is clearly indicated by the circumstances, are exercised only pursuant to (1) a declaration of war, (2) specific statutory authorization, or (3) a national emergency created by attack upon the United States, its territories or possessions, or its armed forces."

Section 3 requires the president to *consult* "in every possible instance" prior to introducing forces and regularly thereafter. While the intent is clear, the specifics of when to consult are vague, and presidents have consistently ignored the intent. With whom the president should consult is also ambiguous. Perhaps most importantly, the meaning of consultation has been abused consistently.[57]

The president is also subject to *reporting* requirements. Reporting and consulting are different and independent. Section 4 sets the requirements for both initial reporting within forty-eight hours and subsequent reports to be submitted at least every six months. Section 4 is the principal source of the Resolution's ambiguity.

Section 5 specifies timelines. Specifically, forces initially deployed under presidential authority must be withdrawn within sixty days after the president submits a report to Congress unless Congress provides a declaration of war or a statutory authorization to continue the use of force. An extension of thirty days may be granted if necessary for the safe withdrawal of forces from hostilities. Congress may also assert that the president *should have* submitted a report, thus retroactively starting the clock.

The exploitable loophole is that, according to section 5(b), the deadlines are triggered only if the initial presidential report cites section 4(a)(1) or if Congress asserts that the report was required. Only Ford explicitly cited section 4(a)(1). Subsequent initial reports included the phrase, "in accordance with the War Powers Resolution," but they did not cite any section or subsection. Thus, presidents later could argue that the time requirements were not triggered.

Section 5 also states that, absent a congressional declaration of war or statutory authorization for the use of force, Congress may require the withdrawal of forces at any time by concurrent resolution—the defective legislative veto—thus requiring Congress to amass a supermajority to override the expected presidential veto of a joint resolution. The authority of Congress to order the withdrawal of forces, as declared in Section 5, has been challenged by successive presidents.

Arrival of the 104th Congress. The 104th Congress was convened 4 January 1995. The new Republican Congress, armed with the so-called "Contract with America," was against U.S. troops under UN command and against UN peacekeeping. As far as the Republicans were concerned, the United States had moved too far toward "globalism." Those sentiments were punctuated by the recent tragedy in Somalia known as Black Hawk Down.[58]

The Soviet Union was no longer a unifying threat, and a strongly ideological Republican majority in Congress was pitted against a Democratic president initially weak in foreign policy and further weakened by events in Somalia, Haiti, and Bosnia. If ever there would be conditions favoring restoration of congressional over presidential war powers, this was it. In the Senate, the Republican Party's presidential aspirations for Robert Dole as well as Newt Gingrich's leadership in the House caused Congress to flail and then fail. Presidential candidates need to appear presidential and not obstructionist. While Speaker of the House, Gingrich argued for a stronger hand for the presidency[59] as did John McCain in the Senate. Establishing a balanced budget took legislative priority over asserting congressional war powers.

Presidential Response to the War Powers Resolution

A pattern of presidential response is clear. Presidents treat the War Powers Resolution as unconstitutional and nonbinding. When Congress attempts to terminate presidential actions, it does so primarily through appropriations. The Court has refused to intervene, and the president is firmly in charge and impotently challenged by Congress. The pattern also includes the "when" and the "with whom" aspects of consultation and the reporting clause that starts the sixty-day clock.

Consulting. Regardless of congressional intent, presidents have chosen to discharge their obligation to consult with Congress by notifying Congress after the decision is made and orders issued but before forces are actually engaged, sometimes only hours before forces are put in harm's way.

With whom a president might consult is uncertain. Several attempts have been made to specify a congressional consultation group. Congress has attempted to address the speed and secrecy issues by having a small and knowledgeable group preselected, but Congress cannot delegate its war-making responsibilities to a subgroup.

Reporting. In their reports to Congress, presidents have avoided reference to Section 4(a)(1) so as to not trigger the sixty- to ninety-day withdrawal deadline. Congress shrinks from the challenge, rarely starting the clock of its own volition.

When presidents have deployed troops without prior congressional authority, they have consistently included language along the lines of, "constitutional authority with respect to the conduct of foreign relations as Commander in Chief of United States Armed Forces." In addition, they have often made reference to treaty organizations like NATO and the UN.

Termination. Congress has a variety of ways to terminate force deployments: funding cutoffs, funding restrictions, and Section 5 of the War Powers Resolution.[60] Congress can also deauthorize the use of force that it has previously authorized. When the legislature and the executive strongly differ on policy, Congress has found that restricting funds is the most effective way of curbing the president's use of force. Congress has withdrawn or reduced funding, and it has imposed significant restrictions on how funding may be used. The power of the purse is a more effective mechanism for checking presidents than are the provisions of the War Powers Resolution. But Congress uses its power timidly and ineffectually.

In general, congressional activity appears to be part of a negotiation with the executive branch. Actual law is passed only after the deal has been struck. Probably more effective than the actual legislation is the friction induced by the public discourse. It is critically important political theater.

Disposition of the WPR

The War Powers Resolution remains problematic. Many in Congress think it has established a process through which they can wrestle with the president; they would prefer shoring up the Resolution. Many whose prejudice lies in preserving the Constitution, its checks and balances, and the rule of law would repeal the Resolution. Presidential imperialists accept the Resolution's weakness and talk around the Constitution.

Repair the WPR. Several proposals have been made to repair the Resolution to deal with the issues of speed, secrecy, legislative veto, judicial review, and redelegation.[61] There is more at stake than providing a workable process of consultation. It is a principle of republican government that the wisdom of the many is superior to the wisdom of one. As Adler reminded us, "an elected president may lack the wisdom, temperament, and judgment, not to mention perception, expertise, and emotional intelligence, to produce success in foreign affairs. Those qualities, which to be sure are attributes of the occupant and not the office, cannot be conferred by election."[62]

Ignore the WPR. Those who favor an imperial presidency need take no specific stand on the Resolution. Since its passage, each president has doubted its constitutionality and refused to be bound by it. Given that modern presidents have refused to be bound by the Constitution, it is doubtful that they would feel bound by a new and improved statute.

Repeal the WPR. A few politicians put the Constitution first and defend the separation of powers.[63] They argue that the Resolution has actually eroded Congress's constitutional authorities. Prior to passage in 1973, "unilateral presidential war was a matter of usurpation. Now, at least for the first ninety days, it was a matter of law."[64] "Our constitutional system is better protected by requiring presidents to act in the absence of law and later obtain legal sanction from Congress, rather than by having Congress authorize in advance, as with the War Powers Resolution, unilateral action."[65]

Rely on the Constitution. Presidents can easily skirt Congress to initiate hostilities, and they often have initial support from a deferential public. But when wars drag on, and the costs mount, the people ask why. Those presidents who did not bother to build the consensus to commitment pay the price. The very process of public debate held in the people's branch engages the wisdom of the many. Congress and the public should adhere to Teddy Roosevelt's admonition that wartime is precisely the time to argue for and against the use of force. Nothing is more democratic, and nothing is more American. Such challenges should be the norm and those who demonize it recognized as the unpatriotic.[66]

Amend the Constitution. David Mervin makes no claim that the Constitution's framers were infallible. They spoke in less than enlightened terms of women, Africans, and American natives. Just as those pronouncements came from an anachronistic value system, so too do congressional war powers.[67] David Adler acknowledges those constitutional defects but counters by saying that those anachronistic positions were altered by the constitutionally prescribed amendment process:

> What is at stake here is nothing less than the rule of law, the marrow of which consists of presidential subordination to the Constitution. . . . If a president strongly, even fervently, believes military force is necessary, he is allowed to argue his case before Congress. But he may go no further if constitutional government is to command any respect.[68]

Either abide by the Constitution or amend it by the constitutional process to grant the president the war making powers of the old European monarchs.

For Consideration

Throughout the Cold War, a political consensus supported a standing military for the first time in American history, and it supported a continual shift in authorities from the people's branch to the executive. The reaction of the Soviet Union had to be factored into every decision concerning U.S. diplomatic and military moves. But with the Cold War over, the Soviet Union no longer checks the presidential use of military force and Congress ceased to play that role.

The shift in war powers from Congress to president is of high consequence, as Arthur Schlesinger notes: "The capture by the Presidency of the most vital of national decisions, the decision to go to war . . . was as much a matter of congressional abdication as of presidential usurpation."[69] The consequence is democracy diminished.

> When presidents rule by decree in even the most routine matters, they diminish democracy. When they and their subordinates ignore, circumvent, and express distain for legislative processes, they diminish democracy. When they create decision-making processes designed to

mute debate and discussion in order to enhance their own power, presidents diminish democracy.[70]

Congress has held a stronger grip on domestic policy, where their constituency lies, while both Congress and the people defer to the president on matters of foreign policy. The terrorist attacks against the United States have blurred the distinction. And "as the distinction between foreign policy and domestic policy diminishes, the president's growing foreign policy powers are certain to take on even greater domestic importance."[71]

Status of the Competition

This is a competition between the legislative and executive branches that is sometimes strengthened by and sometimes diluted by partisan politics. The judicial branch has refused to adjudicate. The chief executive is unchecked and unbalanced. Congress—and the Constitution—are losing badly.[72] The competition between the 104th Congress and the Clinton administration bodes poorly for restoration of constitutional balance. All the conditions at the initiation of the competition favored Congress, but the president won handily. Absent all the enabling conditions present then, there is little reason to believe that Congress will rise to meet its constitutional responsibilities.

Most prominently since Truman, the president expands, Congress acquiesces, and the Court looks the other way.[73] Nixon's excesses caused a strong backlash, but it was short-lived. What could we expect after Iraq?

> In the case of Iraq, the result has been the biggest failure of American power and diplomacy since Vietnam, maybe the worst ever. Will it undermin[e the] power of the presidency? Probably not. Presidents fail, but the presidency adapts. Unfortunately, the adjustments that strengthen the presidency do not reliably produce policies that strengthen the country.[74]

As one of the most distinguished Supreme Court justices, Louis D. Brandeis, reminds us, the point in separation of powers is "not to promote efficiency but to preclude the exercise of arbitrary power."[75]

Democratic Peace

The belief in democratic peace—that democracies tend not to war, or that democracies tend not to war against each other—was used to justify the use of force around the world to spread democracy. However, those things incorporated in the Constitution to make the Republic pacific have been subverted. Presidents ride roughshod over Congress and use force virtually at will. The need to raise an army once required the president to make his case to Congress and to the state governors, but now there is a standing, all-volunteer force, and as predicted, presidents are inclined to use it.

Part 2

National Security Strategies

4   Grand Strategy

Armed with some basic concepts in international relations and the associated language, we are prepared to move toward a discussion of national security strategy. National security strategy, *grand strategy*, is not about winning a war in Iraq or about winning a global war on terrorism. Grand strategy is about assuring the position of the United States in the world, its place in the international system of states, and it is a guide to the exercise of power and influence to attain or maintain the desired position. Grand strategy guides the production and use of national power—*all* instruments of power:

> Grand strategy unites military and diplomatic strategy. . . . It integrates all elements of national power in policies calculated to advance or defend national interests and concerns in light of anticipated trends and events.[1]

Strategic theories ascribe cause-and-effect relationships between the use of power and its consequences. In the following two chapters, we review modern strategic thought, including the several variants of Cold War containment, the strategic alternatives offered after the Cold War, and the pronounced swings in the strategies of post–Cold War administrations. But first, some definitions are in order.

What Is Strategy?

A strategy links ends, ways, and means. The *ends* of a strategy are the objectives or goals to be achieved, the *means* include the multitude of resources devoted to achievement of those objectives, and the *ways* are the methods of organizing and employing those resources to achieve national objectives. Ways are the heart of strategy formulation. Aligning and balancing ends, ways, and means is the *strategic calculation*.

Not every formulation of ends, ways, and means qualifies as a strategy. Stating lofty objectives inadequately supported by resources is not a strategy; that is little more than wishful thinking. At the other extreme, providing resources for all possible objectives—for example, maintaining large standing military forces capable of responding to all conceivable contingencies—squanders resources and leads to overextension. It is all too easy to fall victim to one of these two pathologies. Tough choices must be made to concentrate resources to minimize risks to the most vital interests while accepting some risks elsewhere.

What Constitutes a Good Strategy?

A good strategy guides the use of power as events emerge. Without a good strategy, one can only react to events as they occur, yielding the initiative to the enemy by allowing the enemy to select the time, place, and terms of the competition. Some presidents have possessed an overarching understanding of the geostrategic environment, a view of America's position in it, and a strategy to guide their behavior. Eisenhower, Nixon, George H. W. Bush (41), and Obama responded to crises in the context of a persistent strategy. Other presidents lacked a governing strategic view and allowed crises to dictate responses. Truman, Carter, and George W. Bush (43) reacted to crises outside the context of declared strategy. Presidents are also differentiated by their ability to recognize and seize strategic opportunities. The Nixon and elder Bush administrations offer notable successes in this area.

Presidents have differed in their ability to limit themselves to pursuits they could afford. Large, expanding means do not equate to infinite or even adequate means for all objectives. Some presidents' inability to differentiate between vital and peripheral interests and the threats to them led to a perception of *undifferentiated threats* and to exhaustive responses. Good strategies minimize risks to vital interests and accept some risks elsewhere. Exhaustive responses are all too common, with Truman, Kennedy-Johnson, Reagan, and Bush 43 offering clear examples.

A sustainable strategy is underwritten by public support. Only presidential leadership can build a consensus to commitment. The American public grants the president wide latitude initiating action but withdraws support without a deliberate and sustained consensus-building effort. Even a concerted effort at consensus building will fail if a strategy is inconsistent with the nation's philosophy. Truman, Johnson, and Bush 43 are notable in their failure to build a consensus to commitment to their respective wars. Franklin Delano Roosevelt, although beyond the scope of this work, is notable for his sustained effort at building and maintaining a consensus to commitment.

All instruments of power are brought to bear in a good strategy. There are limits to what can be achieved with any instrument of power, including the hard power provided by the military. Failure to recognize the limits of military power is a dangerous trap. The complementary use of all instruments is more efficient and more effective. Moreover, not all power is in U.S. hands. Other forces can be leveraged, for example, rejecting the sense of monolithic Communism and recognition of the separate nationalistic impulses that allowed Nixon to drive a wedge between China and the Soviet Union.

In short, a good strategy

- pits strength against weakness;
- denies the enemy the ability to determine the time, place, and terms of the competition;
- distinguishes between vital and peripheral interests;
- pursues clear objectives and judiciously applies scarce resources;
- employs all instruments of power;
- is consistent with national values and philosophy; and
- is relevant to the time, that is, is consistent with *contemporary* international politics, military developments, available technology, and domestic attitudes.

How Is National Security Strategy Expressed?

There are many ways to express grand strategy, but the four expressions of a nation's grand strategy below are used in this text:

- declaratory policy,
- employment policy,
- force development policy, and
- force deployment policy.[2]

The traditional four expressions were identified in an era when national security was principally seen as a military problem in search of a military solution. The twenty-first century arguably requires a wider understanding of what constitutes the force or power that can be brought to bear. The four expressions easily extend to include all instruments of power rather than a narrow focus on the military instrument.

Declaratory policy is what we say we will do. The most obvious example of declaratory policy is the president's national security strategy document required by law since 1987. Other statements of public officials also contribute to our declaratory policy. Declaratory policy is communicated to influence enemies, friends, and neutral observers. Such statements deliberately exaggerate some things and deemphasize others. Policy statements are full of *constructive ambiguity*—saying just enough to communicate a position without precommitting to a response to an unpredicted stimulus; good declaratory policy does not draw bright lines.

Employment policy is what we actually do, specifically as our actions relate to the use of force. The overt use of military force is regularly described in the media. But there are uses of covert or paramilitary force that go unannounced. Economic sanctions and foreign aid are also examples of employment policy.

Force development policy dictates what force structure we maintain and what we are developing. It includes, for example, the number of Army divisions and Air Force fighter wings available. It also includes their readiness level, for example, do they require mobilization and training from the reserve forces, or are they ready for immediate employment? Development of next-generation weapon systems is also an expression of national strategy. Maintaining a nation-building capability across the departments and agencies is a broader example of force (or capability) development policy.

Force deployment policy dictates where we position the force in anticipation. Having a small Army force in South Korea, for example, serves as a *trip wire* and deterrent against North Korean aggression far out of proportion to its size. And having a Navy aircraft carrier persistently patrolling within reach of the Persian Gulf is a powerful statement. Where intelligence collection efforts are focused is another example of deployment policy, as is the allocation of linguists.

Preparedness. Declaratory policy generally, and the national security strategy document specifically, sets in motion expensive and laborious processes. If, for example, there is a shift in emphasis from major war to small war, or vice versa, major changes to force development policy follow. The military departments are required by law to organize, train, and equip the four services for the missions the president assigns to the regional combatant commanders. An armored division, for example, had great value in major land war in Europe but much less value to nation building in Afghanistan. Major shifts in declaratory policy require new equipment with logistic support, new organizations, new doctrine, and new training programs. Each costs money, and each takes time. Employment policy not aligned with declaratory policy, or force development and force deployment policy not keeping pace with employment policy, virtually assures unpreparedness of the military and other instruments.

Credibility. There must be an internal consistency to these four expressions of strategy. Having a force unable or poorly positioned to support declaratory policy renders declaratory policy incredible. Failing to follow through on declaratory policy renders it incredible as well. The actual use of force demonstrates both the *will* and the *ability* that underwrites credibility. Achieving deterrent and other influence objectives through credible declaratory policy is less expensive and more sustainable than force employment as a first resort. Repeating a premise of this text, we must expand beyond a narrow focus on military force and consider all instruments of power.

But there's more to credibility than internal strategic consistency. One often hears partisans refer to U.S. credibility as something that must be preserved, even treated as a vital interest, something worth fighting for. But there are competing theories on the source of credibility. The two most prominent theories are Current Calculus and Past Actions theories.

> *Current Calculus* theory concludes that the credibility of a state's threat is the product of the state's *power* to carry out the threat and the state's *interests* involved in the current context.
> *Past Actions* theory posits that the credibility of a state's threat derives from its *past actions*, that is, whether or not it followed through on its declared commitments in the past.

Both theories have been tested by rigorous analysis, always with the same results. The most recent, concise, and convincing examination was carried out by Daryl Press.[3] Rather than analyzing public statements made to persuade, Press examined official transcripts and declassified memos documenting high-stakes decision making by American, British, German, and Russian officials, including steps taken that led to World War II, the Berlin Crises, and the Cuban Missile Crisis. The preponderance of evidence aligns with Current Calculus, and scant evidence aligns with Past Actions, with the overwhelming preponderance of evidence in opposition.

"The credibility of a threat [or promise] is defined as the perceived likelihood that the threat [or promise] will be carried out if the conditions that are supported to trigger it are met," Press writes.[4] Constructive ambiguity in declaratory policy, rather than "bright lines," preserves credibility.

In any given crisis, friends and enemies assess U.S. credibility at its highest when its vital interests are at stake and when U.S. power can compel the desired political outcome. Credibility is at its lowest when only peripheral interests are at stake and when political objectives are beyond the limits of U.S. power or the cost is too high.

Examining the historical record exposes another interesting finding. Decision makers evaluate the credibility of an opponent's threat—a declared commitment to use force—almost entirely by an estimate of the opponent's power to carry out the threat and the importance of the interest involved. Remarkably, however, when deciding to respond to an opponent's threat, decision makers genuinely believe they must act to preserve their own future credibility in the eyes of enemies and friends. In other words, decision makers subscribe to Current Calculus theory but incorrectly believe their opponents subscribe to Past Actions theory.

A theory that doesn't comport with the evidence isn't a theory, but it can survive, even flourish, in the absence of evidence and even in opposition to the evidence. Past Actions will remain a powerful rhetorical tool used to pressure presidents to act even when vital interests aren't at risk or used by presidents to justify contentious policy decisions.

Do theories matter? Countries that invest in a reputation for strong military response are spending money and lives. A strong military response may be a wise response, or it may be a fool's errand that squanders resources.

How Is a Grand Strategy Formulated?

Three broad approaches to strategy formulation are apparent. The well-established majority approach is based on prioritized *state interests*. A recurring and recently resurgent approach is based on addressing *international issues* expected to reduce the sources of conflict. And a third approach is based on acting in accord with *principles* that reflect *national values*. These approaches are not mutually exclusive. The interests-based approach dominates, and the other two assert greater influence periodically.

Stephen Cambone describes the two dominant schools: the interests-based and issues-based schools.[5] His analysis was conducted at the Center for Strategic and International Studies (CSIS) between his service under Bush 41 and Bush 43 while the issues-based approach enjoyed resurgence under Clinton. Apparent throughout American history, the principles-based approach surged under Carter and Bush 43.

Interests-Based Approach

The textbook answer to the question, How is a grand strategy formulated?, is that ends are determined by examining the interests of the state and identifying opportunities and threats, both actual and potential, to those interests.

> The *interests* school sees national security from the perspective of national interests with a focus on the minimization of risks to the United States as a sovereign state in the international system.[6]

The state exists to institute the nation's norms internally and to defend the nation from external threats. The *supreme interest* of the state is survival as a political entity.[7] Challenges to supreme interests lead to war. Further interests are prioritized or simply differentiated as vital or peripheral:[8]

> Vital interests generally include security, well-being, and domestic tranquility. The vital interests of a state include the defense of national unity behind secure frontiers, the security of strategic advantage and its denial to potential enemies, access to resources essential to national power and well-being, immunity from intimidation, and freedom from subversion or intervention in its internal affairs by other states.[9]

The state is highly risk-averse with respect to vital interests. Vital interests leave little room for negotiations and are pursued with all available means, including the threat and use of military force. Honest people can and do disagree on which interests are vital. Perhaps the most consequential disagreement on vital interests is about U.S. credibility. A distant crisis that poses only a minor challenge to U.S. interests will normally provoke a tepid response. But those who believe that credibility is a vital interest worth fighting for will agitate for a strong military response.

Defining vital interests too broadly is the first step to strategic exhaustion. The constraint on available means requires that a strategy concentrate resources to minimize risks to vital interests—means must be subordinated to ends. Resources are shifted to vital interests, and risks are shifted to the less vital. If a strategy—a linkage of ends, ways, and means—cannot secure the state's vital interests, then ways must be reconsidered, additional means must be allocated, vital interests must be narrowed, or greater risks must be accepted. To defend everything is to defend nothing, Frederick the Great reminds us.[10]

The interests-based approach to strategy formulation is consistent with realist thinking. Self-interest, territorial sovereignty, self-determination, and nonintervention dominate.

Issues-Based Approach

A second prominent view is based on issues. American *national* security is best assured by pursuing *international* security. And international security is best assured by addressing the root causes of conflict.

> The *issues* school focuses on global problems that impede the achievement of a fair international system based on the improvement of the quality of life of the world's population. Resolving these issues . . . will address the most obvious sources of human conflict and suffering.[11]

The issues school defines security threats far more broadly than the interests school. For example, the spread of HIV/AIDS and environmental degradation are readily included as threats to security. Other issues include population growth, access to food and water, migration and displacement, the rights of women and children, trafficking in drugs and people, the proliferation of WMD, and access to commercial, financial, and capital markets. Many security threats are transnational and require international solutions.

The international community, perhaps represented by the UN, is a very loose confederation of sovereign states. As such, it is difficult to sustain a consensus to action. Honest people can and do disagree on the issues to address and on their respective importance. The international community establishes norms of behavior between states. It also establishes norms protecting the rights of individuals against the coercive powers of the state. Clearly the major powers have greater influence in establishing international norms, but international norms may not align with American interests or values.

An issues-based strategy formulation process is consistent with idealist, internationalist, institutionalist, and Wilsonian thinking. Such a process rests more on universalism and interventionism and less on self-determination; it endorses limited territorial sovereignty. Peace is indivisible.

Principles-Based Approach

A minority view holds that foreign policy should be constructed by adhering to specific principles rather than by calculating outcomes based on interests. The animating principles might be derived from political, economic, or religious ideology. Spreading market capitalism, spreading democracy, supporting Israel, intervention against genocide, intervention for humanitarian assistance, and noninterference are examples of principles to be followed.

> The *principles* school promotes behavior on the international scene in accordance with specific principles. The goodness of policy action is determined by how it adheres to or diverges from the chosen guiding principles rather than on the consequences obtained.

Morals-Based Approach

There is a distinct subset of principles-based thinking that periodically gains prominence. Its principles are based in religion. Some use *values-based* to describe this approach, but that means many things to many people. *Morals-based* is used here.

According to the morals school, American international behavior should be guided not by calculation of worldly consequences but by following certain principles independent of those worldly consequences. The guiding principles are determined by reference to a biblical interpretation that is believed to be universally applicable. The threat to national security includes multiculturalism, both domestically and abroad. The relative growth of all populations that do not share American values constitutes a threat to the American way of life.

> The *morals* school seeks to project national values by applying to national security decision making principles derived from biblical interpretation believed by its advocates to be universal.

Morality is about right and wrong. A people's norms constitute its "national values by which a nation judges what is right or wrong and what is decent or abhorrent."[12] Different nations have different values, and there is wide recognition of *moral relativism*. The political faction encouraging the morals-based approach observes *moral absolutism* rather than relativism. This faction believes in imposing its version of American values onto the international community rather than yielding to international norms. American values are universal values.

Consistent with vindicationism, the morals school is willing to export values by aggressive foreign policy including the use of military force. It represents the crusading rather than the pacifist Christian tradition. It is Jacksonian, projecting a way of life, not just continentally, but globally.

Reconciling the Approaches

In reality, all of these approaches are simultaneously at work, but the emphasis shifts from one administration to another. A central tendency can be observed in most administrations.

Adherents to the issues-based and principles-based approaches tend to pursue *domestic policies* based on issues or principles, respectively, and then project those same issues and principles onto formulation of *foreign policy*. The interests-based approach, in contrast, does not attempt to project American ways on others, relying instead on exemplarism, self-determination, and noninterference. Where we start with strategy formulation has a lot to do with where we end up.

Interests-based and issues-based approaches hope to achieve consequences (ends) in the secular, temporal, material world. The morals-based approach, as defined here, seeks consequences in the hereafter by following religious principles or doctrine based on the biblical interpretation of religious elites. The empirical analysis of cause and effect that underwrites interests- and issues-based strategy formulation does not serve the morals-based camp.

A cautionary note is in order. Although the orientations to strategy formulation are widely accepted, the labels are not. Sometimes the term "values-based" is used to describe both issues- and principles-based formulation as defined above. Sometimes the values referred to are individual liberty and the rule of law rather than religious in origin. Americans can certainly disagree on what constitutes national values. What Cambone calls interests-based, the Princeton Project calls threat-based,[13] and what Cambone calls issues-based, Princeton calls interests-based. Rather than assuming clear meaning from a label built from words like interests, issues, principles, and values, the cautious thinker must ask which interests, which issues, which principles, and whose values.

The diverse American public is galvanized when it comes to vital interests narrowly defined—that is, national survival and defense of American life, liberty, and property. Presidents will not be forgiven for failing to secure these interests. The same diversity provides fickle support for actions to secure the liberties of others or for promoting values not shared abroad or even domestically. Presidents can create domestic coalitions in opposition to their own actions when the connection to American security is tenuous and the costs are high.

Values always play a role, not just in the morals-based approach. Whether the actual strategy is interests-based, issues-based, or principles-based, it must be communicated to the public in terms of national values to gain and maintain support. Successfully communicating actions in values terms "animates the national will" and "determines fervor." The interests-based approach and its cold calculation of interests especially beg for expression in the language of values. Diplomats abroad must explain U.S. policies to foreign audiences in terms of their values to gain acceptance and support.

All approaches must secure supreme interest and minimize risks to vital interests. That's where the interests-based approach stops and the other approaches continue. Therefore, the issues- and principles-based approaches impose costs over and above the interests-based approach. This explains, perhaps, why the interests-based approach remains dominant and persistent while the others exhibit transient prominence.

Another plausible explanation is the distinction between security and foreign policy. Adherents of the interests-, issues-, and principles-based approaches may reach wide agreement on foreign policy objectives but may diverge wildly over national security. Not all foreign policy objectives are matters of national security. Foreign policy objectives might include advancing human rights in China, but China's failure to guarantee human rights to its citizens, although in opposition to our values, does not constitute a threat to American national security. Maltreatment of coreligionists abroad is not a threat to national security, but it will produce calls for intervention. The interests-based approach to national security strategy formulation maintains a tighter focus on threats and makes a clearer distinction between foreign policy and national security policy. The issues-based approach requires a much broader definition of national security issues and blurs the distinction between foreign and national security policy.

Regardless of the approach taken, a variety of instruments must be resourced to achieve national ends. Instruments include, for example, diplomatic, informational, military, and economic instruments. The mix of instruments must be sufficient to achieve the stated ends, and the resources devoted must be affordable. Alternating approaches every four or eight years creates lurching and contradictory demands on the departments and agencies that house the instruments of power, virtually guaranteeing inadequacy in ways and means.

Who Formulates Grand Strategy?

Statesmen are the men and women in the capital who formulate foreign and national security policy. Most visible are the elected and appointed officials, including the president, cabinet secretaries, and members of the relevant congressional committees. They are supported by long-serving professional staffs in the executive departments and congressional committees. Diplomats, warriors, and spies carry out the policies formulated, often far from Washington. Each group is expected to have mastered the arts of diplomacy, war, and espionage, respectively.[14] Who formulates and who implements is a critically important distinction.

Relationships between States

States are equal in sovereignty, but they are unequal in population, geographic area and location, economic and military strength, interests, and values. Based on their unique characteristics, states enter into a variety of relationships, some formal and some informal.[15]

A dominant regional power may arrogate to itself a *sphere of influence* where it expects a certain degree of deference—regional hegemony. The United States has long asserted hegemony over the Western Hemisphere, and Russia has long asserted hegemony along its periphery. More recently, China is laying claim to a growing sphere of influence in the Asia Pacific where U.S. and Chinese spheres collide. In more extreme cases, weaker states are seen as *buffer states* by their regional hegemon. Russia, a continental power, thought of Eastern European states as a buffer between itself and its historic adversaries in western Europe. The United States, an insular power, had buffering seas from its potential enemies.

Coalitions and Alliances. *Coalitions* are ad hoc, short-lived arrangements formed around challenges to shared interests. They aggregate power at the last minute and expire along with the challenge. *Alliances* form for or against enduring challenges. A common reason for alliance is to aggregate power against a threatening state. A common form of alliance is the mutual defense pact in which each state accepts the burden of defending the other in exchange for the added power. True alliances allow for interoperable equipment and procedures as well as training. Because alliances are enduring, the aggregated power may deter an aggressive adversary and, if necessary, prevail in war. Coalitions have less deterrent effect than a true alliance. And coalitions don't allow for advanced interoperability and training. In war, a coalition of the willing is a weak substitute for a genuine alliance.

But when a powerful state enters into a mutual defense pact with a weak state, the powerful state accepts additional risk and burden with little to show for it. Rather than an alliance relationship, the weaker state is a *protectorate* or *client state* even though it may be called an ally.

A system of alliances or protectorates. The United States deliberately built a system of protectorates at the end of World War II, including Germany and Japan, and it expanded the system during the Cold War to include western Europe, South Korea, Israel, South Vietnam, the Philippines, and Taiwan. U.S. presidents have gone back and forth emphasizing the role of ally or protector. The same mutual defense pacts can serve either purpose. One distinction between the two is *burden sharing*—who carries the main burden, who is supported, and who is supporting. The choice between a system of alliances and a system of protectorates has consequences, including the size of the Defense budget and the tempo of operations. A system of protectorates requires maintenance of a large military force and frequent military intervention—a system of allies less so.

The idea behind a *system of regional alliances* is that regional actors have the most at stake, are best able to understand the problem, and best positioned to deal with it. The United States might provide moral and diplomatic support, advisors, trainers, and equipment, but regional actors shoulder the primary burden and fight their own wars. Only when the outcome appears counter to important U.S. interests would the United States intervene and then only with sufficient force to tip the scales. A regional political loss is preferable to direct intervention in never-ending conflicts where U.S. vital interests are not threatened. The United States is the balancer of last resort. This division of labor shifts the burden away from the United States when our vital interests are not at stake but allows the United States to remain engaged internationally with a demonstrable role on the world stage.

The idea behind extending a U.S. security guarantee to a *system of protectorates* is that secure protectorates won't enter into arms races that could raise tensions and inadvertently increase the likelihood of regional war. A system of protectorates not invested in their self-defense preserves the U.S. position as the last remaining superpower, and only that position makes the United States secure, according to this line of reasoning. To defend its protectorates, the United States must maintain a preponderance of military power and must be willing to use it frequently even when vital interests are not threatened. Advocates of playing the role of global protector claim that the U.S. economy can support this approach.

In the realm of domestic policy, advocates of limited government often argue their positions on the basis of "moral hazard." That is, by creating social welfare programs for the poor, the state creates a dependency that undermines self-reliance and creates a permanent underclass of free riders. Extending the concept of moral hazard into the realm of international security, extending a U.S. security guarantee to a system of protectorates allows them a relatively free ride and little reason to invest in their own defense, thus shifting the burden to the United States, its military, and its taxpayers.

Furthermore, granting unequivocal support may embolden the protectorate to pursue more aggressive policies than are justified by its own power—even in opposition to U.S. policy preferences—thus increasing tensions and the need for a U.S. response.

At the end of World War II, the U.S. economy was the largest in the world while others lay in rubble. Since then Europe and Japan rebuilt, and the economies of South Korea, Taiwan, the Asian Tigers, India, and Brazil grew to represent an ever-larger portion of the global economy. As other economies grew, the expanding U.S. economy represented a smaller and smaller portion of the global economy. Today, the economy of the European Union exceeds that of the United States, with China close behind and gaining. Japan and India have reached rough parity in a second tier along with some EU member states. The U.S. economy went from being the undisputed world leader to being one of several world leaders. With successful postwar economic recovery, the conditions that led the United States to extend a security guarantee are gone, and what role the United States will play is an open question.

U.S. behavior toward other states is a choice, and the fundamental choice is between leadership and domination. As Benedetto Fontana notes, Aristotle and Socrates made an important distinction in the exercise of power: "Leadership or *hegemonia* is exercised over equals and allies in the interest of those over whom that power is exercised, and domination or *despoteia* is exercised over enemies [or] unequals . . . in the interest of those who exercise power."[16]

The Size and Shape of Military Force

Force development policy is an important expression of strategy and is a contentious issue today. It represents preparedness for the present and for the future, and it is about the size and the shape of U.S. forces. The meager public debate is about the size of the Defense budget, an input to the force development process. To a much lesser degree, the discussion centers on the size of the force measured in *end strength*—the number of troops on active duty at the end of the fiscal year. A better indicator than input costs, end strength is an output of the process, but it is a poor measure of the military capability purchased. Rarely discussed is the shape of the force—the missions that the force is organized, trained, and equipped to carry out.

Sizing the Force

How much is enough? One answer is, Just enough to defend the state against aggression—*defensive power*. Another answer is, Enough to defend the state plus enough to tip the scales abroad, possibly in concert with an alliance or a coalition of those who share our interests—*balancing power*. And a third answer is, Enough power to defend the state plus enough to dominate in any conflict in the world and against any coalition that might form in opposition—*preponderant power*. Preponderance is clearly the most expensive answer to the question, "How much is enough?"

Those who favor defensive power and balancing power argue that an aggressive, militarized foreign policy induces opposition and further distances the United States from its friends, creates enemies, and damages the economy upon which national security ultimately rests. Hardliners argue that only a preponderance of U.S. military power and its aggressive use can assure world peace and that the U.S. economy can support it.

There is a great deal of historical evidence going back to the Peloponnesian War on the side of balancing power. But balancing requires deft handling and can fail to prevent war, and history includes examples of miscalculating the balance. There is also historical evidence on preponderance of power. It is the story of Roman, Spanish, English, and Soviet overextension. Preponderance of power, improperly wielded, creates more opposition and a vicious cycle where greater acquisition and exercise of power leads to greater opposition requiring, in turn, acquisition of more power.

In spite of the post–Cold War drawdowns, the United States still holds a preponderance of power. Today's base Defense budget in constant dollars is larger than budgets dating back to the beginning of the Cold War. Defense expenditures exceed the combined expenditures of the next dozen or more countries, including China, and constitute 40 percent of world military expenditures. The question remains, how much is enough: defensive, balancing, or preponderant power?

Shaping the Force

What should the force be organized, trained, and equipped to do? Even before the 1989 fall of the Berlin Wall and the 1991 dissolution of the Soviet Union, the post–Cold War military force drawdown had begun. In the summer of 1992, the highly respected Senator Sam Nunn addressed the Armed Services Committee, urging a thorough overhaul of the uniformed services' *roles and missions*:

> We should not go into the future with just a smaller version of our cold war forces. We must prepare for a future with a fresh look at the roles and missions that characterized the past forty years. We must reshape, reconfigure, and modernize our overall forces—not just make them smaller.

A decade later, after multiple failed reform attempts, the United States entered Iraq and Afghanistan with a smaller Cold War force. The initial invasion force defeated the organized military forces rapidly and decisively. Then the force was given a mission for which it was not designed—nation building under fire. A decade of war temporarily arrested the post–Cold War drawdown, transformed the force under fire, and with the wars winding down, the drawdown has resumed. It appears that reshaping for the evolving geostrategic environment is not a priority.

The four uniformed services have been remarkably successful in resisting clear presidential direction. Examples include development of special operations capabilities and development of joint capabilities instead of separate service capabilities. Legislative intervention was required and even that was met with service resistance.[17]

The defense secretary's responsibilities include both advising and assisting the president on the use of military force (*force employment policy*) and working with Congress on the development of military force (*force development policy*). Force development responsibilities include both maintaining the force (readiness for the present) and developing the future military force (readiness for the future). How the force will be used now and then, however, is anything but certain.

While the president guides the use of force, Congress guides its development. But there's little reason to believe that Congress and the president agree on what military is needed. And the requisite expertise lies in the uniformed services, not in the White House and not on the Hill. The services put the options on the table, Congress authorizes and appropriates, and the executive branch establishes and executes the resulting programs. Once established, programs develop a political constituency and life of their own.

Political capital spent on force development policy will not benefit the sitting president. Due to the lengthy development times, the president will be out of office before new military capability is delivered. The president can only use or misuse the force on hand. If the president does engage in force development policy, the uniformed services know they can undermine or even overturn presidential policy by appealing directly to congressional committees.

Held together by Cold War pressures, artificial states like Yugoslavia (1991), Afghanistan (1992), and Somalia (1993) collapsed and fell into civil war. When called upon to defeat the forces of states, as in Iraq and Afghanistan, military forces designed for state-on-state warfare responded decisively. Those same forces then engaged in years of a type of warfare for which they were not designed. Beyond the military, the broader national security apparatus was unprepared to provide the necessary whole-of-government response, and the larger effort fell to the military that had been organized, trained, and equipped for major war.

The military will be called upon to execute a wide range of missions, not just one. Nonetheless, choices must be made, priorities set, and scarce resources allocated. There is no consensus on what missions U.S. military forces should be organized, trained, and equipped for:

- Some argue that the primary threat will be major-power competition over resources and that a U.S.-based force should be designed primarily to defeat the forces of major powers deployed to fight in the Third World.

- Some argue that the primary threat comes from nonstate actors operating from failing and failed states and that the force should be designed primarily for small wars in the Third World.
- Some agree that the primary threat comes from failed and failing states but believe nation building is too costly and that the force should be designed primarily for standoff warfare emphasizing the ability to project destructive force from a safe distance and the ability to conduct quick in-and-out strikes, raids, and punitive expeditions.
- Still others argue that great-power war continues to be the primary threat to U.S. vital interests, but future great-power wars will be fought not force-on-force but computer-on-computer, and force development policy should emphasize offensive and defensive cyber warfare capability.

Presidential Doctrine

Presidents do not publish an official doctrine under their names. Outside observers—sometimes journalists and sometimes political opponents—identify and assert presidential doctrine. Doctrines can sometimes be traced to a specific piece of declaratory policy, for example, a prominent speech. At other times, doctrines emerge from an observed pattern of declaratory and employment policy. Because they represent the judgment of observers, they are open to interpretation and rebuttal. These doctrines often contain the elements of strategy in crystallized form. Prominent presidential doctrines are presented in the following chapters on grand strategy.

Cold War and Post–Cold War Strategies

To construct a new strategy, we need not and should not begin with a blank slate. Some of the best minds available participated in the national security strategy debate during the Cold War and in the decade that followed. There were eight containment strategies and four proposed post–Cold War strategies. Throughout the Cold War, two other strategies were applied consistently—the offset strategy and a cost-imposing strategy—but they were subordinate to grand strategy. All are covered in the coming chapters.

The various grand strategies examined in the next two chapters are characterized in terms of interests and objectives, major underlying premises, preferred political and military instruments, and policies. Both declaratory policy (as publicly stated for psychological effect) and employment policy (as implemented through plans and action) are examined. No presidential administration has ever "batted a thousand," nor will any future administration achieve anything close. A four hundred batting average is exceedingly rare. Anything above three hundred is exceptional. Any objective examination will find considerable shortcomings.

5 Cold War Strategies

The Cold War is a period of history marked by competition between two great powers. Behind it was the Soviet Union expressly pursuing an expansionist policy through the spread of Marxist-Leninist ideology and its internal political need to project an external threat. U.S. national security strategy in the years 1947 through 1989 is identified with a single term—*containment*—although there were obvious shifts in emphasis across administrations and even within administrations.[1]

According to John Lewis Gaddis, the preeminent scholar on Cold War strategy, one of the most notable shifts in the national security strategy of containment was in the perception of available means. Those presidents who believed their means were limited tended toward *asymmetric* responses to Soviet encroachments, that is, to select the place, time, magnitude, and methods of competition rather than responding tit for tat. Presidents who believed the American economy could produce the necessary means on demand tended toward *symmetric* responses, countering Soviet adventurism wherever and whenever it occurred.

Correlated with the symmetry of response was the acceptance of Keynesian economics, suggesting that increased government spending could produce an expansion in the economy. The belief that government could manage economic expansion without long-term budget deficits, higher taxes, or inflation allowed those presidents so inclined to consider all interests vital, all threats dangerous, and all measures available.[2] Keynesian solutions might apply to a short war but not to an economy on a permanent war footing. Misapplying Keynesian solutions over the long term led to permanent deficit spending and accumulating national debt.

The several administrations' interpretations of containment differed in a variety of ways. Some relied heavily on the military instrument; others favored diplomatic and economic instruments and holding military force in reserve for use when vital interests were at risk. Administrations varied in their ability to differentiate between vital and peripheral interests. Some administrations implemented strategy by centralized decision making, and others favored a decentralized approach. Administrations also varied in their ability to recognize and seize strategic opportunities.

Eight different interpretations of containment are apparent. They include two from the Truman administration, Eisenhower's New Look, Kennedy's and Johnson's Flexible Response, détente under Nixon, Carter's two versions of détente, and Reagan's full-court press.

Strategic Underpinnings

Before sequencing through the presidential administrations, particular emphasis and detail are devoted to the two bedrock views provided by George Kennan and Paul Nitze, both from Truman's State Department. They might be called defensive containment and offensive containment, or rollback.

Kennan's Containment Strategy under Truman

George Kennan provided the original formulation of containment in February 1946. He wrote from his position as *chargé d'affaires ad interim* in Moscow[3] and continued as the director of the State Department's Policy Planning Staff.[4] Kennan's assessment of Russia was that it was incapable of tolerating diversity and would attempt to impose its image on the world—hegemony or universal monarchy—and in so doing would expend huge amounts of energy. Such a policy, Kennan believed, could not be sustained indefinitely and ultimately would be debilitating.

Accepting diversity within the existing world order, on the other hand, is more economical than hegemony. Maintaining balance of power among the contending parties should constitute U.S. policy, Kennan thought. Rather than pursuing its own hegemony, Kennan relied on America's prominent role among the great powers to balance against the Soviet Union and its allies. Kennan looked to Russian history and culture for insight rather than to Communism. He thought Communism to be a mere "fig leaf" and refused to be distracted by it.

Five countries possessed the actual or potential military-industrial capability to qualify as world powers in the middle 1940s: the United States, Russia, Great Britain, Germany, and Japan. Assembling a coalition against Russia and pursuing a balance of power would be more economical than pursuing hegemony, and balance could be sustained indefinitely.

Furthermore, Kennan believed that Russia had no immediate intention of war with the West. For the foreseeable future, the United States could out-produce the rest of the world, control the seas, and strike deep within the Soviet homeland with the atomic bomb if necessary. Kennan was willing to reduce military force structure and rely more heavily on economic and political instruments. Balance of power was ultimately a psychological phenomenon.

By July 1947, Kennan refined his strategy to add a *strongpoint defense* along the periphery of the Asian landmass. The additional defensive perimeter included Japan, Okinawa, and the Philippines as strongpoints and excluded any presence on the Asian continent, specifically China, Korea, Indochina, and Afghanistan. If competition were to take place, then it would be on terrain and with instruments favorable to the United States.

Kennan thought the Soviet Union would eventually exhaust itself by pursuing global hegemony and universalism. He relied on political, economic, psychological, and military measures, and on natural forces of resistance, such as nationalism.[5] Kennan's asymmetry pitted American strengths against Soviet weaknesses. He relied on a strategic nuclear defense and recommended the use of military force only in defense of a few strongpoints whose loss would tip the balance of power and then only when conditions were favorable to the United States. Diplomacy and declaratory policy were used to modify Soviet behavior. Kennan's asymmetry could be sustained indefinitely.

Kennan's containment, as articulated between 1947 and 1949, had three stages. The first was to restore the balance of power in Eurasia following the devastation of the belligerents. The second stage was to fragment the Communist bloc. And the third stage was to modify Soviet behavior with respect to international relations through diplomatic means.

Restoration of the balance of power required the reconstruction of Germany and Japan. The European Recovery Program was the major policy initiative of the period, and occupation efforts in both countries were shifted toward rehabilitation. In March 1947, Truman spoke to Congress about providing aid to Turkey and Greece. Some interpreted the Truman Doctrine to promise aid to everyone, but by September the administration had refined its position to include limits on aid.[6]

The Truman administration implemented the first stage of Kennan's strategy somewhat faithfully. Implementation of the second stage, however, began to depart from the original. The Marshall Plan was consistent with the need to rebuild western Europe and to help splinter the Communist bloc. Truman's rhetoric was oriented against totalitarianism, not Communism, thus allowing separate relations with unaligned Communist countries and splintering the Communist bloc. Kennan opposed the creation of NATO, fearing that Europe would rearm rather than focus on economic recovery. Although Kennan believed the Soviets were not yet a military threat and was willing to accept the near-term risk, the Europeans were not so inclined.[7] He feared that such a military alliance would serve to galvanize rather than splinter the Communist bloc.

Several elements of the Truman administration's strategy did not fit squarely with Kennan's third-stage objectives to change the Soviet concept of international relations without war and without appeasement. The creation of NATO and initiating the H-bomb project worked against Kennan's strategy by building on Russia's historical sense of being surrounded by hostile forces.[8] (The Warsaw Pact emerged in 1955.) However, Kennan's recommendation to tie the level of U.S. military activity in the eastern Mediterranean (force deployment policy) to Soviet activity in Italy and Greece was implemented.

Kennan's containment was based on balancing power, the use of diplomatic over military instruments, and accepting regional losses to Communism as long as the balance of power was not threatened—defensive containment.

Nitze's NSC-68 and the Korean Conflict under Truman

Paul Nitze replaced Kennan as director of the Policy Planning Staff in 1949, and Dean Acheson was appointed secretary of state replacing George C.

Marshall. Nitze and Acheson were more concerned with measurable instruments of Soviet power (means) than Kennan, who was more interested in the Soviet's immeasurable intentions (ends). Kennan was willing to accept some risk, Nitze and the new policy elite less so.[9] Nitze's symmetry required the ability to escalate vertically up and down the ladder to all instances of Communist aggression.

One of Kennan's failings was that he did not articulate his strategy in a form that could be followed uniformly across government. In fact, he felt that the strategy should remain flexible and the particulars left to a few well-qualified elite. Nitze produced a written strategy document to overcome that weakness so that all elements of top government could understand and implement administration policy. The result was National Security Council Paper NSC-68,[10] which contained several strong departures from Kennan's formulation.

First, NSC-68 dropped strongpoint defense in favor of a *perimeter defense*. The underlying rationale was that if the United States failed to stand by *any* country, then American credibility would be damaged. Countries that lacked the power to defend themselves against Soviet aggression might find it more attractive to strike deals with the Soviet Union than to risk invasion or a sustained Communist insurgency. Even strong countries might doubt U.S. resolve. U.S. *credibility as global guarantor became a vital interest.*

Second, the military instrument became primary. This signaled two simultaneous changes: first, a dramatic increase in the area of U.S. interests from a few strongpoints to every country along the perimeter and, second, the increased need for forces that could be projected globally. NSC-68 called for a threefold increase in defense expenditures that certainly would have been hard to sell to Congress and the public. The invasion of South Korea by the North quickly overcame that obstacle.

The balance-of-power view survived, but Kennan's focus on military-industrial strength was lost. NSC-68 stated that "any substantial further extension of the area under the domination of the Kremlin would raise the possibility that no coalition adequate to confront the Kremlin with greater strength could be assembled."[11] No more strongpoints—all points along the perimeter were of *equal* importance. The logic of NSC-68 asserts that the balance of power could shift not just from economic or military developments but also from intimidation, humiliation, or even loss of U.S. credibility.

Under Kennan's strategy, Korea had been a peripheral interest. But Keynesian economics suggested that temporary government actions could grow the economy to finance more military expenditures without long-term budget deficits, taxes, or inflation.[12] Without this constraint, there was no need to distinguish between vital and peripheral interests.

Kennan relied on a variety of instruments, whereas NSC-68 emphasized the military instrument. Kennan's asymmetry pitted U.S. strengths against Soviet weaknesses, but a war by proxy in Korea pitted U.S. weaknesses against Soviet strengths. Furthermore, the U.S. limited conventional response in Korea highlighted its planning overreliance on atomic weapons.

Both Kennan's and Nitze's strategies contained an element of flexible response. To Kennan, flexible meant acting only when vital interests were at stake, conditions were favorable, and the means accessible.[13] To the authors of NSC-68, flexibility meant the ability to escalate vertically, up and down the ladder (*calibration*), wherever and whenever Communist aggression appeared.

NSC-68 did not favor Kennan's third stage. Kennan thought the Soviets could be relied upon to uphold agreements based on mutual interests and that the United States should engage them diplomatically on those grounds. NSC-68 assumed that diplomacy would not work until the Soviet system had changed.

Gaddis closes by noting that the failure of the Truman administration was in not understanding the near-infinite demands that Nitze's containment could entail:

> Beginning with a perception of implacable threat and expandable means, it derived a set of interests so vast as to be beyond the nation's political will, if not theoretical capacity, to sustain.[14]

Nitze's containment was based on preponderant power, military primacy, intolerance of any loss to Communism, and offensive rollback of earlier Communist gains—offensive containment.

Truman 1945–53

After making the monumental decision to employ the atomic bomb against Japan, Truman presided over postwar reconstruction and the beginning of the Cold War. Two starkly different statements of the containment strategy are associated with the Truman administration. Assuming the presidency with no experience in national security, Truman does not appear either to have provided the guiding strategic vision or to have been the strategy's architect. More importantly, he appears to have internalized neither the guiding vision nor the strategy itself.

From 1945 until the middle of 1950, Truman pursued one variant of containment. George C. Marshall was Truman's secretary of state from 1947 to 1949, and George Kennan was director of Marshall's Policy Planning Staff. The threat was from Soviet political warfare and subversion, and the response was to build the political and economic strength of the states that were vulnerable to Soviet initiatives. The Soviet weakness was its internal discord and decay. Under Truman, Marshall and Kennan produced the Truman Doctrine in March 1947 in response to the crises in Greece and Turkey, the European Recovery Act in June 1947, the Berlin Crisis and Berlin Airlift in 1948 and 1949, and the North Atlantic Treaty in 1949.

The belief was that the Soviets would rely on measures short of war—disruption, propaganda, covert action, and support of local Communist parties. Even though they could overwhelm Europe with conventional forces, political warfare would be the chosen way of Soviet strategy. Truman, a fiscal conservative, applied continuous pressure to hold the defense budget to $14 billion. To do so, he relied on the U.S. atomic monopoly against the Soviet conventional force threat. The first formal strategy document, National Security Council Paper NSC-20/4, was signed 24 November 1948.[15]

Truman followed a quite different strategy after his election. After Truman's inauguration in 1949, Dean Acheson replaced George C. Marshall as secretary of state, and Paul Nitze replaced George Kennan as director of the State Department's Policy Planning Staff. Nitze proposed a strategy requiring a massive military buildup, but Truman continued to hold the line on the Defense budget. The 1950 North Korean invasion of the

South led to adoption of Nitze's strategy, and NSC-68 was signed on 29 September 1950.

NSC-68, too expensive to continue, was rescinded in the closing days of the Truman administration.

Review

French Indochina. The Vietnamese fought against the Japanese and their Vichy French collaborators from 1941 to 1945. After Japan was defeated in August 1945, the Provisional Republican Government was established to unify all of Vietnam. In a letter of 16 February 1945, Ho Chi Minh appealed directly to Truman to stand by the wartime statements of the United States and the United Nations to intervene on behalf of Vietnamese independence from France. Ho—both nationalist and Communist—cited the conditions he saw granted to the Philippines and stated his goal as full independence and full cooperation with the United States, "guardians and champions of World Justice." The letter went unanswered.

But the French returned to reclaim colonial prerogatives with military force after Japan's withdrawal. In the *First Indochina War* (1946–54), Ho Chi Minh and General Vo Nguyen Giap led Viet Minh resistance forces. In 1952, Truman authorized $60 million in aid to France.

Greek Civil War. The *Greek Civil War* (1946–49) provided an early Cold War challenge. A competition for the right to govern followed the end of German occupation. Partisans on both left and right waged ugly guerrilla wars. Postwar Britain could no longer provide aid to Greece and Turkey, leaving a power vacuum and the possibility of the Soviets filling it. Both were geographically positioned to be critical in the event of a war between East and West. It was thought that if either country fell, the other would follow. The logic of the domino theory was developing.

The *Truman Doctrine* was announced on 12 March 1947. Truman's speech proclaimed the United States to be the leader of the free world and that it would both support capitalism and oppose Communism. The United States would provide economic and military aid to states threatened by Communism—it was "the policy of the United States to support free peoples who are resisting attempted subjugation by armed minorities or by outside pressure." Although driven by events in Greece and Turkey, the Truman Doctrine was to be a guide to global action.

Greece, governed by a military junta with a record of human rights abuses, was given $300 million. Turkey was given $100 million. Change in force deployment policy included increased U.S. naval presence including an aircraft carrier and battleship. Aid was also provided to assist the governments of Italy and France to resist the growth of the Communist Party; U.S. policy opposed coalition governments that included Communist participation.

The administration's first NSC directive authorized covert intervention into Italy's democratic electoral process to thwart Communist Party candidates. On 24 November 1947, Truman signed NSC-1/1 authorizing psychological warfare in Italy and assigned the responsibility to State. Secretary of State Marshall thought covert operations would damage the diplomatic mission; NSC-4/A, signed on 14 December, reassigned responsibility for psychological warfare to the Central Intelligence Agency (CIA). NSC-10/2 established the principle of *plausible deniability* and authorized the CIA organization for covert actions in June 1948. The three principal offices in the CIA were the Office of Policy Coordination for covert action, including political, economic, and psychological warfare; the Office of Special Operations for clandestine collection; and the Office of Reports and Estimates housing the agency's analysts.[16]

Birth of Israel. The Palestinian Mandate held by Britain was to expire at midnight on 14 May 1948. Jewish and Arab terrorism made the continuation of British involvement untenable, and the United States had no desire to inherit the Mandate. UN Resolution 181, the partition resolution, was issued on 29 November 1947 without Britain or the United States taking a leadership role. Jews embraced the partition establishing a new state, but Arabs did not share in the joy. The result was a violent civil war from December 1947 to January 1948.

The British refused to support international enforcement of the UN partition with troops. Truman came to the same position after receiving near-unanimous advice against supporting an action that appeared to require nearly one hundred thousand troops. Many of Truman's top advisors, including Secretary Marshall, firmly opposed recognition. Warren Austin headed the U.S. team at the UN working on an alternative trusteeship arrangement. Israel announced its statehood before the expiration of the Mandate. Facing an election that many thought he could not win,

Truman reversed course and surprised his UN delegation by announcing U.S. recognition of Israel within minutes after the Palestinian Mandate expired. Khrushchev recognized Israel only hours later. Marshall sent a liaison officer to prevent the mass resignation of Austin's UN team.

First Arab-Israeli War. The First Arab-Israeli War took place in 1948 after Israel announced its statehood and was recognized by the United States and the Soviet Union. The Arab League states of Egypt, Syria, Iraq, Lebanon, and Jordan (with Saudi and Yemini contingents) attacked the new state on 14 May 1948. According to the Arab states in a 15 May statement:

> The only solution of the Palestine problem is the establishment of a unitary Palestinian State, in accordance with democratic principles, whereby its inhabitants will enjoy complete equality before the law, . . . minorities will be assured of all the guarantees recognized in democratic constitutional countries.[17]

For Israel, it was a war of survival. Israel declared the UN partition null and void due to the Arab attack. The partitioning put forward in the UN Resolution was abandoned, and the new Jewish state gained considerable territory as a result of the war.

Berlin Crisis. The Soviets presented Truman with what might have looked to be an insoluble problem. The Soviets closed road and rail access to West Berlin in an attempt to extend their influence over the entire city. The United States and its allies provided fuel and food for 2 million Berliners from 24 June 1948 to 11 May 1949. The *Berlin Airlift* was an extraordinarily complex undertaking and was immensely successful operationally and politically.

Election and Change of Management. Truman's election in 1948 brought considerable change in personnel and policy. Truman's 1949 inaugural address put forward the *Point Four Program* to produce "a better world balance in living conditions." The ways included technical and economic assistance to developing countries in Asia, Africa, and Latin America. East-West and North-South issues would be pursued simultaneously.

Dean Acheson replaced Marshall at State, and Paul Nitze replaced Kennan as director of the Policy Planning Staff. On 31 January 1950, Truman directed State and Defense to conduct a strategy review. The February and March review produced NSC-68 (developed by State, but labeled as an NSC product) in early April.[18] Although no cost estimates were included in the report, Acheson and Nitze estimated them to be between $40 and $50 billion, a tripling of Defense spending. In May, Truman announced a $13 billion target for Defense spending, thus rejecting the strategy.

The driving premise of NSC-68 was that the USSR would be able to deliver a surprise attack by 1954, the *year of maximum danger*. Kennan thought acquisition of atomic bombs would not make the Soviets more aggressive, only more capable. Kennan concentrated on Soviet *intentions*, and Nitze concentrated on Soviet *means*. The estimate was that by the middle of 1954, the Soviets would have two hundred bombs, with half of them deliverable by bomber to the United States. NSC-68 rejected Kennan's defensive containment in favor of offensive, affirmative action to *roll back* Soviet advances. Nitze accepted greater risk of provoking general war, but preventive war was disavowed.

Estimates were that if the Soviets decided to invade western Europe with conventional forces, strategic bombardment would have negligible effect in the critical first ninety days. The conclusion was that NATO needed conventional forces to prevent Europe from being overrun. The United States and its allies required a *preponderance of military power* across the board, including both strategic nuclear and conventional forces. Force development policy followed.

Secretary of Defense James Forrestal wanted a $16.9 billion budget and a more balanced force. Truman supported only a $14.4 billion budget, and although he abhorred the atomic bomb, he relied on it as an economy of force. The inventory of atomic bombs grew from fifty to four hundred between the middle of 1948 and the end of 1950. The Soviet's first nuclear test was in September 1949. Still, Truman lowered the Defense budget to $13 billion in January 1950. He authorized development of the nuclear bomb to augment the atomic bomb on 31 January.

Investments were also made outside the U.S. military. In 1950 and 1951, Truman established Radio Liberty to broadcast into the Soviet Union and Radio Free Europe oriented on Eastern Europe. From 1951 to 1953, the CIA grew from three hundred to six thousand personnel, from less than a $5 million to an $82 million budget, from seven overseas stations to forty-seven, and it experienced a sixteenfold increase in operations. There was little to show for the effort. NATO, too, received considerable funds. But the increase in spending imposed an excessive strain on European economies. By 1952 there was a loss of European momentum for resourcing the NATO alliance.

Loss of China. Truman was dealt a bad hand in China. The Chinese Civil War, beginning in 1927, was temporarily suspended when exploited by the Japanese in 1937. Truman sent Marshall to China in an attempt to prevent resumption of civil war and to form a coalition government with a dominant nationalist party. The civil war resumed in 1946. Mao Zedong's Communists defeated Chiang Kai-shek's nationalists on 1 October 1949. The Communists established the People's Republic of China (PRC) on the mainland, while nationalist forces retreated to Taiwan to establish the Republic of China (ROC). The United States expected the ROC to eventually succumb to the PRC but did not see vital interests at stake.

Korean War. North Korea attacked the South on 25 June 1950. The recent loss of China to Communism took on greater significance. Truman deployed the Seventh Fleet to separate the two Chinese factions. Right-wing partisans in the United States blamed the loss of China on Truman, and some claimed a conspiracy of left-wing Communist sympathizers in the State Department of having assisted. More objective analysis lays responsibility on Chiang's dictatorial behavior that helped drive the population toward Mao and on Chiang's attack on Communist forces, which restarted the civil war in 1946. The era of McCarthyism and the Red Scare (1947–57) exerted considerable political influence throughout the Truman and Eisenhower administrations.

In response to the Korean crisis, and in the shadow of the recent loss of China, Truman appointed George C. Marshall as secretary of defense on 21 September, approved NSC-68 on 29 September, and declared a national emergency on 16 December. By 30 June 1951, Congress had appropriated almost $50 billion for the Defense Department. A later review of the Defense buildup, NSC-114/1, moved the maximum threat up from the middle of 1954 to the middle of 1953, and by October, Congress had increased Defense appropriations to $57 billion. The Strategic Air Command was the biggest recipient.

Cuba. Fulgencio Batista acceded to power in a 1952 coup d'etat and was quickly recognized by the Truman administration. It was not Batista's first coup. The *Revolt of the Sergeants* of 4 September 1933 overthrew the corrupt government of Gerado Machado. Batista declared himself chief of the armed forces and dominated Cuban government through puppet presidents. Recognition by the United States quickly followed. Batista was elected to the presidency from 1940 to 1944. Three months before an election he was sure to lose, Batista evicted another corrupt government and seized power again in the 10 March 1952 coup.

On Secretary of State Acheson's recommendation, Truman recognized the Batista government on 27 March. The two countries had entered into a mutual defense agreement, with Cuba receiving $16 million in military assistance and the United States receiving military presence on the island. Batista was considered reliably pro-American and anti-Communist. He instituted some liberal reforms, acquired considerable wealth through corrupt practices, and was increasingly feared. Batista created the conditions for Fidel Castro's ascendency.

Covert Operations in Guatemala and Iran. Truman lacked experience in national security matters and confidence in political warfare. His director of central intelligence, General Walter Bedell "Beetle" Smith, saw the CIA primarily in terms of collection and analysis, not covert action. But the CIA's deputy director for plans, Allen Dulles, was enthusiastic about covert operations.

Truman authorized Operation PBFortune (PB was code for Guatemala) on 9 September 1952 to support a scheme proposed by Nicaraguan President Anastasio Somoza and exiled Guatemalan General Carlos Castillo Armas. Operational security had been breached and Guatemala presented the evidence of U.S. intentions to a meeting of the Organization of American States. Plausible deniability no longer possible, the operation was terminated a month later.

The British Secret Intelligence Service offered Operation Boot to Churchill in November 1951. Boot would replace Iran's Prime Minister Dr. Mohammad Mossadegh after Iran nationalized its oil industry. The British attempted to enlist the support of the Truman administration. Allen Dulles was positive; Truman was not. Truman would authorize covert actions to minimize Soviet and Communist influence, and Boot did not rise to those standards.

Demise of NSC-68. Charles "Chip" Bohlen's voice added to Kennan's against the premises of NSC-68. He stated flatly that Soviet leaders would do nothing to risk Soviet power in Russia and that the internal political situation would determine their actions. These things, Bohlen argued, were ignored completely in NSC-68. The debate inside State continued between its Soviet experts (e.g., Kennan and Bohlen) and the Washington-bound members of its policy planning staff (Nitze et al.). Truman approved NSC-135/3 on 25 September 1952, replacing NSC-68. Nitze's language of *rollback* and *preponderance of power* was withdrawn. NSC-135/3 called for a report on the resource implications. The response, NSC-141, was delivered to the NSC on 19 January 1953, Truman's last day in office, following his farewell address on 15 January. NSC-68 was gone.

Critique

By the end of Truman's tenure, the United States had returned to Kennan's strategic thinking, having found Nitze's to be unsustainable and misdirected. Still, the rather polemical NSC-68 is considered the definitive version of containment. Truman appears to have allowed the strategy debate to take place in the State Department, but he never truly embraced or internalized either Kennan's or Nitze's strategy. Instead, his employment policy reacted to events on an ad hoc basis independent of declaratory policy.

For the war in Korea, there was no public debate and no meaningful effort to build a consensus to commitment:

> The American people were not prepared mentally or emotionally for the Korean War. War aims were not clearly defined, and the nation never became united in wholehearted, purposeful support. Like Madison and Polk, and unlike Lincoln, McKinley, Wilson, and Franklin Roosevelt, President Truman did not inspire the nation with a sense of purpose in this war effort.[19]

At the end of the administration, despite immediate recognition of Israel, official U.S. policy was to support Arab independence, provide development assistance to the region, oppose Soviet attempts to establish a foothold in the Middle East, and avoid a regional arms race. Maintaining neutrality with respect to the Arab-Israeli Conflict was central to accomplishing those objectives. McCarthy and fellow hard-liners blamed Truman, Marshall, and State for losing China to Communism. Although uncomfortable with covert action, Truman, more than any other president, established the capability and created the major components of the intelligence community in existence today.

Massive Retaliation and the New Look: Eisenhower and Dulles, 1953–61

Eisenhower, from his privileged position as NATO commander, believed that Truman had been erratic and was pursuing an exhaustive strategy. Truman's unpopularity indicated a likely Republican victory, but the Republican Party was deeply divided. Henry Cabot Lodge headed the internationalist wing of the party. Lodge advocated for internationalism and multilateralism to oppose Communism by rebuilding Europe and forging political and military alliances. Herbert Hoover led the noninterventionist and unilateralist wing, which advocated for withdrawal into *Fortress America* and reliance on nuclear weapons for defense. Senator Robert Taft, the leading Republican candidate, endorsed Hoover's isolationist views.[20] Eisenhower was against American withdrawal from the international scene and offered to withdraw from politics if Taft adopted an internationalist approach. Taft declined. Ike won.

Early in Eisenhower's first term, he instituted what came to be called *Project Solarium*. Stalin had died, the Korean War continued, and the nuclear arms race showed no signs of abatement. Eisenhower selected three competent advisors and tasked each to build an interdepartmental team to study and advocate a specific strategy. Team A was assigned a variant on Kennan's strategy of containment through alliances but without provoking general war. Team B was assigned a strategy dividing Europe between free and Communist states; a Soviet attempt to expand Communism into a free state would be regarded as an act of war against the western European allies. Team C was assigned a Nitze-like strategy based on expanding military forces and offensive rollback of Communist gains. After six weeks of study, the three teams presented their strategies to the president and a group of prominent advisors. After a full day of deliberations, Eisenhower announced that his administration would follow the strategy of Team A. Eisenhower plotted a middle course, with a strategy for the long haul that was sustainable and coherent.

Eisenhower, another staunch fiscal conservative, was acutely aware of the debilitating effects that a sustained war effort could have on the economy, destroying the thing he had sworn to defend.[21] His administration reasserted Kennan's asymmetry, stating that the United States would respond at a time and place of its choosing. Secretary of State John Foster Dulles made strong, yet ambiguous, declarations (*constructive ambiguity*) that some interpreted to be the threat of *massive retaliation*. Eisenhower clearly understood massive retaliation as insufficient to deter lesser aggressions. He relied heavily on the diplomatic instrument, and the United States entered into a host of new treaty arrangements to complement NATO, including the Central Treaty Organization (CENTO), also known as the Baghdad Pact, and the Southeast Asia Treaty Organization (SEATO), also known as the Manila Pact.[22] Eisenhower relied on the economic instrument to resolve the Suez Crisis.

The essence of NSC-68's perimeter defense, however, remained along with the perception that the balance of power was so precarious that the loss of any additional state to Communism would tip the scales;[23] the domino theory was by now established. Eisenhower explicitly spoke of the "falling domino" in a 7 April 1954 news conference, referring to what could happen in Southeast Asia (Indochina) and India, but the domino theory quickly generalized beyond the region.[24] The *Dulles Dictum*—"no country not immediately adjacent to the Soviet bloc could be irrevocably lost"—placed higher priority on Communist encroachments along the Soviet periphery than on encroachments in the Third World, thus differentiating the threat.

Eisenhower was not looking for a quick fix. Rather, he was prepared for a sustainable effort over the long haul. The military component of his strategy was a relatively cheap, active response with strategic (intercontinental) and tactical (battlefield) nuclear forces. Force development policy shifted U.S. force structure and Defense spending toward strategic forces favoring the Air Force's bombers and ICBMs and the Navy's ballistic missile submarines over Army ground forces. Perhaps only Eisenhower had the political capital to impose this solution on the military and the Army in particular. For lesser aggressions, the naval services provided carriers and marines for gunboat diplomacy and for expeditionary operations.

Review

Resource Competition over the Jordan River. In 1951, Israel moved heavy construction equipment and military forces into the Demilitarized Zone along the Syrian border contrary to armistice agreements. Seeing a volatile resource competition brewing between Israel, Jordan, Lebanon, and Syria over water in the desert, Eisenhower proposed a water-sharing plan in 1953. The Jordan Valley Unified Water Plan was agreed to by the technical committees of the four riparian contestants. Israel preemptively initiated a secret nine-mile pipeline to divert waters of the Jordan River with around-the-clock construction. Eisenhower secretly suspended financial aid. An unrelated 1953 Israeli attack on a Jordanian village in the West Bank, the *Kibya Massacre*, caused Eisenhower to make public his suspension of financial aid. A deal was brokered that halted pipeline construction and reinstituted financial aid. Only delayed for two years, the pipeline was completed by 1960, and additional steps would be taken in 1964. The United States provided funding for construction of Israel's National Water Carrier (1955–64) and Jordan's East Ghor Main Canal (1957–66).

Political Warfare in Iran. Operation Boot, proposed by Britain to Truman and rejected, was accepted by the Eisenhower administration, renamed Operation TPAjax, and authorized on 25 June 1953. The shah, encouraged by the United States, replaced Prime Minister Mossadegh with royalist General Fazlollah Zahedi on 16 August 1953. The resulting protests caused the shah to flee in panic on 16 August 1953. He returned on 22 August after the CIA arranged "spontaneous demonstrations" in his support.[25]

Post-Stalinist Soviet Union. Stalin died on 5 March 1953, and Nikita Khrushchev soon became general secretary of the Communist Party. On 25 February 1956, Khrushchev denounced Stalin's totalitarianism and announced the end of the "long winter of sacrifice and persecution."[26] He introduced a "new era of socialism" where private lives would be valued. He announced the "peaceful coexistence" of the United States and the

USSR despite their ideological differences. His post-Stalinist approach is referred to as the *Khrushchev Thaw*, spanning the Eisenhower, Kennedy, and Johnson administrations.

Second Arab-Israeli War.[27] The *Suez Crisis* (July–December 1956) provided an early challenge to the Eisenhower administration.[28] The United States withdrew its offer to fund Egypt's Aswan Dam in response to Nasser's anticolonial actions, and the Soviets offered to step in. Instead, Nasser nationalized the Suez Canal—soon to revert from foreign to Egyptian control—to finance the Aswan project. Great Britain, France, and Israel conspired to reclaim the Suez from Egypt by military means. Eisenhower saw it as a continuation of colonialism. Furious with his assumed friends, Eisenhower used the economic rather than the military instrument to quickly resolve the issue in Egypt's favor.[29] Egypt accepted UN peacekeepers; Israel did not.

Having opposed Israel and the colonial powers, the United States left the crisis with some positive influence in the Middle East. British and French withdrawal left a power vacuum and the possibility of the Soviets filling it. Nasser was the big winner, and pan-Arabism was ascendant. Eisenhower's choices were to build on the positive outcome of the Suez Crisis or to recast Middle Eastern issues into the context of the Cold War. Cold War thinking proved irresistible. Official U.S. policy was to remain neutral with respect to the Arab-Israeli Conflict, and U.S. assistance to Israel was primarily food aid.

The *Eisenhower Doctrine* followed directly from the resolution of the Suez Crisis. Economic and military assistance would be provided if requested by nations in the Middle East. National interests and world peace were tied to preserving the independence of Middle Eastern states and the flow of oil. Eisenhower's proposal was submitted to Congress on 5 January 1957, debated, and approved by Joint Resolution on 9 March. The Eisenhower Doctrine was never explicitly invoked, although the administration was actively engaged in the region. By late 1958 the Doctrine was moderated to rely less on military backing, giving greater emphasis to accommodation with Arab nationalists to improve U.S. influence in the region.

Head of Policy Planning Staff Robert Bowie disapproved of the public statement saying that it overstressed the Soviet military threat to the region, which he did not perceive as imminent, and that it relied too heavily on "military cures." Making the Middle East part of the Cold War would stiffen resistance in the region and encourage Arab nationalistic sentiments. Bowie's reasoning followed directly from that of Chip Bohlen and George Kennan.

Poland and Hungary. The *Polish Uprising* (28 June) and the *Hungarian Revolution* (23 October to 10 November) followed Khrushchev's February 1956 liberalizing speech. Soviet interests were significant and U.S. interests few. Presented with the possibility of direct military confrontation between U.S. and Soviet forces, and the attendant risk of nuclear escalation, Eisenhower chose political warfare and defensive containment over offensive rollback.

Lebanon. Lebanon experienced a short civil war and a U.S. military intervention in 1958. Lebanon's population was largely Muslim with a Maronite Christian minority. Camille Chamoun, a Christian, presided over a disproportionately Christian government. The Muslim majority was represented politically by the National Front. But the competition was primarily secular rather than religious. Lebanese Christians were largely pro-Western, and Chamoun leaned toward the Baghdad Pact. Muslims leaned heavily toward pan-Arabism and Nasser. The Eisenhower administration interpreted the Lebanon crisis in the Cold War context.

Pan-Arabism was unifying the region and replacing colonialism. Rather than interpreting it as a positive movement for self-determination deserving of support, it was seen as anti-Western, with the potential to lead the region into being pro-Eastern and pro-Soviet, and therefore as something to oppose.

Chamoun's acceptance of the Eisenhower Doctrine exacerbated domestic tensions and put Lebanon in opposition to Egypt, Syria, and the National Front. The administration secretly funneled funding through the CIA to influence the 1957 parliamentary elections to aid in Chamoun's 1958 reelection. But the funding secret was not well kept, and the National Front initiated a successful military campaign to control the majority of Lebanon two months before the scheduled presidential election.

Chamoun requested assistance in stabilizing the situation. The day after the overthrow of the pro-Western Iraqi government, marines and airborne forces were landed and supported by the Sixth Fleet offshore. An alleged

Syrian plot against the pro-Western monarchy in Jordan met with the landing of British troops in Jordan on 17 July. Chamoun stepped down in September after an acceptable replacement had been found. The head of Lebanon's army, a moderate Christian, assumed the presidency. With resolution of the civil war, U.S. troops were withdrawn on 25 October 1958.

French Indochina. In 1953, Eisenhower upped the U.S. commitment to six times Truman's $60 million support to the French. French Indochina—comprising Vietnam, Cambodia, and Laos—fell in March 1954 after Ho Chi Minh's Vietminh successfully laid siege to French forces at *Dien Bien Phu*. Under considerable political pressure to intervene militarily on behalf of the French, Eisenhower declined by establishing three preconditions for U.S. involvement: U.S. allies would have to provide forces in equal numbers; the French would have to grant independence to Indochina; and the U.S. Congress would have to declare war.[30] He knew those conditions would not be met.

In the same 1950 to 1954 time frame, Ngo Dinh Diem, a Vietnamese nationalist, lobbied European and American elites, with his efforts aided by McCarthyism and the opening of the Korean War. Sponsored by Cardinal Francis Spellman, Diem, a devout Catholic, spent three years in New Jersey and New York seminaries.

The 1954 *Geneva Accords* dissolved Indochina in 1955. Vietnam was divided, with Ho's Vietminh controlling the Democratic Republic of Vietnam in the north and the French-backed State of Vietnam in the south. With the Eisenhower administration's backing, former Emperor Bao Dai named Diem prime minister. The French thought Diem incompetent and protested the appointment. Elections were to be held in 1956 to determine a unifying government. The immensely popular Ho would likely win by a wide margin. Diem had no intention of holding the 1956 election and, along with the United States, did not sign the Accords. The Accords prohibited foreign military forces, but both North Vietnam and the United States quickly violated the prohibition.

Catholics fled north to south in large numbers. Catholics constituted roughly a 10 percent minority amid an 80 percent Buddhist population. The French-trained head of the army despised Diem. Two religious sects and a crime syndicate commanded their own powerful armies. A rigged election in the South provided Diem with 98 percent of the vote. Diem announced the establishment of the Republic of Vietnam three days later, naming himself president and commander in chief on 26 October 1955. The unifying election of 1956 was never held. Diem pursued heavy-handed policies that further eroded public support in the South. As with Chiang Kai-shek in China, the United States was backing a government seemingly doomed to failure. Its appeal was that it was non-Communist.

Guatemala. Eisenhower authorized Operation PBSuccess, a paramilitary war in August 1953 including subversion, psychological warfare, and political action. A Guatemalan force of 150 entered six miles into Guatemala from Honduras on 16 June 1954, supported by aerial bombardment of civilian populations. After a temporary success, a thirty-six-year civil war began six years later. The intervention increased hostility toward the United States throughout Latin America.[31]

Cuba. Fidel Castro, with a force of nine thousand, entered Havana and completed the overthrow of the Batista dictatorship on 8 January 1958. It was seen by many as the replacement of one pro-American regime with another. Castro spoke against dictatorship, including Communist dictatorship, and spoke loudly of Cuban nationalism. But as Castro continued his turn to the left, the United States implemented a trade embargo the next year that continues today.

U-2 Incident. A 1960 incident strained Eisenhower's relationship with Khrushchev toward the end of his administration. In a joint CIA/USAF operation, Operation Overflight, Francis Gary Powers launched a U-2 photoreconnaissance plane from near Peshawar, Pakistan, and was shot down over the Soviet Union on 1 May. Eisenhower refused to apologize for the spy plane intrusions, setting back peace talks for years to come. Khrushchev encouraged and approved the erection of the Berlin Wall in 1961. Powers was released in a prisoner exchange on 10 February 1962.

Critique

According to critics, the Eisenhower administration's heavy reliance on nuclear weapons at the expense of conventional forces risked either capitulation or nuclear retaliation. All administrations accept some risk, and in this time frame, it was a reasonable risk. However, the long-term legacy of the heavy reliance on nuclear weapons had several negative consequences. Most notable is that the Soviets felt compelled to intensify their missile-building programs.

Senator John F. Kennedy and other congressional opponents criticized the Eisenhower administration for allowing a *bomber gap* to develop. The Air Force desired additional bombers and fanned the fear that a gap was developing between the Soviet Union and the United States. Eisenhower was skeptical. Photoreconnaissance flights by the U-2 spy plane refuted the claim, but the president declined to announce the fact so as not to divulge the capability. The 1957 Soviet launch of the Sputnik communications satellite quickly replaced the fear of a bomber gap with the fear of a *missile gap*. Kennedy called a policy failure Eisenhower's preoccupation with an imagined bomber gap that prevented the detection of a real missile gap.

In Congress, those promoting the bomber and missile gaps were led by Senator Henry "Scoop" Jackson (D-WA), nicknamed "the Senator from Boeing" for his strong support of the defense industry. In support of JFK's presidential run, and as a possible Kennedy running mate, Jackson led Eisenhower's congressional critics. With hard-liners opposed, Eisenhower did not or could not capitalize on the Khrushchev Thaw.

Perhaps the most notable accomplishment of the Eisenhower strategy was the return of aligning ends and means. A true fiscal conservative, Eisenhower was fully aware of the many costs of war, more aware than most about the limits of what can be accomplished with military force, and firmly believing that the country's true strength rests on a robust economy. He forcefully expressed the opportunity costs of military expenditures in terms of domestic well-being in his Chance for Peace speech in his first year in office[32] and in his farewell address warning against the influence of the military-industrial complex.

Eisenhower was more comfortable than Truman with using covert capabilities. Eisenhower relied heavily on the threat of strategic nuclear forces to deal with the direct threat from the Soviet Union. But over lower level issues, particularly in the Third World, he relied on political warfare through covert CIA activities and, when necessary, overt military application of carriers, marines, and airborne forces. Eisenhower fulfilled his campaign promise to end the war in Korea, and he left office with no military forces committed to combat anywhere. That would soon change.

Flexible Response: Kennedy and Johnson 1961–69

Kennedy took office after a dozen years that encompassed dramatic changes in international developments. Both the United States and the Soviet Union now had hydrogen bombs and long-range bombers capable of delivering them. International events with implications for U.S. foreign policy took place in the Suez, Strait of Formosa, Lebanon, Iraq, and Berlin. Fidel Castro and Communism had established a foothold in the Western Hemisphere.

Kennedy and Johnson returned to symmetry under the rubric of *flexible response*. At the high end, massive retaliation was replaced by *mutual assured destruction*. As with Nitze, flexible response meant a calibration of the American response to the Soviet offense. Kennedy considered the conventional capability he had inherited to be inadequate, thereby creating the risk of choosing between nuclear escalation and capitulation. Kennedy shifted emphasis from strategic nuclear forces to conventional forces and unconventional forces (for proinsurgency and counterinsurgency) to provide the United States more options to meet Soviet expansion. While reducing the risk of capitulation or escalation, having a full range of options made it possible for the president to engage in more activities and made each step up the escalatory ladder relatively easy. Kennedy became focused on means. Nitze's thinking was reestablished over Kennan's. General Maxwell Taylor's *Uncertain Trumpet*, critical of Eisenhower's approach, was a considerable influence on Kennedy's thinking.

The language of flexible response included taxonomy to subdivide force development policy. High-intensity conflict (HIC) was defined to be conflict characterized by the large-scale exchange of intercontinental nuclear weapons that could be preceded by, accompanied by, and followed by other forms of conflict. Mid-intensity conflict (MIC) had as its dominant characteristic the clash of large-scale conventional forces in one or more theater, but it might be accompanied by isolated instances of strategic and tactical nuclear exchanges. Low-intensity conflict (LIC) was characterized as a clash with irregular forces and militias cast in the context of a political competition for the right to govern.

Low-intensity conflict includes both proinsurgency, to assist indigenous forces undermining an existing government, and counterinsurgency, to assist an existing government resisting indigenous forces perhaps supported by external actors. Either may escalate to civil war. Taylor represented a school of thought espousing counterinsurgency warfare as the appropriate response to Communist-inspired or Communist-exploited insurgency. In the Kennedy administration, the CIA remained responsible for covert opposition to undesirable foreign governments (proinsurgency) consistent with the Eisenhower era. The Pentagon became responsible for countering internal opposition to favorable anti-Communist governments (counterinsurgency). The national policy statement governing operations in this domain is the Overseas Internal Defense Policy of 1962. Adoption of counterinsurgency as a tool of statecraft was a significant step in the evolution of U.S. foreign policy.

The *Kennedy Doctrine* emphasized the East-West competition in Latin America. It continued the containment of Communism globally but also asserted *offensive rollback* of Communism in the Western Hemisphere. The inaugural address of 20 January and the "Alliance for Progress" address of 13 March 1961[33] form the basis of the Doctrine.

The Kennedy-Johnson administrations expanded the perimeter defense to an anywhere, anytime, any-cost global defense. One of the great speeches of modern times, Kennedy's inaugural address was greeted around the world with cheers. But the promise made was patently false and was well beyond the country's capacities to fulfill:

> Let every nation know, whether it wishes us well or ill, that we shall pay any price, bear any burden, meet any hardship, support any friend, oppose any foe, to assure the survival and success of liberty.

As with Truman, Kennedy pursued the East-West competition by addressing North-South disparities. In his inaugural address, Kennedy called upon Americans to enter into "a struggle against the common enemies of man: tyranny, poverty, disease, and war itself." "I have called on all the people of the hemisphere to join in a new *Alliance for Progress*, a vast cooperative effort, unparalleled in magnitude and nobility of purpose, to satisfy the basic needs of the American people for homes, work and land, health and schools."

In his Alliance for Progress address, JFK reaffirmed his pledge to defend threatened nations. He promised food and economic aid, and he encouraged Latin American countries to make social and material progress. Kennedy encouraged greater economic integration in the Western Hemisphere. The Caribbean would be home to the Bay of Pigs, Cuban Missile Crisis, and the crisis in the Dominican Republic.

Khrushchev was ousted by his protégé Leonid Brezhnev in 1964, and the Brezhnev Doctrine replaced the Khrushchev Thaw.

Review

Arms Control. As the United States lost its nuclear monopoly, Defense Secretary Robert McNamara developed the logic of mutual assured destruction to replace Eisenhower's massive retaliation. Initiated late in the Kennedy administration, it was developed through the Johnson years.

Cuba and the Bay of Pigs. The United States initiated a series of covert actions to oust Fidel Castro between 1960 and 1965, including a series of personal attacks and the abortive *Bay of Pigs* invasion. Eisenhower, encouraged by the successful overthrow of the Guatemalan government in 1954 and the Iranian government the year before, had authorized the CIA operation on 16 March 1960. Trained in Central America by the United States, 1,500 Cuban exiles attempted an amphibious assault on Cuba on 17 April 1961. At the last minute, JFK refused to provide the necessary air support, and the invasion failed at considerable political cost to Kennedy and strategic cost to the United States. Kennedy explained his decision by saying that the use of air power would have removed any plausible deniability. Eisenhower responded to Kennedy's naiveté by saying there was no plausible deniability for an overt action of that scale with or without air support. Kennedy approved Operation Mongoose in November 1961, a covert plan to instigate a rebellion leading to Castro's overthrow.

Cuban Missile Crisis. The Cuban Missile Crisis, part of the strategic arms race, brought the world to the brink of nuclear war. U.S. intercontinental missiles were capable of blanketing the Soviet Union, but Soviet missiles could reach only Europe. After the botched Bay of Pigs attempt, Castro was looking for a deterrent against the next U.S. invasion that he was sure would come. Soviet missiles in Cuba met both Castro's and Khrushchev's needs. The Kennedy administration turned in a better performance than during the Bay of Pigs, and Khrushchev was weakened at home.

Seven days after reconnaissance photos revealed the construction of missile sites on 15 October 1962, Kennedy ordered a naval "quarantine" of Cuba to prevent the arrival of additional components (a quarantine rather than a blockade because the latter is an act of war under international law). The situation was made public on 22 October. On 26 October Khrushchev offered to withdraw with a U.S. guarantee not to invade Cuba. A U-2 spy plane was shot down over Cuba on 27 October, and Khrushchev demanded removal of U.S. missiles from Turkey in exchange for the removal of Soviet missiles from Cuba. On 28 October agreement was reached on the basis of Khrushchev's first offer.

Chile. Kennedy authorized covert action to influence the 1962 election in Chile. In 1964 Johnson authorized covert action to support the candidacy of Christian Democrat Eduardo Frei over the pro-Castro, Marxist, socialist Salvador Allende. The action failed, but Allende's government soon proved incompetent, and its economic policies produced its own downfall.

Dominican Crisis. For thirty-one years (1930–61), Rafael Leonidas Trujillo Molina, a brutal right-wing dictator, ruled the Dominican Republic. Trujillo had been trained and installed by U.S. Marines. Trujillo was assassinated in 1961. Juan Bosch was elected president in December 1962, defeating Trujillo's heir apparent, Joaquin Balaquer. Bosch began implementing liberal economic and social reforms opposed by the oligarchy. He was anti-Communist, but he allowed their political activity. A military coup on 25 September 1963 ousted Bosch and abolished the constitution. A popular revolt to reinstate Bosch was opposed by a small military force from the United States. Marines landed 28 April 1965, followed by Army airborne forces. Military presence grew quickly from 500 to 4,500 and eventually to 23,000. U.S. forces left in September 1966 after supervising elections that left Balaquer in power.

The *Johnson Doctrine* followed the Dominican crisis in 1965. Domestic revolution in the Western Hemisphere would no longer be a local matter when "the object is the establishment of a Communist dictatorship."

Indochina. The *Second Indochina War* (1955–75) picked up where the First left off with the United States replacing France as the intervening foreign power but without colonial aspirations. It included what is sometimes called the *Secret War* in Laos (1962–75) run by the ambassador with CIA and USAID resources, the Cambodian Civil War (1967–75), and the Vietnam War (1964–75) beginning with the insertion of U.S. advisors as early as 1955.

Vietnam. At the beginning of his administration, President Charles de Gaulle, recalling the withdrawal of French forces from Vietnam, cautioned Kennedy against deepening the engagement, saying that the United States would sink into a "bottomless quagmire." Diem's heavy-handed political incompetence and his nepotistic administration were increasingly problematic to U.S. interests. His administration favored the Catholic minority and instituted policies unfavorable to the Buddhist majority and Montagnard minority.

General Duong Van Minh overthrew Diem in a 1 November 1963 coup encouraged by the Kennedy administration. Diem and his brother were quickly assassinated. The Vietnamese celebrated in the streets. Kennedy was assassinated three weeks later on 22 November.

Now it was Johnson's war. General Nguyen Khanh overthrew Minh in late January 1964. Khanh lasted a year, his successor half as long. Nguyen Van Thieu came to power in 1965 and remained until 1975. Vietnam became the focus of Johnson's attention, but simultaneously the United States waged a secret war in Laos and bombed North Vietnam's supply lines in Cambodia.

The Army of the Republic of Vietnam (ARVN) was not aggressive, and U.S. nation-building efforts stalled. Hard-liners vilified past presidents for losing China, North Korea, and Cuba to Communism, and Johnson did not want to down as the president who lost Vietnam.

Gulf of Tonkin. Under pressure to look strong during the election campaign, and in response to a minor event off the North Vietnamese coast on 2 August and a nonevent two days later, Secretary of Defense McNamara announced a retaliatory air strike against the North, and Johnson immediately requested congressional support. Congress complied 7 August with what became known as the *Gulf of Tonkin Resolution*. The *Gulf of Tonkin Incident* is considered the first of many major deceptions by the Johnson administration.

The Resolution allowed the president to take actions in "defense of American forces in South East Asia." Retaliatory air strikes dominated. Marines were deployed to defend the Danang air base, but the force quickly went on the offense. *Operation Rolling Thunder* (1965–68)—a major air offensive against North Vietnam—began on 2 March 1965. Johnson's secret bombing of Cambodia began the same year. The escalation to a half million U.S. troops began, joined by forces from South Korea, Thailand, Australia, New Zealand, and the Philippines.

The administration initiated a *Success Offensive* as public opposition to the war continued to grow through 1967. General Westmoreland, Defense Secretary McNamara, and President Johnson made strong assurances that light could be seen at the end of the tunnel. During a 17 November television broadcast, LBJ announced, "We are inflicting greater losses than we're taking. . . . We are making progress." At the National Press Club four days later, General Westmoreland asserted that the Communists were "unable to mount a major offensive." In a *Time* magazine interview the same month, he said, "I hope they try something, because we are looking for a fight."[34] Westmoreland soon got his wish.

Tet Offensive. The *General Offensive, General Uprising* (30 January– 30 August 1968), a multiphased Communist offensive, brought attacks throughout the South by Viet Cong irregulars and North Vietnamese Army regulars. The first phase built up forces in the western border regions of the South and initiated what were called the Border Battles. The intent was to draw U.S. forces away from the population centers along the eastern coast. The next phase was the Tet Offensive against population centers and a simultaneous propaganda campaign to create a popular uprising against the government in the South. Follow-on offensives, mini-Tets, were planned to force a negotiated settlement if the General Uprising failed to materialize. Preparations began in mid-1967, as supplies were stockpiled, Viet Cong forces rearmed, and NVA forces moved down the Ho Chi Minh Trail. In response, Westmoreland redeployed 250,000 troops into the five northernmost provinces. Although subordinates wanted to reinforce the coastal cities, Westmoreland shifted forces from population centers into the field in hopes of pitched battle.

The North laid siege to *Khe Sahn* from 21 January to 9 July 1968 to draw attention to the remote border region and away from the coastal population centers, hoping to deal the United States what they had dealt France at Dien Bien Phu.

On 31 January 1968, Communist forces initiated simultaneous attacks throughout South Vietnam, achieving tactical surprise and considerable initial success, but coalition forces quickly dealt the North an overwhelming battlefield defeat. It became mainstream political thought that the Johnson administration had deliberately deceived the American public. The public and the media saw a *credibility gap* between talk and reality. The Politburo in Hanoi was in disarray from the military defeat. But after seeing the public response in the United States, disarray turned into strengthened resolve. The culminating point had been reached. Light was indeed at the end of the tunnel.

Optimistic estimates, particularly from the field commander, dominated Johnson's perceptions. Negative estimates from the CIA and others were discounted but were becoming the basis of a new consensus. Westmoreland's requested troop increase required an expanded draft, increased appropriations, and increased taxes.[35] McNamara presented the troop request to Johnson on 27 February 1968, recommended deescalation, and stepped down the next day. His replacement, the hawkish Clark Clifford, soon joined the new consensus: another escalation would turn a costly stalemate into an even more costly stalemate. Johnson acquiesced but understood that he personally could not reverse course and continue to lead.

On 31 March 1968 Johnson announced a partial end to Rolling Thunder and his decision not to run for reelection. Later, LBJ bitterly accused Nixon of sabotaging the talks by promising a better deal from the incoming Republican administration.

Resource Competition over the Jordan River. In January 1964, Israel announced its intention to divert water from the Jordan River in the Golan Heights of Syria. At the Arab League meeting that same month, Nasser cited the past lack of unified military action as the source of Arab failure, and the League formed the United Arab Command. The PLO's first attack was aimed at the Israeli pipeline when Israel began diverting water in 1964. Arab states began upstream diversion efforts in 1965 favoring Syria, Jordan, and Lebanon. Israel attacked Arab construction sites in March, May, and August.

A landmine, thought to have been planted by al-Fatah, killed three Israeli soldiers patrolling the border between Israel and Jordan. Israel responded disproportionately with a combined arms attack across the 1949 armistice line into the Jordanian West Bank two days later on 13 November 1966. Dozens of buildings, including homes, were destroyed in the *Samu Incident*.

Israel made repeated threats to topple the Syrian government. Israeli agricultural efforts in a forbidden area were met by Syrian resistance. Small arms exchanges quickly escalated into a major cross-border battle known as the *April 7 Incident*, which included Israeli air penetration to Damascus.

The Soviet Union brokered a Syrian-Egyptian mutual defense pact signed 4 May 1966, and the Soviets claimed that the Samu and April Incidents activated the pact.

Third Arab-Israeli War. Conditions worsened, and in early 1967, the Soviet Union gave unsubstantiated warning to Egypt that Israel was preparing to attack Syria. Some advisors cautioned Egyptian president Nasser against being drawn into a war between Syria and Israel. Others advised Nasser to initiate a preemptive war against Israel. In May 1967, Egypt expelled UN peacekeeping forces, who had occupied the Sinai since the Suez Crisis, moved its own forces to the Egyptian border with Israel, and closed the Strait of Tiran to Israeli shipping, thus denying access to the Red Sea. The Israeli cabinet decided on 23 May to mobilize for an offensive. Jordan and Egypt signed a mutual defense pact on 30 May. The *Six-Day War* began on 5 June 1967 when Israel attacked into Egyptian territory. Another front was opened in the Jordanian West Bank, and a third front against Syria in the Golan Heights. American and Israeli texts tend to refer to the initiation of the war as preemptive, citing the offensive posture taken by Egypt, while Arab and some European texts call it an act of Israeli aggression, citing the defensive posture taken by Egypt. De Gaulle blamed Israel for initiating the war, reversing years of strong French support to Israel.

Arab states announced an oil embargo on 6 June as a deterrent to any state that might provide aid to the Israeli military. The oil embargo was hastily constructed and ineffective. The Khartoum Resolution ended the embargo on 1 September 1967, giving moderate Arab governments the political cover to resume oil exports over the objections of their more radical populations and provided the victims of the war (Jordan and Egypt) annual financial aid. The war also led to formation of the

Organization of Arab Petroleum Exporting Countries to discuss how to use oil for political purposes.

On 8 June 1967 unmarked Israeli jets and torpedo boats attacked the USS *Liberty*, a signals intelligence ship, in international waters, killing thirty-four American sailors, marines, and civilians. Israel launched its assault on the Golan Heights the next day. The attack was covered up by both countries. Johnson and McNamara pronounced it an accident, although, uniquely, the incident was never investigated.

The Six-Day War ended on 10 June. As a result, Israel more than tripled its area, including the Sinai, Gaza, the West Bank, East Jerusalem, and the Golan Heights. The USSR broke relations with Israel, and Egypt broke relations with the United States. Prior to the war U.S. administrations avoided any appearance of favoritism in their Middle East policy. The Johnson administration shifted to a strong pro-Israeli stance. Johnson approved sale of top-line fighter aircraft to Israel in 1968. America began its movement from being the most trusted to the least trusted great power in the Arab Middle East.

The *War of Attrition*, a sustained guerrilla war, began almost immediately to free occupied Arab territory seized by Israel.

Czechoslovakia. De-Stalinization and Khrushchev's liberal reforms were slow to take hold in Czechoslovakia until the Prague Spring (1968). Alexander Dubček was elected as the Communist Party's first secretary on 5 January. Dubček's liberal reforms included decentralizing the economy and shifting from heavy industry to science and technology; granting freedom of press, speech, and travel; and drawing down political surveillance.

The liberal reforms concerned Brezhnev, and the Soviets entered into negotiations with the Czechs. Brezhnev feared loss of an ally, the Czech industrial base, and the buffer against NATO. The Soviet-led Warsaw Pact invaded Czechoslovakia 20–21 August 1968 with two hundred thousand troops and two thousand tanks. Romania opposed the action, and Albania withdrew from the Warsaw Pact. Johnson was fully engaged with Vietnam and wanted to negotiate a SALT arms control agreement with the Soviets. The USSR had strong interests; the United States had none and declined to intervene.

The *Brezhnev Doctrine* followed the Czech invasion late in the Johnson administration.[36] Gone was the Khrushchev Thaw and its liberal reforms. It was a statement similar in nature to the Roosevelt Corollary to the Monroe Doctrine, claiming the right of the Soviet Union to intervene in the affairs of socialist states on its periphery. The Doctrine would remain in place for two decades, although the ability to carry it out weakened continually as time passed. The Brezhnev Doctrine, and its emphasis on a militarized economy, would prove to be the undoing of the Soviet Union that Kennan predicted.

Critique

Early in his administration, Kennedy failed to deter deployment of Soviet nuclear missiles to Cuba. Campaign rhetoric against Eisenhower followed by the 1961 Bay of Pigs fiasco fanned the Soviet's suspicion of Kennedy's militarism. Others thought his perceived militarism induced the Soviets to deploy missiles. Some suggested that his youth and perceived weakness invited the attempt. The subsequent missile crisis reinforced anti-appeasement sentiments and supported the illusion that Communism was monolithic, obscuring Kennan's original goal to splinter the Communist world. Furthermore, Brezhnev accelerated the Soviet intercontinental ballistic missile program. On the positive side, a treaty banning atmospheric testing of nuclear weapons was reached.

The highest-level policy failure of the Kennedy-Johnson administrations was the tenuous credibility of flexible response. Could the United States afford to respond in kind to every local Communist insurgency or Soviet direct or indirect act of aggression? By not responding after strong declaratory policy to the contrary, American credibility would suffer. By committing everywhere, even when the possibility of a positive outcome was minimal, U.S. energy was sapped and the ability to withdraw made difficult. The administration lost sight of objectives (ends), focusing instead on military instruments (means) to support HIC, MIC, and LIC operations. The enemy was allowed to pick the place and time of competition, and American overextension was the consequence.

U.S. involvement in Vietnam is the strongest and most costly example of this policy failure. Insertion of "advisory" forces was an easy early step. Each escalatory step followed with relative ease, and each was harder to reverse. While opposing Communism was considered a just cause, siding with a corrupt and nonviable government and overestimating the effectiveness of the military instrument doomed that opposition to failure. Truman and Eisenhower provided only material support until the South Vietnamese government demonstrated that it could survive. A reverse logic appeared under Johnson; it was concluded that the South Vietnamese government could not survive without direct U.S. military intervention.

After using a contrived incident to secure congressional authorization to use force in Southeast Asia, Johnson deliberately chose not to build a consensus to commitment for the war in Vietnam, fearing the American public would not support both the war and his Great Society domestic programs. Congress passed a 10 percent increase in income tax to finance the war. The large force deployment rested on a conscript army, and an inequitable deferment system helped divide along class lines a public already divided over race. Johnson chose not to pay the political price of deploying the National Guard. An equitable conscription system and deployment of the National Guard would have eroded support rapidly. Support eroded nonetheless. Having been defeated by his own policies, LBJ declined to run again. Nixon campaigned to end Johnson's war just as Eisenhower had campaigned to end Truman's.

With respect to Middle East policy, Kennedy maintained neutrality in the Arab-Israeli Conflict, but Johnson effected a major policy change with his unambiguous support for Israel in the 1967 war. Prior to 1948, the United States was the most trusted foreign power in the Middle East. After the 1967 war, the United States became the most distrusted and even hated foreign power. U.S. policy of avoiding an arms race in the Middle East led to the French being the primary arms supplier to Israel, but the French imposed an arms embargo against Israel in 1967, and the United States moved in to fill the gap.

The Vietnam War and civil rights was forcing schisms in both the Democratic and Republican Parties. Southern Democrats were moving into the Republican Party over the Democratic Party's civil rights positions. Hawkish liberal Democrats, the neoconservatives, were moving into the Republican Party over the war. The Democratic Party was coming apart. The Republican Party was absorbing the southern Democrats that the party was established to oppose.

Détente under Nixon-Ford and Kissinger, 1969–77

Henry Kissinger was the dominant strategic thinker in the Nixon and Ford administrations. Kissinger, like Kennan, strongly preferred maintaining balance of power over pursuing preponderant power and global hegemony. Under *détente*, a relaxing of tensions, the United States recognized that there were different kinds of Communists and that wedges could be driven between them. Kennan's goal of splitting the Communist bloc could be pursued. Nixon created a centralized national security process concentrated in the NSC and freezing the State Department out of the process. The strategy employed resembled Kennan's and was consistent with decades of Kissinger's past thinking. It was based on balance of power theory and *realpolitik*. The Brezhnev Doctrine, announced in 1968, remained in place throughout the Nixon and Ford administrations, although the undergirding Soviet capability continually eroded.

Nixon returned to Eisenhower's international engagement through regional alliances rather than the earlier Republican preference for isolationism. Realism was asserted over idealism and Kennedy's "anywhere, anytime, at any cost" rhetoric. Given Nixon's and Kissinger's strategic predilections, a return to realism was predictable. Annual budget deficits and accumulating national debt associated with the Vietnam War applied additional pressure.

The *Nixon Doctrine* emphasized international alliance structures.[37] The new burden-sharing arrangement required allies to behave less like protectorates. The United States may provide equipment, advisors, and moral support, but the assisted state would have to fight its own wars with its own troops. The Doctrine manifested in Vietnamization—shifting Vietnamese forces to combat and shifting U.S. forces to training and support. It also manifested in the Persian Gulf as a dramatic increase in direct military sales to Saudi Arabia and Iran. Direct intervention in civil wars in Pakistan (between East and West Pakistan) and in Nigeria (secession of Biafra) was avoided.

The Nixon White House, in response to the deep engagement in Vietnam, took steps to avoid involvement in those countries not vital to American interests, such as those of Sub-Saharan Africa. This marked a return to Kennan's horizontal asymmetry (picking the place and time of competition). Another policy shift was the administration's preference for economic instruments over the use of military force. Security assistance was offered to anti-Communists instead of advisors or combat forces. In at least one case, that backfired. By helping to modernize Iran's army, the United States helped to undermine the shah's credibility at home, already tenuous, which later contributed to the clerics' revolution and the storming of the American embassy in Tehran during the Carter administration.

Review

Ending the wars in Indochina was high on Nixon's agenda, but his diplomatic initiatives were not limited to regional concerns in Southeast Asia. Global initiatives in 1972 took Nixon to China (21–28 February) and the Soviet Union (23–30 May) in pursuit of détente. Nixon's détente included diplomatic initiatives with both the Soviets and Chinese negotiating on the basis of their respective self interests. Nixon's strategic diplomacy bore fruit. With détente, and the USSR and China divided, the North Vietnamese position was weakened in Paris. With reduced likelihood of direct great-power conflict, Nixon had greater freedom of action in Vietnam.

Nixon's opening to China is cited by many as the most significant accomplishment of his administration. Nixon's national security assistant, not his secretary of state, made a secret visit to China in July 1971. Nixon followed with a weeklong visit beginning 21 February 1972. Nixon met with Chairman Mao Zedong and had several meetings with Premier Zhou Enlai. The visit resulted in the Shanghai Communiqué announcing a "one-China policy," replacing the United States' recognition of Taiwan as the sole legitimate government of China. Carter later built on the opening and normalized relations with China.

Ending the Vietnam War. Nixon and Kissinger negotiated a withdrawal from Vietnam: not quickly and not painlessly. There were three components to the negotiated withdrawal: Vietnamization, peace with honor, and a decent interval. Under *Vietnamization*, begun under Johnson, responsibility for combat operations shifted from American to Vietnamese units. American forces increasingly trained, advised, and withdrew. *Peace with honor* was a 1968 campaign promise that was repeated when the Paris

Peace Accords were signed on 17 January 1973. After a *decent interval*, the North took the South on 30 April 1975.

Nixon's negotiations began in the context of a narrow presidential victory, peace demonstrations growing in frequency and intensity, close to a half million U.S. troops in Vietnam, and the recent Tet Offensive. Negotiations were stalled from the beginning over issues large and small, including the shape of the table, how to involve the two governments in the South, which refused to recognize each other, whether the NVA would stay in the South or withdraw, and the North's insistence that Nguyen Van Thieu be removed as head of state in the South. Negotiations, Communist offensives against the South, and massive U.S. bombing campaigns against the North all would be on again and off again. Negotiations bore no fruit for three years.

But the real negotiations were conducted secretly by Le Duc Tho of North Vietnam and Henry Kissinger of the United States, who met from 21 February 1970 to 9 January 1973. President Thieu of South Vietnam was not party to the secret negotiations.

Nixon authorized *Operation Menu*, the secret bombing of North Vietnamese supply lines and sanctuaries in Cambodia and Laos, on 17 March 1969. Cambodia was plunged deeper into civil war, including NVA forces. Nixon announced a large-scale combined U.S. Army–ARVN offensive into Cambodia in pursuit of the NVA and VC on 30 April 1970. The offensive began the next day.

Public opposition to the war continued to grow throughout 1970, fueled by continuous news coverage of the *My Lai Massacre* and the battle of *Hamburger Hill*. The Cooper-Church amendment of 22 December prohibited ground forces in Laos and Cambodia. On 13 June 1971 the *New York Times* began publication of the leaked *Pentagon Papers*, which exposed the administration's misrepresentations. Congress repealed the Gulf of Tonkin Resolution on 24 June 1971.

Nixon began 1972 by offering a peace plan on 25 January that was promptly rejected in Hanoi. Hanoi initiated the *Easter Offensive* at the end of March. The North hoped to deal Nixon what Tet dealt LBJ during the presidential election season. Nixon responded to the Offensive with B-52 bombings on 10 April; peace talks resumed in Paris five days later.

But the Offensive continued and the United States and South Vietnam suspended talks 4 May 1972. *Operation Linebacker*, a massive aerial bombardment of the North, commenced 8 May; peace talks resumed 13 July 1972.

In June, Kissinger gave assurances to Zhou Enlai and the Soviets that the United States could accept a Vietnam unified under Communism after a decent interval followed U.S. withdrawal.[38] The United States would withdraw its ground forces, but to ensure the interval, the United States would continue to resupply the South and reinforce with air power. South Vietnam's eventual demise would be due to its government's incompetence.

Kissinger and Le Duc Tho achieved a breakthrough agreement on 8 October 1972. On 22 October, Kissinger presented the secret agreement to Thieu, who felt betrayed; Nixon threatened Thieu with a total cutoff of support if he did not acquiesce; and Operation Linebacker came to an end. Thieu expressed his anger publicly two days later. Hanoi, sensing that the agreement had been sabotaged, also responded angrily in public two days hence. The same day, Kissinger announced that "peace is at hand."

Hard-liners favored Nixon's heavy hand. Antiwar factions grew in number and interpreted the heavy hand as a continuation of LBJ's escalation. The majority middle was shifting and had concluded that initial entry into the Vietnamese civil war was a bad idea in the first place, so the United States should either win or get out, and many interpreted Nixon's actions as an attempt to win. The last U.S. ground combat forces were withdrawn on 23 August 1972. Henceforth, airpower constituted the U.S. response.

Nixon was reelected in a landslide on 7 November 1972, and a week later he attempted to reassure Thieu by promising to reenter the war if the North violated the agreement. Peace talks collapsed when Kissinger presented Thieu's demands to the North on 13 December. Nixon responded with Operation Linebacker II—the "Christmas Bombings" of military targets in Hanoi (18–29 December 1972). The North agreed to resume talks within five days of bombing cessation. Bombing ended on 29 December; talks resumed on 8 January 1973. Kissinger and Tho came to agreement the next day. Nixon announced peace with honor on the 23 January, and the Paris Peace Accords were signed four days later.

The Peace Accords, signed 27 January 1973, had little effect on the North's military operations. The Case-Church amendment of 19 June prohibited U.S. forces in Southeast Asia after 15 August 1973, and Congress dramatically reduced financial support to Thieu's army.

All-Volunteer Force. Nixon established the Presidential Committee on an All-Volunteer Force on 27 March 1969. It was chaired by former secretary of defense Thomas Gates. The free market economist Milton Friedman attributed to the draft 75 percent of the opposition to the war, but he made his argument to end conscription on economic grounds and its effects on the lower socioeconomic classes.[39] The draft and deferment system that rewarded college attendance and early marriage "jams colleges, raises the birth rate and fuels the divorce courts." Joseph Califano, past advisor to LBJ, countered that the volunteer force would be 30 percent smaller and 30 percent more expensive. And he cautioned that above the budgetary costs, the true cost of adopting the all volunteer system would be removal of the "greatest inhibition on a President's decision to wage war."[40] Nixon ended the draft in 1973, largely to aid in his reelection. As Califano predicted, the true costs would be the heavy use of force in post–Cold War strategies. Speaking of the all-volunteer force, Crenson and Ginsberg conclude that

> This is a military better prepared for the idea that war is a normal state of affairs, and whose members are less likely to complain to the media and members of Congress about the hardships they may endure in their nation's service.[41]

War of Attrition. The Arab-Israeli Conflict continued as a war of limited objectives known as the War of Attrition and composed of continuous artillery, air, and commando strikes across Israel's Bar Lev Line on the eastern bank of the Suez Canal. Nasser officially announced the war on 8 March 1969 in an attempt to regain the Sinai occupied by Israel since 1967. Secretary of State Rogers proposed a plan calling for a cease-fire in place. The intent was to buy time to reach agreement on UN Resolution 242's call for Israel's withdrawal from the Sinai in exchange for peace. A cease-fire was reached on 7 August 1970. Egypt accepted the Rogers Plan; Israel did not. Kissinger did not back the plan, and the Nixon administration did not apply the necessary pressure to Israel. Following Nasser's death, Sadat formally ended the War of Attrition on 28 September 1970. Sadat expelled Soviet advisors in 1972, signaling to the United States a willingness to engage diplomatically. Failing that, planning for the 1973 war intensified.

Nigerian Civil War. Civil war erupted in the former British colony of Nigeria when Biafra attempted secession (1967–70). Saddled with the Vietnam War, both Johnson and Nixon imposed an arms embargo, provided humanitarian aid, but declined direct military intervention.

Pakistani Civil War. Civil war erupted in the divided state of Pakistan (1971). West Pakistan brutally suppressed the insurrection in East Pakistan. The Nixon administration, against congressional prohibition, provided material support to the West but declined direct military intervention. India intervened on behalf of the East, and the Indian military decisively defeated the West in short order. East Pakistan became independent Bangladesh, and Indo-Paki relations worsened.

Bretton Woods. On 15 August 1971, Nixon unilaterally withdrew from the *Bretton Woods Accord*. Under Bretton Woods, the value of the U.S. dollar was pegged to the price of gold, and all other currencies were pegged to the dollar. The dollar would now float. The industrialized nations followed suit. Oil exporters decided to peg oil prices to gold rather than to the dollar. Twenty years of price stability was replaced by volatile oil prices.

Arms Control. Nixon and Brezhnev signed the Anti-Ballistic Missile Treaty on 26 May 1972. McNamara's mutual assured destruction was now a matter of international law and became the cornerstone of nuclear deterrence for decades to come. Initiating a nuclear war would result in the initiator's destruction, and a missile defense system could only lead to instability.

Fourth Arab-Israeli War. The *Yom Kippur War* was initiated on 6 October 1973, when Syria and Egypt attacked into territory occupied by Israel since 1967. Initial Arab successes made Israel's position tenuous. The USSR undertook a massive resupply of Syria. On 12 October 1973, the United States initiated an airlift of weapons and supplies to Israel. On 16 October, the Organization of Petroleum Exporting Countries raised the price of oil by 70 percent. The next day, the Organization of Arab Petroleum Exporting Countries placed an oil embargo on the United States and then on Europe and Japan. On 19 October, Nixon proposed $2.2

billion in military aid to Israel. The following day, Libya, Saudi Arabia, and other producers joined the embargo. The war ended on 26 October 1973 in Arab defeat.

Although the United States failed to find a diplomatic solution that would prevent the war, it played an important role in ending it and in postwar negotiations. When Israel was in its weakest position, Prime Minister Golda Meir requested military resupply from Nixon. Kissinger argued to delay the response and to let Israel "bleed" to reinforce his postwar negotiating position. But fortunes reversed, and Israel trapped the Egyptian Third Army. Kissinger, seeing an opportunity, made clear to Israel that the destruction of Egypt's army was unacceptable. Egypt withdrew its request for Soviet assistance. After the war, Kissinger was able to pressure Israel to withdraw from Arab lands occupied since 1967. Thus enabled, Sadat initiated what became a real Israeli-Egyptian peace.

Oil Crisis. The *Oil Crisis of 1973* followed from Nixon's withdrawal from Bretton Woods and the Arab-Israeli War. The Organization of Arab Petroleum Exporting Countries instituted an embargo against the United States for its support of Israel. Secretary of State Kissinger announced Project Independence to achieve independence from imported oil on 11 February 1974. The embargo ended (with the exception of Libya) on 17 March 1974. The price of oil had quadrupled from three dollars to twelve dollars per barrel. The United Kingdom and France had been unaffected by the embargo because they remained neutral, refused U.S. access to their airfields, and embargoed arms to both Israelis and Arabs.

Chile. The Marxist Allende government brought about its own demise through incompetence and disastrous economic policies. Nixon entertained covert intervention as early as 1970, but Kissinger was not persuaded. General Augusto Pinochet was prepared to lead a coup against Allende. The first attempted coup was suppressed on 29 June 1973. The 11 September 1973 coup succeeded. Allende died during the storming of the presidential palace.

Angola. The Angolan War of Independence (1961–75) gave way to the Angolan Civil War (1975–2002). Having gained independence from Portugal, the warring factions turned on each other in a naked contest for power. The most powerful factions were nationalistic and left-leaning but not ideologically committed. External support was minimal, but to wage a civil war, they required additional resources, and that required taking sides in the superpower competition. The war was brutally prosecuted with all forms of human rights abuses committed on all sides.

The Popular Movement for the Liberation of Angola (MPLA), the National Union for Total Independence of Angola (UNITA), and the National Front for the Liberation of Angola (FNLA) were the major contestants during the War of Independence and the Civil War that followed. To curry favor with the superpowers, the MPLA claimed to be Marxist-Leninist, and UNITA renounced Marxism and claimed to be anti-Communist. The MPLA continued to pay Cuban advisors (and later combat troops) and received support from the USSR. The FNLA received support from China, Zaire, and the United States. UNITA allied with South Africa and received aid from China, Zambia, and the United States.

The MPLA captured the capital of Luanda and declared independence from Portugal on 11 November 1975. By late January 1976, MPLA and Cuban forces defeated the South African, UNITA, and FNLA coalition. The international community recognized the MPLA as the legitimate government of Angola, with the United States, Israel, and South Africa the notable exceptions.

State and the CIA had long favored the MNLA. Assistant Secretary of State for African Affairs Nathaniel Davis and CIA Angolan Task Force Chief John Stockwell argued against secretly funding UNITA, predicting that it would result in increased Soviet funding to the MNLA and create the conditions for a larger regional conflict. And they argued that the effort was too large to be kept secret. Against strong opposition from State and CIA officials, Ford authorized Operation IA Feature, covert aid to the nominally anti-Communist factions, the FNLA and UNITA, on 18 July 1975. Davis resigned.[42]

With Vietnam still in the news, and as predicted by Davis and Stockwell, the covert aid became public. The Clark Amendment barring aid to *nongovernment* groups conducting military operations in Angola passed both houses of Congress by large, bipartisan margins. Ford signed it into law on 9 February 1976. But Kissinger found a Communist outcome unacceptable, and Director of Central Intelligence George H. W. Bush concluded that the Clark Amendment did not bar all funding for the war.

Working around the prohibition, the administration turned to South Africa as military lead and to Israel as the proxy weapons provider. As predicted, the Soviet Union expanded its covert aid as well. Angola became a proxy war drawing in several neighboring states.

Fall of South Vietnam. North Vietnam violated the Peace Treaty on 13 December 1974 without a counter from President Ford. Ford would not and could not honor Nixon's promise to defend the South with airpower and financial support to its army. The North began planning for the final offensive on 18 December. The offensive began on 10 March 1975, and the South quickly folded. Thieu resigned 21 April and left the country a wealthy man, rightly claiming that he had been betrayed by the United States. The North Vietnamese Army entered Saigon on 30 April 1975. The last American troops, ten marines, departed the embassy roof the same day. The war had lasted too long, cost too many lives, divided the country, and damaged U.S. reputation and influence on the world stage.

Critique

The Nixon and Ford administrations are marked by strategic coherence, major successes at the global policy level, and some failures at the regional level. Perhaps paramount was the recognition of the growing split between China and the Soviet Union and the deliberate exploitation of it by opening diplomatic relations with China. Communism as a monolith was now exposed as myth. The ability to play Moscow against Peking dramatically changed the balance of power equation on the Asian continent, including wider latitude to negotiate an end to the war in Vietnam. Regional failures included Soviet adventures in the Horn of Africa and Afghanistan encouraging hard-line detractors to equate détente with appeasement.

The enabling condition for the period of détente was the fact that the Soviet Union had reached nuclear parity with the United States. It was now possible to negotiate arms control. Again, the administration recognized the condition and was able to capitalize on it. Related policy successes include anti-ballistic missile and strategic arms limitation treaties with a freeze on offensive weapons. However, the Soviets continued arming missiles with multiple warheads.

The Paris Peace Accords was another success of the administration withdrawing the United States from a costly military commitment on the Asian continent. However, the bombing of Cambodia contributed to its collapse and misery for years to come. Neocons and other Democratic hardliners saw U.S. withdrawal from Vietnam as appeasement.

The strategic successes of this administration are overshadowed by the public's loss of trust in its government. The elected vice president, Spiro Agnew, was driven from office for corruption and was replaced by Representative Gerald Ford. A host of felony convictions associated with the Watergate scandal drove President Nixon from office in disgrace. Ford, elevated again, almost immediately pardoned Nixon, freeing Ford to concentrate on his presidency but leaving justice unserved and the public suspicious.

The expression "credibility gap" was coined toward the end of the Nixon-Ford era and retroactively extended to include Kennedy's false rhetorical claims of bomber and missile gaps. After Nixon, the media took on a more adversarial role with government. The credibility gap between reality and presidential claims has since remained a constant. Gone was the trust in government earned by recovery from the Great Depression and the defeat of fascism in World War II. But the 9/11 attacks immediately created a deferential press that failed in its watchdog function.

Détente under Carter, 1977–81

As with Truman, two distinct strategies are apparent during the Carter administration: Truman's, separated by initiation of the Korean War, and Carter's, separated by the Soviet invasion of Afghanistan.

Principals of the Carter administration entered office believing that the Cold War was coming to a close. The East-West power struggle no longer served as an organizing principle for U.S. foreign policy. Instead, modernization of social and governmental structures cast in the disparities between North and South should be elevated. Carter entered office pledging to remove combat forces from Korea, reduce the nuclear arsenal, and reduce foreign military sales; foreign aid would be linked to human rights performance.

In his first policy speech Carter encouraged the abandonment of containment, to move beyond the belief that Soviet expansionism is inevitable and be "free of that inordinate fear of communism which once led us to embrace any dictator who joined us in our fear." Instead, Carter called "for a new American foreign policy, a policy based on constant decency in its values and on optimism in our historical vision."[43]

Gaddis says that the Carter administration was marked by "surface innovation with subsurface continuity."[44] Gaddis goes further to say that there was no apparent foreign policy, no apparent priorities, and no dominant strategic thinker. Carter lacked a single voice to formulate strategy. Secretary of State Cyrus Vance and National Security Assistant Zbigniew Brzezinski held fundamentally different views on important issues. Decision making was decentralized in contrast to the Nixon era.

Saddled with rampant inflation from a decade of the heavy costs of Vietnam, Carter did not have the Keynesian option of symmetric response. Prior to the Soviet invasion of Afghanistan, "Carter retained an asymmetrical approach of differentiating between vital and peripheral interests, distinguishing between levels of threat, and of keeping responses commensurate with means."[45] According to Gaddis, after the Soviet invasion of Afghanistan, Carter appeared to "embrac[e] the undifferentiated view of interests and threats characteristic of symmetrical response."[46]

Review

Africa. Africa was rife with violent conflict during Carter's tenure. In East Africa, Ethiopia was attacked by Somalia and lost a separatist war with Eritrea. In Central Africa, Idi Amin's brutal Ugandan dictatorship was overthrown by Tanzania. In Western Africa, Morocco and Mauritania contested sovereignty over Western Sahara. South Africa attempted to hold on to apartheid capitalism and to impose regional dominance over leftist black neighbors across southern Africa. U.S. destabilization efforts included military interventions in Namibia, Zimbabwe Rhodesia, Mozambique, and Angola. South Africa tested a nuclear weapon on 22 September 1979.

In general, the administration sided with left-leaning black African movements pursuing majority-rule and self-determination after centuries of colonial domination. But that meant siding against white minority-ruled regimes that were generally pro-Western and anti-Communist. International condemnation of South Africa's repressive apartheid government was growing, and domestic politics in the United States were racially charged. The administration had harsh criticism for South Africa's human rights abuses and imposed economic sanctions.

Regionalists in the administration, led by Cyrus Vance, interpreted events primarily as matters of badly drawn colonial boundaries, self-determination, and human rights to be adjudicated through diplomacy. *Globalists*, led by Brzezinski, interpreted them as part of the global East-West competition to be met with military force even if it meant supporting right-wing authoritarian regimes responsible for human rights abuses. Carter leaned toward the former before the Soviet invasion of Afghanistan and toward the latter after.

Angola. The Front for the National Liberation of the Congo (FNLC) launched an invasion from Angola into Zaire on 7 March 1977. MPLA and Cuban complicity was alleged, but Carter doubted Cuban involvement and provided only nonmilitary aid. Having predicted that Ford's IA Feature would create the conditions for a widening regional conflict, CIA Angolan Task Force Chief John Stockwell resigned.[47] The Clark Amendment barring support to private military groups contributed to Carter's slow and ambiguous response. Brzezinski argued for the amendment's repeal in 1980.

Ogaden War. The Ogaden Desert—inhabited by nomadic Somalis—had been arbitrarily divided by colonial powers and constitutes a very large part of Ethiopia, northern Kenya, and Somalia. The Ogaden War (1977–78) began when Ethiopia fell into civil war and Somalia attacked into Ethiopian Ogaden. Initially, Ethiopia was backed by the United States, and Somalia by the USSR. Ethiopia switched to Soviet backing, causing the United States to shift support to Somalia. For a brief period, the Soviets backed both sides. Ethiopia has since achieved some degree of recovery; Somalia has not.

Relations with Israel and Middle East peace. Immediately upon entering office, Carter began aggressive diplomatic efforts in the Middle East, leading to the Camp David Accords. In Carter's first year in office, he met with heads of state from Egypt, Jordan, Syria, and Israel. Building on Kissinger's end state in the 1973 war and Anwar Sadat's initiative, Carter preferred an even hand in dealing with Israel and Palestine. To complicate matters, the right-wing Likud Party displaced the Left for the first time with the election of Menachem Begin in 1977. Likud took a more hard-line stand on occupied lands and settlements. Carter's pressure on Israel to withdraw from occupied Palestinian territory and for a Palestinian

Homeland was unwelcome. Rather than Kissinger's "shuttle diplomacy" and bilateral negotiations, Carter pursued an intense multilateral approach between Israel, Egypt, and the United States. The Camp David Accords were signed by Sadat and Begin on 17 September 1978. A peace treaty between Egypt and Israel followed in 1979. But Israel did not withdraw from occupied Palestinian territories.

Terrorism. The convincing 1967 Israeli defeat of Arab forces motivated some to shift to a different strategy. Europe became the battleground for Arab terrorists as well as for homegrown dissidents originally brought together against the war in Vietnam. Israeli athletes were attacked at the 1972 Munich Olympic Games. In July 1976, Israeli special forces conducted a hostage rescue at the Entebbe Airport in Uganda. A dozen Hanafi Muslim terrorists stormed three buildings in Washington DC, in March 1977 and held them for thirty-nine hours. In October 1977, Germany's counterterrorist unit successfully executed a hostage rescue from Arab terrorists aboard a hijacked Lufthansa passenger jet grounded in Mogadishu, Somalia.

The German hostage rescue prompted the new President Carter to ask whether the United States had similar capabilities, and he received assurances from the Pentagon that it did. America's approach to these special operations was the *hasty response option*. Talented people from across the services were assembled at the last minute for a daring rescue. It was a formula for unpreparedness and an example of the lesser-included-case thinking of the big services. A month later, November 1977, the Army established a special operations unit for counterterrorism, Delta Force. The Navy dedicated a SEAL team to the mission in late 1980.

Southern Lebanon. On 11 March 1978, eleven Fatah militants conducted a raid into Israel killing thirty-seven Israelis, mostly civilians, in the *Coastal Road Massacre*. Israel responded three days later with an invasion force of twenty-five thousand, killing between one and two thousand, mostly civilians, and resulting in the flight of a quarter million refugees.

The year 1979 was unkind to Jimmy Carter. Iranian nationalism asserted itself—significantly induced by past interventions in its internal affairs—and erupted into the Iranian Revolution that deposed the pro-Western Shah Pahlavi and resulted in a drawn-out hostage situation. The revolution disrupted the oil-based economy and damaged military cohesion. Iraq seized the opportunity and initiated a war with Iran. The Soviet Union invaded Afghanistan at year's end.

Iranian Revolution. Anti-shah demonstrations began in January 1978. Martial law was announced on 7 September, and some demonstrators were killed by the shah's forces the next day. Demonstrations and strikes continued from August through December. The shah fled Iran on 16 January 1979, and the exiled Ayatollah Khomeini returned on 1 February to establish the first modern Islamic theocracy. Hundreds of the shah's supporters were subsequently executed.

The revolution contained populist, nationalist, and Islamic facets. But extremists offered the only options. A heavy-handed, modernizing monarch was pitted against a heavy-handed, reactionary theocrat. Carter could not decide whether to back the shah all the way, abandon the shah, or ride out the storm. Brzezinski and Energy Secretary Schlesinger favored support to the Iranian army. Carter's preference was to fashion a moderate civilian government backed by the military that would limit the power of the clerics.

In a controversial decision, the Carter administration granted the shah entrance to the United States to be admitted to the Mayo Clinic on 22 October 1979 for cancer treatment, fueling suspicions of another U.S.-backed coup to reinstall the shah. On 4 November, Iranian Islamic students stormed the U.S. embassy in Tehran, taking sixty-six hostages.

Vance and Brzezinski disagreed over the best course of action. The secretary of state placed higher value on long-term relations with Iran and favored a negotiation with the new regime. The national security assistant favored a military rescue of hostages and the president's political fortunes. Brzezinski prevailed.

The Algiers Accord, agreeing to the release of the remaining hostages, was signed on 19 January 1981 by Warren Christopher, Carter's deputy secretary of state. As a final expression of disrespect to Carter, the hostage release was delayed until the following day, Reagan's inauguration day. Reaganites claimed that fear of President-elect Reagan forced the Iranians to the negotiating table.

Iran-Iraq War. Iraq had severed ties with the United States over U.S. backing of Israel in the 1967 Arab-Israeli War. The Iranian Revolution swept away the shah and removed Iran as the guarantor of U.S. interests in the Persian Gulf region. Iraq was seen by many in the West as a counter-balance to the unknown revolutionary Iran. The Carter administration initiated a rapprochement with Iraq and found Saddam Hussein receptive. The Iranian Revolution incited fears and passions associated with the suppressed Shia minority in Iraq. Old border disputes, including oil-rich land, and the possibility of a Shia insurgency, coupled with Iran in political and military disarray, proved irresistible to Saddam. Iraq attacked Iran on 22 September 1980. The war continued until 20 August 1988 with no apparent outcome other than large-scale personal and economic loss to both countries. The United States backed Iraq.

Oil Crisis. Like Nixon before him, Carter presided over a national energy crisis rooted in the Middle East. The Iranian Revolution caused a serious disruption of Iran's oil sector. The sector performed erratically and at a significantly reduced level. The Iran-Iraq War devastated both countries' oil output. Carter's Crisis of Confidence speech urged public action to conserve energy to reduce dependence on foreign oil.[48] The world market overreacted. Other exporters responded by increasing output. The resulting overproduction and reduced demand led to declining oil prices from 1980 to 1986.

Pakistan. Muhammed Zia-al-Huq installed himself as a military dictator favoring a fundamentalist theocracy. His tenure (16 September 1978 to 17 August 1988) roughly corresponds to the Soviet occupation of Afghanistan. He replaced parliamentary law with an Islamic legal system. He favored the Saudi Wahhabist interpretation of Islam and established madrasas to build a fundamentalist political base and to oppose the Soviets. Saudi funding and young Afghan refugees followed.

Afghanistan. The Afghan Communist Party successfully executed a coup and seized power on 28 April 1978 in the *Saur Revolution*. The new government immediately initiated a socialist agenda, including state-approved atheism and suppression of Islam, land reform, and equal participation of women, all of which aggravated more conservative Afghans. Opposition developed quickly, and the Soviet Union invaded on 25 December 1979 to prop up the fledgling government.

On 3 July 1979 Carter signed a directive to aid opponents of the pro-Soviet government in Kabul, Afghanistan. The opposition, the mujahideen, comprised a half dozen or more factions. The U.S. goal was to draw the

Soviet Union into a long, costly, draining war in Afghanistan and to induce dissent in the Soviet Union's internal Central Asian population. It would be the largest covert operation since World War II.[49] Already leaning in that direction, the Soviet Union invaded Afghanistan on 24 December 1979.

Having achieved what it hoped for, the administration had a choice. Rather than interpret the Soviet incursion into Afghanistan as a response to turmoil on its periphery, Carter interpreted it as increasing the potential for Soviet hegemony in the Persian Gulf. "The Soviet Union is now attempting to consolidate a strategic position," that constitutes "a grave threat to the free movement of Middle East oil." The *Carter Doctrine* was announced in his third State of the Union address, given in January 1980. In it, Carter said, "An attempt by any outside force to gain control of the Persian Gulf region will be regarded as an assault on the vital interests of the United States of America, and such an assault will be repelled by any means necessary, including military force."[50]

To make the declaratory policy credible, Carter had to match it with force development and force deployment policy. He initiated the Rapid Deployment Joint Task Force, which grew into the U.S. Central Command under Reagan. He also increased naval presence in the Indian Ocean and the Persian Gulf region. He authorized continued covert support to the mujahideen and imposed economic sanctions on the USSR.

Panama. Carter negotiated two Panama Canal Treaties. The first gave the United States the right to intervene if neutrality of international access to the Canal was challenged. The second set 1 January 2000 as the date Panama would assume full control of canal operations and primary defense responsibility. The United States had controlled the Canal since 1903. By popular vote, Panamanians approved the treaties in October 1977. The U.S. Senate gave its consent in early 1978. Carter succeeded where Johnson, Nixon, and Ford had failed to overcome hard-liner opposition.

Nicaragua. The Carter administration waffled on whether Nicaragua's right-wing dictator should be removed for human rights abuses or kept in support of U.S. anti-Communist pursuits. Anastasio Somoza Debayle, the corrupt, repressive U.S.-backed dictator, was overthrown in 1979. The socialist Sandinistas assumed power, pursued domestic policies favoring the large, poor majority over the small oligarchy, and gave another apparent victory for Communism in the Western Hemisphere.

Critique

Apparently the administration's early view of a Soviet threat in decline was accurate. But the invasion of Afghanistan—perhaps the last convulsion of a dying empire—demonstrated that looking beyond the Cold War was a bit premature. The Brezhnev Doctrine continued its decline into obsolescence in the second half of the Carter administration.

Some high-level appointees in the Carter administration represented an agenda placing human rights over military confrontation with the forces of Communism. But as Cold War hostilities continued, his staff remained divided, and Carter did not resolve the contradictions. In November 1979, Iran collapsed, and in December, the Soviet Union invaded Afghanistan. The administration announced a new containment policy for the Persian Gulf region on 23 January 1980 *after* events had overrun his earlier policies.

Carter had no persistent strategy from which to respond to events. Instead, events drove employment policy in an ad hoc, reactive fashion. Where Nixon demonstrated strategic coherence and global successes, Carter showed a lack of global coherence and some regional successes. Regional successes include the Camp David Accords, reclaiming Egypt from the Soviet sphere, and the Panama Canal Treaties. The SALT II Treaty was withdrawn from the Senate after the Soviet invasion into Afghanistan. Other policy failures include the administration's inability to affect the timely release of hostages in Tehran and support of a dictator in Nicaragua.

While Carter vacillated between promoting human rights and supporting regimes violating human rights, it appears that his efforts contributed to permanently elevating human rights in African politics.

The Panama Canal Treaties were controversial. For opponents, the treaties relinquished U.S. sovereign territory. For the mainstream, the treaties were a success and did much to improve the U.S. position in Latin America. But conditions were set for invasion under Bush 41.

In force development policy, Carter misspent his political capital killing an Air Force bomber acquisition early in office and was later unable to kill the MX missile program. Carter proposed an increase in defense spending in February 1979, and after the invasion of Afghanistan, Carter initiated what later became known as the Reagan buildup of military forces.

Rollback and Full-Court Press under Reagan, 1981–89

If Nixon is labeled a geopolitical strategist, and Carter labeled a values and decency president, then Reagan must be called an ideologue.[51] He turned the Cold War into an ideological crusade, a crusade for freedom. He proclaimed America's support for freedom fighters (who commonly employed terrorist tactics). He was antidétente, anti-Communist, and initially anti–arms control. Reagan returned to the language of "offensive rollback" from Nitze's NSC-68. Reagan took greater risks of nuclear war (HIC), made major resource investments in conventional forces (MIC), but primarily employed proinsurgency against Communist countries and counterinsurgency (LIC) to support pro-Western regimes, often right-wing dictators. Rhetorically, Reagan went on the offense with a "full-court press" making use of all instruments of national power his declaratory policy.

Reagan felt that Nixon's and Carter's détente had shifted the balance of power to the Soviet Union. Détente, including arms control, was a one-way street favoring the Soviets. Reagan's campaign rhetoric claimed that the Soviet Union had achieved across-the-board superiority in strategic nuclear capability, combining JFK's missile gap and bomber gap. The Soviets retained their long-held quantitative lead in conventional forces. A *window of vulnerability* was the underlying premise to his strategy. Reagan's force development policy included a buildup of both strategic nuclear and conventional forces.

Détente under Nixon and Carter was intended to diffuse tensions with the Soviets to facilitate bargaining. Reagan returned to the earlier confrontational stance. His 1976 and 1980 campaigns were aggressively anti-Communist. On 20 May 1982 he signed NSDD-32, the top secret National Security Strategy citing an alleged Soviet lead in military strength and including the objective to "contain and reverse" Soviet advances. On 17 January 1983 he signed NSDD-75, "U.S. Relations with the USSR," elaborating on the strategy.

The Carter Doctrine rested on the use of military force to keep the Soviets out of the Persian Gulf region. The *Reagan Corollary* extended the Carter Doctrine to include military intervention into the internal affairs of the region without reference to the Soviet Union or Communism. The Corollary was announced in October 1981 in response to the Iran-Iraq

War (1980–88). The United States would intervene to protect Saudi Arabia's independence, which was perceived to be threatened by the Iraqi invasion of Iran following the Iranian Revolution.

Based on an article written late in the Carter administration, the *Kirkpatrick Doctrine* provided the intellectual justification for the Reagan Doctrine that followed. According to Jeane Kirkpatrick, the Carter administration's policy favoring human rights and opposing right-wing dictators was deeply flawed.[52] She concluded that right-wing dictatorships are *authoritarian* and easier to overturn than are left-wing *totalitarian* Communist dictatorships. The article attracted Reagan's attention and led directly to her appointment as U.S. ambassador to the UN.

The *Reagan Doctrine* supported anti-Communists everywhere with a special interest in Central America, a return to a JFK-like posture. The Doctrine was more anti-Communist than prodemocracy. Under the Doctrine, Reagan supported the efforts of Nicaraguan counterrevolutionaries (Contras) to overthrow the Sandinista government, supported the right-wing Salvadoran government against Communist insurgents, supported the mujahideen against the Soviets in Afghanistan, and supported the bloody civil war in Angola.[53]

The Heritage Foundation, established to advocate for the New Right, translated the Kirkpatrick and Reagan Doctrines into concrete policy recommendations. The first step was to deepen Carter's aid to anti-Soviet forces in Afghanistan and then to broaden that policy across the Third World. The Heritage plan targeted nine countries for rollback—Afghanistan, Angola, Cambodia, Ethiopia, Iran, Laos, Libya, Nicaragua, and Vietnam. The American Enterprise Institute was also supportive, but Cato withheld support, claiming that vital interests were not involved.[54]

Review

Brink of Nuclear War. Reagan's bellicose campaign rhetoric did not fall on deaf ears in the Soviet Union. Things came to a head in 1983. Reagan delivered his Evil Empire speech to the National Association of Evangelicals on 8 March (and said he regretted it only weeks later). His Strategic Defense Initiative speech followed quickly on 23 March. The basis of deterrence was a shared belief that a nuclear war could not be won regardless of which side fired first, but Soviet leadership interpreted Reagan's

Strategic Defense Initiative (SDI) as evidence that the United States now thought it could win. Navy exercises aggressively probed Soviet airspace. NATO's Able Archer exercise to test nuclear release procedures was viewed as a possible cover for initiating war. The USSR initiated the largest intelligence collection effort in Soviet peacetime history and was prepared to initiate nuclear war if U.S. launch preparations were detected. When later told of the Soviet interpretation, Reagan expressed surprise. In a 16 January 1984 speech, Reagan said, "My dream is to see the day when nuclear weapons will be banished from the face of the earth."

Iran-Iraq War. Reagan continued and deepened Carter's post–Iranian Revolution rapprochement with Iraq and named Donald Rumsfeld as his emissary. The United States became heavily invested in an Iraqi victory in the Iran-Iraq War (1980–88), covertly providing technical assistance, access to weapons, unconventional warfare training, battlefield advice, intelligence, and WMD elements. The United States acquiesced when Iraq used chemical weapons on Iraqi Kurds. A tanker war ensued in 1984, the United States reflagged Kuwaiti tankers, and the U.S. and Soviet navies provided support. The costly war ended in stalemate on 20 August 1988, with Iraq having failed to capture the disputed Iranian oil fields. Iraq invaded Kuwait two years later and became a U.S. enemy.

Proxy War against Libya. Following Carter's Iran Hostage Crisis, Reagan was determined to take a strong stand against terrorism, and Libya was connected to many recent terrorist acts. In the opening days of his administration, Reagan designated terrorism as a primary threat to world order and signed a presidential finding that initiated a covert war (1981–90) against Libya using Chad as proxy.

Four thousand Libyan troops invaded in November 1980 and soon occupied most of Chad. In January 1981, the possible merger of Libya and Chad was announced. Backed by the Reagan administration, two thousand rebel troops led by Hissène Habrè entered the Chadian capital of N'Djamena and effected a coup on 7 June 1982. Habrè's eight-year rule included all forms of human rights abuses, including political assassination, torture, and tribal massacre. Idriss Dèby's rebels, supplied and funded by Libya, returned to overthrow Habrè on 31 November 1990.

Fifth Arab-Israeli War. Reagan deployed marines to Lebanon in 1982 and 1983. The two deployments took place in the context of a civil war in

Lebanon (1975–91), the Fifth Arab-Israeli War (1982–84), the Syrian occupation of Lebanon (1976–2005), and the Israeli occupation of Lebanon (1982–2000). They were preceded by growing Palestinian refugee camps from the earlier Arab-Israeli wars and the expulsion of Palestinian militants from Jordan, leading to the Christian-Muslim Conflict (1975–76) that drew Arab League peacekeeping forces, including Syrians who later came to dominate. Southern Lebanon became a state within a state.

Citing the assassination attempt of an Israeli ambassador by Abu Nidal, Israel invaded Lebanon on 6 June 1982, hoping to drive the PLO and Syria from Lebanon and install a pro-Israeli Christian government. Israeli forces laid siege to Beirut from 14 June to 21 August 1982, an attack that eventually included car bombing and saturation bombing and left Beirut in rubble. The televised Israeli bombing produced extensive civilian casualties. Reagan phoned Israeli prime minister Menachem Begin on 12 August to protest the civilian casualties and said, "you must stop." Reagan pressured Begin to allow the PLO to withdraw from Lebanon and briefly deployed marines, matched by French and Italian forces, to provide security while the PLO departed on 24 August. Lebanese prime minister Bachir Gemayel, installed by Israel, was assassinated on 14 September 1982 by Syrian extremists. Lebanese Christian Philangist militia massacred civilians in the Sabra-Shatila Palestinian refugee camps (16–18 September 1982) facilitated by Israeli forces.

Hezbollah was born to oppose the Israeli occupation. The U.S. Sixth Fleet provided fire support from carriers and surface combatants including the battleship *New Jersey* and was seen as part of the occupation. Osama bin Laden later cited the falling towers in Beirut as motivation for the 9/11 attacks.

Reagan deployed marines again on 29 September 1982. This deployment, with no clear mission, was opposed by the secretary of defense, chairman of the Joint Chiefs of Staff (JCS), and members of Congress. The U.S. embassy in Beirut was bombed on 19 April 1983, with casualties including State, CIA, and USAID personnel (63 killed, 17 Americans). Representative John McCain said on 28 September 1983, "I do not see any obtainable objectives in Lebanon." The French embassy and the marine barracks were bombed on 23 October 1983. The French lost 58 paratroopers and the

United States lost 220 marines, 18 sailors, and 3 soldiers. Reagan soon withdrew the surviving marines.

Grenada. Two days after the marine barracks bombing, the United States invaded Grenada and overthrew its democratically elected government with friendly ties to the Soviet Union. The UN General Assembly condemned the action as a flagrant violation of international law by a vote of 108 to 9 with 27 abstentions. Even Canada and Great Britain opposed the invasion. Margaret Thatcher was "deeply disturbed" by the action. Reagan's popularity spiked after completion of the Grenada operation, masking the political consequences of the marine barracks bombing.

Delayed until Reagan won reelection on 6 November 1984, the *Weinberger Doctrine* was announced later in the month. The Doctrine constituted an attempt to state a policy for the use of military force to fill the alleged vacuum following Vietnam. It was most recently provoked by Weinberger's deep personal reflection on the marine barracks bombing.

- The United States should not commit forces to combat unless the vital national interests of the United States or its allies are involved.
- U.S. troops should only be committed wholeheartedly and with the clear intention of winning. Otherwise, troops should not be committed.
- U.S. combat troops should be committed only with clearly defined political and military objectives and with the capacity to accomplish those objectives.
- The relationship between the objectives and the size and composition of the forces committed should be continually reassessed and adjusted if necessary.
- U.S. troops should not be committed to battle without a "reasonable assurance" of the support of U.S. public opinion and Congress.
- The commitment of U.S. troops should be considered only as a last resort.[55]

The Weinberger Doctrine resonated with the generation of military officers who received their trial by fire—militarily and politically—in Vietnam. It would later evolve into the Powell Doctrine.

Iran-Contra. The Iran-Contra scandal developed as the administration attempted to solve two disparate problems. The first problem was providing assistance to guerrilla forces opposing the Sandinista government of Nicaragua. The second problem was resolving a hostage crisis that Reagan, like Carter before him, had in the Middle East.

Lebanon Hostage Crisis. The Lebanon Hostage Crisis (1982–92) included the taking of nearly one hundred hostages, mostly Westerners, by a small number of men from clans within Hezbollah, strongly aligned with Iran. Hostages were held as insurance against reprisals for terrorist attacks against the United States and France and to induce Americans to apply pressure against Israel, who had invaded Lebanon pursuing the PLO.

The hostages were held in Lebanon while the Iran-Iraq War dragged on. Although subject to a U.S. arms embargo, Iran secretly sought weapons in 1985. In spite of the embargo, Reagan authorized the transfer of weapons from Israel to Iran in exchange for Iran's intervention with the terrorists holding hostages in Lebanon. The United States later replenished Israel's arms inventory. Proceeds from the sale were used to fund the Contras in Nicaragua, support that Congress had expressly prohibited. Declaratory policy to not negotiate with terrorists was contradicted by employment policy.

Nicaragua. The left-wing Sandinistas overthrew the U.S.-backed right-wing Nicaraguan government in 1979 and quickly turned to support left-wing guerrillas opposing the U.S.-backed right-wing Salvadoran government. Reagan signed NSDD-17, authorizing the CIA to organize right-wing factions into the Contras in January 1982. Congress soon prohibited the expenditure of funds to support the Contras. The Contras conducted sabotage and terrorism in Nicaragua, and Nicaragua brought suit in the International Court of Justice. The court found in Nicaragua's favor and ordered the United States to cease support for the Contras and to pay reparations. The United States refused.

Panama's Manuel Noriega supported U.S. anti-Communist efforts in Central America but was under indictment for drug trafficking. Through diplomatic channels, Reagan encouraged Noriega to step down but rejected military options to depose him advanced by hard-liners like Elliot Abrams. Reagan also rejected military options to intervene in Nicaragua, saying of his advisors, "Those sonsofbitches won't be happy until we have 25,000 troops in Managua, and I'm not going to do it."[56] Hard-line observers called Reagan a "pussycat" in July 1985.[57]

Afghanistan. Reagan arrived in 1981 with a Democrat-controlled Congress eager to increase funding for Carter's covert war in Afghanistan. Reagan continued and escalated the program. The Soviets withdrew in 1989 leaving a power vacuum. Regional powers—for example, Iran, Pakistan, and Saudi Arabia—pursued their interests unfettered by great-power interference. The country quickly descended into civil war (1989–92), with the various mujahideen factions struggling for control in the countryside. The results included widespread killings, refugees, chaos, and eventually fiefdoms under local warlords. Several cleavages were apparent and rose and fell over time: modernist versus traditionalist, Communist versus non-Communist, Sunni versus Shia, Pashtun versus non-Pashtun, and warlord versus warlord.

Pakistan. Coincident with the Soviet occupation of Afghanistan (1979–89), Muhammed Zia-al-Huq headed a military dictatorship in neighboring Pakistan (1978–88). Zia favored a fundamentalist theocracy and established Wahhabist madrasas to educate a generation of political supporters. Saudi funding followed, as did young Afghan refugees displaced by the war.

Angola. Secretary of State George Shultz opposed support to UNITA. Rather than ostracizing South Africa as done under the Carter administration, Assistant Secretary of State for African Affairs Chester Crocker proposed "constructive engagement" to establish an environment "conducive to compromise and accommodation with South Africa."[58] New Right conservatives were suspicious of Crocker's regionalism and doubted his loyalty to the Reagan Doctrine. The war accelerated.

Ford's earlier support to Angolan forces was expanded. The Heritage Foundation lobbied Congress to repeal the Clark Amendment prohibiting aid in Angola. The bipartisan effort comfortably passed the Senate in June 1985 and the House in July. Angola's government announced that it could no longer accept the United States as an honest broker in negotiations.

By the late 1980s, Soviet support for client states and independence movements was in severe decline correlated with Gorbachev's ascendancy. South Africa was overextended. Congress passed the Anti-Apartheid Act of 1986 over Reagan's veto. By 1988, UNITA was close to collapse. And in

1989 reports of UNITA atrocities—using boy soldiers, using girls as reward to soldiers, cutting off ears and noses, indiscriminate laying of landmines—came more frequently.

The recognized governments of Angola, South Africa, and Cuba signed the Tripartite Accord at UN headquarters on 22 December 1988. South Africa agreed to end support to UNITA. On 6 January 1989 Vice President Bush, the president elect, informed UNITA's Savimbi that U.S. financial support would continue, thus prolonging the conflict.

Terrorism. Challenges continued unabated in Reagan's second term. Terrorism was on the rise. Reagan signed NSDD-166 on 27 March 1985, authorizing a major escalation in covert aid to the mujahideen, but he softened his stance against the Soviet Union and achieved a significant arms control agreement. The Iran-Contra scandal became public in November 1986 and congressional hearings followed. In May 1987, 32 percent of the public thought Reagan should resign before the end of his term, and 62 percent thought the country was on the wrong track in July.

In his failed 1976 campaign, with memories of marine helicopters lifting off the Saigon embassy roof still fresh, Reagan promised "no more Vietnams." During his successful 1980 campaign, Reagan promised that the United States would never negotiate with terrorists, and in 1981 he pledged "swift and effective retribution" against terrorists. His promises were tested in his second term. During the Hezbollah hijacking of TWA flight 847, U.S. Navy diver Robert Stethem was killed and his body dumped on the Beirut tarmac on 15 June 1985; four embassy marines were killed in El Salvador on 19 June 1985; and a spate of terrorist attacks in 1985 and 1986 were traced back to Libya. When offered retaliatory strikes, Reagan consistently asked his advisors about the potential for collateral damage and said that "killing innocent civilians in a retaliatory strike is itself a terrorist act."[59]

In the hope of securing the release of fifty Palestinians held by Israel, the Palestinian Liberation Front hijacked the *Achille Lauro* cruise ship on 7 October 1985. (The hijacking was preceded by the Israeli bombing of a PLO headquarters in Tunisia on 1 October that killed sixty, which in turn was preceded by the killing of three Israelis on a yacht off Cyprus by the PLO on 25 September.) Reagan put Delta Force and SEAL Team Six hostage rescue forces on alert. Syria rejected the ship, but it was allowed to dock in Egypt. Egypt negotiated release of the ship and hostages in exchange for safe air passage to Tunisia for the four hijackers. Reagan ordered the aircraft intercepted and put down at a NATO base in Italy. The hijacking is most remembered for the brutal killing of an elderly Jewish man and his wheelchair-bound body being dumped overboard. But the operation also exposed sovereignty issues met by hostage rescue forces. Egypt demanded an apology for diverting the aircraft, and SEALs were in a five-hour standoff against Italian Carabinieri at the Sigonella airbase in Sicily.

Terrorist acts with a Libyan linkage shown or suspected included the *Achille Lauro* hijacking in October 1985 by the PLF; Abu Nidal attacks at the Rome and Vienna airports on 27 December 1985 that killed twenty; and the Libyan bombing of La Belle, a West Berlin nightclub, that killed two U.S. servicemen, a Turkish civilian, and injuring hundreds on 5 April 1986.

Something beyond the Chadian proxy war was necessary. Reagan put aside his concern about collateral damage, and launched a complex retaliatory air strike against Libya, including early-morning attacks against multiple targets within a ten-minute period on 15 April 1986. Dozens were killed, including Colonel Gaddafi's fifteen-month-old adopted daughter; two of his sons were wounded. France, Italy, and Spain denied overflight rights. Libya's retaliation included the bombing of Pan Am Flight 103 on 21 December 1988, killing 270 at Lockerbie, Scotland.

Arms Control. Reagan and Gorbachev met in Reykjavik, Iceland, on 11–12 October 1986. Both were willing to consider banning all nuclear weapons, but Reagan's insistence on SDI brought the Reykjavik Summit to a close. Representative Newt Gingrich said the meeting could be "the most dangerous summit for the West since Adolph Hitler met with Chamberlin in 1938 at Munich." Reagan delivered his Tear Down This Wall speech on 12 June 1987. The Intermediate Nuclear Forces Treaty was signed on 8 December 1987, eliminating 859 American and 1,836 Soviet missiles with ranges of 300 to 3,400 miles, corresponding to roughly 4 percent of nuclear forces.

Eastern Europe. When confronted by the successful 1989 rise of the Solidarity Party in opposition to the Communist Party, the Soviets did not invade Poland. The Brezhnev Doctrine, underwritten by Soviet power in decline since its announcement in 1968 due largely to Brezhnev's crippling military-industrial economic policy, officially came to an end under Mikhail Gorbachev. It was replaced by the facetiously named "Sinatra Doctrine," playing on the "I did it my way" song and allowing former client states to pursue self-determination.

Critique

Reagan lacked a Kissinger to formulate strategy, and the underlying strategic premise (window of vulnerability), the economic sustainability, and the military necessity of his strategy were questionable. Neither the CIA's threat assessment nor the Scowcroft Commission supported Reagan's asserted window of vulnerability. Reagan's declaratory policy and force development policy were hawkish primacy, but his employment policy was quite restrictive. Declaratory policy included spiritual and rhetorical support to movements in Poland and elsewhere in Eastern Europe with positive effects. U.S. interventions in Lebanon and Grenada are widely considered policy failures, but they are overshadowed by the Iran-Contra scandal.

Reagan's worldview was shaped by the unambiguous prosecution and victory of World War II, tempered by the ambiguous lessons of Vietnam. The moral clarity of World War II was carried over to the Cold War, clouding Reagan's ability to differentiate threats. Reagan claimed that the terrorist attacks in Lebanon and the spread of Communism in the Western Hemisphere were part of the same phenomenon. British prime minister Margaret Thatcher rejected the linkage. John McCain called the Middle East policy "confused," arguing against treating it as part of the Cold War.

Reagan saw a "Soviet strategy of wars of liberation rather than one of Soviet support and exploitation for its own benefit of indigenous conflicts."[60] Conflicts between plutocrats and impoverished peasants in Central America were interpreted through the Cold War lens, asserting a different morality than that seen by Carter. But Reagan's employment policy relied on covert support for proxy wars rather than direct Vietnam-style intervention. The Grenada intervention was the only use of offensive ground forces in Reagan's eight years.

Reagan continued and expanded Carter's covert support to Afghanistan. The Afghan resistance contributed to the subsequent withdrawal of Soviet forces. The Soviets were arguably backing the better side. But blind U.S. opposition to the Soviet Union and support to the mujahideen would have negative consequences in the long term.

A new détente emerged late in the administration as Reagan found a reliable negotiating partner in Gorbachev. Not only could nuclear arms levels be negotiated, but regional conflicts, like those in southern Africa, could also be resolved through diplomatic means.

The Reagan administration began the isolation of Libya with a punishing air strike in response to Libya's connection to terrorist acts. The subsequent administrations of Bush, Clinton, and Bush continued debilitating economic sanctions that contributed to Libya's eventual yielding to international inspections of its WMD facilities. The sustained effort, initiated by Reagan, can be considered a policy success.[61] The value of the initial bombing was challenged by allies. The Chadian proxy war was more costly to Libya than the bombing.

In force development policy, Reagan continued and expanded Carter's arms buildup. Former president Nixon counseled Reagan upon entry to office that the United States could afford an arms reduction. Eisenhower and Nixon established the postwar Republican alignment with Kennan's thinking. Reagan aligned with Nitze, a position previously associated with Democratic administrations. Nitze was one of the defense intellectuals promoting the massive arms buildup. Following the Able Archer event, Kennan wrote that the U.S. government and the military establishment were committed to an arms race and a "march toward war."[62] The United States should now be the object of self-containment. As in the Truman, Kennedy, and Johnson administrations, Nitze's thinking led to overextension and reexamination of strategy. The costs of the buildup were extraordinary. In the words of ABC's Hugh Downs:

> The Reagan-Bush years took America from the heights of a rich creditor nation down to a pit of the world's worst debtor nation. The reason was weapons purchases. No other expense came close.[63]

The Reagan boost in military expenditures produced no change in Soviet expenditures contrary to the assertion that Reagan's massive arms buildup forced the Soviets to spend themselves into exhaustion. The Soviets were already spent, having reached the culminating point in December 1979, when they invaded Afghanistan during the Carter administration. The overextension was not caused by Carter or Reagan. The overextension is attributable to the Brezhnev Doctrine and is consistent with Kennan's predictions.

Like Nixon, history presented Reagan with a strategic opportunity, but Reagan was slow to recognize it. The most notable example was the failure to make greater progress on arms reductions while Gorbachev was in power to militate against later nuclear proliferation. When recognition came, however, Reagan and Gorbachev eliminated an entire class of nuclear weapons and implemented on-site verification procedures. The arms reduction and the recognition of Gorbachev as a trustworthy negotiating partner are arguably Reagan's greatest contributions to peacefully ending the Cold War.

Subordinate Strategies

Throughout the Cold War, important subordinate strategies were pursued. A wise strategy pits one's enduring strengths against the enemy's enduring weaknesses and vulnerabilities. NATO's offset strategy is one example. And for decades the United States quietly pursued a cost-imposing strategy.

Throughout much of the Cold War, NATO employed the *offset strategy*. The strength of the Warsaw Pact was in numbers. The West's strength was in technological sophistication. NATO relied on its technological advantage to offset quantity with quality.

The economy underpins a nation's strength, and economic competitions can be decisive. A *cost-imposing strategy* guides decisions in this type of competition, and such a strategy was conducted quietly during the Cold War. An enduring weakness of the Soviet Union was the need to defend the longest perimeter in the world compounded by the stultifying effects of its command economy. America's strength was in technology. The existence of a fleet of American strategic bombers required the Soviets to invest heavily in air defenses of radar, surface-to-air missiles, and supersonic fighter-interceptors. Announcing a bomber that could fly under the radar rendered the air defense system irrelevant. After heavy investment in research, development, and fielding of a new defense system, announcement of a stealth bomber rendered the new system irrelevant again. Even if these penetrating and stealth bombers had never been built and fielded, their development encouraged the Soviet Union to spend itself into defeat as Kennan had predicted.

U.S. interventions in Korea and Vietnam are instructive examples. In both cases, the U.S. committed hundreds of thousands of troops while the Soviets provided mostly advisors. The USSR was on the right side of a cost-imposing strategy and was able to pick the time, place, and conditions of the competition.

Summary of Cold War Strategies

While the Carter administration may have been in greater disarray in its four-year tenure, the Kennedy-Johnson administration had the worst Cold War national security strategy based on the costly involvement in Vietnam. The cost in lives, capital, and credibility—both foreign and domestic—was large, and the effects still loom large on the national psyche. Vital national interests were not involved. Means were not subordinated to ends. The effectiveness of military force to achieve political objectives was grossly misjudged. Although by now a common presidential practice, involvement in the internal affairs of another country was not consistent with the American public's philosophy. There was no consensus to commitment built.

The Eisenhower administration earns high marks for national security strategy. It clearly subordinated means to ends, and the strategy was demonstrated to be adequate during Eisenhower's tenure. Its long-term implications, however, include a backlash in the Kennedy-Johnson years focusing on conventional and unconventional forces; the focus on military means proved to be a costly trap. The Nixon administration demonstrated the best national security strategy, achieving strategic coherence and a set of priorities that achieved global successes while enduring some regional failures. The pre–Korean War Truman administration (Marshall and Kennan) also scores high marks.

Presidents responding symmetrically (tit for tat) to Communist expansion tended to favor military over diplomatic and economic instruments. Those responding asymmetrically (choosing the time, place, and terms of competition) relied more on diplomatic and economic instruments while reserving military force for those times when vital interests were at stake and the terms of the competition favorable. Those presidents responding symmetrically failed to differentiate between vital and peripheral interests and made large demands on military forces.

Throughout the Cold War, the potential of the military instrument deterred major war through standing strategic nuclear and conventional forces. The actual uses of military force were for small wars that were assumed to be lesser-included cases of the major-war capability.

A partisan progression played out during the Cold War. Republican isolationism was gone. Internationalism and balance of power were pursued through alliances instead. Kennan's realist thinking was prominent, including the restrictive use of military force and the balanced use of instruments. Democratic administrations, in contrast, favored Nitze's focus on military means—specifically expansive force development policy and heavily interventionist employment policy. The pattern survived until the Carter-Reagan era. Carter vacillated. Reagan adopted the earlier Democratic pattern with respect to force development policy and the Republican pattern of cautious employment policy.

There is also considerable continuity across parties and administrations, more evolutionary in substance than partisans like to present to the public. The Truman Doctrine, the Point Four Program science and technology assistance to Latin America, and economic assistance to countries in Europe resisting its spread all focused on containing Communism. The Eisenhower Doctrine continued the same policies but shifted greater emphasis to the Middle East and increasing trade relations with Latin America. The Kennedy Doctrine was global, but his Alliance for Progress focused on Latin America, influenced by Cuba falling to Communism. Eisenhower and Kennedy were committed to Saudi Arabia and Iran as the two pillars of Middle East policy. Johnson pressed the shah for social reforms—land redistribution, women's rights, and educational opportunities—to match the rapid growth of industry and the military.

Cold War administrations interpreted threat differently. Kennan's strongpoint defense differentiated threats based on the potential capacity for industrial-age warfare. Nitze's perimeter defense lost the focus on military-industrial strength. The Dulles Dictum refined perimeter defense by explicitly distinguishing between threats to states along the Soviet

Union's perimeter and those beyond. Eisenhower spoke of the domino principle with respect to Southeast Asia. Kennedy extended the domino theory globally to an "anywhere, anytime, at any cost" response with a particular focus on Latin America. The Kirkpatrick Doctrine differentiated the threat posed by right-wing authoritarian and left-wing totalitarian governments. Reagan returned to a view similar to Kennedy and Nitze.

Truman, Eisenhower, and Kennedy established a policy of neutrality in the Arab-Israeli Conflict; Johnson and Nixon took a pro-Israeli position; and Carter attempted a return to neutrality. Reagan, despite his vocal opposition to the Israeli strike against the Osiraq nuclear power plant in Iraq and the Siege of Beirut, was rated the most pro-Israeli administration by AIPAC and other elements of the Israel lobby. Arab resentment increased accordingly.

Several arguments are advanced identifying the proximate cause of the Soviet Union's collapse. Republicans credit Ronald Reagan.[64] The Roman Catholic Church claims the victory for Pope John Paul II, and the Afghan mujahideen claims the victory for itself. Gorbachev cites the rollout of the personal computer (12 August 1981) and his country's inability to adapt to modern technology as the reason for the Soviet Union's demise. The Chernobyl disaster offered painful corroboration.

Margaret Thatcher gave explicit credit to application of the Reagan Doctrine in the Third World, citing the Nicaraguan rejection of the Sandinistas in the 1990 election, the Soviet withdrawal from Afghanistan, and Savimbi's resistance in Angola leading to Soviet and Cuban withdrawal in 1989. Others attribute the withdrawals to Gorbachev's arrival and his policies of solving problems with diplomatic negotiations, solutions mutually assured by the United States and the USSR, and return to reliance on international bodies like the Organization of African Unity and the UN.[65] Critics said the Reagan Doctrine supported terrorist regimes that abused human rights, distributed weapons and landmines, fueled violence, and contributed to blowback and Islamic opposition to U.S. policies. Moralists remind us that the ends do not justify the means. Realists remind that national security is amoral.

In *At a Century's Ending*, Kennan called the idea that any American administration toppled the Soviet system "silly and childish." He added that Reagan delayed the Soviet demise by giving Moscow hard-liners the political capital to oppose Gorbachev's reforms:

> The more American political leadership was seen in Moscow as committed to an ultimate military, rather than political, resolution of Soviet-American tensions, the greater was the tendency in Moscow to tighten the controls by both party and policy, and greater the braking effect on all liberalizing tendencies within the regime. Thus, the general effect of Cold War extremism was to delay rather than hasten the great change that overtook the country at the end of the 1980s.[66]

Most credible is that the collapse was a result of the over extension predicted by Kennan four decades earlier and achieved by consistent application of a U.S. containment strategy underwritten by a potent Western alliance against a corrupt and dysfunctional economic system. The Brezhnev Doctrine and its emphasis on a militarized industrial economy replacing Khrushchev's economic liberalization was the fulfillment of Kennan's projections. Gorbachev and the elder Bush deserve a great deal of shared credit for a peaceful end. The revolutions of 1989 through 1991 were truly remarkable. Self-determination would have its way over imposed hegemony.[67]

For Consideration

Undifferentiated Interests and Threats

Elected officials—executive and legislative—must make choices. If all interests are vital, then all must be defended and every transgression must be countered. Failing to differentiate between vital and peripheral interests, and between challenges to those interests, yields the initiative to the enemy. The enemy is allowed to pick the time, place, and terms of competition. A strategy based on undifferentiated interests is a formula for exhaustion and self-defeat. A long war, like the Cold War, requires a sustainable strategy.

Undifferentiated threat is related to undifferentiated interests. Many saw Communism as a monolithic threat. Early on, Truman was able to differentiate between Marshal Tito in Yugoslavia and Joe Stalin's brutal totalitarian leadership of the Soviet Union. Nixon was able to distinguish between the Soviet Union and China recognizing the two different and powerful nationalistic forces independent of Communism. Having made the distinction, Nixon was able to exploit it to advantage, altering the equation in Asia.

Terrorism is a tactic, not an enemy. Terrorists use the tactic to achieve a wide range of political objectives, not all of which are threats to U.S. national security. Terrorism as a monolithic enemy does not serve strategic thought. Attempting to counter an undifferentiated, monolithic enemy can induce an exhaustive rather than a strategic response.

War waged by nonstate actors employing terrorist tactics is not a long-term technological competition or an arms race between two powerful peers. Terrorists' weapons are *bricolage*—an assemblage of readily available materials. Still, there is an almost irresistible American urge to respond with technology. While technology may be helpful, the strategic competition lies elsewhere. Al-Qaeda's strategy explicitly identifies the U.S. economy as the center of gravity.

The United States is now on the wrong side of a cost-imposing strategy. The American response to a few countries possessing a small strategic nuclear capability is to ring the perimeter of the United States and Europe with an expensive ballistic missile defense system. On another front, those employing terrorist means have an infinite set of targets. Allocating resources to successfully defend civilian air traffic will result in terrorist attacks shifting to other civilian targets. The enemy can pick the time, place, and conditions of the competition.

Resisting forceful intervention and remaining neutral in disputes pays dividends, allowing the United States to be a force for fairness and honest broker in negotiations between disputants. Elected officials may feel pressured by domestic politics to react to each apparent transgression, thus yielding the initiative. Hard-liners demand a response to challenges real or imagined. When a national response is deemed inadequate, hard-liners assert appeasement and isolationism, the Beltway version of calling someone "chicken." Resisting the playground name calling requires maturity, strategic thought, tough choices, and leadership. A strong response is not necessarily a wise response.

Picking Winners and Losers

More than one president has backed the wrong horse; in fact, good horses have been hard to find. In ongoing competitions, the United States backed Chiang Kai-shek against Mao Zedong in China, backed Ngo Dinh Diem against Ho Chi Minh in Vietnam, and later backed Duong Van Minh against Diem.

More than one reason has been cited for forcible regime change. Some may govern through tyrannical methods that offend American values. Some may be too weak to govern and require assistance in meeting their nation's needs. Some may be insufficiently supportive of U.S. policies. And there is more than one way to replace the undesirable head of state, including covert political manipulation, supporting a military opponent, or direct military intervention.

Overthrowing the undesirable head of state is the easy part. A replacement must be chosen from a pool of candidates who lacked the political or military acumen to seize and hold power on their own. There is little reason to expect them to be able to govern once installed. If the state is divided into violent factions, only someone of extraordinary political skill, or someone capable of violent suppression of political opposition, can be expected to govern.

The track record in China, Vietnam, Africa, and Latin America gives little reason for optimism, but the lesson remained unlearned during the Cold War. The experience was relived post–Cold War in Africa, Iraq, Afghanistan, and Libya. Entering into another nation's internal affairs is tricky business.

Consensus to Commitment

Building a consensus to commitment is critical to the conduct of a long war. As World War II began to develop in Europe, many Americans were opposed to participation, and many preferred supporting the other side. Italian and German Americans had strong loyalties. Scandinavian immigrants were likely to lean toward Germany. Irish Americans were not so much pro-German as they were anti-British. From this beginning, FDR skillfully, steadily, and deliberately built a consensus to commitment delaying entry to the war until the time was ripe. Truman successfully initiated a presidential war, but by bypassing Congress and public debate, he failed to build a consensus to commitment. Johnson, exploiting a contrived incident to gain congressional authorization, chose not to build a public consensus to commitment. Presidents can easily start wars by trickery or sleight of hand, but those who fail to build the consensus to commitment are eventually reined in and their policies overturned after the damage to the United States has been done.

The clear lesson, well known to the framers, is that the president must thoroughly engage the people and the people's branch to build the consensus to commitment required for a sustained war effort. No one knew that better than General George Washington and those who persevered through the Revolutionary War. In large measure, consensus to commitment was once indicated by the president's ability to get a declaration of war from Congress, to gain authorization and appropriation to raise an army, and the ability to convince the state governors to provide their militia for federal service. After building commitment it must be maintained for the duration. A consensus to commitment is a presidential responsibility and the ultimate measure of leadership. Leadership is a scarce resource not bestowed by election to office.

6   Post–Cold War Strategies

International relations theories and American political traditions assumed only a supporting role during the Cold War as containment and deterrence of the Soviet Union dominated strategic thinking and forged a political consensus. Lacking a clear and agreed-upon perception of threat, theories and traditions reasserted themselves in the post–Cold War debate. This chapter begins with the national security strategy debate that followed the end of the Cold War. Nothing has yet to serve as a political rallying point as did the idea of containing Communism, and nothing appears on the horizon.

Nonetheless, several alternative strategies have been proposed and debated. They differ as to whether American interventionism is the solution to or the cause of threats to national security. The alternatives also differ over the ends to which military means are applied. Some advocate the use of force whenever and wherever it might advance American interests, including economic advantage, social values, and the spread of democracy, arguing, "Why have a military if you can't use it?" Others advocate more restraint, using force only to prevent war between great powers or only to defend the homeland.

Alternative post–Cold War strategies are presented in the next section followed by the real strategies of the post–Cold War administrations. The chapter concludes with issues for future consideration.

Strategic Alternatives

The grand strategy alternatives are characterized below in terms of interests and objectives, major underlying premises, and preferred political and military instruments. They differ fundamentally on the reasons for using military force, ranging from the conservative to the liberal use of force. Post–Cold War strategies examined include primacy, collective security, selective engagement, and homeland defense. These summaries rely heavily on "Competing Visions for U.S. Grand Strategy" by Barry Posen and Andrew Ross.[1] Two variants, cooperative security and offshore balancing, are also covered.

Collective security is most strongly correlated with Wilsonian idealism. True global collective security was impossible during the bipolar Cold War due to the veto power in the UN Security Council and the ensuing deadlock. But the strategy was reenergized by the end of the Cold War. Selective engagement contains the strains of realism, balance of power, Hamiltonian logic, and Kennan's containment. Defensive realism and the isolationist thinking of Adams still resonate with many citizens and find voice in today's restrictive homeland defense strategy, but they attracted little support from the policy elite until the global economic recession and resurgence of libertarianism. Global hegemonic primacy was also enabled and energized by the end of the Cold War and the "unipolar moment" that followed.

Offensive realism predicts the progression from isolationism to primacy as the United States grew from weak power to lone superpower. The predilection to global hegemony can be seen in its precursor, regional hegemony, in Jackson's bellicosity and desire to expand American empire farther westward under Manifest Destiny, and in the Monroe Doctrine with respect to the Western Hemisphere. And one can see the continuation of Nitze's preponderance of power.

Hegemonic Primacy

Advocates of a *primacy strategy*, or *hegemonic primacy strategy*, see the rise of a peer competitor as the greatest threat to international order and, therefore, the greatest risk of war involving the United States.[2] They seek to preserve the unipolar moment that arrived at the end of the bipolar Cold War. Furthermore, proponents believe that only a preponderance of American power ensures peace. Adherents of this school often refer to *preponderance* rather than primacy. The objective, then, is for the United States to act to retain a *benign* global hegemony and prevent the rise of competing powers. Primacy focuses on inhibiting (containing) Russia and China but includes inhibition of the European powers of Great Britain, Germany, and France, as well as the Asian powers of Japan and India.

Proponents of the more restrictive strategies subscribe to the theory that states *balance against power*. If primacy were pursued, then the United States would be the power against which to balance. In the long term, the United States may find itself isolated when confronting rising powers. Primacy advocates are more likely to subscribe to the theory that states *balance against threat*. Primacists argue that by using force prudently the United States will be seen at worst as a benign, nonthreatening hegemon, and, therefore, states will not balance against it.[3] Others assert that foreign nationalism will brace against even benign American hegemony and cause the problems the strategy is designed to prevent—countervailing alliances and arms races, for example.[4]

The Cold War practice of aggregating power through coalitions and alliances is insufficient. Primacists are skeptical of international institutions but believe that they can be used as a strategic asset in the pursuit of American interests.[5] For example, to inhibit Russia, they might expand NATO into Central Europe; to counter China they would perhaps rebuild SEATO and include Vietnam.

The primacy strategy requires large overseas presence. Stationing military forces in Europe is seen as an effective means of preventing Germany from forming an independent foreign policy. Forces should remain forward deployed in the Middle East and Southwest Asia to safeguard oil reserves and to discourage India from ambitions of regional hegemony.

Primacy advocates are not a homogeneous group, but they share preference for the military over other instruments. The more extreme have contempt for the other instruments and consider vindicationism the right and duty of the dominant power. Of the strategic alternatives, primacy poses the greatest demand for force structure. Advocates are unilateralist, thus requiring the force to be sized and shaped without regard for coalition contributions. Some argue for offensive air, land, and sea forces that are superior to the combined forces of the next two, three, or even four major powers.[6] A strong second-strike nuclear force should be maintained to deter major aggression, especially aggression with weapons of mass destruction. One can easily see the logic of Nitze's NSC-68 and preponderance of power.

Primacists assert that the U.S. share of the global economy is sufficient to sustain a strategy of primacy. They argue that American power and influence are far more than that reflected in the gross domestic product (GDP).[7] Primacy's detractors believe the strategy is economically unsustainable in the long run and will likely result in imperial overstretch, destroying what it intended to protect.[8] And they predict coalition formation and blowback directed against the United States.

Homeland Defense

Proponents of a *homeland defense strategy*[9] assert that the United States is an economically powerful nation with vast protective oceans and an overwhelming nuclear arsenal. Its security is thus assured from many, but not all, threats. Adherents of this school often use the words *restraint, disengagement,* or *restrictive* instead of homeland defense. Hard-line opponents use the term *isolationism* as a pejorative and dismissive term. While primacy is the most ambitious of America's strategic choices, homeland defense is the least. It defines national interests so narrowly that internationalism is neither required nor desired. The only vital American interests are the life, liberty, and property of the American people.[10] Adherents are more inclined to see as major threats the flow of illegal immigrants, terrorists, and drugs and therefore to see border control as the priority solution.

The homeland-defense belief system includes the premise that promoting values abroad generates resentment and that American intervention is the cause of trouble for the United States, not a preventative solution. Adherents of this strategy believe in staying out of foreign conflicts and not using military power to impose world order, spread democracy or American values, or advance American economic interests. Promoting economic advancement is best left to the private sector. One can see defensive realism, pre-Eisenhower Republican thinking, and today's libertarian movements.

Moreover, for political instruments, adherents to homeland defense see very little need for international actions, for international organizations, or for traditional alliances. Alliances like NATO obligate the United States in advance to unimagined future crises around the world. Restrictivists recognize the threat posed by weapons of mass destruction but argue that the risk of attack is proportional to U.S. involvement in foreign conflicts. Therefore, the United States should withdraw from such entangling alliances and reduce foreign engagement to only those conflicts that threaten U.S. vital interests.[11] The force structure required to support this strategy should take less than 2 percent of GDP, a nontrivial but modest near-term defense savings.

Those favoring this most restrictive strategy suggest the use of force almost exclusively to protect the homeland. They argue, therefore, for significant reduction of conventional military forces and a shift toward the use of the National Guard and Reserve. They would retain a small naval expeditionary force to protect our vital interests abroad, modest air and missile defense, and a second-strike nuclear capability. In the long run, the country would require a robust mobilization capability rather than a standing military. Mobilization requires a strong strategic intelligence apparatus and a prescient understanding of events that might lead to major-power war. It also requires the ability to mobilize public support so as to wrest resources from the private sector. In the meantime, the low force level would offer reduced options to the president. To the adherents of a restrictive use of force, this is more a blessing than a shortcoming.

In the absence of security provided by the United States or by a U.S.-led coalition, according to opponents of this strategy, other countries might expand their militaries to provide their own security. An expensive and dangerous spiral of militarization could ensue. In the absence of a global leader, regional powers might assume only local resistance to their attempts at regional hegemony. The result could be more war, not less. Some argue that the low military force level would imply low international influence[12] giving short shrift to the potency of other instruments of national power.

Collective Security

A *collective security* strategy is based on the premise that a threat to one nation is a threat to all. Peace is indivisible. And American national security is best assured through international institutions. The original idea of collective security applied to the global community of nations principally represented by the UN. During the bipolar Cold War, however, the idea degenerated into two distinct and opposed collective security systems represented militarily by NATO and the Warsaw Pact. Liberal (idealist) political factions could see NATO as a collective security arrangement, and realist factions could see it as an aggregation of power through a traditional alliance structure. Political consensus was thus possible.

Collective security is implemented through a multinational coalition to deter or defeat an aggressor that has amassed sufficient power to pose a threat to other states. American security, indeed, the security of the free world, was bolstered through the NATO alliance. The Persian Gulf War was less ambiguously based on a collective security strategy. One sovereign state invaded another, and the international community responded collectively to return to the status quo ante. A collective security arrangement developed throughout the twentieth century and had become the accepted norm by the end of the Cold War. One can easily see the aspirational logic of post–World War I Wilsonian idealism, liberalism, and institutionalism in a collective security strategy.

Another premise is that peace is indivisible. Because wars spread, the United States has an overriding interest in preserving global peace. The credible international institutions do not yet exist, and a principal objective of this strategy is to build them over the long term. Without such institutions, small regional powers might calculate that local aggression would be overlooked by major powers because they have no interests at stake. International institutions that respond consistently over time will alter that calculation and deter small aggressions that might grow into larger regional conflicts.

The implications of the collective security strategy for force structure are demanding.[13] The strategy assumes a large American overseas presence. Internationally, it requires some countries to maintain forces sufficient for the defense of their homeland plus a force subordinated to international institutions. The U.S. contribution—the *reconnaissance strike complex*—would complement other nations' forces. The complex is essentially the Desert Storm force and its power projection capability, command and control systems, and precision guided munitions. A strong second-strike nuclear capability would be maintained.

The criticisms of the collective security strategy are easy to anticipate and can be inferred from the various schools of thought that advocate the alternatives. Perhaps the two loudest criticisms come first from those who advocate primacy and who reject the subordination of American interests and forces to an international body, and second from those realists who suggest that there is no historical reason to believe that a new world order based on nations subordinating their own interests is achievable. Given the degree of internal strife worldwide, the demands are extreme.

Cooperative Security

Cooperative security is a recent variation on collective security.[14] "Cooperative security differs from the traditional idea of collective security as preventive medicine differs from acute care." Whereas a collective security strategy is implemented through an international coalition to deter or defeat an aggressor that has already accumulated sufficient power to pose a threat to other states, the architects of cooperative security seek to prevent war by preventing any country from assembling the means to aggress against others.[15] The implications of this difference are significant.

Pursuing cooperative security requires standing international organizations with domestic and international legitimacy.[16] International institutions authorize or take military actions against aggressor states, maintain arms control and confidence-building regimes, and prevent proliferation of weapons of mass destruction. The new international arrangement "must begin with the central principle that the only legitimate purpose of national military forces is the defense of national territory or the participation in multinational forces that enforce UN sanctions or maintain peace." Furthermore, "it requires that any effort to change borders by force be disavowed."[17]

One premise of cooperative security is that democracies do not war with each other, and because major powers are democracies (or on the road to becoming democracies), war between major powers is not the pressing problem seen by other schools of thought. A focus on preventing a state from assembling aggressive means moves the proliferation of weapons of mass destruction to the forefront. Accumulation of conventional forces sufficient to threaten neighbors and accumulation of a power projection capability is thought to be less of an immediate problem.

Those advocating a cooperative security strategy ascribe special meaning to the word *prevention*:

The central purpose of cooperative security arrangements is to prevent war and to do so primarily by preventing the means for successful aggression from being assembled, thus also obviating the need for states so threatened to make their own counter preparations.[18]

Cooperativists rely heavily on arms control and nonproliferation arrangements.[19] If these diplomatic efforts fail, they will not hesitate to use military force as a last resort. Using force to prevent proliferation may be preferable to using force later with WMD more widely held. If local aggressors hold such weapons, they may be more inclined to aggress against neighbors and assume that great powers will be deterred from intervening.

Like collective security, the cooperative security strategy simultaneously pursues humanitarian interests in the near term and the political principle of internationalism in the long term. Cooperative security inherits the criticisms of the collective security strategy. But using force to *prevent* a sovereign state from *acquiring the means of aggression* rather than using force to counter *real aggression* constitutes a major departure from past strategic thinking and international order. As with primacy, one can see Nitze's focus on means and preponderance of power rather than Kennan's focus on intentions and balance of power. As with primacy, one can see the seeds of preventive war.

Selective Engagement

The goals of a *selective engagement strategy* are twofold.[20] The first goal is preventing war between the major powers, including Russia, China, Japan, and the European powers. The second goal is preventing proliferation of weapons of mass destruction to hostile, ambitious powers, including Iran, Iraq, and North Korea.[21]

The first goal is premised on the belief that any major-power war in Eurasia is a threat to the United States. The industrialized regions of Europe and Northeast Asia and the resource-rich and politically volatile region of the Middle East and Southwest Asia are the primary areas where competition will take place. Loss of easy access to Middle East oil will lead to great-power competition.

Proponents of selective engagement believe that states balance against power, inducing friction or outright opposition in international relations, and if the United States exerts power indiscriminately, countries will balance against it. Adhering to the realist school, advocates recognize that resources are scarce and must be jealously husbanded. The threat of major-power war and proliferation argue for engagement. Balance of power theory and resource scarcity dictate the need for engagement to be selective. One can see this strategy lying between defensive and offensive realism or in Eisenhower's moderate Republicanism.

Selective engagers believe the public will not support the global police mission. Forces engaged in peace operations may be difficult to disengage and redeploy and may not be ready to participate in major regional war. Because assuring major-power peace is this strategy's principal objective, engaging in humanitarian assistance and disaster relief operations should be decided by domestic politics and only entered into when prospects for success are good and risks and costs are low.

According to advocates, the United States must be prepared to act unilaterally if great-power peace is threatened. Traditional alliances, such as NATO, are viewed as beneficial to the extent that they either prevent or allow the United States to respond to threats to major-power peace. While they may be beneficial, there is little or no need to enlarge NATO or the web of alliances.[22]

To support this strategy, the United States needs the ability to deter major-power wars in regions of competition and, if necessary, to fight and restore peace. The force structure logic of the Cold War remains; the United States must have the force structure to fight and win two nearly simultaneous major regional wars. The second would be fought with an opportunist aggressor that might be emboldened by substantial American involvement elsewhere. The United States must maintain a strong nuclear deterrent. In addition to deterring attack on the homeland, America should signal to non-nuclear states that its force stands behind the status quo powers.[23]

While this strategy is founded in the realist school, critics contend that focusing on Eurasia isn't selective enough to husband scarce resources and might lead to grand strategy mission creep. Given that engagement in peace operations is left to domestic politics, implementing the strategy might be buffeted by the media and fickle public interest. The resulting employment policy, appearing random and lacking any coherent vision, would likely lose public support over time. A series of uninspiring peace operations could further erode public support.[24]

To opponents of selective engagement, engaging selectively means the United States leads only when its vital interests are at risk. Its prestige and ability to lead in the international community would likely suffer. The result would be that the United States could not affect others in important matters, thus forcing U.S. unilateral action when multinational action would be preferable.

Offshore Balancing

Offshore balancing is a restrictive variant of selective engagement that maximizes geographic advantage. Based on balancing power, it can also be called a tipping strategy. The United States' insular condition, like Great Britain's, gives it relative advantage over noninsular, continental, powers on the Eurasian landmass. Continental powers share borders and compete with neighbors. Insular states have the option of balancing from offshore. The United States enters the equation only when its vital interests are threatened and then only as a balancer of last resort.

Making distinctions is an important part of any critical examination. The distinctions made by Posen and Ross are a positive contribution and allow identification of the political factions that might coalesce around each strategy. Christopher Layne—a realist of the selective engagement camp—makes different distinctions. Rather than the Posen and Ross taxonomy—neo-isolationism, selective engagement, cooperative security, primacy—Layne differentiates grand strategies as being based either on *balancing power* or *preponderant power.* And he further argues that preponderance has been the strategic choice since the end of World War II, throughout the Cold War, and throughout the post–Cold War era—strategic continuity. Tacitly, cooperative security and primacy are both based on preponderance of power, with cooperativists' *initial* preference for projecting power through multilateral institutions, and primacists' *initial* preference for projecting power unilaterally. "Initial," because collectivists will act unilaterally if multilateral institutions are not cooperative, and primacists will accept coalitions of the willing to support

U.S.-initiated actions. Thus, the distinction between cooperative security and primacy is a distinction without difference.[25] For Layne, the only distinctions that matter fall entirely within the realist school.

Painted as an isolationist and dismissed by some cooperativists and primacists, Layne rejects the notion that the United States was isolationist (defensive power) through the first half of the twentieth century, asserting instead that the United States chose to be the balancer of last resort (balancing power), entering the world wars late and tipping the scales.

But that changed during the Cold War. Not only did the United States hope to contain the Soviet Union, it hoped to contain Germany and Japan by providing their security through *extended deterrence.* The United States guaranteed the security—the supreme interest—of Europe and Japan, adding other protectorates, including South Korea, Israel, South Vietnam, the Philippines, and Taiwan. Europe and Japan understood that their survival outside the Soviet sphere was considered a vital interest to the United States. The recognized threat posed by the Soviet Union made U.S. preeminence acceptable to its protectorates. The acceptance of U.S. preeminence has faded, however. After the dissolution of the Soviet Union, the United States extended its *security guarantee* into eastern Europe by expanding NATO.

Layne *explains* post–World War II behavior in the language of offensive realism and preponderant power, but he *prescribes* U.S. behavior in language closer to balancing power than to preponderant or defensive power.

Comparison of Post–Cold War Strategies

The various strategies show significant disagreement on several points. There is disagreement on what distinguishes American vital and peripheral interests. That, in turn, leads to disagreement on when the use of military force is justified. Moreover, there is disagreement on whether using military force increases or decreases the threat. When using force, there is disagreement on whether it generally should be employed unilaterally or through international institutions.

Primacy, collective security, and cooperative security all have the potential to make the United States the world's policeman: primacy through unilateralism, collective and cooperative security through multilateralism and international institutions. Both primacy and cooperative security have the seeds of preventive war, and both contain the seeds of overextension by expanding the U.S. security umbrella.

Primacy, collective security, and cooperative security have some common implications for force deployment policy, force development policy, and force employment policy. Forces are structured for a broad range of missions similar to Nitze's NSC-68 and Kennedy's force structure. And forces are deployed and employed worldwide in that broad range of missions.

The homeland defense, offshore balancing, and selective engagement strategies differ significantly from the other strategies. Force deployment policy brings force structure home to the United States, and the force is employed sparingly. Force development policy produces a narrower spectrum force structure for conventional warfare and returns the reserve component to a strategic reserve.

Post–Cold War Administrations

No real administration adopts a strategy in pure form. The world is too complex and deals presidents unimagined events. But one can easily discuss the post–Cold War administrations in the language of the strategy options presented above. And one will see ad hocery over strategy in some cases.

The post–Cold War period saw the simultaneous decrease in the size of the force and increase in the use of force. End strength is a measure of the number of troops on active duty (including National Guard and Reserve forces on active duty) on the last day of the fiscal year, 30 September.[26]

The post-Vietnam drawdown began under Nixon and Ford and continued through the first half of the Carter administration. The Carter-Reagan buildup began after the 1979 Soviet invasion of Afghanistan and continued through most of the 1980s. End strength was virtually unchanged during the Reagan administration, expenditures going toward the acquisition of weapon systems rather than toward manpower. The steep post–Cold War drawdown began under the Bush 41 administration, even as the Gulf War was being prosecuted, and continued through most of the Clinton years. Bush presided over a nearly 20 percent decrease in four years, and Clinton presided over a nearly 19 percent decrease in eight years. The end of the Clinton administration saw a modest reversal of the downward trend. The Bush 43 administration continued the slight upward trend briefly before returning to the levels existing at the end of the Clinton administration. The Bush force was augmented to an extraordinary extent by private contractors. Obama initially held force levels steady and then began a drawdown following the end of the Afghan and Iraq wars.

An old saw is that a general's most important decision is when to commit the reserve. After the inevitable drawdown began following the Cold War, force deployments increased. Evidence of overcommitment of the military began to build almost immediately. Toward the end of Clinton's second term, compared to Cold War levels, operational tempo estimates for the Air Force were up more than 400 percent and up over 300 percent for the Army and Marine Corps.[27] From those high levels, optempo accelerated dramatically under Bush 43 with the invasions of Afghanistan and Iraq. The reserve was committed early. The Reserve and National Guard, a strategic reserve for once-in-a-generation mobilization became an operational reserve with recurring mobilization.

George H. W. Bush, 1989–93

The Cold War came to an abrupt end under the first Bush administration. Three different strategies emerged at the same time that force structure was in rapid decline. It would be a pivotal point in grand strategy formulation. The president directed a major strategic review in the National Security Council's NSR-12. Everything was on the table, including the president's national security strategy, the chairman's national military strategy and the associated array of strategic plans, and the defense secretary's defense planning guidance. Declaratory, development, deployment, and employment policy were all subject to review. Strategy would be guided by Eastern Establishment appointees rather than by Reagan's New Right.

As chairman of the JCS, Colin Powell put forward the *National Military Strategy* consistent with selective engagement.[28] After Vietnam, Powell watched budget and force structure enter a free fall without adequate planning into what became known as the *hollow force*, and he wanted to avoid a repeat. In a major force development policy initiative, the Bush administration established a *Base Force*, a force structure below which the United States could not meet its putative obligations as the last remaining superpower. The administration managed a 20 percent reduction in end strength and fell below Base Force levels. In force deployment policy, Powell called for a return of forces to garrison in the United States organized under a Contingency Command. Nuclear forces would be consolidated under a Strategic Command. To remain engaged globally, he called for forward presence to be maintained by rotating U.S.-based forces through the Atlantic and Pacific Commands, long the custom of naval forces. Secretary of Defense Dick Cheney approved Powell's proposal.

The secretary of defense is responsible for producing the *Defense Planning Guidance* (DPG) driven by the White House strategy. The DPG collects inputs from across the Department and translates them into action. The under secretary for policy, Paul Wolfowitz, and Cheney's chief of staff, Scooter Libby, produced Secretary Cheney's DPG. Large segments of it were less defense planning guidance and more foreign policy statement— the domain of the State Department. It was decidedly an expression of a primacy strategy, including preventing the rise of a peer or near-peer competitor, preventing European allies from developing their own foreign policy, and providing global security so that no potential competitor would need to aspire to greater power—preserving the unipolar moment and maintaining U.S. hegemony. Some in the Pentagon found the language of the classified document so disagreeable that they leaked it to the *New York Times*.[29] Talking primacy was as politically incorrect as talking isolationism. The White House ordered a rewrite, but the thinking would resurface in the next Bush administration post 9/11.

The White House's *National Security Strategy* document[30] was consistent with the JCS view. It explicitly rejected withdrawal into isolationism, just as it rejected the role of world policeman. It paid considerable attention to managing the effects of the Soviet Union's implosion and to WMD proliferation. It included favorable language about the increasing international roles of Japan and the European powers rather than the inhibiting DPG language. It advocated burden sharing by other major powers. It accepted the inevitability of force reductions but specified a Base Force. The roles of the Contingency, Pacific, Atlantic, and Strategic Commands were in line with Powell's approach. It nodded to collective security by referring to the indivisibility of peace and security. The president was prepared to unveil the new strategy on 2 August 1990, the day Iraq invaded Kuwait. Bush's planned speech was never delivered, and the strategy never executed.

Congress established a new category of alliance—major non-NATO ally—that became law in 1989. Benefits included important exemptions to the Arms Export Control Act. Designated allies were authorized to enter into defense research and development projects, possess prepositioned U.S. war reserve stocks, and participate in some counterterrorism efforts. Initial designees were Australia, Egypt, Israel, Japan, and South Korea.

In employment policy, the Bush administration was selective but more inclined than Reagan to intervene directly. Bush executed a rapid military intervention (1989–90) his first year in office deposing Panama's head of state. The Gulf War (1990–91) was the major intervention of the administration. He took a standoff approach with respect to Haiti and initiated a humanitarian intervention in Somalia late in his administration. Bush continued Reagan's indirect intervention in southern Africa.

Review

Arms Control. Building on the modest reduction of nuclear forces between Reagan and Gorbachev, Bush recognized and seized the opportunity to unilaterally withdraw tactical nuclear weapons in 1991 rather than negotiate for further reductions. Bush's bold unilateral action reduced domestic pressures in Moscow, and Gorbachev, in an equally courageous move, followed suit almost immediately. Other reductions followed rapidly. The Strategic Arms Reduction Treaty (START) was signed 31 July 1991, resulting in an additional 30 percent reduction in strategic nuclear weapons. Congressional leadership initiated the Cooperative Threat Reduction program, popularly known as Nunn-Lugar, in 1992. The program provided funds to dismantle and destroy Soviet weapons of mass destruction and their supporting infrastructure. Collectively, these efforts were a major policy success of the administration, reducing the spread of WMD as the Soviet Union lost control. Depending on the accounting method, overall reductions may be as high as 80 percent.

Panama. Reagan rejected advice to depose Panama's president Manuel Noriega with force, using personal diplomacy instead. Bush, in contrast, executed a rapid military intervention (1989–90) his first year in office ending in Noriega's extraction. Whatever positive feelings Carter gained in the region were lost.

Persian Gulf. Several months later, Iraq's Saddam Hussein invaded Kuwait, and there was fear that he threatened Saudi Arabia. Bush led a coalition to return conditions to the status quo ante. Residual forces remained to protect Iraqis in the north and south. When Iraq launched missiles into Israel, the Bush administration extended a security guarantee and provided antimissile defenses. It was feared that Israel's entry to the war would cause Egypt and Syria to withdraw from the carefully constructed coalition. Israeli politicians courageously held back. Gulf States in the coalition gave unprecedented access to U.S. forces. Force deployment policy made some basing options permanent, including establishment of the Fifth Fleet headquarters in Bahrain.

Relations with Israel. Bush returned to a more even hand with regard to the Arab-Israeli Conflict. Secretary of State James Baker, in a 22 May 1989 speech to AIPAC, urged Israel to abandon its expansionist policies. Seeing an opportunity following the Gulf War, Bush delivered a 6 March 1991 address to Congress urging a territory-for-peace exchange and political rights for Palestinians. Bush's efforts led to the Madrid Conference in October to establish procedures and restart the process. The Conference was hosted by Spain, cosponsored by the United States and the USSR, and attended by Syria, Lebanon, and Jordan in addition to Israel and Palestinian representation. Prime Minister Yitzhak Shamir (Likud) requested another $10 billion in loan guarantees prior to the Conference but refused to verify that previous loan guarantees were not used to expand settlements. Had Bush bowed to Shamir's demand U.S. credibility as mediator would be damaged. Opposed to Likud's pro-settlement policy, and against efforts by the Israel lobby, Bush petitioned Congress to delay discussion of loan guarantees. Yitzhak Rabin and the Labor Party defeated Likud in July 1992. Rabin promised to end Shamir's policies. Labor soon approved a partial halt to housing developments in the occupied territories. Loan guarantees were extended.

Angola. Bush supported the national reconciliation process in Angola that led to a cease-fire 31 May 1991 and elections 29 and 30 September 1992. The U.S.-backed UNITA lost the election and returned to open warfare. The United States continued its support prolonging the civil war.

Afghanistan. The Soviet withdrawal from Afghanistan left a power vacuum that no outside power was willing to fill. The handful of Afghan warlords no longer had a unifying external threat, and the country sank into a civil war in a competition for the right to govern. One of the factions entered and took Kabul in 1992. In 1994, the Taliban (Pashtu for students) emerged from the refugee camps along the Afghanistan-Pakistan border, many products of madrasas funded by the United States, Britain, and Saudi Arabia during the Soviet occupation. They were refugees and orphans who had never known their country without war. This virulent form of Islam had no roots in historic Afghanistan. In September 1996, the Taliban captured Kabul with the aid of Pakistan.

Haiti. Bush applied an economic embargo, adopted a forcible return policy for refugees, but declined direct intervention into a chaotic Haiti (1992).

Somalia. Bush initiated a humanitarian intervention into Somalia (1992) his last month in office after losing the election to Bill Clinton.

Critique

While declaratory policy from the White House took on the more acceptable mainstream language of collective security or selective engagement, the administration's employment policy was ambivalent and subject to interpretation. In total, the Bush administration's combination of declaratory policy and employment policy can be seen fairly either as a successful implementation of primacy, including the role as *benign* hegemon, or as an implementation of selective engagement. Given the more traditional conservative view expressed in President Bush's national security strategy and Chairman Powell's national military strategy, selective engagement is arguably the more accurate characterization.

The invasion of Panama to remove a head of state is an example of a willingness to use force unilaterally. It is easy to interpret the Panama invasion as a continuation of the Monroe Doctrine and regional primacy in the Western Hemisphere rather than as a trend toward global primacy.

The Gulf War, however, can be seen as an example of collective security: one state violated the territorial sovereignty of another, and the international community under UN authorization returned conditions to the status quo ante. Or it can be seen as primacy: a benign hegemon leading a coalition of the willing in service of global order. Or it can be seen as selective engagement: aggregating power through a coalition of the willing when shared vital interests are threatened.

The humanitarian intervention in Somalia can be seen as consistent with all but homeland defense and a restrictive selective engagement strategy. The response to Haiti—employing diplomacy and economic embargo rather than a military intervention—can be interpreted similarly.

Bush did not invest heavily in building a consensus to commitment in support of his employment policy, but it proved inconsequential by design. The invasion of Panama had initial public support, as is frequently the case, and the military intervention was over before public opinion could shift. The damage to U.S. relations with Panama was significant and persists. The Gulf War was conducted under what is often called the *Powell Doctrine*, going in with overwhelming force. The results were decisive and concluded before public sentiment could turn. With public support, Bush chose a humanitarian assistance intervention in Somalia.

In general, the instruments of power were considerably weakened. The Bush national security strategy and Powell national military strategy calling for the return of forces to the United States did not come to pass. By the end of the Bush administration, the size of the conventional force had been reduced by almost 20 percent while adding residual overseas commitments in northern and southern Iraq. The military instrument was somewhat weakened. After twelve years of large-scale deficit spending, the economic instrument was greatly weakened, and the economy was the dominant campaign issue. The power over opinion was mixed. The demise of the Soviet autocracy and Communism appeared to be affirmation of democracy and market capitalism. The U.S.-led collective response to the Iraqi invasion of Kuwait offered evidence that the world could act together through the UN once the bipolar stalemate of the Cold War was broken. The invasion of Panama increased resentment in Latin America.

William J. Clinton, 1993–2001

The campaign leading to the 1992 election paid scant attention to foreign policy and national security issues; domestic issues prevailed. "It's the economy, stupid," was the contemporary mantra. Following his election, President Clinton gave speeches apologizing for the Cold War and

American preoccupation with power.[31] The administration explicitly rejected balance of power in favor of Wilsonian internationalism.[32] Clinton inherited a post–Cold War world that was redefining itself and demanding attention, including crises in Somalia, Haiti, Rwanda, Yugoslavia, and Korea. Militant Islam was expanding, changing, and metastasizing.

The premises underlying the Clinton strategy are drawn from cooperative security, selective engagement, and primacy. So, too, are its goals. Its strategy shares none of the characteristics of the restrictive homeland defense strategy; declaratory policy denounced any and all aspects of withdrawal into isolationism. It rejected the principle of noninterference. The administration's eventual grand strategy was a soup of selective engagement, cooperative security, and primacy that mixed idealist international, liberal, and offensive realist views. Critics said there was no strategy at all.

Each of the administration's seven national security strategy documents[33] was decidedly oriented on cooperative security, assuring world peace and nonproliferation through arms control regimes. An international community that proved less supportive than hoped for led the administration to adopt some of primacy's unilateralism in subsequent strategy statements. A desire to intervene internationally coupled with unwillingness to risk American casualties and popular support for those interventions led to technology-enabled standoff warfare. As time passed and military overextension become more obvious, the administration's declaratory policy began to stress the need to be selective in its engagement. Simultaneously, it expanded its military presence overseas in Southeast Asia, Northeast Asia, and Central America.

Clinton's employment policy was mixed. He frequently employed standoff methods rather than deploying ground forces, including the air war in Kosovo. He used punitive strikes against Iraq in retaliation for an assassination attempt against President Bush and in Afghanistan and the Sudan in retaliation for terrorist attacks against U.S. embassies in Kenya and Tanzania. Clinton's tendency was dubbed *cruise-missile diplomacy* by his critics, but it was the modern equivalent of gunboat diplomacy.[34] It is a practice that past presidents would have understood as a sustainable use of military force, but for hard-liners, it showed weakness and lack of commitment.

North Korea. Clinton's employment policy toward North Korea began with the aggressive application of diplomatic and economic instruments and held out the possibility of both preemptive and retaliatory strikes but not preemptive or preventive war. The administration came close to employing military force. Later, during the second Bush administration, Clinton's out-of-office cooperative security proponents argued for the aggressive use of military force to prevent North Korea from acquiring nuclear weaponry.[35]

Secretary of Defense William Perry made significant strategic contributions. He coauthored the cooperative security strategy prior to the election. He responded to the breakup of the Soviet Union by assisting some of the former states to develop legitimate defense establishments under democratic rule. Simultaneously, the administration expanded the Nunn-Lugar effort to gobble up WMD. Jordan joined Israel and Egypt as major non-NATO allies in the Middle East.

Yugoslavia. The former Yugoslavia was leaning toward civil war and genocide. The Clinton administration was thus confronted with a situation that seemingly required NATO for the first time to respond to other than the Warsaw Pact. General Wesley Clark, then NATO commander, conducted operations in Kosovo through the alliance with allies providing valuable diplomatic throw weight even if they were militarily a bit underweight. According to Clark, "A coalition of the willing is a poor substitute for a real alliance in that regard."[36]

Haiti. A military coup in Haiti during September 1991 put an end to the government of Jean-Bertrand Aristide, and the Bush administration responded with withdrawal of economic aid, a leaky economic embargo, and a forced return of fleeing refugees. Clinton criticized the policy during his campaign but initially continued the policy after entering office. Clinton later ordered a military intervention, including peacemaking, peacekeeping, and nation building.

Rwanda. The tiny country of Rwanda has borne more than its share of misery. Past outbursts included the brutal killing of tens and hundreds of thousands of lives and the displacement of millions. A new cycle began in late 1993 that produced another million killed and 2 million refugees.

The UN authorized an intervention by African forces, but the effort stalled over who would pay for U.S. armored personnel carriers. The UN authorized French forces to intervene to break the impasse. Both the UN and the Clinton administration specifically refused to use the word *genocide*. The administration deployed forces to evacuate U.S. nationals in April 1994 and to provide humanitarian assistance in December 1996. In a personal visit in 1998, Clinton acknowledged that "we did not act quickly enough."

Somalia. Bush's humanitarian mission (a mission that generally garners support from the American public) evolved under Clinton into a peacemaking and peacekeeping mission (a mission that generally lacks public support).[37] The evolution, called *mission creep*, is common to interventions into humanitarian disasters.

Genocide. After Kosovo, Rwanda, and Haiti, Clinton was on the horns of a dilemma in American strategic thought. Genocidal war drew a strong American response in Kosovo but not in Rwanda. When people in another country are killing each other, how many American lives shall be spent to stop it? For many Americans, the answer is damned few to none. But for others, "never again" is a promise sincerely made after the Holocaust.

Angola. With respect to the civil war in Angola, Clinton returned more to the posture of the Carter administration emphasizing trade, encouraging national reconciliation and power sharing between the factions, and extending diplomatic relations to the Angolan government. But conditions had changed considerably. There was no longer the overarching East-West competition. It was now a competition for power and resources. Without superpower financing, the government turned to Chevron and oil, and insurgents turned to De Beers and diamonds.

After losing the September 1992 elections, the U.S.-backed UNITA returned to open warfare terrorizing the countryside and drawing no response from the Bush administration. Soon after entering office, Clinton extended diplomatic relations to the government of Angola on 19 May 1993. Clinton signed Executive Order 12865 on 23 September 1993, calling the formerly U.S.-backed UNITA a "continuing threat to the foreign policy objectives of the United States." By late 1998 the Angolan Armed Forces and UNITA were engaged in full-scale warfare. Jonas Savimbi was killed in combat on 22 February 2002, and without Savimbi's personal ambition for power, UNITA dissipated.

South Lebanon. The conflict in South Lebanon flared twice during the Clinton administration while Hezbollah waged a guerrilla war against occupying Israeli forces and their Lebanese proxies, the South Lebanon Army.

Hezbollah rocket attacks into the Israeli-occupied security zone killed five IDF soldiers in late June, and Israel launched Operation Accountability on 25 July 1993. In the seven-day operation, thousands of buildings were destroyed, including two thousand houses, more than one hundred were killed, almost all civilians, and another three hundred thousand were displaced. Hezbollah responded with rocket attacks on Israel. The United States negotiated a cease-fire.

Another violent exchange took place in April 1996. An Israeli missile killed two civilian workers in Lebanon on 30 March; Hezbollah responded with twenty rockets. A roadside bomb killed a Lebanese boy on 9 April; Hezbollah responded with thirty rockets. Israel initiated Operation Grapes of Wrath on 11 April. The sixteen-day operation included a blockade of Lebanese ports and massive artillery and aerial bombardment that destroyed two thousand buildings, power stations, and bridges employing over a thousand air attacks and twenty-five thousand artillery rounds. On 18 April, an Israeli barrage struck a UN compound in Qana, killing 106 Lebanese civilians who had taken refuge there. Up to a half million fled. The United States brokered an agreement. The disproportionate Israeli response caused the Lebanese to close ranks behind Hezbollah. Mohamed Atta dedicated himself to martyrdom, and Osama bin Laden cited the bombing of Qana and the falling towers in his declaration of war against the United States.

Relations with Israel. In the Middle East, Clinton attempted an even hand, but the United States was increasingly seen as other than an honest broker. His administration expended considerable energy in negotiating Palestinian-Israeli issues. The next round of negotiations took place in Oslo, Norway, enabled by Bush's efforts at Madrid. Clinton reopened dialogue with the PLO on 10 September 1993; Israel and the PLO agreed to mutual recognition the same day. The Declaration of Principles on Interim

Self-Government Arrangements was signed three days later by the PLO, Israel, the United States, and Russia. The Oslo Accords allowed for a Palestinian Authority and called for Israeli withdrawal from the West Bank and Gaza. Permanent agreement was to be concluded within five years.

Some progress followed while the Labor Party was in power before this round ran its course. Jordan and Israel signed a peace treaty on 26 October 1994. Yitzhak Rabin was assassinated on 13 July 1995 by a right-wing radical over the Oslo Accords. He was followed by Shimon Perez. Another interim agreement between Israel and Palestinians was reached on 28 September 1995.

After the April 1996 flare-up, Likud's Benjamin Netanyahu took office on 18 June 1996 and soon expanded settlements in the occupied territories over Clinton's objections. The Wye Agreement was signed 23 October 1998 but was soon suspended by Israel. Labor's Ehud Barak took office on 17 May 1999. By then, progress appeared stalled. Negotiations in July 2000 failed.

Terrorism. Islamic terrorism was on the upswing. The World Trade Center was attacked with a truck bomb on 26 February 1993. Another truck bomb exploded in front of an American facility in Riyadh on 13 November 1995. And another truck bomb was used to attack the Khobar Towers apartment complex in Dhahran. The U.S. embassies in Nairobi, Kenya, and Dar es Salaam, Tanzania, were attacked by car bombs on 7 August 1998. Just prior to the 2000 election, the USS *Cole* was attacked on 12 October at Aden, Yemen. The White House was informed that Osama bin Laden was planning attacks on the United States in a memorandum from the DCI's counterterrorism center entitled, "Bin Laden Preparing to Hijack U.S. Aircraft and Other Attacks," dated 4 December 1998.

In many cases, the response to terrorist attacks was after-the-fact investigation and prosecution. Investigations were hampered by less than forthcoming cooperation from Saudi Arabia and Yemen, but the Saudi monarchy was beginning to see itself as a target for Islamic terrorism. The embassy bombings in East Africa, in contrast, resulted in cruise missile attacks on Afghanistan and Sudan in a nearly successful attempt to kill bin Laden on 20 August 1998.

Clinton's response to terrorism was made an issue in the 2000 presidential campaign and again after 9/11. His preventive closure of

Pennsylvania Avenue at the White House after the 19 April 1995 Oklahoma City bombing was called "hysteria" by Republican opponents. The Bush campaign criticized the after-the-fact law enforcement actions as being too little, too late. The cruise missile attacks on Osama bin Laden were dismissed as a diversion from the Monica Lewinski scandal.

Southwest Asia. Clinton implemented a major policy shift in Southwest Asia. Up to and through the Bush 41 administration, the United States balanced between Iran and Iraq. The Iranian Revolution severed U.S.-Iran relations, and economic sanctions remained in place. The Iran-Iraq War weakened both, and the Gulf War weakened Iraq further. Iran backed Hezbollah, the spoiler in attempts to address Israeli-Palestinian issues, and Iran was linked to the Khobar Towers bombing. Clinton announced a dual containment policy toward Iran and Iraq, and he reiterated Bush 41's offer to open dialogue without preconditions.

Critique

In the end, the administration lacked a strategy to guide the use of force. Its employment policy, instead of following a strategy, followed a *constructivist path of ad hoc responses*. Clinton's second national security advisor, Sandy Berger, said "grand strategies were after-the-fact rationales developed to explain successful ad hoc decisions."[38] The Clinton administration's strategy made demands on military force structure not substantially greater than that required to underwrite selective engagement. But rather than forces standing at the ready under selective engagement, the force was divided, deployed, and employed simultaneously in multiple theaters.

A major initiative was attempted in force development policy. The administration conducted a *Bottom-Up Review* that began with multiple post–Cold War scenarios to derive the necessary force structure, bottom-up rather than the top-down budget-driven process alleged of Bush's Base Force review. It, too, failed to arrest the free fall of forces. Following Bush's 20 percent end strength reduction over four years, Clinton managed another 19 percent reduction in eight.

One significant driver of force structure was the previously described reconnaissance strike complex for major theater war in Southwest Asia and elsewhere. A land- and sea-based air force was proposed as the U.S.

contribution to a major theater war on the Korean Peninsula. A forward-deployed naval expeditionary force was required for prosecution of the many small-scale contingencies requiring American attention. Rather than a separate force oriented on small-scale contingencies (including peace operations), the reconnaissance strike complex is to be divided, dispersed, and employed until major theater war demands its reconstitution—a risky proposition at best.

The eight years of the Clinton administration reversed the weakening of the economic instrument but continued the decline of the military. The economy had recovered, the budget was balanced, and a budget surplus was handed to the next administration. Positive economic conditions improved the U.S. power over opinion at home and abroad. The expansion of NATO into eastern Europe was seen as threatening to Russia but was welcomed by the former Soviet states who received the security guarantee; U.S. commitments expanded without benefit. The intervention into the disintegrating Yugoslavia was seen as heavy-handed by NATO allies and added to residual overseas military commitments. The military instrument was clearly overextended.

George W. Bush, 2001–9

In the language of selective engagement, the 2000 Bush campaign argued against the Clinton strategy—specifically against "misuse" of the military for *nation building*. After 11 September 2001, the administration quickly went from one end of the strategic spectrum to the other and adopted a strategy of hegemonic primacy, and then just as quickly moved beyond primacy. The overwhelming international support for the United States reversed as quickly. The predictions of those who argued against the primacy strategy came to pass. The extraordinary optempo of the Clinton administration was accelerated and the evidence of military overextension was pronounced.

The Bush campaign's national security strategy was quickly discarded after the 9/11 attacks. A security focus on the rogue states of Iraq, Iran, and North Korea—the axis of evil—however, remained. Associated with presidential campaigns, *Foreign Affairs* provides space for each campaign to put forward its candidate's view of foreign affairs and national security. Condoleezza Rice wrote for the Bush campaign,[39] and a comparison with the Bush administration's first national security strategy document is in order. During the campaign, Rice articulated a lack of urgency with respect to these three rogue states by saying that "they were living on borrowed time" and "there need be no sense of panic about them."[40] She further communicated a veiled threat of nuclear retaliation if any of them employed (not acquired) weapons of mass destruction.

She went on to say that U.S. intervention in "'humanitarian' crises should be, at best, exceedingly rare." Rice reversed the Clinton position and invoked the principal of noninterference by saying that frequent involvement in humanitarian crises through the UN will communicate to great powers that the United States "has decided to enforce the notion of 'limited sovereignty' worldwide in the name of humanitarianism." She further hinted at the unilateralism of primacy and selective engagement by suggesting that by showing too great a reliance on the United Nations we are "implying that we will do so even when our vital interests are involved." Limits were put on what constituted vital interests. An "overly broad definition of America's national interest is bound to backfire as others arrogate the same authority to themselves." Continuing to speak from selective engagement, Rice favored the use of the military to deter and fight major conflicts rather than for nation building. "America's military is the only one capable of this deterrence function, and it must not be stretched or diverted into areas that weaken these broader responsibilities."[41]

The 2002 national security strategy document was delivered several months late.[42] In contrast to the campaign's strategy, the document contains a great deal of language reminiscent of Wilsonian internationalism and the Carter administration's human rights agenda. "American values are universal," Rice wrote.

> The U.S. national security strategy will be based on a distinctly American internationalism that reflects the union of our values and our national interests. The aim of this strategy is to help make the world not just safer but better.[43]

The national security strategy document also contains language common to cooperative security and primacy emphasizing proliferation of WMD. Overall, the Bush strategy document is dominated by the language of primacy. The strategy takes an undifferentiated view of terrorism:

The enemy is terrorism—premeditated, politically motivated violence perpetrated against innocents. We make no distinction between terrorists and those who knowingly harbor or provide aid to them. [T]errorism will be viewed in the same light as slavery, piracy, or genocide.[44]

The strategy employs the language of the system of states to deal with the nonstate threat by speaking of campaigns "to localize the threat to a particular state" and to then "ensure the state has the military, law enforcement, political, and financial tools necessary to finish the task."[45] Having campaigned against Clinton's *nation building*, the Bush administration coined the term *capacity building* to refer to the process of providing these tools. Bush's employment policy relies heavily on the military instrument for combat and for nation building. The second national security strategy document of 2006 makes the spread of democracy its central tenet—liberalism.[46]

Review

Arms Control. Early in the administration, on 16 June 2001, President Bush and President Vladimir Putin met in Slovenia for the first time. The two countries were divided over NATO expansion and U.S. plans to deploy missile defenses in Poland and the Czech Republic. On 13 December 2001, the United States gave Russia the required six-month notice to withdraw from Nixon's 1972 ABM treaty, a move opposed by Russia, China, and many U.S. allies. The treaty had been the international basis of stability for almost thirty years. The Strategic Offensive Reductions Treaty (SORT) was signed on 24 May 2002, leading to a reduction from about 6,000 warheads each to no more than 2,200 each by the end of 2012, when the treaty expired.

Attacks of 9/11. Despite the terrorism emphasis given by Sandy Berger and Richard Clarke to the Bush transition team, coupled with an "anything but Clinton" attitude, the administration was unprepared for the events of 9/11. A month before the attacks, during the 6 August 2001 presidential daily briefing, the CIA briefer told the president that bin Laden was determined to strike the United States; the president responded, "All right. You've covered your ass, now."[47] When the attacks came, subsequent employment policy bore no resemblance to the declared strategy of the political campaign. International support for the United States peaked after the 9/11 attacks. Public support for presidential action peaked as well. On 18 September, Congress provided the president almost carte blanche with the "Authorization for the Use of Force Against Terrorists," and the president signed it into law the same day.

Terrorism. During a 13 March 2002 White House press conference, the president was questioned about what appeared to be a shift in emphasis away from Osama bin Laden and responded, "I am truly not that concerned about him." The wars in Afghanistan and Iraq had taken center stage.

Afghanistan. No UN authorization was requested for operations against Afghanistan under the premise that they were an act of self-defense. The president acted under the authority provided by Congress a week after the 9/11 attacks. Objectives included dismantling al-Qaeda, overthrowing the Taliban, and installing a democratic government. A coalition was formed by the United States, Great Britain, and the Northern Alliance. After the Taliban refused to turn over Osama bin Laden, the coalition began air strikes on 7 October 2001. With considerable skill and rapidity, a small and sophisticated contingent of CIA paramilitary, special operations, and local forces initiated actions against Kabul, Mazari Sherif, Kandahar, and Tora Bora. Operatives from the CIA's Special Activities Division (SAD) had been establishing relationships with the Northern Alliance since the Clinton administration. The Taliban abandoned Kabul on 13 November, and Kandahar fell on 7 December. Bin Laden escaped from Tora Bora.

The U.S. military hierarchy initially recommended a larger invasion force but was overruled by Defense Secretary Rumsfeld, who held to a new economy-of-force approach. Bin Laden's escape was attributed to the smaller footprint. The UN authorized establishment of the International Security Assistance Force on 20 December 2001, and the mission transitioned to NATO in 2003. The U.S. mission was planned for termination in 2014.

Iraq. The Bush administration invested months attempting to elicit domestic and international support for a war on Iraq to "disarm Iraq, to free its people and to defend the world from grave danger." The domestic effort succeeded, but the UN rejected the U.S. request for authorization. The U.S. Congress provided the "Authorization for Use of Military Force

Against Iraq Resolution of 2002," enacted 16 October 2003.[48] Failing to gain UN authorization, the administration cited past UN resolutions associated with Iraqi disarmament and as an act of defense due to a claimed linkage between Iraq and al-Qaeda. Large antiwar demonstrations were held around the world.

The coalition invasion began on 19 March 2003. As with Afghanistan, the military hierarchy's initial war plan was overruled by Rumsfeld in favor of a smaller invasion force. As in Afghanistan, CIA SAD and U.S. special operations forces initiated operations, but the majority of activity was conducted by conventional forces. The defeat of Iraqi military forces was quick and impressive, but the force was insufficient to establish security after the military victory. The coalition was unprepared for follow-on security and years of nation building. On 14 December 2008, the president signed an agreement to remove all U.S. forces by the end of 2011, leaving withdrawal to the next administration.

Caucasus. Since the dissolution of the Soviet Union, the provinces of South Ossetia and Abkhasia had been geographically part of Georgia but politically largely independent and backed by Russian forces. Mutual provocations led Georgia to intervene and Russia to counter. With no interests involved, Bush declined direct military intervention, responding instead with declaratory support for Georgia, some humanitarian aid provided by navy destroyer, and airlifting Georgian troops back from Iraq. The French brokered an end to the Russo-Georgian War with Russia, effectively annexing 20 percent of Georgia.

Southern Lebanon. Hezbollah again engaged Israel from southern Lebanon in the summer of 2006. Hezbollah launched missiles as a diversion for a ground attack, capturing two Israeli soldiers to exchange for four Lebanese soldiers whom Israel had previously agreed to return. Israel responded with disproportionate force beginning with artillery and air strikes. The Beirut airport was attacked and closed, seaports blockaded, and the main road to Damascus closed. Hezbollah missile-launching sites were destroyed. IDF ground forces crossed over into southern Lebanon on 23 July 2006. Hezbollah launched four thousand rockets into Israel, many into population centers. Cluster munitions were used in Lebanon and remained as unexploded ordnance. Civilian casualties and displacements were significant. Both sides suffered; both sides claimed victory.

Unable to control southern Lebanon, the Lebanese government pleaded to the UN Security Council for a cease-fire. Secretary Rice and U.S. ambassador to the UN, John Bolton, unequivocally rejected the cease-fire. Instead, the U.S. sold jet fuel to support Israeli operations.

Relations with Israel. U.S.-Israeli relations were mixed under the Bush administration. Prime Minister Ariel Sharon (Likud) accused the United States of appeasing Palestinians to curry Arab support for the war on terrorism on 4 October 2001. Bush objected but received no retraction. According to some, Bush waffled in his demands on the Palestinians and Israelis.[49] Bush expressed disapproval of settlements but didn't follow through on implementation. The United States extended loan guarantees to Israel during its 2003 economic slump. Some small evacuations in Gaza and the West Bank were completed on 23 August 2005. Secretary Rice named no special envoy to work Arab-Israeli issues. During the 2006 Israel-Lebanon Conflict, the administration provided material support to Israel but refused to intervene diplomatically or militarily.

Critique

After campaigning on a selective engagement strategy, Bush adopted primacy and then went beyond primacy by invading Iraq and losing the appearance of a benign hegemon. The predictions of primacy's opponents in the 1990s strategy debate, as presented in Posen and Ross, came to pass.

The United States national debt historically hovered around 35 percent of GDP with the exception of World War II, when it peaked at 100 percent. Bush inherited a *budget surplus* of 1 percent of GDP from Clinton, and there was talk of paying off the national debt. At the end of the Bush administration, the *budget deficit* had reached 3.2 percent of GDP, and per-capita public debt rose by 50 percent. The chief contributors were the 2001 and 2003 tax cuts, which reduced revenues compounded by increased expenditures on the unfunded Medicare prescription-drug benefit and the wars in Iraq and Afghanistan. "The eight years of the Bush administration saw the largest fiscal erosion in American history," write Roger Altman and Richard Haass.[50]

Carr's military power, economic power, and power over opinion were all in decline. Bush accelerated the use of force, already high under Clinton, resulting in an increasingly overextended military. The administration left office with U.S. forces committed to lengthy wars in Iraq and Afghanistan. The events of 9/11 created a great deal of international support, strengthening the power over opinion, but the invasion of Iraq in defiance of the UN quickly reversed that. In much of the world, the United States was seen more as rogue state than as benign hegemon. Bush scores high marks, even from his opponents, in regards to U.S. policy in Africa. Large-scale deficit spending greatly weakened the economic instrument, again making the economy the dominant campaign issue and further eroding power over opinion.

Barack H. Obama, 2009–17

Barack Obama entered office constrained by serious economic decline. Just as Clinton campaigned on the weakened economy at the end of the Reagan-Bush era, Obama campaigned on the weakened economy at the end of the Bush 43 administration. At the beginning of the campaign, however, national security and foreign policy were important issues. Obama opposed the war in Iraq from the beginning. Like many, he considered it a distraction from the war against al-Qaeda and associated movements (AQAM). As the public's opinion soured on the war in Iraq, Obama's position and logic appealed to an increasing portion of the electorate. Of the Democratic presidential candidates, only Senator Joe Biden could claim any meaningful foreign policy experience by virtue of his long service on the Senate Foreign Affairs Committee.

International opinion opposed to Bush-Cheney policies shifted quickly and positively with Obama's election, but it deepened the growing gap in American politics. A speech given in Egypt early in the administration was well received and improved optimism in the Arab world, but it was viewed negatively by U.S. hard-liners. In a preemptive act of its own, the Norwegian Nobel Committee awarded Obama the Peace Prize in his first year (nominations were due during Obama's second week in office).

The war in Iraq that Obama campaigned against was brought to closure. Obama announced the end of combat operations in Iraq on 31 August 2010, and force withdrawal was complete on 18 December 2011. Emphasis and troops were shifted to Afghanistan, and a timetable set for withdrawal there as well.

Nation building had become the primary way in the ends, ways, and means of strategy in Iraq and Afghanistan. Under Obama, emphasis shifted from Iraq to Afghanistan, and the way of strategy shifted away from nation building and toward a manhunt increasingly carried out by unmanned drones and by small special operations raids. Somali pirates were dealt with personally rather than by attempting nation building in Somalia. Terrorist attacks were thwarted by law enforcement and intelligence operations.[51] Osama bin Laden was killed on 2 May 2011 in Abbottabad, Pakistan, by special operations forces aided by CIA operatives. Drones attacked al-Qaeda targets in Yemen.

Review

Arms Control. Obama, like Bush 41 and Clinton, extended an invitation to open dialogue with Iran, but Iran rejected the offer. The offer was seen as weakness by U.S. hard-liners, but the offer and rejection garnered additional support from European powers in imposing increasingly stringent economic sanctions. Iran's nuclear ambitions caused increased tension in the region, including Arab states and especially Israel. The New START agreement was signed on 8 April 2010 following Bush 43's SORT agreement and reducing nuclear inventories by half.

Arab Spring. Internally generated political movements for responsive government—referred to as the Arab Spring—spontaneously erupted in Tunisia, Egypt, Libya, Syria, Jordan, Bahrain, and Morocco.[52] In general, the Obama administration responded with diplomatic, economic, and informational rather than military instruments. Effects on power over opinion were mixed. Some in the Arab world hoped for stronger support against Middle Eastern and North African autocrats, and their opinion of Obama began to decline. Others, many youthful activists who wanted to claim their own destiny and conduct their own political revolution, were happy that the United States did not intervene further. The administration's approach was tailored to each country, and critics in the United States claimed the strategy was confused and inconsistent.

In the case of Libya, the administration responded with limited military strikes from offshore, without ground forces, with UN authorization, without U.S. congressional authorization, and through NATO. The French and British urged intervention. Burden sharing followed from stakeholder analysis. Libyans had the most at stake, followed by European states along the Mediterranean with large North African populations. Libyans carried the main effort themselves. The French led in enforcing a no-fly zone and air interdiction (Qatar provided its entire complement of French Mirage fighters, and its transport fleet ferried supplies and weapons to the rebels). The United States provided what only the United States could provide, precision guided munitions and the intelligence, surveillance, and reconnaissance assets necessary for targeting. Protected from Kaddafi's air forces and mechanized land forces, Libyans on the ground won their own hard-earned freedom. Kaddafi was killed on 20 October 2011. The tipping action cost the U.S. $1 billion and no American lives. But, as is often the case following forced regime change, there was no one to govern.

Hawks like Senator John McCain argued that the United States should have responded earlier and with more direct intervention, criticizing the administration's "leading from behind" approach. Other critics on the right, including Newt Gingrich and Michelle Bachman, claimed that the United States had no interests in Libya and should not have intervened at all.

In the case of Syria, the administration declined direct military intervention and, seeing no partners capable of achieving a military and political solution, chose humanitarian and nonlethal assistance. McCain argued for intense bombing of Syrian military installations.

Relations with Israel. Relations were strained between the Obama and Netanyahu administrations. Obama made an Arab-Israeli peace settlement a high priority upon entering office. Under pressure, Netanyahu agreed on 14 July 2009 to enter into negotiations over a Palestinian state. A ten-month freeze on housing settlements was agreed to but with exceptions, including settlements in East Jerusalem, a deal breaker for Palestinians. Obama secretly authorized the sale of bunker-busting bombs in 2009 that gave Israel the ability to destroy Iranian nuclear facilities deeper underground, thus delaying Israel's decision to strike and buying the United States more time to resolve the issue diplomatically.

Vice President Biden traveled to assure Israelis of U.S. commitment to Israeli security and to restart peace talks. On 9 March 2010, Biden spoke of "absolute, total, unvarnished commitment to Israel's security."[53] Within a few hours, Israel announced its intentions to restart construction of 1,600 new homes in East Jerusalem. Secretary of State Hillary Clinton denounced the decision as "deeply negative." The president instructed the secretary to issue an ultimatum to Netanyahu. Obama and Netanyahu had a tense meeting in the White House on 26 March 2010. On 19 May 2011 Obama called for a return to pre-1967 borders and land exchanges. On 2 October, Secretary of Defense Leon Panetta cited Israeli policies as the reason for its increasing isolation in the region. He argued that Israel needed to begin negotiations with Palestinians and improve relations with Turkey and the new Egypt.

Ukraine. Viktor Yuschenko, president of the Ukraine (2005–10), vowed to eject Russia's Black Sea Fleet from Crimea. His successor, Victor Yanukovych (2010–14), signed an agreement to extend Russia's lease until 2042. The country was divided between those who wanted greater movement toward the European Union and those who wanted strong relations with Russia. Yanukovych was ousted, and Russia moved to annex the Crimea. With Russian interests high and U.S. interests few, Obama, like Bush 43, declined direct military intervention in the region and responded with economic sanctions focused on Russian plutocrats.

Iraq Redux. Arguments for overthrowing Saddam Hussein were made and rejected during the Reagan and Bush 41 administrations. Counterarguments always included the prediction that without an autocratic ruler, the country would disintegrate into warring Sunni, Shia, and Kurdish factions. And the decades-long practice of balancing between Iran and Iraq no longer being an option, the region would be destabilized favoring Iran, long considered the biggest threat by Gulf States. Predictions came to pass as Sunni militias formed in Syria quickly captured large swaths of Iraq. The Iraqi army built over a decade of U.S. capacity building crumbled in the face of a small but violent force.

Prime Minister Nouri al-Maliki failed to form an inclusive government. Seeing no military action that would lead to a political solution in Iraq, the Obama administration initially declined direct military intervention. Marines were sent to bolster security in the Baghdad embassy; four U.S. warships were sent to the Persian Gulf, including an aircraft carrier, missile-carrying cruiser and destroyer, and an amphibious ship with five hundred marines; and special operations forces were sent to assess, train, and advise the weakened Iraqi army. Iran, Jordan, Lebanon, and Turkey had significant interests at risk.

Shift to Asia/Pacific. The administration announced a shift in foreign policy emphasis to the Asia/Pacific and away from the Middle East and Europe. In force deployment policy, the administration made small, incremental changes similar to those of Clinton and Bush. A small number of Navy ships were re-ported and a small Marine Corps unit was redeployed to northern Australia.

Critique

Although collective or cooperative security is the established Democratic strategy, the Obama strategy most closely resembles selective engagement, and even more closely the offshore balancing or tipping variant. The predictions of selective engagement's opponents in the 1990s strategy debate, as presented in Posen and Ross, came to pass.

The Obama strategy implemented multiple shifts from the previous administration. The first and most obvious was a shift in emphasis and forces from Iraq to Afghanistan. The war in Iraq was brought to closure. Following a temporary surge in Afghanistan, forces began a drawdown and withdrawal. The less obvious shift was away from invasion, forced regime change, and nation building under fire and toward a manhunt conducted by intelligence operations and *direct action* by special operations forces. The effects on military power, economic power, and power over opinion were mixed.

Protectorates responded more strongly to the offshore balancing employment policy than to the Asia/Pacific declaratory policy. The developing burden-sharing arrangement caused Japan to shoulder its defensive burden more directly and signaled European allies to do the same.

The drawdown of forces from Iraq and Afghanistan allowed the force to recuperate and strengthen after extreme use under Clinton and Bush, but recovery takes time. Fiscal concerns defer recapitalization. The conventional force began a drawdown in the administration's second term, but special operations forces continued operating at high tempo, and their budgets continued to grow. In the second term, special operations forces shifted emphasis from direct action to training and relationship building in countries threatened by extremism.

Economic power continued in a weakened state. While annual budget deficits declined, the national debt continued to grow. Mainstream economists argued for deficit spending on infrastructure investments in a deep recession that will pay dividends in the future, but that spending will inarguably increase the current debt. The opposition party insists instead on fiscal discipline that it was unwilling to impose on presidents of its own party and for a return to policies that produced the Great Recession.

The power over opinion abroad improved considerably after the Bush years, but things slowly degenerated. As the world watched the crippling partisan stalemate in Washington, power over opinion, at home and abroad, declined.

Subordinate Strategies

Threats to American national security interests are far broader than those posed by AQAM, but those threats have played a prominent role in national security policy post 9/11. The al-Qaeda strategy and the U.S. counterstrategy deserve attention.

Al-Qaeda's Strategy to the Year 2020

Al-Qaeda's strategy contains elements of both classic insurgency strategy and cost-imposing strategies. Insurgents commit terrorist acts in the hope of provoking an exaggerated response that will drive the target civilian audience to the insurgents' side in a competition for the hearts and minds of the public. Cost-imposing strategies hope to provoke exhaustive responses over time.

Insurgencies are a competition for the right to govern. Whether the established government is corrupt, tyrannical, or foreign, insurgents consider it illegitimate. Insurgents often have separate political and military wings. The political wing may participate in the legitimate political process, may develop a shadow government in waiting, and may provide social services to attract the contested population. The military wing commits terrorist acts to demonstrate that the established government cannot provide security and hopes to provoke an exaggerated response from the established government that will drive the target civilian audience to their side. But if not properly calibrated, the focus and scale of attacks may have the opposite effect. As the insurgency advances, the military wing may field militias to directly oppose government forces. The eventual victory will be ushered in by a *General Uprising* of the masses in Maoist doctrine, or a *Grand March* of the *umma* in ibn Taymiyya's teachings.

Ayman al-Zawahiri, al-Qaeda's intellectual lead, formulated its grand strategy. Abdel Bari Atwan claims that al-Zawahiri relied heavily on Paul Kennedy's *The Rise and Fall of the Great Powers*. According to Kennedy, past empires fell because of the increasing costs of internal security, the increasing costs of military operations, and the growing strength of economic competitors. Al-Qaeda's strategy followed.[54]

In 1996, Osama bin Laden declared war on Americans occupying the Arabian Peninsula, the land of two holy mosques.[55] Bin Laden made explicit his casus belli. Former CIA station chief for al-Qaeda, Michael Scheuer, lists six U.S. policies considered by bin Laden to be anti-Islamic:

- U.S. support for Israel that keeps Palestinians in the Israelis' thrall.
- U.S. and other Western troops on the Arabian Peninsula.
- U.S. occupation of Iraq and Afghanistan.
- U.S. support for Russia, India, and China against their Muslim militants.
- U.S. pressure on Arab energy producers to keep oil prices low.
- U.S. support for apostate, corrupt, and tyrannical Muslim governments.[56]

The objective of al-Qaeda's strategy is the establishment of a regional and then worldwide caliphate. The center of gravity, the point at which all effort is directed, is the U.S. economy. Suicide bombers, irregular military forces, and the Internet are the primary means of the strategy. "Al-Qaeda wishes to foment a 'clash of civilizations,' with Christian fundamentalism opposed to Islamic fundamentalism," building on the crusading spirits of both.[57]

By committing terrorist attacks against the United States (e.g., 9/11, embassy bombings, USS *Cole*), al-Qaeda hoped to draw the United States into invading a Muslim country (e.g., Somalia, Afghanistan, Iraq) where AQAM had the advantage in a war of attrition. The presence of Western forces will have the desired effect of enraging the *umma*. Local resistance will form, outside jihadists will be attracted, and neighboring Muslim states will be drawn in.

By committing terrorist acts against other Western powers (e.g., Madrid, London), al-Qaeda will drive a wedge between the United States and its allies. An increasingly isolated United States will bear the costs of war alone.

Violence is accompanied by two-pronged explanatory rhetoric aimed at people rather than governments. All al-Qaeda and Western actions are explained through the lens of the widely held Arab narrative. The narrative includes the Crusades and the heroic, unifying figure of Saladin, the *Great Betrayal* following World War I, the establishment of Israel after World War II, and the long humiliation of colonialism. Rhetoric is also aimed at Western publics explaining that their own governments' actions brought violence to their homeland.

Actions are to be taken in parallel with terrorist acts to transform al-Qaeda from an organization into a movement. Information technology, including the Internet, will be exploited to promulgate an ideology, guiding principles, and a common set of operating procedures. With ideology and procedures widely distributed, global operations can continue without centralized command from al-Qaeda.

Economic collapse is the inevitable outcome of an increasingly isolated United States engaged in too many wars of attrition. Collapse of the worldwide economic system and global political instability will quickly follow and create the conditions for the *Grand March*, enabling establishment of the caliphate.

The events of 9/11 led the United States to invade Afghanistan and deny the movement's primary sanctuary. Al-Qaeda's operations were severely disrupted. But the U.S. invasion of Iraq played into the movement's hands. Arabs had been disadvantaged in Pashtu-speaking Afghanistan by language and geography. Arabic speakers in states neighboring Iraq had family, clan, and tribal relations that allowed easy movement throughout the region. Jihadists flowed easily and rapidly into Iraq to oppose the presence of foreign powers. Iraq has far more significance to Arabs than Afghanistan. Iraq, the Land of Two Rivers, has more holy places than Saudi Arabia, the Land of Two Holy Mosques. And Baghdad has extraordinary historical significance to Arabs and Muslims as the home of the Abbasid Caliphate during the Islamic Golden Age (750–1258).

Al-Qaeda's strategy to induce overextension of the United States bore fruit after 9/11. China and India provide the economic competition.

Terrorist acts committed against the U.S. homeland increased the costs of internal security. Commitment of U.S. military forces to Iraq, Afghanistan, and elsewhere entail extraordinary costs for military operations abroad.

U.S. Counterstrategy

The ends of the U.S. counterstrategy include reducing the likelihood of attack, the severity of attack, and the number of people ready to take up arms against the United States. There are a variety of ways in a strategy to counter al-Qaeda, including invasion and major combat operations, regime change, proactive and reactive law enforcement, intelligence operations, nation building, and strikes and raids. The various strategies—distinguished by their emphasis on ways—must be evaluated according to their blowback, sustainability, the need for international cooperation, and the need for interagency cooperation requiring the reorganization of government. The ways chosen create varying degrees of opposition and additional means are required to overcome additional opposition.

Unlike the Cold War, there is no agreement on the nature of the current conflict environment or on the strategic response.[58] Counterterrorist and counterterrorism conceptions are possible. A *counterterrorist* conception is more of a manhunt than a war. It focuses on the individuals who plan and execute terrorist acts. Overt military strikes and raids, in and out, are used when appropriate. A *counterterrorism* conception, as implemented under the label of the "global war on terrorism," involves protracted war beginning with regime change and followed by nation building under hostile conditions.

Both conceptions beg for international support, but mobilizing public support for information sharing and cooperative law enforcement under a counterterrorist conception is less demanding and easier to sustain over time than is support for continuous war, regime change, and nation building under a counterterrorism conception. Nation building, in turn, makes greater demands for orchestrating all instruments of power.

Periodic, discrete strike operations, whether conducted by air or land forces, are more sustainable than invasion, occupation, and nation building. Certainly they are more sustainable economically. They also conserve military forces for application when only military power will do. It is easier to maintain public consensus to commitment for periodic strikes than for continual war. The continuous application of all instruments of power, supported by periodic strikes and raids, is sustainable indefinitely.

States or Terrorists? According to Richard Clarke, former national security advisor on terrorism, the principal failure of U.S. decision makers was to direct its efforts not at al-Qaeda but at its state sponsor, protector, or enabler. Specifically, a primary way in extant U.S. strategy is state-centric, leading to the invasion of Afghanistan and Iraq followed by nation building amid insurgency. Since the Obama administration, the United States appears to have effected a shift in the ways of its strategy. Less emphasis is given to wars and nation building, and more emphasis is given to a manhunt for the al-Qaeda leadership.

Religion or policy? According to Mike Scheurer, chief of the CIA's former bin Laden task force, the principal failure of U.S. decision makers is viewing the source of the conflict in terms of fundamentalist religious beliefs rather than as a reaction to U.S. policies toward the region: "They hate us for what we do, not for who we are." The nature of twentieth-century terrorism—largely the product of leftist, secular organizations including the Palestinian Liberation Front and Popular Front for the Liberation of Palestine—supports Scheurer's conclusion. And content analysis of bin Laden's public statements also supports the conclusion that AQAM are responding to U.S. policies often cast in the language of religion.[59]

Blowback. Forced regime change followed by occupation and periodic strikes and raids both will produce blowback from the affected populations. Both are an offense to nationalism. Periodic strikes, raids, and punitive expeditions should produce less blowback than occupation.

Summary of Post–Cold War Strategies

Like their Cold War predecessors, post–Cold War administrations had varied national security strategies. But unlike Cold War administrations that retained a core strategy of containment, post–Cold War administrations showed no stability in strategy. Clinton and Bush 43, however, did share a strong tendency to military intervention and nation building as a way in the ends-ways-means strategic linkage.

More like Eisenhower and Nixon, the elder Bush held to a consistent strategic conception and responded to crises from that conception. More like Kennedy and Johnson, Clinton responded to crises on an ad hoc basis rather than from a consistent strategic conception. And more like Truman and Carter, the younger Bush professed one strategy and immediately abandoned it when a crisis emerged. Arguably, Truman, Carter, and Bush 43 did not believe in their declared strategies, instead preferring ad hoc to strategic response. Like Eisenhower and Nixon, Obama is winding down inherited wars that had lost public support and adopting a balancing strategy reminiscent of the Nixon Doctrine. An emphasis in the ways of strategy has shifted from nation building to strikes and raids.

The public often rallies around presidential action initially, but opposition generally grows over time. A consensus to commitment is not required when operations are completed within the public's tacit grant of support. Nation building takes considerably more time. Bush 41 chose to build a consensus to go to war but not to long-term commitment. He chose instead military operations that could be completed quickly. Like Truman and Johnson, Bush 43 chose not to build a consensus to commitment for his wars.

Throughout the Cold War, there were observable swings in grand strategy, but there remained a strong central tendency around containment. Exhibiting no central tendencies, there have been abrupt, discontinuous changes in post–Cold War strategies. The predictions of the pre-9/11 debate against primacy are showing true. There is no sign of settling on a stable strategy. The public debate on the wars in Iraq and Afghanistan has faded, and the public's attention shifts from crisis to crisis, but no debate on national security strategy is apparent.

Relations with Israel and Arab states are the Gordian Knot of U.S. national security post Cold War. During the Cold War, having a strong and reliable European ally astride the strategic Suez Canal and a strong intelligence source on the USSR made Israel a valuable ally. But the Cold War is gone. Today, Iran, China, Russia, and Israel maintain the largest espionage efforts in the United States. Islamic terrorism is driven by U.S. and Israeli policies, while the United States and the industrialized West are dependent on Arab oil. The rising economies of China and India stake an additional claim on the same oil.

Regardless, there can be no public debate about U.S.-Israel relations. Israelis vigorously debate, and even protest, their own government's policies, and U.S. citizens are willing to debate Israeli policies on a case by case basis. But American politicians must all profess unquestioned support for Israel or face condemnation by right-wing Christians on religious grounds and powerful pro-Israel lobbyists on grounds of survival. Discussion of Cuba policy is similarly off-limits. Self-examination of U.S. policies is also a political taboo. Philosophical conservatism has long elevated the principle of personal responsibility, but political conservatism labels those willing to examine U.S. polices as the "blame America first" crowd. Change is unlikely in this regard.

Achieving a political consensus on strategy and commitment to consensus will be accomplished only through open debate. No individual or small group has the answer. A strategy developed in secrecy will eventually be exposed and result in loss of public support. Close-hold decision making relies on the wisdom of the few rather than the wisdom of the many. Security achieved at the expense of civil liberties damages public support in the long term.[60]

For Consideration

What the national security strategies presented in this chapter have in common is a logic of when to use military force. According to Sharon Caudle's studies of international trends in national security strategies, other countries around the world, including our traditional allies and our competitors, are redefining their vital interests in ways that defy military solution. Allies and competitors have shifted the emphasis of their national security strategies to economic interests and the welfare of their citizenry, while the United States' strategic orientation emphasizes physical threats that can be countered with military force.[61] The very meaning of national security is in question, enabled by the end of the Cold War, challenged by the phenomenon of globalization, and brought into sharp focus by the global economic downturn.

National security is in jeopardy when vital interests are threatened. Vital interests, according to the international trend, include territorial sovereignty, financial security, ecological security, physical safety, and social and political stability. The persistent classic threats include interstate warfare resulting from deteriorating international conditions and international terrorism. Emerging threats rising in prominence include immigration flows that threaten existing social cohesion, large-scale natural disasters potentially exacerbated by climate change, global pandemics (natural or deliberate), and the threat of attacks through cyberspace on critical infrastructure and financial systems.

The new list of threats to interests requires a whole-of-government response, and even a whole-of-society response including industry and nongovernmental elements of civil society. The trend includes a merger of strategies for internal and external action as opposed to separate national security and homeland security strategies. And, accordingly, the strategies affect traditional military establishments as well as organizations oriented on internal security and safety.

Expanding on Caudle's case studies, Leslie Gelb compares U.S. to international adaptation post Cold War:

> Most nations today beat their foreign policy drums largely to economic rhythms, but less so the United States. Most nations define their interests largely in economic terms that deal mostly in economic power, but less so the United States. Most nations have adjusted their national security strategies to focus on economic security, but less so the United States. Washington still principally thinks of its security in traditional military terms and responds to threats with military means.[62]

A national security strategy oriented on economic strength would reinvigorate the U.S. economy by improving public schools and critical infrastructure, reducing public and foreign debt, creating jobs, and reducing dependence on foreign oil:

> Leaders throughout history have pursued economic strength as the foundation of state power, but power itself was equated with military might. Today, the prevailing idea is that economic strength should be applied primarily toward achieving economic—not military—ends.
>
> Money is what counts most, so most nations limit their spending on standing armies and avoid military interventions. What preoccupies most leaders is trade, investment, access to markets, exchange rates, additional riches for the rich, and a better life for the rest.

To counter terrorist threats, rather than waging costly protracted wars as in Iraq and Afghanistan, the United States should be

improving police and intelligence operations at home and abroad, hunting terrorists in rogue states with air and missile strikes and commando raids, helping friendly states battle terrorists, and greatly upgrading homeland security.[63]

In the more narrow Cold War tradition, national security was assured with military means, and all military matters were matters of national security. Throughout the Cold War, Congress paid considerable legislative attention to shortening, clarifying, and strengthening the chain of command from the president to the combatant commander in the field. Similar attention was given to legislating and relying on processes internal to a single department—the Defense Department. The processes of the president's National Security Council and Defense Department annually aligned policy priorities and influenced the budgeting cycle that allocates resources to organize, train, and equip military forces for assigned missions. No comparable legislative attention was given to the other departments and agencies.

Formulation of the national security strategy identifies vital interests, threats to those interests, and counters to those threats. Strategy formulation begins the process of setting policy priorities and the annual budget cycle. The budget process allocates resources that build the capabilities necessary to counter threats to vital interests. Significant change in interests and threats are accompanied by changes in the capabilities needed to assure interests against threats. Building new capabilities or rebalancing existing capabilities may take a decade or more. The alternative to a strategy-led process is ad hoc response to crisis amid emotion and media sensationalism by cobbling together capabilities designed for other purposes.

Part 3

National Security Apparatus

7   Instruments of Power

The notion of instruments of national power is an abstraction. Terminology in this domain is not widely agreed upon, but neither is it the subject of contentious debate. In many contexts the named instruments are merely quick jumping-off points on the way to discussing the concrete capabilities of the departments and agencies that house the instruments. In this book, I attempt to develop the idea of instruments a bit more fully before the necessary and inevitable shift to orchestrating the instrumental capacities housed in the departments and agencies—the mechanisms of national power. The perspective developed is not widely held, but it should not be controversial.

Power, in the context of foreign affairs, can be defined as the ability to influence the behavior of others to achieve a desired outcome. And diplomacy projects power, including the potential for war. The seminal work of Edward Carr in 1939 provides a good starting point in discussing the instruments of power.[1]

> Political power in the international sphere may be divided, for purpose of discussion, into three categories: (a) military power, (b) economic power, (c) power over opinion. . . . But power is an indivisible whole; one instrument cannot exist for long in the absence of the others.[2]

Carr's formulation was later supplanted. During the Cold War, the acronym DIME was used as a common shorthand for the diplomatic, informational, military, and economic instruments of national power. By the 1960s the instruments were housed in the State Department, the U.S. Information Agency, the Defense Department, and the U.S. Agency for International Development, respectively. There is no such simple correlation of instrument to agency in the twenty-first century, but the DIME acronym remains in use.[3]

More recently, MIDLIFE—military, informational, diplomatic, law enforcement, intelligence, financial, and economic—has gained some currency, reflecting the greater complexity in the ways and means of pursuing national security in the twenty-first century.[4] Other meaningful lists are too long to be presented here.[5]

Why is it that Carr did not include diplomacy as an instrument of power? One possible extrapolation of Carr's definition of power is that diplomacy is the art of applying the instruments of power rather than a separate instrument itself. The diplomatic instrument is often called the political instrument, and Carr's definition actually defines *political power* as being subdivided into the three instruments. This formulation leaves the image of the diplomat negotiating with friends, enemies, and neutrals backed always by the potential application of American military power, economic power, and power over opinion. And the diplomat may be the traditional Foreign Service Officer from State negotiating with peers representing other states, or it may be a young Marine Corps captain negotiating with a village chief.

> Negotiation is the central task of diplomacy. Negotiation is a search for common ground between parties with disparate interests, objectives, and perspectives.[6]

It is also worth noting that Carr identified power over opinion rather than the power of information. As Carr emphasizes, the three elements of power are indivisible, and none can exist long in the absence of another. The substitution of informational power for the power over opinion was a significant innovation, but it is not at all clear that it was an improvement. How the United States uses its military and economic power communicates volumes and affects domestic and foreign opinion. Positive domestic opinion represents strategic staying power, and negative opinion can bring down a president's policies. Foreign opinion can create either opposition or support for U.S. policies. There is but one message. It is the sum of action and word. Considering the information instrument as a message separate from action creates contradiction, dysfunction, and distrust. Moreover, governments' ability to control information has been in rapid decline.

Some also distinguish between *hard power* and *soft power.*[7] Hard power is the power to *coerce.* That is, what can be compelled by military force or economic sanction or what can be purchased with economic incentives. Soft power is a shorthand for the power to *attract.* Soft power is far closer to Carr's power over opinion than is the information instrument of DIME. Soft power also includes U.S. influence abroad exerted through private commerce and society rather than through direct government effort. Some inaccurately equate hard power to that provided by the military and soft power to that provided by civilian departments and agencies.

And there is talk of *smart power.*[8] But there is nothing smart about power, only the smart *application* of power—the orchestration of all instruments of power. The label is a not-too-veiled slap at the Bush administration's use of military power thought to be other than smart.

Instruments

Each of the instruments is briefly described below. A partial mapping of instrument to agency is begun, but a detailed discussion of the relevant departments and agencies is deferred to subsequent chapters. Some of the more contentious issues related to the instruments are highlighted here.

The Military Instrument

The military instrument includes, but is not limited to, the capabilities present in the armed forces of the United States—the Army, Navy, Marine Corps, and Air Force. It also includes the capability of the Coast Guard when configured for military operations rather than for its other missions including, for example, law enforcement, public safety, and environmental protection. But these are organizations, not instruments. Instead, when discussing instruments, it is more appropriate to look across these organizations at their collective ability to conduct military operations.

One useful taxonomy includes the ability to conduct high-intensity (HIC), mid-intensity (MIC), and low-intensity (LIC) conflict. These are roughly equivalent to strategic nuclear warfare, force-on-force interstate warfare with conventional weapons, and unconventional warfare. Unconventional warfare includes both the ability to promote and to counter insurgency, generally intrastate. Some military operations at the lower end of the conflict spectrum have been called *military operations other than war*. These include peacemaking, peacekeeping, humanitarian assistance, and disaster relief.

Standoff warfare—attacking targets from a safe distance over the horizon with air-delivered ordinance including cruise missiles launched from aircraft, submarine, or surface combatant ship—is the modern equivalent of gunboat diplomacy (or coercive diplomacy) when used in tandem with diplomatic efforts. The same standoff capability can be used alone for punitive strikes or for interdiction, but it is almost always part of a larger diplomatic or military effort.

Not all military operations are conducted by the uniformed services of the Defense Department. The capability of civilian intelligence agencies to conduct paramilitary operations, directly or through surrogates, is properly considered part of the military instrument rather than the intelligence instrument, but that is debatable.

A major issue for the military instrument is *force development*. In the late Cold War era and the decade following, *transformation of the force* was widely discussed across the defense establishment. The more popular notion was of transforming the industrial-age force designed for great-power war into the information-age force designed for great-power war—the *revolution in military affairs*. The less popular notion was of transforming from the industrial-age great-power force to a force for small wars or low-intensity conflict. The Defense Department pursued the equipment-centric revolution in military affairs and failed to provide the field commanders with the types of forces required for the wars actually being waged.

The military has become the default choice of instruments, the first choice, because the other instruments are weak or disdained by some political decision makers. Military operations can represent hard, coercive power, or soft, attractive power, for example, when providing humanitarian assistance. Military operations can be judged on whether they increase or decrease the power over opinion at home and abroad. Using the military instrument consumes resources and weakens the economic instrument, although military force can be used for economic benefit, for example, assuring the free flow of oil and freedom of the seas.

The Information Instrument

The information instrument disseminates and collects information. Narrowly defined, as the term is used here, it is limited to U.S. government efforts to disseminate information to, and collect information on, foreign audiences—public audiences. Government information exchanges with foreign public audiences is often called *public diplomacy.* When addressed to domestic audiences, it is referred to as *public affairs.* And government-to-government exchange, that is, information exchanged through official interstate channels, is discussed separately under the diplomatic instrument.

A central objective is to communicate America's story, its image, to the world. The message is about who we are and what we hope to achieve. The most prominent programs associated with the information instrument are Radio Free Europe, Voice of America, public-access libraries established abroad, and cultural and educational exchange programs.

The information instrument also collects information about the histories, cultures, and attitudes of foreign populations. This puts the information instrument in apparent competition with the intelligence instrument. The DIME construct includes the information instrument but neglects the intelligence instrument; MIDLIFE includes both.

There are two major issues associated with the information instrument. The first is about defining the target audience. The United States has taken a strong position on separating dissemination of information to domestic and foreign audiences. Agencies authorized to disseminate abroad are strictly prohibited from addressing domestic audiences. But given the advances of the information age, enforcing a strict division is virtually impossible. There are serious privacy issues to address when it comes to collection.

Truthfulness is a second major issue regarding the information instrument. The strong majority position is that the information disseminated must be the truth, the whole truth, and nothing but the truth. Lies and half truths eventually will be exposed and discredit the entire effort. This position is arrived at independently for reasons of morality and for effectiveness. The minority view is that the objective is to influence an audience and manipulating the facts may be necessary and therefore acceptable.

The American story includes slavery and residual racism, unpopular wars and violent public protest, and displacement and genocidal warfare waged against an indigenous population. Attempting to project an American image that minimizes these aspects of history is seen as false and casts doubt on the positive history. A lie of omission poisons the message. Telling the entire story, good and bad, communicates honestly and portrays self-examination and progress on the ills that plague all mankind—it portrays hope. Some choose to minimize (or even reject) the darker aspects of American history even for domestic consumption, and it logically follows that they would project only a positive, albeit incomplete, image abroad.

The U.S. Information Agency (USIA) was the organization chartered to communicate the American message abroad. The Agency fell victim to reforms as part of the "peace dividend" imagined due at the end of the Cold War. USIA was disestablished in 1999. After 9/11, it became clear that the need to communicate an image abroad persisted. The culture at State and Defense gives priority to gathering, analyzing, and protecting information. State gives additional priority to official communications between governments. USIA's culture, in contrast, is about engaging foreign societies and explaining U.S. policies to them. Attempts to re-create the capability in the State Department and separately in the Defense Department failed miserably. There is no functioning information instrument today.

Perhaps the greatest issue is how the current view of the information instrument differs from Carr's earlier description of the *power over opinion*. Carr's earlier admonition that power is inseparable still applies. The United States' power over opinion rests collectively on its military, economic, and cultural substance. The current view is of an information instrument somehow separate and isolated from the other instruments of power. Talking about America, through a variety of media, cannot be separate from the reality of American action. The message is the sum of action and word. The message is indivisible.

The Intelligence Instrument

The intelligence instrument was excluded in the original DIME construct but its conspicuous absence quickly required that it be subsumed under the information instrument. Intelligence is considered separately and explicitly under MIDLIFE. It is inarguable that intelligence is an important mechanism that helps guide the application of Carr's instruments, but it is arguable whether or not intelligence is an instrument.

Intelligence operations include the collection and analysis of information, some of it jealously guarded by foreign actors. Valuable intelligence is increasingly gathered from open sources. Counterintelligence—denial of undesirable information collection efforts—is also included under the intelligence instrument. Intelligence operations might also inject false information into foreign decision-making processes, deception.

The Central Intelligence Agency is the best-known organization responsible for intelligence collection and analysis, but the Intelligence Community is large and distributed widely across the departments and agencies of government. The Community's collection methods include human intelligence (HUMINT), signals intelligence (SIGINT), image intelligence (IMINT), and measurement and signatures intelligence (MASINT). *All source analysis* brings these different sources together. A major issue for the Community is restoring the HUMINT capability that once lost favor to technical means.

Not all intelligence operations concern collection, analysis, or protection of information. Elements of the Intelligence Community are authorized to conduct operations that influence or disrupt political processes abroad. Historically, these operations have been referred to as political warfare, psychological warfare, and strategic operations. Along the spectrum of warfare, these operations are adjacent to operations conducted by the special operations forces of the military. Accordingly, these operations are considered to be part of the military instrument. Another possibility is to include it as part of the diplomatic instrument. Associating these capabilities with the military or diplomatic instruments may be minority views, and the association certainly is arguable by honest and knowledgeable people. Attempting to resolve the issue here would require effort without reward.

The most prominent and persistent issue for the Intelligence Community is that its work is cloaked in secrecy, and where there is secrecy there is suspicion. Some detractors prefer the abolition of certain agencies, and a larger group argues for greater transparency and oversight. The majority view is that intelligence operations are a necessary even if unattractive activity. Before the Vietnam era, most in Congress preferred not to know what the Intelligence Community was doing.

Another major issue for the Intelligence Community is the politicization of the intelligence process. Some administrations have influenced the process to produce intelligence estimates that supported the desired political action. Cherry-picking supportive evidence is common. Such politicization is usually detected, but, more importantly, it is a key component of faulty decision-making processes that produce bad policy.

Secrecy works against the Intelligence Community in other ways. The Community cannot advertise its successes, and it cannot defend itself against accusations of failure. Congress and the president find the Intelligence Community to be a convenient scapegoat for their own poor decision making. The public's expectations for the Intelligence Community are unrealistically high, approaching perfection.

Senior decision makers must make critical decisions based on information that is incomplete, out-of-date, inaccurate, and even contradictory. Information provided by the Intelligence Community is and always will be flawed. Intelligence officers and mature decision makers know and acknowledge that fact. Only the decision maker is responsible for his or her decisions.

The Economic Instrument

Wielding the economic instrument leverages the nation's wealth to influence others. Narrowly defined, the economic instrument includes economic sanctions and foreign aid. More broadly defined, the instrument includes export controls and trade policies that range from granting liberal to restrictive access to U.S. markets. Such use of the economic instrument is a hard, coercive use of force. In its broadest definition, it includes the sheer size of the U.S. economy as having an influence on the rest of the world. The vitality of the U.S. economy and the attendant standard of living is a soft, attractive power felt around the world. Every move in U.S. economic, fiscal, and monetary policy has global effect.

Perhaps the most traditional view, however, is that the economic instrument is wielded abroad by providing or withdrawing foreign aid to developing countries and imposing economic sanctions on those who oppose U.S. policies. A major issue with the economic instrument is that sanctions (sticks) and aid (carrots) have not worked with dictators, and especially not with dictators who rule over an extractive economy (e.g., with a nationalized oil industry). The common result is the punishment of innocents. The government we are trying to influence through sanctions is able to ignore the sticks and carrots and live comfortably, while the population at large goes without food, water, and public services.

Foreign aid comes in at least two major forms: *military assistance* and *foreign assistance*. Military and foreign assistance differ in kind as well as in delivery mechanism. Foreign assistance tends to concern the development of the economy and the institutions of government, and the preponderance of aid is delivered through USAID-administered contracts with foreign nationals. Military assistance tends to be training- and equipment-related and is delivered directly by DOD personnel.

Beyond the difference in kind and delivery mechanism, a tension exists between military and foreign assistance. The military is more inclined to shift aid to countries where immediate benefit may accrue to the United States in dealing with the crisis du jour.[9] USAID tends to take a longer-term, steadier approach.

The State Department has the responsibility to guide both USAID's and DOD's efforts and to balance the objectives of the different missions in accordance with overall foreign policy objectives and long-term strategic interests. The Defense Security Assistance Agency, later renamed the Defense Security Cooperation Agency (DSCA), is the dominant organization administering military assistance. DSCA has increased its share of foreign aid from 7 to 20 percent in recent years.[10]

In the broadest definition of the economic instrument, the effects of the massive U.S. economy are included. National security rests on a robust economy. In this broad view, Federal Reserve Board policy on money supply and interest rates, promotion of international trade activity by the Commerce Department, State Department, and the American Trade

Representative, are all considered applications of the economic instrument. So, too, are activities conducted via a variety of international organizations supported by the United States.

Increasingly, the economic instrument addresses issues that inhibit economic development. Health issues like HIV/AIDS, malaria, and avian flu can swamp local government capacities and prevent any type of development, either economic or governmental. The Department of Health and Human Services' Centers for Disease Control and Prevention bring capability to bear. And other departments, like the Agriculture Department, have significant contributions to make in developing countries.

Historically, developmental efforts abroad have not been supported by any natural constituency in the United States. Funding is miniscule by federal standards. A burst in the foreign aid budget does not result in a larger administrative staff. The same number of staff disperses more money and oversees more programs. Some money inevitably goes to unsavory characters and enterprises. Stories of fraud and corruption attract negative attention and damage the entire effort. Detractors of foreign aid argue that private industry, rather than government, is better at pursuing economic development through investment abroad. But the private sector does not assist in governmental development.

In the traditional view, the U.S. Agency for International Development (USAID) is the dominant organization administering foreign assistance. It focuses on economic development in states receiving aid, but it does more. It is also the vehicle through which the United States assists states in developing the institutions of government. One aspect of good governance is establishment of the rule of law, including legislation, independent courts, and law enforcement. USAID has never attempted quick fixes. Theirs is a deliberate process designed not to outstrip the pace suited to the nation assisted. In small wars, the DOD plays a dominant role in development and attempts an accelerated process. In this more complete view, the economic instrument might be more accurately called the *developmental instrument*.

The Developmental Instrument

The developmental instrument has already been introduced under the economic instrument. This section focuses on a major issue facing U.S.

developmental efforts specifically and Western efforts more generally. Modernization is ideology that rests on the assumption that modernization is good and necessary. Next is deciding whose version of modernization should govern. Economic and governmental systems are both objects of modernization, and there are competing views on both.

William Easterly takes a critical look at the West's past development efforts in the underdeveloped world.[11] Easterly asserts that Western development efforts are characterized by centrally planned economies in developing countries, something Westerners would never tolerate at home. He argues instead for grassroots, bottom-up efforts like those fostered by microgrants and loans.

Rudyard Kipling encouraged the United States to "pick up the white man's burden" in 1898 after the United States defeated Spain in the Philippines. The Old World powers were in decline, but the European sense of cultural supremacy was not. Europeans had the right and moral duty to bring civilization to the uncivilized. In the colonial era, one spoke of civilized, semi-civilized, and uncivilized societies. During the Cold War, one spoke of the First World (the West), the Second World (the East), and the Third World (the South). In the post–Cold War era, one speaks of the developed, developing, and underdeveloped worlds. The labels have changed but the assumptions and logic of white man's burden remain.

There are different motives for U.S. development efforts. Some may be acts of simple generosity. Some may derive from a sense of supremacy. And other developmental efforts may be the result of enlightened self-interest, the belief that developing other societies will provide greater security and access to wider markets. Progressives in the targeted states are more likely to embrace modernization. Conservatives will view it with cautious suspicion. Fundamentalists and reactionaries will oppose it, some violently, and prefer a reversion to past ways. How the international community interprets U.S. motives increases or decreases American *power over opinion.*

The Financial Instrument

The financial instrument is implicitly included in the economic instrument under the DIME construct, but it is called out separately under the new MIDLIFE construct. Developing countries require access to the financial markets of the developed world. The United States assists directly and assists indirectly through international bodies such as the International Monetary Fund, multilateral development banks, and the Export-Import Bank. The financial instrument includes the ability for restructuring the debt of underdeveloped countries. The financial instrument—specifically the World Trade Organization and International Monetary Fund supported by the U.S. government—is vigorously opposed by a complex collection of small, disparate political factions who often call for debt forgiveness, among other things, for the developing world.

The Law Enforcement Instrument

The law enforcement instrument is a new addition to the list of instruments of power, but there is a significant legacy. Law enforcement agencies are numerous and diverse, including local, national, and international agencies. Law enforcement, narrowly defined, includes the investigation and prosecution of crime. Its successful employment requires cooperation with foreign and international law enforcement agencies. A broader definition—required when considering the nation-building mission—includes developing the law enforcement capacities of failed and failing states. Because these broader activities involve building the governmental capacities of weak states, they might better be included under the development instrument.

The law enforcement approach to terrorism attributed to the Clinton administration was much maligned by the Bush campaign of 2000. After-the-fact collection of highly reliable evidence followed by prosecution, in court or perhaps with military means, was considered too little too late. But conspiracy to commit crimes, including terrorist acts, is also a crime, and the law enforcement instrument has shown its ability to prevent terrorist acts and to disrupt terrorist networks just as it has demonstrated the ability to disrupt organized crime.

But the nation-building mission requires a much broader definition of law enforcement, and history offers lessons. In the decades surrounding World War I, the U.S. Marine Corps conducted nation-building operations—typically in Central America and the Caribbean—under the rubric of small wars.[12] It was not uncommon for marines to establish a judiciary and a *constabulary*. After deposing a dictator and building a constabulary, it was not uncommon for a new dictator to rise up from the constabulary and use it to seize and hold power. And the marines would come again.

Providing aid to foreign police reemerged in the 1950s.[13] In 1961, Kennedy initiated the Public Safety Program under the new Agency for International Development. The program was to build police forces for internal security as part of Kennedy's efforts to counter Communist-inspired insurgencies.[14] After the United States sided with right-wing dictators against Communist encroachment, U.S.-trained internal security forces were accused of human rights abuses while quashing political opposition. In response, legislation in the post-Vietnam era prohibited "U.S. agencies from using foreign economic or military assistance funds to assist foreign police."[15] Kennedy's Public Safety Program was specifically terminated in 1974. The prohibition did not apply to funds beyond the Foreign Assistance Act, for example, the Department of Justice's Federal Bureau of Investigation (FBI) or Drug Enforcement Administration (DEA) activities.

Since 1981, Congress began adding numerous exemptions from the prohibition, and the law is now effectively neutered. Allowed activities include training for criminal investigation, patrolling, interrogation and "counterinsurgency techniques," riot control, and weapon use. Weapons, communications, and transportation equipment may be provided.

Nation building often requires development of internal security forces to provide for public safety. Training and equipping foreign police in countries with a long tradition of authoritarian rule will likely prove to be a bad idea in some cases. There is no effective unifying oversight of the many efforts of the departments and agencies.

Today, the Justice Department houses the principal national law enforcement agency, the FBI, as well as significant capabilities in the Bureau of Alcohol, Tobacco, Firearms and Explosives (ATF), and the DEA. The State Department administers programs to train foreign police in international narcotics control and counterterrorist activities. The Defense Department is authorized to assist national police forces. The Coast Guard, until recently part of the Treasury Department and now part of the Department of Homeland Security (DHS), houses significant law enforcement capabilities in the maritime. The Federal Law Enforcement Training Center also resides under DHS. The Treasury Department houses the Financial Crimes Enforcement Network (FinCEN), which contributes a significant capability to law enforcement efforts by monitoring money flows associated with the illicit narcotics trade, money laundering, financing terrorist organizations, or common tax evasion.

Much has been made of "the wall" that exists between those investigators pursuing courtroom-quality evidence and those conducting intelligence collection operations. The issue is that they stem from distinct legal authorities. Authority to conduct a wiretap while investigating a common crime is granted through the federal courts. A separate court, the FISA court,[16] grants wiretap authority in intelligence cases. Mixing the evidence acquired under these distinct authorities is problematic. One issue is that the accused have the right to confront their accuser, and evidence presented in open court may reveal critical intelligence sources. The conservative approach was to put a wall between evidence collected from the different sources. Considerable effort has been, and continues to be, expended in breaching "the wall."

The Diplomatic Instrument

The diplomatic instrument is sometimes called the *political instrument*. It represents the power of persuasion. Narrowly defined, diplomacy includes negotiations pursued through international institutions like the UN and NATO, and it includes negotiations pursued through bilateral relations—state-to-state negotiations. It produces treaties and lesser international agreements. Broadly defined, diplomacy includes the above and all declaratory policy statements issued to influence others and is underwritten by the other instruments of power. The State Department is, of course, the principal organization housing the diplomatic instrument.

Two important facts characterize the international system of states: the interests of states are divergent, and states are unequal in power. Foreign policy describes the objectives of states, and diplomacy is the intercourse between states attempting to achieve their foreign policy objectives. Not all foreign policy objectives are matters of national security. Foreign policy objectives might include advancing human rights in China, but China's failure to guarantee human rights to its citizens does not constitute a threat to American national security. Foreign policy objectives include security, trade, and investment.

Diplomacy is the power of suasion—convincing foreign governments to take desired actions without resort to more forceful methods. General George C. Marshall—who after serving as the Army chief of staff during World War II, secretary of state, and secretary of defense—said that "military force without diplomacy is pointless, and diplomacy not backed by military force is mere posturing."[17] One can easily add other types of force to the military. Diplomacy is conducted backed by all the instruments of power.

Most diplomacy—influencing the behavior of other governments—takes place outside public view. Examples include moderating foreign police treatment of U.S. citizens and gaining access to foreign markets for commercial products. Strong relations between states make easier the resolution of specific issues, and weak relations make resolution harder. Relations must be built and maintained, and State Department personnel make long-term relations a high priority. Foreign embassies in Washington and American embassies abroad provide early warning of crisis and the opportunity to understand host nation interests.

Diplomacy takes place through the enunciation of U.S. policy and negotiations. Ensuring that U.S. positions are known in advance might well avoid misunderstandings and confrontations. Negotiating agreements is another important function of diplomacy, whether those negotiations are public or private and whether they are formal or informal. These functions take place more fluidly when regular relations are maintained, and the maintenance of relations is itself an important function of diplomacy.

While there is a great deal of information exchange associated with diplomacy, information exchanged between the U.S. government and other sovereign states is properly viewed as part of the diplomatic rather than the information instrument. Diplomacy is the standard way the United States interacts with the international system of states to communicate its intentions and views. It achieves influence through bilateral and multilateral agreements, negotiations, and engagement with states, the UN, nongovernmental organizations, and other international organizations.

Other negotiations within the purview of the diplomatic instrument include nuclear arms control, conventional arms control, cooperative threat reduction, confidence building regimes, nonproliferation of weapons of mass destruction, and export controls. These functions were under the purview of the Arms Control and Disarmament Agency until merged into the State Department in 1999.

The diplomatic instrument includes the *power of recognition*. Through recognition, the United States receives representatives of other sovereign states and recognizes them as equals, but recognition does not imply approval of the recognized state's policies. The quick recognition of Panama by Teddy Roosevelt in 1903 after it was "liberated" from Colombia and of Israel by Truman in 1948 is demonstration of the power of recognition. The refusal to recognize is equally important. Below refusal are the recall of U.S. diplomats and the ejection of foreign diplomats. Through diplomatic channels, the United States expresses its official dissatisfaction with the "demarche" and the "strongly worded demarche" before resort to more coercive actions.

The major issue facing the diplomatic instrument today is its relevance and role. It once was the preeminent instrument that orchestrated all instruments of power. When negotiating an agreement with another country, the diplomat is well positioned to consider the specific issue on the table in the context of all other issues between the two states, and the diplomat can put options on the table that draw from the resources of the other instruments of power. One view, recently prominent, is that diplomacy is tantamount to appeasement. From this camp, the military instrument is preferred and is perceived as the dominant instrument through which foreign policy and national security objectives are pursued.

To equate the diplomatic instrument with the State Department is simply wrong. While the great majority of State's work is diplomacy, and State may lead in many diplomatic efforts, the diplomatic instrument is spread across the departments and agencies of the executive branch. And since the Vietnam War, the legislative branch became increasingly involved in diplomacy as congressional delegations rose in prominence.

The Defense Department challenges State in diplomacy. The office of the under secretary of defense for policy is sometimes referred to as the state department inside the Pentagon. The under secretary and assistant secretaries lead in diplomacy through the military alliance structure, including NATO (1949–), CENTO (1955–79), and SEATO (1955–77). The Joint Staff policy and planning staff (J5) plays an important role, and its director is the military advisor to the U.S. ambassador to the UN. The regional combatant commanders are deeply and continuously engaged abroad through the European, African, Pacific, Central, Southern, and Northern Commands. Their regional orientation generally gives them greater diplomatic weight than ambassadors representing U.S. interests in single countries. The Defense Department also places defense attachés in foreign embassies.

Several single-issue agencies also perform diplomatic functions, making public statements, negotiating agreements, and conducting their missions through international organizations. The former USIA led in educational cultural exchange efforts and in communicating to foreign publics. USAID leads in economic and governmental development. The U.S. Trade Representative, with direct reporting responsibilities to both Congress and the president, has responsibility for bilateral trade negotiations and can deny or grant access to U.S. markets.

Other departments contribute to the diplomatic effort. The Treasury Department leads in foreign investment and engages with international financial institutions like the World Bank. The Departments of Agriculture and Commerce play strong roles. The Department of Health and Human Services and its National Institutes of Health and Centers for Disease Control and Prevention continually engage with international health organizations. The Justice Department conducts liaison with foreign police agencies.

The State Department, in general, is not structured to plan or operate programs (exceptions include counterdrug, counterterrorism, and refugee issues). Each of the single-issue agencies provides staff with specialized skills and knowledge. The agencies typically lead in policy formulation and execution with overall State Department policy guidance. The president's National Security Council, national security advisor, and presidential special envoys compete with State.

For Consideration

Carr defined the instruments of power in a highly abstract way that remains useful today. Carr's instruments—military power, economic power, and the power over opinion—convey a three-legged stool upon which national security rests. The instruments must be strong and in balance. If one leg is weak, the imbalanced stool tips over. Our strategic actions, in addition to achieving objectives, must be evaluated as to whether they increase, preserve, or weaken the instruments of power that assure national security. The stool needs to remain strong and balanced.

First we'll use Carr's instruments as a way to consider the current strategic condition, and then we'll turn to more recent interpretations of the instruments of power.

Status of the Instruments

The well-being of the military and economic instruments receives a great deal of public attention. But the power over opinion is neglected by many. And some realists equate power solely with the military instrument. But as Carr reminds, no instrument can long stand alone. Roger Altman and Richard Haass provide a recent assessment of the instruments with an emphasis on fiscal profligacy.[18] They argue that reduced expenditures are necessary to stop the deficit spending and that increased taxes are necessary to pay off accumulated debt.

The United States reached its peak of power relative to the rest of the world's economies at the end of World War II. Much of Europe's and Japan's industrial base lay in rubble and their workforces were dislocated. As the world recovered, U.S. relative economic power declined. The increasingly integrated economy of the European Union exceeds that of the United States. The strengthening of Brazil, Russia, India, and China represents continuing relative economic decline for the United States. And relative economic decline implies a weakened ability to "lead and shape international relations."[19]

American power over opinion is weakened on two fronts, making the ability to lead and shape international relations more of an uphill climb. During the Cold War, the "thriving economy and high standard of living" of U.S. capitalism compared to conditions of Soviet Communism contributed greatly to U.S. power over opinion in the Third World. But during the recent global recession, the United States was compared not to the Soviet Union but to China, whose economy continued its expansion while the West's contracted. The Chinese system; "a top-heavy political system married to a directed hybrid form of capitalism," has greater appeal in the developing world than does the U.S. system with little government "oversight and regulation." The world sees a country debt-ridden and unable to cope as congressional Republicans and a Democratic president agreed to postpone the inevitable and continue to borrow from China.[20]

On another front, the Guantanamo prison and incidents at Abu Ghraib weakened the U.S. claim on the rule of law. Military operations in Iraq and Afghanistan have created more negative than positive sentiment in the Muslim world. Waging war in Iraq in opposition to international sentiment expanded the divide between the United States and its allies in Europe and East Asia.

Offensive realism predicts expansion of U.S. interests following the demise of its Cold War competitor. In the words of Altman and Haass, Paul Kennedy's 1989 *The Rise and Fall of the Great Powers* concludes that "the costs of carrying out an ambitious overseas policy can undermine the economic foundations of a state."[21] The United States spends more on defense than China, the European Union (including its NATO member states), Japan, and India combined. Rather than narrowly deterring actions against the United States, deterrence was extended to western Europe, South Korea, Taiwan, Japan, and Israel during the Cold War. Extended deterrence was expanded into eastern Europe after the Cold War.

Pursuing preponderance of power, whether in the name of primacy or cooperative security, extends the U.S. security umbrella even further. Proponents of both strategies assert the responsibilities of the last remaining superpower. No national, international, natural, or biblical law is cited as the basis for these putative responsibilities. The last remaining superpower is well positioned to choose its obligations, and it is the ultimate act of responsibility to choose those obligations carefully and wisely.

There are political forces that demand a strong response under the assumption that a *strong* response is an *effective* response. To be effective, U.S. actions must be judged on whether they preserve, erode, or expand U.S. power. As the late Walt Kelly, creator of the *Pogo* comic strip, said, "We have met the enemy and he is us."

From Instrument to Mechanism

Carr's meaning has been supplanted over time. DIME moved us away from Carr's instruments and toward assignment of responsibilities to departments and agencies. The more recent MIDLIFE and longer lists moved us even further from Carr's formulation. Today, *instrument* is often used as a synonym for the concrete *capabilities* or *mechanisms* spread across the departments and agencies of government—action channels. In the context of ends, ways, and means, some use these concrete capabilities as an expression of means. Means are assembled and applied to produce the ways of the strategy. Orchestrating these widely distributed instruments is exceedingly problematic.

DIME and MIDLIFE convey more of a mechanistic or tool mind-set. Other than normal wear and tear, the mechanic isn't inclined to think much about whether using a wrench increases or decreases its value. The tool is there to use. As Madeline Albright said, "What's the point of having this superb military . . . if we can't use it?"[22] Still, the tool kit must be balanced, like Carr's instruments, but that is a matter of investment, what the military calls force development policy. The uniformed services have well-developed and rigorous force development processes, and Congress pays considerable attention. No such emphasis is apparent for the other instruments of power.

As a guide to action, Carr's instruments support strategic thought at the highest levels. As a guide to organizing government and allocating resources, DIME and MIDLIFE appear better suited. The departments and agencies are action channels, or mechanisms of power, that can be applied to achieve the objectives of state. The capacities of the departments and agencies must be adequate to carry out the national security strategy. The next chapter surveys the relevant parts of the departments and agencies that house the mechanisms of power, that is, the capacity to implement policy.

8   Mechanisms of Power

The principal departments comprising the national security apparatus are the State Department and the Defense Department. There are several independent and semi-independent agencies that also contribute, including the Central Intelligence Agency, the U.S. Agency for International Development, the former U.S. Information Agency, and others. These agencies are presented first, followed by State, Defense, and the Intelligence Community.

The national security apparatus has evolved considerably since the constitutional convention. The Spanish-American war of 1898 ushered in a new era, with the United States finding itself with imperial outposts in the Caribbean and the Philippines. The requirements of World War I led to the creation of wartime organizations that were quickly stood down after the war and had to be re-created for World War II. These same organizations were made permanent after World War II and throughout the Cold War. The Second World War exposed deep organizational problems in conducting great-power war, and those problems were the subject of unification hearings following the war. The current national security system is rooted in the National Security Act of 1947, a product of postwar deliberations.

Major amendments to the act were made in 1949, 1953, 1958, and 1986. Truman and Eisenhower both pursued reorganization through formal mechanisms, specifically the Commission on Organization of the Executive Branch of Government. The first commission stood between 1947 and 1949, and the second between 1953 and 1955. Both were headed by former president Herbert Hoover and are typically referred to as the Hoover Commissions.

The 1960s also produced change. The decolonization of Africa was followed by a great-power competition there. Kennedy initiated an era of counterinsurgency that required new organizations and nation building in the Third World to counter Communist-inspired insurgencies. The era led to costly policies in Latin America and Southeast Asia that brought down Johnson and Nixon. Backed by popular support, Carter led reform efforts aimed at the military and intelligence agencies. Those reforms, too, proved costly.

The end of the Cold War produced reform in the context of a personal and ideological competition between Speaker of the House Newt Gingrich and President Bill Clinton. Clinton's and George W. Bush's reliance on military intervention and nation building underlies reform efforts today.

Common Themes

Departments and agencies represent experience, specialized knowledge and skills, and the statutory authorities to do the work of government. They also provide institutional memory and continuity of effort across presidential administrations. As such, they represent a conservative force that presidents must overcome to pursue their agendas. To assist in the pursuit of a chosen policy agenda, presidents have the authority to appoint, subject to Senate confirmation, their own management team. The highest-level appointments include secretaries and deputies for the cabinet departments (see figure 4).

A great deal of a department's work is conducted under the auspices of assistant secretaries. Congress limits the number of assistant secretaries per department but allows the department to determine their purpose. Where the executive branch has failed to perform certain functions, Congress establishes specific assistant secretaries by statute. For example, the Defense Department is required by law to have an assistant secretary of defense for special operations and low-intensity conflict.

As assistant secretary positions proliferated, Congress authorized an intermediate layer of under secretaries as a span-of-control mechanism to reduce the number of offices reporting directly to the secretary and deputy secretary. Under secretaries and assistant secretaries have a variety of deputies and assistants that are also political appointees that do not require Senate confirmation.

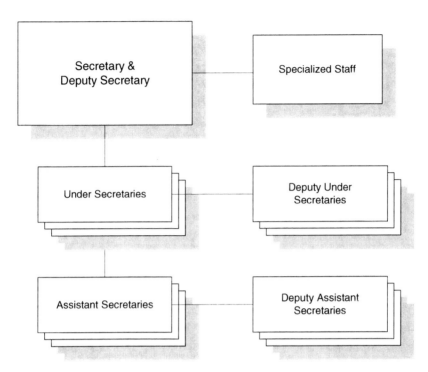

FIG. 4. Nominal cabinet department management hierarchy

The permanent departmental bureaucracy is made up of Civil Service and Senior Executive Service employees. Metaphorically, the political appointees steer at the behest of the president and the permanent staff rows. Agencies are headed by directors and deputy directors with a similar management structure of political appointees and civil servants.

There are frequent calls to reduce the number of political appointments (more than seven thousand positions).[1] Some appointments are doled out as political patronage. Appointees often lack the necessary specialized knowledge and executive skills. Positions often go unfilled for long periods while members of the Senior Executive Service fill in capably. Some positions are temporarily filled by appointees who lack Senate confirmation and full authorities. Presidential initiatives are stunted by the lack of Senate-confirmed appointees.

The president's appointees have responsibilities that are difficult to reconcile. They are at once the president's representatives embedded in the bureaucratic hierarchy with the responsibility to ensure that the president's guidance is followed, and they are the department's or agency's champion to Congress and the White House. If they wish to be respected in their department, they must challenge the president. If they wish to be trusted by the president, they must challenge their department. In addition to their departmental duties, these same appointees have significant responsibilities as principals on the interagency committees of the National Security Council. They extend the president's reach deep into the executive branch hierarchy.

The demands on secretaries in particular are complex and even contradictory. Secretaries are the senior advisor to the president in their specific policy domain. They are also the president's principal assistant and are responsible for carrying out the president's decisions through departmental action. The president's direction may be at odds with the expert opinion of the department's permanent staff. The secretary is also responsible for the long-term health of the department, including budgetary support from Congress, and for the morale of career staff.

At the assistant secretary level, where much of the work gets done, there are often specialized organizations oriented on geographic regions or on functions with global implications. The regional organizations tend to dominate the functional. The departments and agencies divide the world into regions in a way that makes sense for their unique missions. The different regional subdivisions complicate interagency coordination. Regionally oriented organizations tend to subdivide internally by function, and functionally oriented organizations tend to subdivide by region.

Perhaps more important than boundary issues is that the regional offices of most departments and agencies are in Washington, while the Defense Department's regional organizations are in the field and well resourced and thereby wield greater influence abroad. DOD has capacities beyond those of other departments. No other department comes close to Defense's planning capacity. No other department has the excess capacity that allows rapid response to crises with personnel and resources. And no other department has the consistent support of Congress in appropriations.

Noteworthy Agencies

Several agencies deserve mention prior to discussion of the two principal cabinet departments with national security responsibilities. Some agencies survived post–World War II reorganization, including the predecessors of the U.S. Information Agency (USIA). The National Security Act of 1947 established the CIA and gave statutory authority for the existing Joint Chiefs of Staff. The act initiated major reform, but the need for reform continued. Urgency was added by the Soviet launch of the Sputnik communications satellite in 1957. Legislation late in the Eisenhower administration, followed by implementing executive orders issued early in the Kennedy administration, established several new organizations, including the Agency for International Development (USAID), the Defense Security Assistance Agency (DSAA), and the Arms Control and Disarmament Agency (ACDA). The State Department Operations Center was established in April 1961, providing a capability for worldwide communications.

In the late 1950s, Congress saw the need to retire post–World War II mechanisms and transition to something more general and sustainable for the long haul of the Cold War. Much of postwar reconstruction efforts had been conducted through the military and an army of occupation. The Marshall Plan and its siblings had been successful, but something new was needed. In September 1961, Congress passed legislation requiring the separation of *foreign assistance* and *military assistance*, with State determining which countries needed assistance. Later the same year, by executive order, Kennedy established USAID to administer foreign assistance to developing countries and established DSAA to administer military assistance.

A round of consolidation took place in the context of the 104th Congress, specifically House Speaker Gingrich's "Contract with America" and the Clinton/Gore "Reinventing Government" initiative. All foreign affairs agencies were targeted, including USAID, USIA, and ACDA. A congressional attempt at consolidation in 1995 failed, but by 1997 the Clinton administration concluded that the time for consolidation had come. The Foreign Affairs Restructuring and Reform Act of 1998 and the ensuing reorganization resulted in the functions of USIA and ACDA being merged into State in 1999.[2] USAID retained its status as an independent agency. The various agencies merged their respective public affairs and inspector general offices into State.[3]

U.S. Agency for International Development

The United States Agency for International Development (USAID) houses the preponderance of capability to assist countries in developing their economies and their institutions of government. As with other departments and agencies, USAID has both regional and functional bureaus, and the regional bureaus dominate. The bureaus are creatures of Washington. Each of the regional bureaus—for example, for Africa, Latin America and the Caribbean, East Asia and the Near East, and Europe and Eurasia— has field offices around the world where aid is administered directly. The functional bureaus for Democracy, Conflict, and Humanitarian Assistance and for Global Health also have field offices.

Unlike USIA and ACDA, USAID remained a distinct agency with a separate appropriation. But the secretary of state is responsible for coordinating all development activity in accordance with broader foreign policy objectives. To that end, the reforms created the position of *director of foreign assistance* at the deputy secretary level reporting directly to the secretary of state. The director also serves as *administrator of USAID*.

During the Vietnam era, USAID personnel numbered approximately 15,000. By the Reagan administration, its numbers had fallen to approximately 9,600. Today, its personnel count is a bit above 2,000. Approximately 80 percent of its workload is contracted out to businesses and other nongovernmental organizations abroad.

Defense Security Cooperation Agency

The Defense Security Assistance Agency (DSAA) was established in 1961 in parallel with USAID. DSAA had execution authority to administer military assistance, with the State Department having policy responsibilities. The name was changed to the Defense Security Cooperation Agency (DSCA) in 1998 under Clinton. The Agency gained execution authority for the humanitarian assistance demining mission, and it retained its execution authorities for security assistance (or security cooperation) programs. State retained guidance, approval, and policy oversight authorities.

U.S. Information Agency

Before its post–Cold War demise, the U.S. Information Agency (USIA) mission was to promote a positive American image abroad to counter foreign propaganda. It was an important component in the ideological competition of the Cold War. Disestablished in 1999, it was unavailable for the ideological competition of the post-9/11 world. The Agency was legally prohibited from distributing informational material to domestic audiences inside the United States—*public affairs*. The USIA mission included three distinct functions:

- dissemination of information to foreign publics—*public diplomacy,*
- promotion of mutual understanding through operation of educational and cultural exchange programs, and
- frequent collection of foreign attitudes toward the United States and presentation to the secretary, president, and National Security Council.

The Agency's organizational history is one of creation and destruction and of moving in and out of the State Department. The World War I Committee on Public Information was the first large-scale attempt at a government information capability. After dormancy in the interwar era, information operations were resurrected in 1938 to counter the Axis Powers' propaganda targeting Latin America. The Voice of America (VOA) was established in 1942 and the Office of War Information quickly followed.

Post–World War II legislation mandated a peacetime exchange program[4] and chartered a peacetime program to disseminate information abroad.[5] In 1949, the Hoover Commission and the Advisory Commission on Information recommended moving the foreign information program out of State and into an independent agency—the USIA. Truman established Radio Liberty in 1950 to broadcast into Russia and established Radio Free Europe in 1951 for Eastern Europe. The USIA was officially established by Eisenhower in 1953 as an independent agency to consolidate existing organizations and activities. Educational exchange remained under State.

The major issue facing USIA and its broadcasting components was whether it would be a messaging body for the United States or an outlet for legitimate news. The mission was to provide news to those living under oppressive regimes by countering Axis propaganda during World War II and countering Communist propaganda during the Cold War. But in 1976, President Ford signed legislation stating that VOA was to broadcast "accurate, objective, and comprehensive" news. This became a persistent component of the Agency's professional ethic.

A major reorganization was approved by Carter in 1977. The International Communications Agency (ICA) was created in 1978 from the merger of the State Department's Bureau of Education and Cultural Affairs and Eisenhower's USIA. Carter expanded the mission to include understanding foreign cultures and perceptions—information gathering in addition to information distribution. The director advised the president, secretary of state, and National Security Council on foreign public opinion about the United States and its policies. The ICA was renamed USIA in 1983 under Reagan.

The Agency was subjected to a 1997 reduction in force, and at the time of the 1999 merger the Agency had a staff of about 6,715. About 1,000 of those were in the Foreign Service, with about half deployed abroad at any given time. Another 3,000 were employed in civil service and mostly posted in Washington DC, with two-thirds involved in international broadcasting and the remainder supporting educational and informational programs. Prior to its disestablishment in 1999, the USIA budget was about $1 billion. The senior USIA official in American embassies was typically the embassy's public affairs officer and a member of the ambassador's country team.

Upon disestablishment in 1999 its remnants and personnel were merged into the regional bureaus of the State Department. The global perspective was thus lost, and personnel from the distinct USIA culture were neither well received nor truly integrated into State. Their distinct career path was gone. The under secretary of state for public diplomacy and public affairs assumed USIA functions but has failed in its mission. The White House staff is the preferred communications mechanism of most administrations.

In 2014, after Russia effectively employed its propaganda machine in the Ukraine, the House and Senate agreed to a bill that consolidated broadcasting outlets under the new nonfederal U.S. International

Communications Agency and, reversing Ford's emphasis, elevated influence over objectivity.

Arms Control and Disarmament Agency

The Arms Control and Disarmament Agency (ACDA) is another example of post–World War II mechanisms being updated. After the war, disarmament and demobilization consumed a great deal of U.S. and international effort. In 1961, ACDA was created with the mixed mission of continuing postwar disarmament plus initiating arms control to inhibit the new arms race as the number of nuclear weapons grew rapidly.[6] ACDA was merged into the State Department in 1999.

The directors of ACDA typically have been highly qualified and high-powered in the area of arms control rather than underqualified partisans. And they have often been selected because of their position on arms control. The director can be in conflict with secretaries of state or national security assistants. In one case, national security assistant to President Carter, Zbigniew Brzezinski, chose to chair NSC arms control meetings specifically to challenge the arms control positions of ACDA director Paul Warnke and Secretary of State Cyrus Vance.

In 1983, Barry Blechman, an assistant ACDA director during the Carter administration, summarized the organization's position:

> Born in controversy in 1961, ACDA has always been a headache of every President since John F. Kennedy. Repeatedly purged, always distrusted, criticized by its friends, savaged by its enemies, the Agency has been the center of turmoil and discord for more than 20 years. . . . [The conflicts] are neither trivial nor transitory. They represent immutable conflicts—characteristics which can coexist only in the most artificial and unstable circumstances. Little wonder that the Agency has been consistently beset by controversy.[7]

Congressional support for ACDA waxed and waned but generally moved in a downward direction. In 1997 Clinton directed ACDA's absorption into the State Department, and the merger was accomplished by 1999. ACDA functions were placed under the renamed under secretary of state for arms control and international security. In the Bush administration, appointees were selected because they opposed arms control and limitations all together, e.g., John Bolton served as under secretary of state for arms control (2001–5). By 2006, morale was low and experienced professionals were seeking other employment.[8]

One-Off Missions

There are other significant activities in the departments that are applicable to national security. Many are only secondary to the primary mission of the owning department. For example, the Department of Energy has offices to address nuclear terrorism and nuclear proliferation.

The Department of Homeland Security (DHS), established hastily after 9/11, was the recipient of security-related capabilities from existing departments and agencies. DHS now houses the Coast Guard, which can be used to guard the maritime approaches to the United States or to patrol contested waters around the world where Navy surface combatants are poorly suited. The Immigration and Naturalization Service was reoriented from soliciting and processing applications for entry into being a restrictive gatekeeper.

The Treasury Department deals with foreign actions that might affect fiscal and monetary policy and with terrorist financing. Treasury's Financial Crimes Enforcement Network brings a significant capability to track money flows. Treasury houses the Secret Service, and until recently, the Customs Service and the Bureau of Alcohol, Tobacco, and Firearms. The ATF underwent a name change to the Bureau of Alcohol, Tobacco, Firearms, and Explosives on 24 January 2003 and was transferred to the Department of Justice. The U.S. Customs Service, with a largely tariff-collecting mission, was dissolved and its capabilities transferred to the Homeland Security Department as Immigration and Customs Enforcement and the Bureau of Customs and Border Protection.

The Justice Department's Federal Bureau of Investigation has responsibilities to penetrate national and international networks, terrorist organizations, foreign intelligence services, and WMD proliferators. Justice also houses the Marshals Service and the Drug Enforcement Administration. The DEA, with 4,500 agents, conducts operations against organized criminal organizations trafficking in illicit drugs. Those same organizations may be complicit in terrorist activities. Approximately 4,000 marshals hunt fugitives and might be expected to bring valuable skills.

Department of State

The State Department is the oldest department, and the secretary enjoys seniority among cabinet members. State represents U.S. policies to foreign governments, foreign publics, and international organizations. It negotiates treaties and lesser agreements on behalf of the U.S. government, including issues of arms control, international development, illicit narcotics trafficking, environment, economics and business, and science and technology. It manages the allocation of resources for foreign relations. And State oversees and coordinates the activities of other U.S. agencies abroad.

Foreign affairs responsibilities were first considered to be properly centered in the Senate, but the Constitution's framers changed their minds and assigned them to the president, as head of the executive branch. It quickly became clear that the president needed assistance, and two years later Congress authorized the Department of Foreign Affairs; the name was changed to Department of State later the same year. State was the first federal agency established under the Constitution, and for several years it was the only federal agency. State accumulated domestic duties until the creation of additional federal agencies allowed State to concentrate on foreign affairs. In the early years, most overseas posts were seeking markets for American industrial output. Preferring to avoid foreign political entanglements, Congress authorized the position of ambassador only in 1893.

The State Department serves in two distinct roles. First, it serves as a staff advisory body to the president. Second, it serves as a line organization of executive government. As a line organization, State has statutory authorities to *implement* American foreign policy. State is also the principal point of contact for foreign states and international organizations. And State is responsible for overseeing and coordinating the efforts of other government agencies where foreign policy implications exist.

In Washington, State has strong ties to otherwise independent agencies. Three of those agencies are USAID, the now-defunct USIA, and the former ACDA. The latter two have been absorbed into State. Each has been briefly discussed above. Each has an important contribution to make with respect to twenty-first-century national security.

State's Washington bureaucracy competes in policy formulation, planning, and budgeting processes. State Department officials often chair National Security Council committees. But some of State's most important work is conducted in embassies and consulates far from Washington. In the field, the ambassador is the president's personal emissary to the government of the host nation. The ambassador oversees and coordinates the activities of the other in-country agencies through the *country team*. There are more than thirty government agencies operating overseas carrying out U.S. policy. In some embassies, State Department officials are outnumbered by personnel from other agencies.

State's lead role in many interagency activities rests on one simple, inescapable fact. Relations with other sovereign states are bilateral, and the State Department is responsible for negotiating all treaties and lesser agreements and for ensuring their faithful execution. State is also responsible for conducting multilateral relations with the UN and other international organizations,

The number of State Department personnel is small, especially when compared to the Defense Department. There are approximately 11,000 Foreign Service Officers serving rotational assignments abroad, and approximately 8,000 civil service employees mostly working in Washington posts. An additional 31,000 foreign nationals are employed abroad. State suffered a 50 percent budget reduction in the decade surrounding the end of the Cold War. The rate of resignations for Foreign Service generalists doubled between 1994 and 2000, while the resignation rate of foreign service specialists quadrupled. State's 2008 operating budget request was for $7 billion. For all additional purposes, including operations in Iraq and Afghanistan, and for foreign aid, the total budget request was for $42 billion, or about 6.5 percent of the Pentagon budget request.

Secretary of State

The *secretary of state* serves as principal advisor and assistant on foreign affairs to the president. Advisory responsibilities are conducted informally in private settings and formally as a statutory member of the National Security Council. As assistant, the secretary is the principal representative of U.S. policies to foreign and domestic audiences, chief negotiator, and chief executive officer charged with the long-term health of the State Department.

It is difficult to imagine someone with the disparate skills that the position requires. Academics like Madeleine Albright (Clinton) and Condoleezza Rice (Bush 43) were trusted advisors but lacked significant executive experience. Several retired Army generals have served with varying success. Some, like George C. Marshall (Truman) and Colin Powell (Bush 43), brought both significant executive skills and mature advice. Marshall was successful in both roles. Powell was marginalized as advisor but was successful as chief executive. Alexander Haig (Reagan) was "wound too tight" for the task. John Foster Dulles (Eisenhower), Dean Rusk (JFK-LBJ), and Henry Kissinger (Nixon) emphasized their presidential advisory role. William Rogers accepted the role of State Department custodian in the Nixon administration. Warren Christopher (Carter), an international lawyer, undertook significant departmental reforms. The career diplomat, as another option, might bring a good balance of negotiating, diplomatic, and executive skills, but as secretary would be seen as a champion for the State Department rather than trusted agent of the president. According to Leslie Gelb:

> Recent Presidents have probably concluded some time during their first year that they cannot trust anyone in the State Department below the Secretary—and perhaps one or two others. . . . This puts the Secretary in a horrendous position. Either he can disassociate himself from his own department to preserve his standing with the President, thereby letting his institution flounder, or he can become an advocate for his department and end up being suspect himself.[9]

Organization

The State Department's management hierarchy is headed by the secretary and deputy secretary.[10] The deputy may be chosen to complement the skills of the secretary and establish a division of labor between the two that covers all the functions. Chief operating officer is a common assignment for the deputy. The secretary and deputy are supported down the line by several under secretaries (see figure 5).

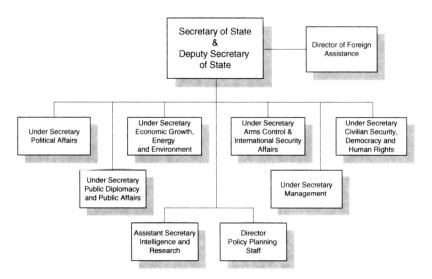

FIG. 5. Department of State organization

Two significant restructuring efforts have taken place post Cold War. The Clinton administration undertook a restructuring in 1999. The first Quadrennial Diplomacy and Development Review (QDDR) of 2010 resulted in the most recent restructuring in 2011.

As part of the 1999 Clinton initiatives, the position of director of foreign assistance was created within the State Department reporting directly to the secretary. The director holds status at the deputy secretary level and is simultaneously administrator of USAID, which retains its independence in execution authorities.

Much of the State Department's work is done in "the bureaus." Bureaus generally are headed by assistant secretaries that report upward to a specific under secretary. Some State Department organizations, however, report directly to the secretary. The offices of the under secretaries most closely related to national security are covered first, followed by the relevant direct reporting offices.

Political Affairs

The mainstream State Department mission is conducted in the regional and functional bureaus reporting to the *under secretary for political affairs,* the number three officer in the State Department.[11] The bureaus are headed by assistant secretaries who advise the under secretary and guide the diplomatic mission in their regions. A chain of authority might be imagined from the secretary, under secretary, and assistant secretary to an ambassador abroad, but ambassadors jealously guard their direct relationship with the president. Beyond American shores, the ambassador dominates.

In Washington, there are regional bureaus for Near Eastern, Western Hemisphere, African, East Asian and Pacific, South and Central Asian, and European and Eurasian Affairs. The regional bureaus have *country desk officers* who provide a two-way link between Washington and the embassies. They provide the same linkage with foreign embassies in the United States.

The functional Bureau of International Organization Affairs represents U.S. interests with the UN, UN-affiliated organizations, and other international organizations.

Economic Growth, Energy, and Environment

The *under secretary for economic growth, energy and environment* provides an important component of the economic and financial instruments. The under secretary is assisted by assistant secretaries for economic and business affairs, energy resources, oceans and international environmental and scientific affairs, and chief economist.

Arms Control and International Security Affairs

The *under secretary for arms control and international security affairs* is the senior advisor to the secretary of state and the president on matters of arms control, nonproliferation, and disarmament. And the under secretary heads related interagency committees of the NSC. The under secretary's purview includes conventional, nuclear, biological, and chemical weapons.

Bureaus of Arms Control and International Security. The office of the under secretary was created by the integration of ACDA into the State Department late in the Clinton administration. ACDA bureaus were disassembled and then reassembled under the *Bureau of International Security and Nonproliferation* and the *Bureau of Verification, Compliance, and*

Implementation, the latter established in statute. The existing Bureau of Political-Military Affairs was assigned to the new under secretary.

Bureau of Political-Military Affairs. The *Bureau of Political-Military Affairs* provides the principal liaison between the State and Defense Departments, and the links are many. Certain Defense activities are subject to State approval and oversight. The Bureau participates in planning processes, deals with internal defense plans, military assistance programs, and arms and munitions exports, and ensures that DOD actions are consistent with broader U.S. foreign policy objectives.

The Bureau has responsibility for a wide range of negotiations related to the military. These include status of forces agreements for military forces stationed abroad and defense cooperation agreements with friendly countries. The Bureau also has responsibility for negotiating bilateral Article 98 Agreements to exempt U.S. persons from the jurisdiction of the International Criminal Court. The Bureau also negotiates overflight, aircraft landing, port visit, and basing agreements with other sovereign nations.

A *Pol-Mil Action Team* is on call 24/7. State participates in time-sensitive planning with the JCS and the combatant commands. If forces must deploy, the secretary of defense must issue a deployment order that is first coordinated with State to ensure the deployment's consistency with U.S. foreign policy. The Pol-Mil Bureau coordinates with the appropriate regional State bureaus and instructs the relevant embassies to seek host nation support. If embassy and other personnel are threatened by local hostilities, noncombatant evacuation operations using DOD capabilities are coordinated by the Bureau.

The Bureau plays a leading role in security assistance. It prepares budget requests to Congress to fund grants to foreign nations to buy U.S. military equipment, for conducting peacekeeping operations, and for expanding foreign peacekeeping capabilities. The Bureau is also responsible for approving foreign military sales and to assure the consistency of sales with overall foreign policy. The Bureau assures that military exchanges and multinational military exercises are consistent with foreign policy objectives. DOD executes the security assistance programs.

The Pol-Mil Bureau provides support to a variety of interagency working groups. It provides *political advisors* to the uniformed service chiefs, the combatant commanders, and others like NATO's supreme allied commander. It also provides State Department personnel at the next lower level to joint interagency coordinating groups, increasingly constructed within those combatant commands that employ U.S. government capabilities beyond military forces.

Public Diplomacy and Public Affairs

The *under secretary for public diplomacy and public affairs* has responsibility for communicating to foreign publics (*public diplomacy*) and for communicating to the American public (*public affairs*). The objective is to explain U.S. policies and to promote understanding. Much of the USIA's capability was parceled out to the State Department's regional bureaus. Three separate offices report directly to the under secretary: Education and Cultural Affairs, Public Affairs, and International Information Programs.

Having formulated policies contrary to the advice of friendly Middle Eastern heads of state, the Bush administration had difficulty explaining its policies to Middle Eastern audiences. Well into its second term, Karen Hughes returned to the administration as the under secretary. She was a trusted advisor to the president and had been highly successful explaining Governor Bush's domestic policies to Texans. She was not as successful in explaining his foreign policies to Middle Eastern audiences. Policy actions that are objectionable to foreign audiences, sugar-coated with talk, remain objectionable. There are limits to public diplomacy; words and actions comprise a single message. The under secretary's job is complicated by the fact that most presidents prefer to communicate through the White House director of communications.

Civilian Security, Democracy and Human Rights

The majority of QDDR reforms of 2010 affected the *under secretary for civilian security, democracy and human rights*. The under secretary has responsibility for a variety of global issues, that is, functional issues that span multiple regions. Responsibilities include international population, refugee, and migration issues, for promoting democracy, human rights, and labor rights, and for combating human trafficking. The under secretary is also responsible for counterterrorism, conflict and stabilization operations, international narcotics and law enforcement, and global criminal justice.

Congress authorized the position in 1995.[12] The position was initially named *under secretary for global affairs* and was given the name *under secretary for democracy and global affairs* in 2005 to reflect the emphasis of the Bush 43 administration on promoting democracy abroad as part of the "global war on terrorism." It was little more than a name change. The 2010 QDDR resulted in more substantive reform, consolidating some former direct reporting offices and capturing other offices from other under secretaries. The new position was renamed the *under secretary for civilian security, democracy and human rights.*

Bureau of International Narcotics and Law Enforcement Affairs. The Bureau of International Narcotics and Law Enforcement Affairs deals with international drug trafficking and international crime. The Bureau also supports foreign criminal justice systems and law enforcement agencies with respect to international terrorism.

Bureau of Counterterrorism. State is the lead agency for counterterrorism, and the Bureau of Counterterrorism exists to carry out that departmental responsibility. The Bureau coordinates and supports the development and implementation of all U.S. government policies and programs for countering terrorism abroad.

The Office for Combatting Terrorism was established in 1972 during the Nixon administration after the Munich Olympics terrorist attack. The Office was responsible for policy initiatives and for day-to-day coordination of counterterrorism activities. The Office was redesignated in 1985 as the Office of the Ambassador-at-Large for Counterterrorism, and again in 1989 as the Office of the Coordinator for Counterterrorism. Congress mandated the Office in 1995[13] and its mission was refined by law in 1998.[14] The 2010 QDDR changed the reporting relationship from the secretary to the under secretary.

The Bureau head is appointed by the president with the advice and consent of the Senate and holds the rank of ambassador-at-large. Guided by the president's national security strategy, the coordinator is responsible for producing a national strategy for combating terrorism.[15] According to the national strategy document:

The mission of the [Bureau] for Counterterrorism . . . is to develop and lead a worldwide effort to combat terrorism using all the instruments of statecraft: diplomacy, economic power, intelligence, law enforcement, and military. [The Bureau] provides foreign policy oversight and guidance to all U.S. Government international counterterrorism activities.[16]

The Bureau has four functional directorates, each headed by a deputy coordinator. The Homeland Security Directorate maintains liaison with the White House National Security Council and the Department of Homeland Security. The Operations Directorate maintains liaison with the Defense Department and participates in the development and implementation of policies. The Programs, Plans, Press and Public Diplomacy Directorate is responsible for building the will and capacity of foreign governments to deal with terrorism. The Regional and Trans-Regional Office oversees the development, coordination, and implementation of national, regional, and multilateral counterterrorism policy.

The "Programs Directorate" is responsible for counterterrorism capacity building through a broad range of foreign assistance programs designed to train and equip foreign agencies for counterterrorism operations, including law enforcement, border control, banking regulations. Programs include the Anti-Terrorism Assistance Program, the Counterterrorism Finance Program, the Terrorist Interdiction Program, and with the Defense Department, the National Interagency Combating Terrorism Research and Development Program. The Directorate participates in State's budget process and manages the Bureau's relations with Congress, including production of the annual Department of State Country Reports on Terrorism, required by statute, to assist lawmakers in understanding the nature of the threat.

The Regional and Trans-Regional Directorate has two subordinate offices. The regional office has six regional subdivisions—Western Hemisphere, Europe and Eurasia, Near East, Africa, and East Asia and Pacific—designed to work through the regional offices of other departments and agencies. The Office also conducts liaison with the National Counterterrorism Center and the Intelligence Community. The Trans-Regional and Designations Office designates individual terrorists and

Foreign Terrorist Organizations (the Treasury Department designates terrorist fund-raisers, front companies, and supporters). These designations allow legal sanctions, for example, freezing the designee's assets. The Office also represents U.S. counterterrorism policies to international organizations like the UN and Group of Eight (G8).

The Operations Directorate assists the Defense Department in developing and implementing overseas counterterrorism policies. The Directorate also provides a Foreign Emergency Support Team, an interagency, on-call capability to respond to overseas terrorist events on short notice.

Bureau of Conflict and Stabilization Operations. After the 2003 invasion of Iraq, State established a *coordinator for reconstruction and stabilization* (CRS) as a direct reporting agency. It was blessed in statute by authorizing legislation. Congress authorized State to reprogram existing funds but refused meaningful appropriations. Assigned personnel were demoralized and since inception busied themselves in anticipation of disestablishment or neglect. The 2010 QDDR elevated the office to a bureau under an assistant secretary and changed the name to the *Bureau of Conflict and Stabilization Operations* (CSO) in November 2011. Personnel morale improved as they were better able to participate in budget processes, but the longevity of the mission after Iraq and Afghanistan remains a question.

Failing, failed, and postconflict states are breeding grounds for terrorism, trafficking, and other crimes. A variety of complex emergencies befall these states. The Bureau's mission is to prevent or prepare for the complex emergencies and to put states on a sustainable path to peace, democracy, market economy, development, and the rule of law. In the past, the national and international response has been ad hoc, requiring the re-creation of relationships and techniques. The Bureau is to make the capability permanent and to *lead a whole-of-government response.* Although a State Department entity, the Bureau is an interagency organization staffed by representatives from State, USAID, Defense, Justice, and others.

The Clinton administration responded to failed-state situations in Somalia, Haiti, Bosnia, and Kosovo. The presidential decision directive, PDD-56, Managing Complex Contingency Operations, was not entirely embraced by Defense or Congress, but the process and organizational relations were initiated and experience accumulated. Having campaigned against military interventions for nation building, the Bush administration revoked PDD-56 without replacement. Upon initiating operations in Afghanistan and Iraq, the administration lacked the capacity to define the desired end state and to orchestrate all instruments of power toward that end. The Bush administration had no way to develop a whole-of-government plan to achieve a desirable end state.

Those with extensive experience in foreign aid recognize a "golden hour," a brief period of time following a failure of central government when outside intervention can prevent a spiraling out of control that will be increasingly costly to arrest and reverse. The request for an appropriate response capability came from several agencies in April 2004. To that end, the Bush administration requested $100 million to be available to immediately fund operations in the golden hour. Long-term funding for sustained operations would continue to be requested through normal appropriations channels. Congress authorized reprogramming of existing funds to create the office in July 2004. Secretary Powell announced establishment of CRS on 5 August. And in November 2005, the House denied the request to establish a Conflict Response Fund at State. Officials at State and Defense were both supportive of the Fund. After the House refused the funds, Defense Secretary Donald Rumsfeld requested authority to transfer up to $200 million of Defense funds to State to conduct operations. In December, CRS's first director, Carlos Pascual, resigned.[17]

Pascual faulted "The [Bush] administration's lack of political will to get fully behind the capacity it set out to create, and the Congress' consistent rejection of the Administration's meager requests." He went on to say that CRS had weak representation on the NSC, and that the White House must use the capacity it created in CRS rather than circumvent it. "The necessary vitality at senior levels [the president]" was absent. Furthermore, Congress needs to allow more flexibility across accounts. There are now about twenty foreign affairs accounts, and account managers jealously guard them, making unity of effort problematic.

Direct Reporting Organizations

Some State Department organizations report directly to the secretary rather than through an under secretary. Most relevant to national security are the Bureau of Intelligence and Research and the Policy Planning Staff.

Policy and Planning Staff. Although the *Policy and Planning Staff* is typically shown as a line organization, it historically serves as a personal staff to the secretary. It has always been small, between ten and twenty, and a prestigious brain trust that focuses on the long term. After World War II, it served as the principal policy formulation body for foreign and national security policy. George Kennan and Paul Nitze—authors of the Cold War containment strategy—served successively as director.

Since creation in 1947 by Secretary of State George C. Marshall, the Staff has remained in a prestigious position but has lost prominence and influence as the National Security Council staff matured. It more recently has been dragged into current operations and troubleshooting. The Staff serves as tutor to the secretary when important issues arise requiring the secretary's personal attention. Although the Staff is headed by a director, directors enjoy status at the under secretary level.

Bureau of Intelligence and Research. The *Bureau of Intelligence and Research* is a prominent member of the Intelligence Community, and it participates in the production of National Intelligence Estimates. It exploits the information available from the diplomatic missions around the world and the expertise available in the regional bureaus. It has no covert or clandestine responsibilities. The Bureau of Intelligence was originally established in 1957 and has earned a superior reputation based on a long history of competence at the strategic level, but it lacks the sophisticated technical means available elsewhere in government and is unable to contribute significantly to real-time, tactical processes.

Department of Defense

Prior to the Second World War, there were three separate and equal Departments of State, Navy, and War (see figure 6). In times of crisis, the president requests a declaration of war or an authorization for the use of force that required Congress to exercise its constitutional authority to raise an army. The War Department stood by with the planning capacity to raise that army. Below the threshold of declared war, the president could conduct foreign affairs—including diplomacy, coercive diplomacy backed

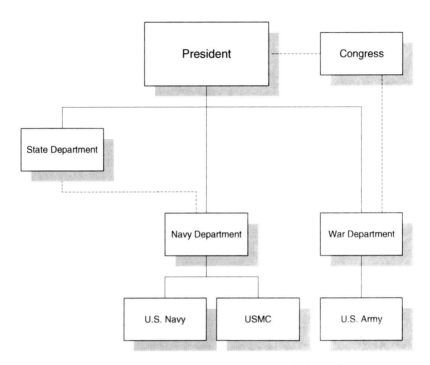

FIG. 6. Pre–World War II national security organizational relationships

by force, or small wars—through the State and Navy Departments. Marines were often referred to as State Department troops during this era.

This dual organizational arrangement, in line with constitutional authorities, presented significant problems when waging a declared major war like World War II. Dozens of coordinating boards were established to coordinate the activities of the State, Navy, and War Departments. The National Security Act of 1947 created the National Military Establishment to unify the Departments of Army, Navy, and Air Force. The Establishment's name was soon changed to the Department of Defense. The ability to conduct great-power war was improved, but something was lost.

The Defense Department is the largest employer in government and has the largest budget. In 2008, there were more than 1.3 million uniformed military on active duty, with another 1.1 million in the reserve. The Department also employs almost seven hundred thousand civilians.

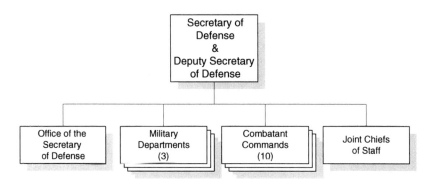

FIG. 7. Defense Department organization

Beneath the secretary and deputy secretary are three military departments—Army, Navy, and Air Force—the Office of the Secretary of Defense, the Joint Chiefs of Staff, and the Combatant Commands (see figure 7).

Military Departments

The National Security Act of 1947 replaced the War Department with the Department of the Army and the Department of the Air Force. The Department of the Navy remained intact. The military departments provided civilian oversight of the uniformed services. Aviation assets—aircraft, bases, and personnel—were systematically transferred to the new Air Force. The secretaries of the military departments soon were removed from the chain of command governing the *use* of force and lost cabinet status. Their duties were eventually restricted to the *production* of force. The military departments and constituent uniformed services *recruit, organize, train, and equip* the force for *use* by the combatant commanders.

Each of the services has its own conception of war. Major war has been the dominant organizing principle for the Army, Navy, and Air Force. The Marine Corps, albeit with a major war mission of amphibious assault, retains a strong small-war culture as does the special operations community. *Transformation* was the post–Cold War watchword. The dominant service cultures preferred transformation of the industrial-age force for major war to the information-age force for major war: the *revolution in military affairs* (RMA). Others argued for a transformation to a small-wars

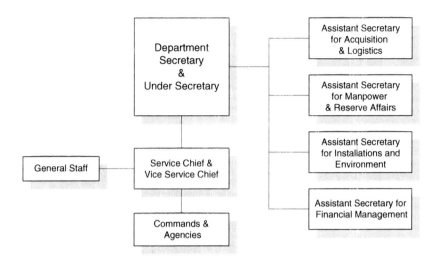

FIG. 8. Military departments

force for the interwar period. The producer chain of command pursued the RMA while the small wars of the interwar period erupted, leaving the combatant commands with a force poorly suited to the mission.

While there is some variability in the organization of the three military departments, they have more in common than not. Figure 8 shows a notional organization. Each has an assistant secretary for the acquisition of next generation weapon systems. This assistant secretary is the Service Acquisition Executive (SAE) with specific statutory authorities. Each department has an assistant secretary for manpower and reserve affairs with responsibilities for human resource functions, including personnel, education, and health-care policies. Each has an assistant secretary for budget and financial issues: the department's chief financial officer. And each has an assistant secretary to oversee the service's installations, including infrastructure and environmental issues. The service chief reports to the secretary and has a separate staff. The Navy Department has two service chiefs, the chief of naval operations and the commandant of the Marine Corps.

Office of the Secretary of Defense

The Office of the Secretary of Defense (OSD) was originally established to assist the secretary in managing the military departments (see figure 9).

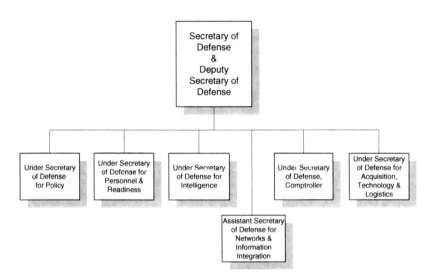

FIG. 9. Office of the Secretary of Defense

Over time, functions common to the uniformed services were con-solidated in newly created *defense agencies*. Originally assigned to the Joint Chiefs of Staff, the defense agencies were eventually transferred to OSD, typically under an assistant secretary. There are currently seventeen defense agencies and eleven DOD field activities in the Defense Depart-ment. This evolution shifted OSD from staff to line. One might ask an independent staff about the status of military training and have some expectation of a credible answer. If, on the other hand, one asks the head of the line organization responsible for training, one might expect a self-serving answer. Staff and line exist for entirely different reasons. OSD has a certain amount of dysfunction built in.

Policy. The *under secretary of defense for policy* (USD(P)) is the principal staff assistant and advisor to the secretary and deputy secretary on mat-ters of defense and national security policy and for overseeing its implementation. The under secretary is supported by a principal deputy under secretary, two deputy under secretaries, and three assistant secre-taries. The under secretary often sits on the deputies committee of the National Security Council.

- ASD (International Security Affairs)
- ASD (Strategy and Threat Reduction)
- ASD (Special Operations and Low-Intensity Conflict)
- DUSD (Policy Support)
- DUSD (Technology Security Policy)
- Defense advisor to the U.S. Mission to NATO

The under secretary exercises authority over the Defense Security Cooperation Agency through the ASD for international security affairs.

DOD's increased influence in foreign policy formulation is attributed to the strengthening of USD(P). Through USD(P), Defense arguably achieved dominance over State and the National Security Council under Rumsfeld.

Intelligence. The Defense Intelligence Agency, National Security Agency, National Geospatial-Intelligence Agency, and National Reconnaissance Office all report to the *under secretary of defense for intelligence* (USD(I)), and all are important members of the broader Intelligence Community. The CIA was established by law in 1947, but the defense agencies were established by executive order under DOD control.

The Defense Intelligence Agency (DIA) was formed in the early 1960s and was initially populated by recently retired military intelligence officers. Its collection efforts are focused on foreign military capabilities. The DIA's estimates were more likely to justify Defense budgets than were CIA estimates. The DIA once reported to the chairman of the JCS as the joint staff intelligence directorate. During Rumsfeld's tenure, it was moved to OSD, reporting to the secretary through an under secretary. The DIA also provides a *military attaché* to the ambassador's country team in foreign embassies.

The National Security Agency (NSA) is the primary collector of signals intelligence (SIGINT)—electromagnetic eavesdropping—and ensurer of communications security. Initially established by executive order, it gained statutory authorities in the National Security Agency Act of 1959. A 1972 presidential directive promoted full participation by the military components responsible for SIGINT under the Central Security Service (CSS). Focused on technical means, it employed mathematicians and computer scientists, and the post-9/11 era found the Agency short of linguists and analysts. The NSA underwent a rejuvenation, acquiring new skills and youth while losing experience to obsolescence and retirement.

The National Geospatial-Intelligence Agency (NGA) is somewhat new and a product of rapid technical change. The old Defense Mapping Agency—formed in 1972 by consolidating existing service capabilities—provided paper maps to the Department. It was largely a print shop. It turned abruptly to digital maps and electronic distribution and became the National Imaging and Mapping Agency (NIMA) in 1996. The CIA's National Photographic Interpretation Center (NPIC), reporting to the Directorate of Intelligence in 1958, was moved to the Directorate for Science and Technology in 1973, and merged with NIMA in 1996. More rapid technological change and mergers late in 2003 led to the NGA with a principal focus on image intelligence (IMINT) under the new designation of geospatial intelligence (GEOINT).

The National Reconnaissance Office (NRO) was first established in 1960. Soon after Frances Gary Powers was shot down over the Soviet Union flying a U-2 spy plane, Eisenhower initiated a study to determine the feasibility of photo reconnaissance conducted by satellite. Jointly sponsored activities of the CIA and Air Force the year before provided the foundation. The NRO acquires, launches, and operates the necessary overhead assets.

Personnel & Readiness. The *under secretary of defense for personnel and readiness* (USD(P&R)) performs the same functions as the assistant secretaries for manpower and reserve affairs in the military departments. The under secretary is supported by two assistant secretaries and two deputy under secretaries. The defense agencies for commissaries, education, human resources, and health care report to P&R.

Comptroller. The *under secretary of defense (comptroller)* is the Department's chief financial officer. The under secretary is supported by a principal deputy under secretary. The office administers the all-important Programming, Planning, and Budgeting System. The Defense Contract Audit Agency and the Defense Finance and Accounting Service report to the under secretary.

The Director of Program Analysis and Evaluation (PA&E) was created by Defense Secretary Robert McNamara to look across service programs at the total force, for example, to assess the totality of strategic nuclear forces of the Air Force and Navy.[18] Prior to PA&E, each service budget was considered separately. The services, resenting the second-guessing, quickly countered with their own PA&E organizations to challenge the findings of OSD. The chairman of the JCS also was given budgetary and oversight authorities in 1986 legislation.

Acquisition, Technology, and Logistics. The *under secretary of defense for acquisition, technology, and logistics* (USD(AT&L)) is the principal advisor and assistant to the secretary and deputy secretary for all matters relating to DOD acquisition. The under secretary is the Defense Acquisition Executive (DAE) with specific statutory responsibilities. The office largely establishes policies in accordance with law and oversees compliance with those policies. But several defense agencies with line responsibilities are organized in the office of AT&L.

The DAE and the service acquisition executives in the respective military departments are responsible for all defense acquisitions and for huge budgets. Work is carried out by private defense contractors. Acquisition programs are managed by the services. No other department or agency of government has the acquisition capacity of the Defense Department.

A separate and semi-independent director of operational test and evaluation reports on operational testing of major weapon systems. The director sits between the secretary and the under secretary. It is not uncommon for the secretary to hear about budget, schedule, and development problems from the *Washington Post* before hearing from the defense and service acquisition executives.

USD(AT&L) exercises authority over several defense agencies. The *Missile Defense Agency* has acquisition responsibilities for ballistic and cruise missile defense systems. Logistics functions common to the uniformed services were consolidated under the Defense Supply Agency in 1961. The name was changed to *Defense Logistics Agency* in 1977. The *Defense Threat Reduction Agency* (DTRA), established in 1998, consolidated DOD's capabilities to deter, reduce, eliminate, and counter weapons of mass destruction, including chemical, biological, radiological, nuclear, and high-yield explosive weapons. The Agency is primarily oriented on the acquisition of equipment, but it has some operational capability as well. DTRA reports to USD(AT&L) for the former and to STRATCOM for the latter.

Networks and Information Integration. The *assistant secretary of defense for networks and information integration* (ASD(NII)) is the Department's chief information officer. The office has acquisition authority to build the network that supports the defense establishment. The position was more recently known as the assistant secretary for command, control, communications, and intelligence (ASD(C3I)), an office mandated by Goldwater-Nichols legislation in 1986. ASD(C3I) had responsibility for overseeing policies and operations of the NSA, DIA, and NIMA, and it had acquisition authorities like USD(AT&L). The office's acquisition responsibilities are now centered in ASD(NII), and the policy and operations responsibilities were reassigned to the new USD(I).

Joint Chiefs of Staff

The Joint Chiefs of Staff (JCS) was initially a committee of service chiefs with no one in charge. When a chairman was authorized, he had no vote and little authority, only the responsibility to induce agreements among the service chiefs. The Joint Staff worked for the JCS, not for the chairman, and was constituted from personnel on loan part-time from the service chiefs' staffs.

Today's JCS is different. By law, the chairman of the JCS (CJCS) and the vice chairman (VCJCS) are the two top officers in the uniformed military. The chairman has true authorities and a permanent Joint Staff that reports through a director to the chairman to assist in carrying out the chairman's many statutory responsibilities. The JCS and the Joint Staff structure is depicted in figure 10. The combatant commands have similar joint staffs, typically including only the J1 through J5.

An important Pentagon process deserves attention: the *Joint Strategic Planning System*. The system produces three documents: the Unified Command Plan (UCP), the Joint Strategic Capabilities Plan (JSCP, jay-scap), and the Forces for Combatant Commands (Forces For) Memorandum. The UCP and JSCP are the responsibility of the chairman's J5. The Forces For Memo is the responsibility of the chairman's J8.

The UCP establishes the combatant commands and assigns regional and functional responsibilities. The JSCP directs the combatant commands to develop plans for specific possible uses of military force. Forces are

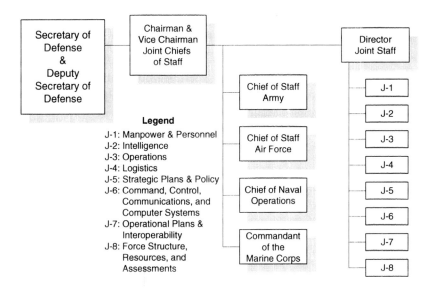

FIG. 10. Joint Chiefs of Staff and Joint Staff

apportioned to the combatant commands for purposes of planning. The JSCP is a collaborative process of the chairman's J5 and the J5 of the respective combatant command. The Forces For Memo *assigns* forces to combatant commands, which are then responsible for preparing forces for assigned missions.

As a crisis emerges, the chairman's J5 and the respective combatant command's J5 select the most relevant operational plan (OPLAN, oh-plan) and begin to tailor it to the current situation. Moving military forces to a theater of operations requires a deployment order (DEPORD, dep-ord) signed by the secretary of defense. The DEPORD is first coordinated by the State Department to assure approval from the sovereign states affected by the deployment. As operation commencement time approaches, a *warning order* passes from the chairman's J3 to the combatant command's J3. When the president and secretary of defense give final approval, an *execute order* passes between the J3s. The OPLAN becomes the operational order (OPORD, op-ord), and forces are *allocated* to the combatant command, giving the combatant commander legal authority to employ allocated forces to execute the designated operation.

At the end of the Cold War, forces began to return to the United States, forces were reduced in numbers, and the presidential use of force accelerated rapidly. Where forces were once dedicated to a specific region and war plan, the scarcity of forces today must meet the requirements of all regions and all war plans. But operations in Iraq and Afghanistan made it difficult to prepare for other contingencies.

Combatant Commands

All military operations are conducted under the legal authorities of one of the combatant commanders. Combatant commands are either *unified* (all services) or *specified* (single service). Although authorized in law, there are currently no specified commands; the Strategic Air Command was one of the last specified commands disestablished in 1992. Unified commands are either *regional* or *functional*, although this distinction is not mentioned in statute. Functional commands tend to enter into a supported/supporting relationship with a regional command with respect to a specific war plan or an ongoing operation. Each command is briefly covered below.

Central Command. The *Central Command* (CENTCOM) is a regional unified command, headquartered in Tampa, Florida. Its area of responsibility spreads across South and Central Asia, including the "stans," the former Soviet states, and much of the Middle East (excluding Mediterranean states). It recently lost the Horn of Africa to the new Africa Command.

The region did not warrant a combatant command during most of the Cold War. The 1973 Arab-Israeli War and increased growth of Chinese, Cuban, and Soviet presence in Sub-Saharan Africa by 1976 brought greater attention to the region and a rapid sequence of ad hoc solutions. The Soviet's 1979 invasion of Afghanistan precipitated the Carter Doctrine with respect to the Persian Gulf area. Carter ordered establishment of the Rapid Deployment Joint Task Force to back up the Doctrine. Reagan approved establishment of CENTCOM on 1 January 1983 from Carter's RDJTF.

From birth, CENTCOM was only a secondary theater in Cold War planning.[19] The Gulf War (1990–91) completed CENTCOM's transition from a backwater to become the country's principal war-fighting command.

Iraq's aggression against Kuwait provided the United States with unprecedented access to bases and facilities in the region.

European Command. The *European Command* (EUCOM, you-comm), headquartered in Stuttgart, Germany, is a regional unified command. The EUCOM commander is dual-hatted, with the grandiloquent title of Supreme Allied Commander, Europe (SACEUR, sack-yur), the top NATO position. EUCOM is the command most affected by the shift from great power to interwar period. EUCOM was a planner and provider of U.S. forces to NATO, headquartered in Mons, Belgium. As a force provider, EUCOM dominated Army and Air Force thinking on training and doctrine and set the norms worldwide for both. EUCOM epitomized the major-war culture.

After the fall of the Berlin Wall, EUCOM undertook the task of aiding the former states of the Soviet Union through the Partnership for Peace. It is impossible to quantify the stabilizing force provided by EUCOM's presence during the Cold War and during the difficult transition following.

Until recently, EUCOM's area of responsibility spanned the Scandinavian countries, the European landmass including Turkey, Middle Eastern countries bordering the Mediterranean, Africa excluding the Horn, and the surrounding waterways. In 2007, it stood up a subordinate unified command for Africa, which became a full unified combatant command in 2008.

Africa Command. The *Africa Command* (AFRICOM) was first established in October 2007 as a subordinate unified command under the European Command. Its headquarters was established and developed in Stuttgart, Germany, and it became an independent unified command in October 2008. AFRICOM's area of responsibility includes the continent of Africa formerly under EUCOM. Parts of East Africa remained under CENTCOM but soon transferred to AFRICOM. Its focus is on building the host-nation capacities to prevent and respond to crises through military-to-military relations and increased presence on embassy country teams.

Pacific Command. The *Pacific Command* (PACOM) is a regional unified command headquartered in Honolulu, Hawaii. PACOM has the largest area of responsibility (AOR) of any unified command, over half the earth's surface, including vast expanses of empty waters and almost 60 percent of the world's population. The command's AOR spans the Pacific Ocean and includes China, Mongolia, Japan, the Koreas, India, Southeast Asia, the Philippines, and Indonesia. PACOM has considerable organizational infrastructure oriented on humanitarian assistance and disaster relief and has responsibilities should conflict emerge on the Korean Peninsula or across the Taiwan Strait. The Command has wielded considerable diplomatic influence in the region in the absence of a State Department authority of any comparable consequence.

Southern Command. The *Southern Command* (SOUTHCOM) is a regional unified command headquartered in Miami, Florida. SOUTHCOM was established in June 1963, subsuming the area and responsibilities of the Caribbean Command, which dates to the opening of the Panama Canal and World War I. Responsibilities shifted from defending the southern maritime approach from European powers to conducting political-military interactions within Latin America. Defending the Canal remained a core mission throughout. Assigned forces are minimal, mostly limited to counterdrug operations. Headquarters moved from Panama City to Miami in 1998.

SOUTHCOM is better understood as a political command rather than a war-fighting command. South America has been the most militarized continent in past decades but has never been home to a great power. Latin American presidents commonly wore the uniform of an army general, and their preferred communications path to the United States was not through the State Department or CIA but through SOUTHCOM's Military Advisory Groups and a U.S. Army colonel. Not until the Carter administration, accompanied by post-Vietnam antimilitary sentiment, did diplomatic relations take on a more traditional appearance.

The transition to an interwar period has forced other unified commands to shift from a war-fighting orientation to a theater-engagement orientation, the norm in SOUTHCOM for many years.

Northern Command. The *Northern Command* (NORTHCOM) formed in response to the 9/11 attacks. While most of the Defense Department *defends forward*, NORTHCOM defends the homeland and the air, land, and sea approaches extending five hundred miles beyond the coast. The homeland defense mission has not been taken seriously for a very long time. The command has regional responsibility for North America (including the Gulf of Mexico, Puerto Rico, and the U.S. Virgins Islands) and is headquartered in Colorado Springs, Colorado.

NORTHCOM's mission includes *consequence management*—military assistance to civil authorities in the United States after a natural or man-made disaster. This mission is perhaps NORTHCOM's most critical contribution to national security and the most problematic. A great many working relationships between federal, state, and local agencies must be defined, built, and exercised. NORTHCOM cannot solve these problems; it is not in command. These problems are beyond even the highest level of the federal government, given the fact that governors, mayors, local law enforcement, and emergency medical services are not federal and will always carry the heaviest burden in consequence management.

Also at issue are the roles of the active and reserve military organizations, particularly the role of the National Guard. The Guard is ideally suited to integrate with state and local agencies for consequence management but prefers to organize as combat forces and is deployed abroad with regularity. The reserve units well suited to consequence management in the United States (military police, engineers, transportation, medical, and civil affairs units) are in heavy demand for nation building overseas and are unavailable for use by governors. NORTHCOM cannot solve these problems, either.

Special Operations Command. The *Special Operations Command* (SOCOM, so-comm) is a functional unified command responsible for providing special operations forces to the regional combatant commands. SOCOM, headquartered in Tampa, Florida, was established in 1987, but only after legislation demanded it. Legislative action resulted from long-running conflict within the executive branch between the president (user of military force) and the services (producers of military force). The services steadfastly neglected the function, preferring instead to provide conventional forces for major war. Special operations, civil affairs, and psychological operations forces are assigned to SOCOM by law.

The command is unusual in that it has characteristics more like a service providing forces organized, trained, and equipped to the regional combatant commands for employment. It has specialized acquisition authorities.

Secretary Rumsfeld bypassed the Joint Strategic Planning System and directly assigned SOCOM the Defense lead in the global war on terrorism, a role it was ill-suited to perform. Simultaneously, large numbers of its forces, including Army Special Forces and Navy SEALs, were assigned bodyguard duties in Iraq. Conventional force commanders commonly employ special operations forces in ways for which they were not designed.

Joint Forces Command. The *Joint Forces Command* (JFCOM, jay eff-comm), headquartered in Norfolk, Virginia, was a functional unified command without area or global responsibilities. The command had authority over assigned forces in CONUS not assigned elsewhere, and it was responsible for providing CONUS-based forces from all services to the regional combatant commanders, the users of force. JFCOM was the force provider. The Atlantic Command, an almost exclusively naval command, became Joint Forces Command in October 1999 with little more than a name change.

From inception, JFCOM had been the force provider for conventional forces (readiness for the present), but Secretary Rumsfeld assigned JFCOM the additional mission to *transform* U.S. forces (readiness for the future). Like SOCOM, JFCOM's mission was more like a service than a combatant command. After more than a decade, JFCOM had failed to establish its own identity, and its relevance was questionable. It failed in the transformation mission, leaving the transformation problem for CENTCOM to solve under fire. Defense Secretary Robert Gates announced his intention to disestablish the command in August 2010. Formal disestablishment came in August 2011.

Strategic Command. The *Strategic Command* (STRATCOM) is a functional unified command with global responsibilities for strike in support of the global war on terrorism, for missile defense of the continental United States, and for space and information operations in support of the other combatant commands. STRATCOM is headquartered near Omaha, Nebraska, with strong remnants of the former *Space Command* (SPACECOM) remaining in Colorado Springs.

Early in the Cold War, the services independently developed their nuclear delivery mechanisms and separately targeted the Soviet Union.

In 1960, the Joint Strategic Target Planning Staff was established to produce the Single Integrated Operational Plan (SIOP, sigh-op). A 1969–70 blue-ribbon panel recommended the establishment of STRATCOM, with strategic bombers, intercontinental ballistic missiles (ICBMs), and ballistic missile submarines (SSBNs)—the nuclear triad—assigned. But STRATCOM was not established until 1992, *after* the Cold War.

Secretary Rumsfeld bypassed the Joint Strategic Planning System and directly assigned STRATCOM a new mission—global strike. On 1 October 2002 the old STRATCOM was disestablished and a new command established with the same name and the new mission. STRATCOM is now responsible for short-notice attacks on, for example, heavily fortified, high-value targets. Furthermore, the potential for STRATCOM attacks—to be conducted within a regional combatant command's area of responsibility—created unresolved command relationships. Nuclear and conventional munitions as well as conventional forces are within the new STRATCOM purview.

The new STRATCOM also subsumed SPACECOM and inherited its mission for space and information operations. All military space-based assets—for example, communications, navigation, weather, warning, or intelligence gathering assets—are under STRATCOM. The U.S. Cyber Command headquartered with the National Security Agency was established as a subordinate unified command in June 2009 and reached full operational capability on 31 October 2010.

Transportation Command. The *Transportation Command* (TRANSCOM) is a functional unified command with global responsibility for movement of troops and supplies. TRANSCOM, established in 1987, and headquartered in East St. Louis, Illinois, consolidates all strategic lift assets under one commander. Given the United States force posture to defend forward, the command is of critical strategic significance. TRANSCOM's functional responsibilities include management of air, sea, rail, and road assets from bases in the United States to delivery to the theater of operations. In addition to the global transportation responsibility, the command was given responsibility in 2003 for distribution of equipment and supplies.

The National Guard and Reserve

The National Guard derives from the state militias during the early days of the country, spanning the revolution, the Articles of Confederation, and the framing of the Constitution. There was a distrust of a standing army, the existence of which would incline presidents toward war. The federal army would be a small cadre of professionals during peacetime, and combat power would be in the governors' militias. Should the president chose war, Congress would have to be convinced to raise an army, and the governors would have to be convinced to contribute their militia. All this was to be a check on the presidential power to wage war. The professional federal army would keep the arts alive during peace and bring the militia up to professional standards in war.

For several decades, the National Guard (Army and Air Force) and the Reserve (Army, Air Force, Navy, and Marine Corps) have constituted a *strategic reserve.* That is, they stood at various levels of readiness should Congress declare war or authorize the use of force in a conflict requiring a major mobilization to protect the country's vital interests. Volunteers typically committed one weekend per month and two weeks per summer to training. The Reserve provided mostly individual replacements and augmentation to the high-echelon staffs required for major wars. The National Guard was mostly organized as units of combat power, e.g., armored divisions and fighter wings. Those days are long gone. Today's post–Cold War National Guard and Reserve constitute an *operational reserve.* Individuals and units conducted multiple deployments in Iraq, Afghanistan, and the Horn of Africa.

According to the U.S. Commission on the National Guard and Reserve, the change from strategic to operational reserve is driven by two concurrent trends: the post–Cold War drawdown of military forces; and the post–Cold War increase in military interventionism. Both political parties clearly participated in both trends. It is a post–Cold War phenomenon and not a Republican, Democratic, liberal, or conservative phenomenon. It is a matter of chosen strategy. Force development policy has seen a reduction in the size of the force. Force employment policy has seen an increase in the use of military forces for nation building. When Iraq and Afghanistan were both active, *there was no strategic reserve.*

The Intelligence Community

The Intelligence Community (IC) is spread across the departments and agencies. Sixteen members are part of a cabinet department with specific roles and missions. Each of the uniformed services, for example, has intelligence components designed to meet its specific needs. Only the CIA and the Office of the Director of National Intelligence lie outside a cabinet department.

From 1947 to 2002, the director of central intelligence (DCI) had dual responsibilities. The DCI, sitting at the head of the intelligence community, was the president's principal advisor on intelligence matters and a statutory advisor to the National Security Council. The DCI was also the director of the CIA. Responding to the 9/11 Commission,[20] the responsibilities were separated, and distinct positions of director of national intelligence (DNI) and director of the CIA (DCIA) were established. The responsibilities associated with head of intelligence community were assigned to the new DNI, including responsibilities for managing the broader intelligence budget.

Office of the Director of National Intelligence

The Office of the DNI includes the National Intelligence Council (NIC, nick). A dozen or so national intelligence officers (NIO) comprise the NIC. Each is a senior analyst drawn from across the Intelligence Community and from the private sector. Each has a regional or functional orientation. There are regional NIOs for Europe, Russia and Eurasia, Latin America, Near East and South Asia, East Asia, and Africa. There are functional NIOs for Economic and Global Issues, Transnational Threats, Military Issues, Intelligence Assurance, Warning, and WMD Proliferation.

The NIOs produce national intelligence estimates (NIEs). Typically an NIO tasks an analyst in one of the intelligence agencies to draft the estimate and analysts from across the community review the draft. The NIE is forward-looking, not an assessment of the current situation. Draft NIEs are reviewed and approved by the President's Foreign Intelligence Advisory Board, a group of no more than sixteen presidential appointees. The DNI is also responsible for the President's Daily Brief and for the Senior Executive Intelligence Brief disseminated to the heads of departments and agencies.

Central Intelligence Agency

The Central Intelligence Agency (CIA) was established by the National Security Act of 1947 as an independent agency reporting to the president's NSC. Issues too contentious at the time were deferred until the Central Intelligence Agency Act of 1949. Throughout the Cold War it served as the integrating function from the intelligence capabilities spread across the departments and agencies of the executive branch. The Agency retains the ability to collect its own intelligence, the ability to analyze intelligence from all sources, and the ability to conduct operations.

The State Department found disagreeable the aggressive intelligence gathering and covert political action of World War II. If those functions were to continue into the Cold War, then a separate organization was required—the CIA. The Agency advised the NSC; made recommendations to the NSC on coordinating intelligence activities; correlated, evaluated, and disseminated intelligence; and performed additional activities deemed necessary by the NSC.

The Agency quickly became the primary organization responsible for intelligence analysis, clandestine human intelligence collection, and covert operations. *Covert* operations are those that, if discovered, can be plausibly denied by the sponsor—that is, the act may be overt and seen by all, but the actor is obscured. In contrast, it is common knowledge that the United States is an actor involved in *clandestine* intelligence collection, but the act itself is obscured. Perhaps more significantly, covert operations require a presidential finding and congressional notification, and clandestine operations do not.

The director of the CIA has deputy directors sitting at the top of four directorates. The Directorate for Science and Technology operates the technical means employed by the Agency, and it includes an acquisition authority. The Directorate for Intelligence houses intelligence officers organized into regional and functional bureaus. The Directorate for Operations, recently renamed the National Clandestine Service, has responsibilities for collecting human intelligence (HUMINT) and for covert and clandestine operations.

The senior CIA representative in a foreign embassy is known as the *chief of station* and is a prominent member of the ambassador's country team. HUMINT is collected by *case officers* who manage *agents* who are foreign nationals. CIA officers may be assigned to other agencies of government and provided with official cover and diplomatic protections. They are referred to as *nominals* because they are outwardly employees of the host department or agency. A smaller number are without diplomatic cover as *nonofficial cover* (NOC, nawk) personnel.

Federal Bureau of Investigation

Part of the Justice Department, the FBI is the premier federal law enforcement agency and is an important part of the Intelligence Community. The FBI traces its birth to 1908, although the name was not formally bestowed until 1935. Born during Theodore Roosevelt's administration (1901–9), it carried the Progressive Era's emphasis on professional competence over political patronage and an expanded role for the federal government. The newly appointed FBI Director J. Edgar Hoover (1924–1972), himself a Progressive, aggressively returned the Bureau to professionalism after Taft's cronyism.

There were few federal crimes to enforce in the early days, only those issues that crossed state lines. National banking, antitrust, and peonage (compulsory servitude) cases consumed much of the Bureau's energy. Advances in communications and transportation technologies created new opportunities for interstate crime, and new laws followed requiring enforcement. The Bureau increased its support to state and local law enforcement, including an increasingly sophisticated crime laboratory.

Emphasis shifted over time. Prohibition (1920–33), the Stock Market Crash (1929), the Great Depression (1929–39), and the massive fraud and failure of the savings and loan industry of the 1980s led the FBI to shift emphasis to white-collar and organized crime. World War I, World War II, and the Cold War led the FBI to shift emphasis to espionage, sabotage, and violation of selective service laws. It also included a foreign intelligence function until the CIA was established for that purpose in 1947.

The 1970s and 1980s were dynamic and resulted in the establishment of FBI national priorities. Director Clarence M. Kelley (1973–78) established three national priorities for the Bureau: (1) foreign counterintelligence (preventing intelligence collection by hostile states' intelligence agencies), (2) organized crime, and (3) white collar crime. In response to increased terrorist activity in the 1980s, William H. Webster (1978–87) added (4) counterterrorism. Following terrorism at Munich, the FBI unveiled its *Hostage Rescue Team* at the 1984 Summer Olympics in Los Angeles. The massive fraud in the failure of the savings and loan industry led to a reemphasis on its traditional area of white-collar crime. Acting Director John Otto added (5) counterdrug in 1987. In 1989, William S. Sessions (1987–93) added (6) violent crime.

The formal dissolution of the USSR at the end of 1991 caused a rapid reorientation of FBI efforts. Three hundred special agents were reassigned from foreign counterintelligence to violent-crime investigations. Director Louis Freeh (1993–2001) undertook numerous reform initiatives to reorient the Bureau for the post–Cold War environment. He urged *prevention* over *prosecution*, that is, investigations to penetrate, disrupt, and thwart terrorist organizations rather than after-the-fact investigations to bring perpetrators of terrorist acts to justice. Freeh also expanded legal attaché (*Legat*) representation in embassies abroad and emphasized the Middle East. He encouraged greater cooperation between the Legats and the CIA chief of station in the embassies. He also expanded and deepened international police partnerships.

The 1990s included some highly publicized events. The disasters at Ruby Ridge (1992) and Waco (1993) led to the creation of the FBI's *Critical Incident Response Group*. The same period included successful FBI investigations of the World Trade Center bombing (1993), the Murrah Federal Building bombing (1995), and the Unabomber (1996).

In 1998 the FBI designated *counterterrorism* as its top priority, and the five-year plan included a program to build counterterrorism professionals. But senior FBI officials in Washington and the field offices resisted the redirection. In 1999 separate counterterrorism and counterintelligence divisions were established. The Counterterrorism Division was to complement the CIA's counterterrorism center, but resources did not follow. In 2000 there were twice as many agents devoted to counterdrug as to counterterrorism.

The Washington Field Office is generally responsible for overseas operations, but standard operating procedures grant persistent authorities to the *office of origin*. Because the New York Field Office had investigated the World Trade Center bombing (1993), it investigated the East Africa bombings (1998) and the attack on the USS *Cole* in Yemen (2000). Knowledge of al-Qaeda was concentrated in the New York office rather than shared across the fifty-six field offices.

In 2001, the FBI was not properly oriented on the threat of al-Qaeda and associated movements (AQAM). Decentralization favored local over national priorities. Collection on the new threat was weak due to lack of language and cultural skills. Human resource policies did not shift toward the counterterrorist profession, nor did they elevate the role of analysts and analysis. Information systems were outdated, and information was not adequately shared. Agents and offices were credited for their arrests, indictments, prosecutions, and convictions. Promotions went to criminal investigators and not to those agents engaged in intelligence or counterterrorism. Senior agents had little counterterrorism experience.

Robert S. Mueller (2001–13) was appointed director a week before the 9/11 attacks. Under his charge, the Bureau conducted a massive investigation including domestic and foreign law enforcement agencies. He pushed again Freeh's shift in emphasis from investigation to prevention of terrorist acts, this time with greater organizational cooperation. James Comey was appointed director on 4 September 2013 and is increasing emphasis on cyber crime.

As of 2014, counterterrorism and counterintelligence remain top national security priorities. The FBI employees 35,000 personnel assigned to Washington, the fifty-six field offices, and sixty-three international offices (Legats). Its budget has more than doubled to over $8 billion since 9/11. In addition to its mainline investigative capabilities, it has national and regional SWAT teams, national and regional Hostage Rescue Teams, and 141 Evidence Response Teams, some specialized, including teams for evidence collection underwater, in hazardous (WMD) environments, and from computer systems.

Production and Application of Power

Achieving a unity of effort from a diversity of means has at least two components: the *production* of the necessary means and their *application* to objectives. A president can apply only capability previously built. A change in president, or a change in environment, may result in a change in strategy. A change in strategy may result in a change in presidential demands on the mechanisms of the departments and agencies. And a dramatic change in strategy may make demands on mechanisms ill-suited to the task. Producing a mature mechanism may take a decade or more, and then only after the shortcoming is recognized and addressed.

The necessary means—whether called instruments, mechanisms, capabilities, or tools—must be made available, and they must be in the right balance. Unless unlimited resources are available, too much of one results in too little of another. There is no reason to assume that the tools suited to the Cold War great power conflict are equally suited to the twenty-first century. Even if the same instruments are appropriate, there is no reason to assume that they are in the right balance. Adjustments must be made, and adjustments take time. Overcoming Cold War inertia requires sustained legislative and executive energy.

Production and application of means are shared responsibilities of the legislative and executive branches of government. It is useful to view Congress as leading in the production of capabilities and the president and cabinet in leading in the application of capabilities within statutory grants of authority. But the president certainly has an important role to play in the production of capability. The president and heads of departments and agencies must convey to Congress their needs in terms of additional statutory authorities and budget. The legislative and executive branches must then come to agreement. This bargaining produces the capabilities available for use by the president.

The president dominates in the application of force. Over time, the president assigns a range of missions to the components of the executive branch, and the capabilities spread across the branch need to be assembled and directed in common cause—orchestrated—in a whole-of-government response.

In general, departments and agencies are produced by congressional authorizing legislation. However, some agencies (e.g., some defense agencies) are created by executive order signed only by the president. Agencies created by executive order operate under the parent department's existing statutory authorities. Regardless of the basis of their existence, only Congress can appropriate funds for the agencies. And Congress can check a president's creation of an agency by refusing adequate appropriations.

The executive branch dominates in policy formulation. Soon after World War II, the State Department led in policy formulation. But since then, the National Security Council, designed in law to assist the president in *coordinating* policy developed in the departments, now plays the dominant role in *formulating* policy. Members of Congress represent small and diverse constituencies; the president represents the entire nation and sits atop the entire executive branch hierarchy. With a carefully selected staff, the president is better able to set an agenda and guide policy formulation with a single hand. According to one analyst:

> [Congress] is chaotic, non-hierarchical, and fragmented. . . . It is inherently political . . . and responds to political stimuli. [Congress] is particularly well structured to react to many publics (including other governmental institutions) and, in reacting, to criticize, refine, promote alternative proposals, bargain, and compromise. [Congress] is a representative forum for national-level debate and deliberation, a place where consensus is built and retained.[21]

> Congress is not now and never has been well designed to create its own agenda and act on it in a coordinated way to produce a unified domestic or foreign policy program.[22]

In more dramatic cases, when the executive has demonstrably failed, Congress takes the lead. Examples include the post–World War II unification of the armed forces hearings that led to the National Security Act of 1947, the failures of joint military operations that led to Goldwater-Nichols of 1986, the failure of special operations that led to the Nunn-Cohen Amendments in 1987, and the failure to prevent the 9/11 terrorist attacks that led to the USA Patriot Act of October 2001[23] and later to establishment of the 9/11 Commission in November 2002.[24]

Production of Power

The two houses of Congress design their committee structures independently. Committee structure can change more rapidly than the organizations of the executive branch. Committee names can change even more quickly, but committee jurisdictions are relatively stable. In addition to authorization and appropriation, Congress has a third important role to play—*oversight* of executive branch operations. Oversight is affected by committees in the House and Senate, often as a matter of after-failure investigations, and too often to seek partisan advantage.[25]

Budget Process. The annual process begins with development of the president's budget request for agencies and programs and its transmission to Congress. The congressional budget committees provide upper bounds for the twenty or so major budget functions, for example, National Defense, International Affairs, and Administration of Justice. The relevant authorizing committees put upper bounds on line items in their respective budgets. Authorizing committees also write enabling legislation. But it is the appropriations committees that actually put dollars to line items and produce twelve appropriations bills. Theoretically, money cannot be appropriated for programs not previously authorized. But appropriators have, in fact, written authorizing legislation of their own. And appropriators have declined to fund programs authorized by the relevant authorizing committees.

Authorizing Committees. Even though the two houses design their committee structures independently, there is considerable congruence. Both have standing authorizing committees for foreign affairs and international relations;[26] both have standing committees for defense and the armed forces;[27] both have standing committees for homeland security;[28] and both have select committees for intelligence oversight.[29]

The House and Senate authorizing committees on foreign affairs subdivide into a handful of regional subcommittees and a couple of functionally focused subcommittees. Given that the different executive departments and agencies regionalize the world differently, it is impossible for the congressional subcommittees to align well with an executive branch that isn't aligned internally.

The House and Senate authorizing committees for the armed services subdivide into several functional subcommittees. Separate subcommittees exist for strategic nuclear programs, Army and Air Force programs, and Navy and Marine Corps programs. Other subcommittees have jurisdiction over personnel, force readiness, installation and facilities, research and development, and procurement issues. During the long-term technological competition of the Cold War, subcommittee design was dominated by acquisition of weapon systems. Post Cold War, each house established a subcommittee of the armed services committee that looks toward emerging threats. Many of the topics considered fall under the Cold War label of low-intensity conflict, but they are driven largely by terrorism and associated threats.

Appropriations Subcommittees. Each house has a committee for appropriations separate from the committees that authorize actions and expenses.[30] Both the House of Representatives and the Senate appropriations committees have defense subcommittees with jurisdiction narrowly defined to include the Defense Department and the Intelligence Community. There are strong domestic constituencies for weapon system acquisition programs.

Both houses have an appropriations subcommittee with wide-ranging jurisdiction over the foreign operations—particularly economic assistance—of State, Defense, Treasury, USAID, and a long list of U.S. organizations associated with international development. Also included are the U.S. organizations dealing with the UN and related international organizations. There is no domestic constituency for these functions.

Both houses have separate appropriations subcommittees for military construction. Jurisdiction extends to military facilities within the United States, giving subcommittee members the ability to direct funds to their home districts.

In addition to the twelve annual appropriations bills, Congress typically considers two or more supplemental bills each year that bypass normal procedures. Supplemental appropriations pay for emergencies like disaster relief and military operations abroad.

Application of Power

We have discussed the most prominent departments and agencies comprising the national security apparatus in the executive branch, the capabilities they possess, and in some cases their evolutionary development. Now we turn our attention to the various organizations charged with producing a unity of effort from this diversity of means.

Orchestrating the instruments of power occurs at many levels. In Washington the president's multitiered NSC is the primary orchestrating mechanism. The ambassador's country team is the primary orchestrating mechanism in most countries. The combatant commanders provide a military-led regional orchestrating mechanism. And in countries undergoing extensive nation-building efforts, the provincial reconstruction team orchestrates localized interagency operations.

Policy plays a central role in applying and orchestrating the instruments of power. Policy must be formulated, policy must be implemented, and policy makers must effect oversight to ensure that policy is faithfully implemented and verify that policy is effective or is in need of modification.

National Security Council. The NSC is not a department or agency. The NSC has no authority to implement policy. The National Security Act of 1947 authorizes the NSC to advise the president in integrating foreign, domestic, and military policy as it relates to national security. The unstated premise in 1947 was that policy would be formulated in the departments and agencies with the statutory authorities and specialized skills and that the NSC would assist the president in integrating the various policies into a coherent whole. Many knowledgeable observers and experienced participants argue that advising and integrating is the proper role for the NSC. Formerly, policies were formulated in the departments and agencies and the NSC assisted the president in coordinating those policies, but since establishment in 1947, the NSC slowly established its dominance in policy formulation with varying degrees of success. When the NSC formulates policy, the departments and agencies are weakened and the White House becomes a bottleneck. The importance of the NSC requires detailed examination in a subsequent chapter.

State Department Bureaus. The State Department's Bureau of Counterterrorism and Bureau of Conflict and Stabilization Operations lead in their respective policy domains. But they lack resources and real power, and they are overshadowed by Defense.

Country Team. In countries where normal diplomatic relations exist, the country team is the primary orchestrating mechanism. The ambassador is the direct emissary of the president and is responsible for representing and carrying out U.S. foreign policy in the designated country as allowed by bilateral agreements. Typically, weekly meetings at the embassy are chaired by the ambassador and attended by the senior officers of each department and agency operating in the host country. Where normal relations don't exist (e.g., Somalia), an embassy in a neighboring country (e.g., Kenya) may house a watch office.

Combatant Commands. The combatant commands, born of the needs of World War II and honed throughout the Cold War, establish a regional presence around the world. Each is headed by a four-star general or admiral. The combatant commands represent a tremendous organizational capacity for planning and for bringing resources to bear for contingencies ranging from humanitarian assistance and disaster relief to war. They are powerful representatives of U.S. foreign policy, not just military policy, and they generally trump the influence of ambassadors. Post Cold War, combatant commands have augmented their staffs with personnel from the civilian departments and agencies, including, for example, a senior diplomat from State as a political advisor (POLAD, po-lad) to the military commander.

Provincial Reconstruction Teams. In countries where stabilization and reconstruction efforts are being carried out, as in Iraq and Afghanistan, the provincial reconstruction team (PRT) is an important orchestrating mechanism. In underdeveloped countries or countries with widely divergent ethnic groups, U.S. operations must be tailored at the province level. Where security is the primary issue, the PRT is led by a military officer and security forces are most prominent enabling U.S. civilian agencies and nongovernmental organizations to conduct their specialized operations. Where security is at an acceptable level, development personnel and operations dominate, and the PRT may be civilian-led.

For Consideration

Capabilities for achieving national security ends are spread across the departments and agencies of government. On paper, it appears that the State Department is best suited for leadership on national security issues. Defense, however, can also claim lead. Abroad, State leads at the country level under the authority of the ambassador through the country team, while Defense leads at the regional level under the authority of the combatant commander. The National Security Council, depending on the president's preference, can lead in policy formulation, or the president can lean toward either State or Defense lead.

Defense Department Lead

Rather than accept external orchestration of the instruments of power, a strong manager may attempt to consolidate authority over the various instruments of power in a single department. Secretary of Defense Donald Rumsfeld attempted to acquire the information instrument rather than rely on State. He also attempted to expand an intelligence instrument that he could drive rather than rely on the CIA. Defense has unmatched planning capacity. And Defense is the only organization possessing the excess capacity necessary for emergency deployments and the excess capacity necessary to keep a significant part of its workforce continually involved in professional development through education and training. The economic or development instrument seems increasingly independent of State and applied through Defense.

The Joint Strategic Planning system—and all major Pentagon processes—move slowly. Slowness is attributed to two factors. The first is the conservative nature of the military, which prefers incremental to radical change. The second is the exhaustive *staffing* of every written product. Each draft is circulated around the Pentagon, soliciting concur or nonconcur positions section by section. The final product is often a lowest-common-denominator document including only those things on which everyone could agree.

Secretary Rumsfeld understood the process and chose to make bold changes and accept risks rather than endure the glacial pace associated with Pentagon processes. The basic premises underlying Rumsfeld's change of mission to JFCOM, NORTHCOM, STRATCOM, and SOCOM need to be reexamined. But all of these need to be considered in the broader context of a national security strategy and in the context of all instruments of power.

State Department Lead

The Pentagon does not have a monopoly on sluggish staffing processes. The State Department also staffs its written products into submission. Presidents are frequently frustrated by the Departments' systems, which they consider unresponsive. Once dominant in national security policy formulation, State now appears to be a distant third behind the National

Security Council and the Defense Department. Once State had policy-making and oversight authorities over the semi-independent agencies of USIA, ACDA, and USAID. It is heavily invested in the diplomatic instrument. State has lead for whole-of-government response for counterterrorism and for conflict and stabilization operations. Under a wide range of conditions, the ambassador is the interagency leader through the country team.

Within a single country, and according to the "Kennedy letter," the ambassador is the uncontested interagency lead. But increasingly Defense leads abroad through the regional combatant commands, organizations created to command separate theaters of war in Europe and the Pacific in World War II. Third World countries and authoritarian regimes understand the dominant political role played by their own armies. It is part of their national narrative. By leading abroad with a military command, the United States communicates the wrong image. It is difficult to encourage civil government with a military lead.[31] According to Carlos Pascual, first coordinator for reconstruction and stabilization:

> [It] is critical that we maintain a civilian character to the nature of our operations. . . . There are too many countries that would love to have authoritarian control imposed by the military as a mechanism for governance internally within their countries. And if their perception of the United States at a decentralized level is that we have combatant commands run by the military where the civilians are simply part of that, . . . I think it would be counterproductive.[32]

National Security Department Lead

There is, of course, no national security department. There is no national security committee in Congress. And there is no national security budget. The next chapter presents the National Security Council, the principal and top-level organ for assuring national security. The penultimate chapter is devoted to prominent reform proposals that address the perceived shortcomings of a system designed for the twentieth century and the serial application of instruments.

9   National Security Council

National security policy is not an easily defined domain. Foreign policy is both more and less than national security policy. Military policy and domestic policy, too, are both more and less than national security policy. The instruments available to pursue national security are scattered across the departments and agencies of government. Assuming that the instruments exist in the proper mix, assuring national security is a matter of orchestrating the many instruments. No cabinet secretary is subordinate to another. Only the president sits atop the departments and agencies, and the National Security Council system is the president's principal mechanism for achieving a unifying national security policy and overseeing its implementation.

Up to and throughout World War II, the executive branch included separate departments of State, Navy, and War. Foreign relations were conducted through State. When necessary, the Navy and its Marine Corps provided the muscle behind coercive diplomacy. The War Department stood by with mobilization plans to raise an army should Congress declare war.

In the run up to World War II, President Roosevelt assumed the position of commander in chief of the armed forces and acted as his own secretary of state. The Joint Chiefs of Staff was established as a committee of service chiefs with no one in charge. By the end of the war, there were nearly twenty major joint boards established to coordinate activities across State, Navy, and War. They, too, were committees with no one in charge. Committee chairs lacked directive authority and could at most induce agreements.

After the war, unification was sought as an alternative to the plethora of coordinating committees. Unification of State, Navy, and War, including a central intelligence function, was the objective of some, but that proved to be too ambitious. The span of unification quickly receded to the Navy and War Departments. A single Defense Department was created on top of three subordinate departments of Army, Navy, and Air Force. Some joint boards survived but one by one were subordinated to the Defense Department. The State Department remained outside the unified solution as did the new Central Intelligence Agency. The National Security Council (NSC) was established to integrate policies across the various departments and agencies. The subordinate CIA provided integrated intelligence to the NSC.

New agencies were born in the early 1960s. The U.S. Agency for International Development (USAID) was established to administer foreign aid. Defense administered military assistance. The U.S. Information Agency (USIA) was established to project the message. A weak form of unification was established by allowing State to set objectives and priorities but granting USAID and USIA independence in execution. The relationship and the agencies decayed after the Cold War.

The result is a mixed bag. There is strong unification over the military instrument in the Department of Defense. There is weak unification over the diplomatic, economic, and information instruments in State, USAID, and the remnants of USIA. Other instruments—law enforcement, financial, and intelligence—are scattered across the executive branch, including State, Treasury, and Justice.

The separation of the military and diplomatic instruments may have served the country well during great-power conflicts like World War II and the Cold War. But the current geostrategic environment requires unity of effort from all the instruments of national power. Only the president's authority spans the entire executive branch.

Given the radical reorganization to be imposed on the War and Navy Departments after World War II, establishment of a national security council was at most of secondary importance. After an inauspicious beginning under Truman, the NSC system matured and grew in importance until it took center stage, allowing the president to steer the ship of state toward the administration's security objectives. The NSC system is the principal mechanism for achieving unity of effort. The highest-level committee is chaired by the president, who has directive authority over all the departments and agencies. The chairs of the remaining lower-level committees in the hierarchy have no directive authority. They are committees with no one in charge.

The NSC system is principally involved in policy formulation. Unity of effort is accomplished by establishing overarching national policy to be followed across government and by overseeing its faithful execution. The NSC system is best characterized as a decision support system for presidential decision making. The NSC is not a decision-making body. Decision making and crisis management are generally handled in the Oval Office, with elements of the NSC system providing support. As currently configured, the NSC system is not suited to day-to-day operational decision making. That authority is delegated to the departments and agencies.

Since 1949, the *statutory members* of the NSC have been the president, vice president, secretary of defense, and secretary of state. The director of central intelligence and the chairman, Joint Chiefs of Staff have been *statutory advisors*. With the creation of the Arms Control and Disarmament Agency and U.S. Information Agency in the early 1960s, their directors have been *special statutory advisors*. The secretary of energy was added as a statutory member in 2007. It is common in the literature to see *NSC principals* used to include the statutory members and statutory advisors.

This chapter begins with short summaries of the ad hoc interdepartmental solutions used during World War II, the system established soon after the war, and its evolution during the Cold War. The main body of the chapter summarizes the strengths and weaknesses of the National Security Council system from Truman to Obama. The chapter concludes with issues of concern for future presidential consideration.

National Security Act of 1947

Mobilizing for and fighting World War II—the largest great-power war in history—exposed a variety of shortcomings in America's national security apparatus. The surprise achieved at Pearl Harbor, among other things, suggested the need for a central intelligence organization to bring together the disparate intelligence capabilities spread across government. There were matters of *efficiency* attributed to redundancy between the Army and Navy. There were matters of *effectiveness* due to coordinating across the services rather than achieving unity of command over the services. Some were too difficult to address during the war and were deferred. Of necessity, the United States developed ad hoc solutions demanded by the war.

As the war grew in Europe, FDR assumed the position of commander in chief of American armed forces. Roosevelt's system included a weak State Department, allowing him to act as his own secretary of state, and he relied heavily on his generals to lead in diplomacy and intelligence and to influence operations. Roosevelt relied on trusted White House advisors like Admiral William D. Leahy, who served as liaison to the uniformed service chiefs in the Pentagon. In a sense, Leahy served as chairman of the joint chiefs before the position was formally created.

To formalize the U.S.-U.K. alliance, the United States created the Joint Chiefs of Staff (JCS) to meet with the British equivalent. The JCS first met in February 1942. Initially it had a small, part-time staff borrowed from the several service staffs. It was a committee of service chiefs with no one in charge. The State-War-Navy Coordinating Committee was established in 1944 to coordinate the actions of the civilian departments at the assistant secretary level. The next year, the secretaries of state, navy, and war—the "Committee of Three"—began meeting weekly.

For many, the experience of World War II showed the inadequacy of joint and interdepartmental coordinating committees. *Unification* was the proposed solution. Some wanted unification of the three departments, but that was a bridge too far. Unification of the Departments of War and Navy would have to do.

The Army and Navy took opposing positions on unification. The Army wanted unity of command as the way to achieve unity of effort. The Navy claimed that joint coordinating committees had demonstrated their ability to achieve unity of effort during the war. Secretary of the Navy James Forrestal commissioned a study by Ferdinand Eberstadt, who proposed three military departments—army, navy, air force—each headed by a cabinet secretary.[1] From the Department of War, Lieutenant General J. Lawton Collins produced recommendations that reflected the Army's desire to have more centralized command favoring a single secretary of defense.[2] In the near term, Eberstadt's study had greater influence with the authors of the 1947 act. But the logic of Collins's study proved irresistible, and subsequent reforms eventually implemented the single-department solution.

Merging the two powerful organizations, each with its own long history, proved to be a monumental undertaking. Given the magnitude of change suggested by unification of Navy and War, the proposal for a National Security Council was at best of secondary interest. The reasons for proposing the NSC were varied. Sensing too much power in the presidency of FDR, Congress hoped that working with the military through the NSC would inhibit unilateral presidential action. Congress specifically doubted Truman's experience in foreign affairs, and some in Congress doubted Truman's broader abilities. Perhaps an advisory body like the NSC would militate against his perceived shortcomings. For Congress, the NSC could both rein in too powerful a president and bolster a weak president. Secretary Forrestal and the institutional Navy were opposed to strong unification of the uniformed services. With the secretaries of army, navy, and air force as statutory members, Forrestal saw the NSC as an alternative to unification.

The National Security Act of 1947

The National Security Act of 1947 is the basis of the system we have today. The effect of major-war thinking was clear in the purpose statement of the act. The military instrument had primacy, and other instruments were at best secondary, not even warranting explicit mention in the purpose statement. The purpose of the act, enacted on 26 July 1947, was

> to promote the national security by providing for a Secretary of Defense; for a National Military Establishment; for a Department of the Army, a Department of the Navy, and a Department of the Air Force; and for the coordination of the activities of the National Military Establishment with other departments and agencies of the Government concerned with national security.

There was some reform of the uniformed services. Air power enthusiasts wanted three coequal services, one each for air, land, and sea forces.

But that was not to be. The Army was split between land and air forces, resulting in two separate services. But the Navy successfully retained its aviation and its naval infantry. And the Marine Corps retained its own aviation but did not achieve status as a service separate from the Navy.

To provide civilian control, four departments replaced two. The Department of War was replaced by separate and coequal Departments of Army and Air Force above the two respective uniformed services. The Department of the Navy continued to preside over the uniformed Navy and Marine Corps.

The act authorized the position of secretary of defense with a small staff to head the overarching National Military Establishment. The secretary had weak authorities as a coordinator between the Departments of Army, Navy, and Air Force. The name was changed to Department of Defense two years later.

A War Council was established comprising the secretaries of Army, Navy, and Air Force Departments, the three uniformed service chiefs (the commandant of the Marine Corps was not included), and the new secretary of defense chairing. The chair's function was coordinating, not directive.

The Joint Chiefs of Staff, a World War II creature of necessity, was given statutory authority to continue. It was established as a committee of service chiefs with no one in charge. A Joint Staff was authorized as well.

The Office of Strategic Services was removed from the JCS and given independent status as the Central Intelligence Agency (CIA). The intelligence components of the various departments remained, but the CIA provided a centralized, integrating capability to support national decision making. The CIA initially was placed under the NSC as an advisory body, but the director of central intelligence attended NSC meetings as an observer rather than as a member.

Some joint boards survived. The National Security Resources Board remained responsible for industrial and civilian mobilization in time of war. The Munitions Board replaced the Joint Army and Navy Munitions Board, and the Research and Development Board replaced the Joint Research and Development Board. The joint boards were fundamentally committees composed of representatives of the uniformed services with no one in charge.

The NSC was placed under the immediate direction of the president. The act specifies the function of the National Security Council as follows:

The function of the Council shall be to advise the President with respect to the integration of domestic, foreign, and military policies relating to the national security so as to enable the military services and the other departments and agencies of the Government to cooperate more effectively in matters involving the national security.

Statutory members of the NSC were the secretaries of state, defense, army, navy, and air force and the chairman of the National Security Resources Board. Other members were allowed subject to the Senate's advice and consent.

The act allowed for a permanent staff to assist the president in integrating national security policy. The NSC, composed of statutory members, was an advisory body with no executive authority. The NSC staff was to be small and to review, not duplicate, the work of executive branch departments and agencies. The substantive policy work was initially conducted in the departments, but as the permanent NSC staff developed, substantive work shifted from the departments and secretaries to the White House and the president.

Reforms

The National Security Act of 1947 has been amended but never replaced. Meaningful reforms have been made since 1947, specifically the legislative acts of 1949, 1953, 1958, and 1986.

The National Security Act Amendments of 1949 made significant changes. The Army, Navy, and Air Force Departments were designated *military departments* rather than *executive departments*. Their secretaries lost cabinet rank and their memberships on the NSC. The National Military Establishment was renamed the Department of Defense and was designated the executive department over the military departments. The secretary of defense retained cabinet status, was designated principal assistant to the president for defense matters, and retained a seat on the NSC.

The Key West Agreement of March 1948 designated the JCS—the committee—as principal advisor to the president. The 1949 amendments authorized a chairmanship for the JCS, but the chair had no vote. The JCS remained a committee with no one in charge.

Reforms continued in 1953 and 1958. The largely independent joint boards lost statutory authority in 1953, and their responsibilities were transferred to the increasingly powerful Defense Department. The Department of Defense Reorganization Act of 1958 authorized a true, full-time staff, replacing the part-time staffs on loan from the services.

The next few years saw the creation of new agencies. In the Defense Department, new agencies included the Defense Nuclear Agency in 1959 and the Defense Communications Agency and Defense Intelligence Agency in 1961. Elsewhere in the executive branch, the Arms Control and Disarmament Agency, U.S. Agency for International Development, and the U.S. Information Agency were established.

The Vietnam War sapped congressional and presidential energy. The next major reform effort occurred late in the Cold War. The Goldwater-Nichols Act of 1986 is the landmark legislation that topped off previous reforms and, according to most, produced the more unified military action displayed in the Gulf War. The chain of command from the president to the commander in the field was direct and unambiguous. The chairman of the JCS, rather than the JCS committee, was made the principal military advisor to the president. Many suggest that what is needed in the twenty-first century is a Goldwater-Nichols for the interagency.

In the 1940s, "joint" often meant a committee of service representatives with no one in charge. "Interdepartmental" meant a committee of State, Navy, and War representatives with no one in charge. Today, "interagency" similarly connotes a committee of representatives from the departments and agencies with no one in charge. The purpose of joint and interagency solutions is to produce a unity of effort. For our purposes here, unity of effort includes direction toward common national objectives, minimum overlap of activity, minimum gaps in activities, and minimum friction at the seams.

The military instrument was the focus of reform following World War II, and that focus continued through the Cold War. Similar attention has not been paid to the other instruments of power, which have been in relative decay. The result is an imbalance in instruments, a superb military instrument isolated from the other instruments, and a weak system for orchestrating the instruments.

NSC System in Practice

The title "National Security Council" refers to different things in context. The legislative meaning of NSC denotes a small number of statutory members and statutory advisors, possibly extended by presidential invitation. Sometimes, a reference to the NSC embraces the NSC staff and the entire interagency committee hierarchy from the formal NSC down to the working groups that do the NSC's detailed business. When necessary to avoid ambiguity below, "NSC proper" refers to the highest-level committee, "NSC" refers to the entire committee hierarchy and support staff, and "NSC system" includes the NSC organization and its process.

NSC Functions

At the highest level, the NSC system performs two distinct functions—*advising* the president in regard to national security matters and assisting the president in *integrating* domestic, foreign, and military polices to achieve national security objectives. Although the NSC has statutory authority to advise the president, presidents seek counsel beyond the NSC and often prefer less formal settings that allow more candid discussions.

Actual presidential *decision making* and *crisis management* generally take place separately and outside the NSC proper. The United States has a *presidential* rather than a *cabinet* government in the proper British sense. In Great Britain, the various prime ministers have their own political base, and the cabinet bears a collective responsibility for decision making. In the United States, cabinet members advise, the president decides, and cabinet members carry out presidential decisions.

Still, several U.S. administrations have claimed cabinet government. Reading between the lines, these administrations claim to have strong department heads, and the president delegates significant authority to them, reserving only the most important and cross-cutting decisions for presidential decision making.

The NSC system is designed primarily to perform the integration of domestic, foreign, and military policies. Independently developed policies could percolate bottom up from the individual departments for integration, but the typical process injects presidential guidance from the top down. Following initial guidance, the ideal process is a collaborative, interagency effort producing integrated national security policies from the bottom up.

Within the integrating interagency process, three functions have been apparent in the several decades since the establishment of the NSC—*policy formulation, oversight of policy implementation*, and *policy implementation*. The literature often applies terms like *operations* and *implementation* to the work done within the NSC system when, in fact, the Council at most exercises *oversight* of operations and policy implementation. The Reagan administration is an exception, having engaged in implementation with disastrous results. Only the departments and agencies have the statutory authority and the capacity to implement policy.

NSC Organization

Congress did not rigidly specify NSC organization. The organization should conform to the individual management style of the chief executive it is designed to serve. Typically, each new administration designed an NSC system to overcome the perceived shortcomings of the previous administration. The result was a pendulum swing with some modest forward progress. The elder Bush administration established organizational stability at the end of the Cold War.

Organizationally, the NSC system is a hierarchy of interagency committees—the NSC itself, a cabinet-level committee, a subcabinet-level committee, and a layer of working-level committees (see figure 11). Presidents often seek advice outside the formal NSC system from their inner circle of trusted advisors.

The formal National Security Council is at the top of the interagency committee hierarchy. NSC meetings are attended by statutory members and statutory advisors. Others may be invited depending on the issues on the agenda. In recent history, the *statutory members* of the NSC have been the president, vice president, secretary of defense, and secretary of state. President Ford vetoed legislation in 1975 to add the treasury secretary, who attended regularly under some administrations. The director of central intelligence and the chairman of the Joint Chiefs of Staff are *statutory advisors*. Since the creation of the Arms Control and Disarmament Agency

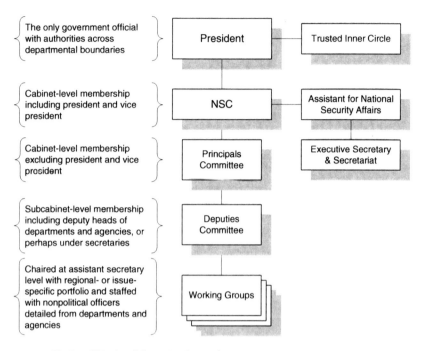

FIG. 11. Notional National Security Council system organization

and U.S. Information Agency, their directors have been *special statutory advisors*, although both were disestablished in 1999. The secretary of energy was added as a statutory member in 2007 without much notice. It is common in the literature to see NSC *principals* used to include the statutory members and statutory advisors.

Some administrations limited attendance at NSC meetings to principals, while some allowed principals to be accompanied by support staff. With staff in attendance, principals were more likely to represent their agencies than to act as presidential advisors. After the Iran-Contra scandal in the Reagan administration, the Tower Commission clarified the respective roles of NSC members:

> When they sit as members of the Council they sit not as cabinet secretaries or department heads but as advisors to the President. They are there not simply to advance or defend the particular positions of the

departments or agencies they head but to give their best advice to the President.

The NSC is only advisory. It is the President alone who decides. When the NSC principals receive those decisions, they do so as heads of the appropriate departments or agencies. They are then responsible to see the President's decisions are carried out by those organizations accurately and effectively.[3]

The *Principals Committee* sits directly below the formal NSC and is chaired by the president's assistant for national security affairs. The president's time is scarce and the NSC principals often meet without the president when an issue can be resolved without presidential intervention. Without being convened formally, Principals Committee meetings often take place informally just prior to an NSC meeting so as to make best use of the president's time. The Principals Committee also serves a quality-control function over the outputs of the interagency process prior to presidential consideration.

The *Deputies Committee* sits below the Principals Committee in the hierarchy. It is chaired by the president's deputy national security assistant. Membership on the Deputies Committee is drawn from the same departments and agencies represented on the NSC and the Principals Committee. The deputy secretaries or deputy directors typically represent their organizations. State and Defense each has an influential under secretary with responsibility for policy and planning. That under secretary may attend instead of the deputy.

The Deputies Committee meets more frequently than the Principals Committee and NSC. The deputies attempt resolution of interagency issues at their level elevating only the most difficult up the hierarchy. A great deal of NSC work gets done at the deputies' level, but the detailed interagency work is conducted at the next-lower level. The Deputies Committee decides which working groups to establish, gives them specific tasking, assures the quality of upward-moving products, and assures that the mix of tasking downward is responsive to the president's agenda.

Attendees at the top three level committees in the NSC hierarchy—NSC, Principals Committee, and Deputies Committee—are the president's political appointees subject to Senate confirmation. They have broad, departmentwide portfolios. Their purpose is to steer the ship of state according to the president's will. But eventually someone must row.

The detailed interagency work is done in *working groups* staffed by nonpolitical career civil servants and uniformed military detailed from across the departments and agencies of government. Working groups are chaired at the assistant secretary level. The chair—a political appointee—has a narrow regional or functional focus. A regional focus might be on Europe, Latin America, or the Middle East. A functional focus might be arms control or terrorism. Rather than periodic meetings characteristic of the higher-level committees, the working groups are continually engaged.

With reasonable foresight and a measure of luck, an NSC working group will be continuously engaged in a policy area when a crisis emerges. The working group is best capable of shifting into a support role for presidential crisis management. Crisis management is often conducted in the White House by the president and the closest advisors, not in the NSC.

NSC Process

Driven by the president's agenda, the NSC system formulates interagency policies for presidential consideration. Early in an administration, issue-focused studies may indicate the need for new or updated policy statements. Studying issues and reviewing policies prepares the administration for action. It builds familiarity within elements of the NSC organization and it frequently produces written policy statements to be promulgated to the departments and agencies for implementation.

The NSC system workload changes over time. The opportunity for change is short. More studies are initiated early in an administration. Later in an administration, preparation and planning is often overtaken by events—crises emerge and demand attention. Administrations that do not prepare early can only be reactive.

The need to review existing policy or to initiate new policy can be recognized anywhere in the committee hierarchy. But a policy study is initiated from the top through an NSC directive. Guidance comes from the top, the work is done at the bottom of the hierarchy, and all intermediate levels perform a quality-control function. Several iterations may be required before the study produces an output for presidential consideration. The output of a study is often a new policy statement, developed through the interagency process, approved by the president, and promulgated to the affected departments and agencies of government. Some more immediate decisions are promulgated without lengthy studies.

The NSC's interagency process has produced documents for three purposes.[4] Many documents are used to task the NSC to conduct single- or multiple-agency studies. Others promulgate official policy; the policy is often the output of a previously commissioned study. A third type directs specific actions. But administrations have employed either one or two types of directive. Most make the distinction between study directives and decision directives. Decision directives are used either to promulgate policy or to direct action. Administrations have typically chosen to rename their documents to distinguish them from the documents of the previous administration.

Although the process clearly produces paper, something intangible and no less important is also produced. By engaging the president's appointees in the process, the president's agenda drives the process. By engaging the expertise resident in the departments and agencies, implementation of the policies produced are more likely to be feasible. Bad ideas are more likely to be exposed, as are good ideas that may entail excessive risk, work cross purpose with other policies, or lack the necessary resources. The departments and agencies that participate in policy formulation are more likely to see it as their own and implement it more faithfully. The process that produces documents prepares the executive branch to be proactive rather than merely reactive when crises erupt. Process is critically important.

Models for National Security Assistants

The position of *national security assistant* deserves special attention. The position has no specific basis in law. The original 1947 legislation allows for an executive secretary to manage the permanent staff and the staff process. The Eisenhower administration established a new position of *special assistant to the president for national security affairs.* The holder of the new position was a process manager without policy agenda. (The position of executive secretary remained and retained the authorities that the title implies. At Eisenhower's request, Truman's executive secretary, James Lay, continued in the position.) Kennedy's national security assistant, McGeorge Bundy, was the first to have a substantive policy-making role rather than acting as a policy-neutral process manager. The Nixon administration shortened the title to *assistant to the president for national security affairs*, but the president informally used the title of *national security advisor*, reflecting his relationship with Henry Kissinger, and the informal title continues in common use today. Carter's national security assistant, Zbigniew Brzezinski, is the only assistant to hold cabinet rank, a presidential designation. The national security assistant is appointed through the president's authority to appoint White House staff without Senate confirmation.

While there is general agreement that Kissinger is the exemplar of the most powerful national security assistant—the deputy president for national security affairs—many are equally quick to nominate Brent Scowcroft as the exemplar to emulate—the honest broker.[5]

Kissinger and Nixon shared a strategic vision, and Kissinger enjoyed the president's trust and confidence. A highly visible national security assistant and a weak secretary of state resulted in power concentrated in the White House. Kissinger designed the NSC committee structure and chaired the committees he chose to dominate. Kissinger set the NSC study agenda. The president wanted to be presented with multiple options. Kissinger's position as committee chair allowed him to control the study agenda and the committee debate, and his direct access to the president allowed him to skew the discussion in private advisory sessions with Nixon.

Brent Scowcroft also enjoyed the trust and confidence of the president, George H. W. Bush. Scowcroft focused his efforts on his role as assistant to the president and substantially delegated management of the interagency process to his deputy, Robert Gates. Scowcroft had direct access to the president, something that can raise the suspicions of department and agency heads. But the NSC principals trusted Scowcroft to fairly and accurately represent their positions to the president. When the president asked, Scowcroft expressed his independent views. Scowcroft maintained a low public profile, allowing the NSC principals to enunciate the administration's position to domestic and foreign audiences. Scowcroft's low public profile and honest broker approach was a critical enabler of collegiality in the Bush administration. His quiet competence allowed trust and avoided destructive competitions.

NSC Staff Organization and Size

It is common for an administration to come into power thinking the past administration's NSC staff was too large and unwieldy. It was also common to see staff size reduced initially only to see it grow back later under the pressures of geostrategic events. Still, there is an apparent consensus that the NSC staff should be lean and focused.

The true numbers may change day to day, and one can legitimately quibble over who should and should not be counted. Precision is not a realistic option, but there are clear general trends. The NSC staff counted barely over a dozen during the Truman administration. It was near eighty under Eisenhower. It fell precipitously back to Truman's levels upon Kennedy's inauguration, but it then began a steady upward climb across administrations with a large spike under Reagan. Bush 41 returned staff size to pre-Reagan numbers, and the steady upward climb began again until it peaked at nearly one hundred under Clinton.[6]

The Clinton administration added a National Economic Council in parallel with the NSC, and NEC staff members are not counted in the one hundred. The Bush 43 administration established a separate Homeland Security Council and staff. The Obama administration consolidated the NSC and HSC staffs into a unified National Security Staff. These innovations make the value of further comparison questionable.

Each administration organizes its NSC secretariat differently, but there is some level of regularity. *Divisions* are staffed by a small number of professional staff members. Some are political appointees, and some are detailed from government. A division has a regional or functional focus. Figure 12 gives an example from late in the Clinton administration showing the staff organized into regional divisions on the left and functional divisions on the right. The number in parentheses indicates how many staffers were devoted to the division.[7]

Administrations in Review

From Truman to Ford, the NSC system has been tailored to each president's individual style. The elder Bush created a system that achieved some

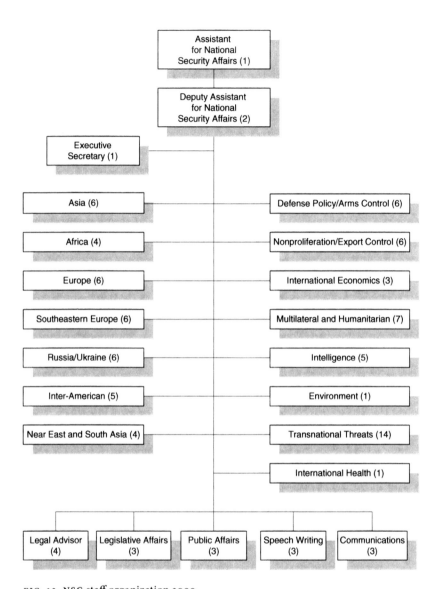

FIG. 12. NSC staff organization 2000

stability and was adopted by subsequent administrations. The earlier NSC systems differ in meaningful ways. Some presidents used the NSC to foster collegiality while others used it to control competing agencies.[8] In some administrations the NSC was weak relative to the Departments of State and Defense, and in others it appeared as a peer or even as a superagency. Some presidents turned to the NSC as their principal source of advice, and others sought advice in private, informal settings. Rather than simply as a source of advice, some presidents used the NSC system to deeply engage the expertise resident in the departments and agencies of government in the policy formulation process.

The strength of the NSC relative to the State and Defense Departments has varied across the administrations. The NSC system was formative and underused by Truman until the Korean War. Truman initially believed that the NSC would be constraining, thinking it a congressional attempt to impose cabinet government over his presidential prerogative. He rarely attended meetings until the outbreak of the Korean War. During the war, meetings were frequent, and he attended regularly. Toward the end of his administration, the president and all that attached, including the NSC, were rendered ineffective. Throughout, the State Department dominated both the NSC and the fledgling Defense Department.

The NSC system was perhaps strongest under Eisenhower, reminiscent of a general staff. Ike's NSC conducted both policy formulation and oversight of policy implementation in two distinct boards. One board developed policy and passed it vertically to the departments and agencies for implementation and horizontally to a parallel board to oversee policy implementation in the departments and agencies. The president's national security assistant was a policy-neutral process manager. The process was criticized as not much more than a paper mill by the opposition party and the Kennedy presidential campaign. The departments and agencies were thoroughly engaged in policy formulation, and they were able to continue to pursue the president's policies even while Eisenhower was seriously ill late in his administration. State remained dominant.

Informality and ad hocery weakened the NSC under Kennedy and Johnson.[9] Both preferred to receive advice in more intimate and informal settings. Their NSC systems continued the policy formulation function but dropped the oversight function under the assumption that the departments and agencies would follow presidential policies. As a result, policies often failed in implementation. Kennedy's NSC was reactive. Johnson's NSC was almost completely consumed by the Vietnam War. Secretary of Defense Robert McNamara built a powerful civilian staff in the Pentagon.

Nixon was determined to run foreign policy from the White House rather than from Foggy Bottom. A powerful national security assistant and NSC staff were key. So, too, was the deliberate choice of a secretary of state, William Rogers, lacking foreign policy strength. By now, the Defense Department clearly could hold its own against State. Nixon referred to Henry Kissinger, his assistant for national security affairs, as his national security advisor, and the informal title stuck. In Nixon's second term, Kissinger became secretary of state and for a time simultaneously held his position of national security assistant. Nixon's impeachment further strengthened Kissinger's hand. Ford continued Nixon's NSC system. Throughout, Kissinger served almost as deputy president for national security.

In the aftermath of Watergate and the unpopularity of the Vietnam War, there was a strong and common sense that Kissinger had amassed too much power personally and that too much power organizationally had collected in the White House. Carter's response was to attempt cabinet government. Carter continued with a strong national security assistant in Zbigniew Brzezinski. He also selected a strong secretary of state in Cyrus Vance. A visible competition developed between Vance and Brzezinski. Carter sat above the competition without resolving it.

Like Carter, Reagan wanted a form of cabinet government but without a strong national security assistant like Kissinger or Brzezinski. Retired Army general Alexander Haig was Reagan's first secretary of state, and Casper Weinberger served as secretary of defense. A competition quickly developed between Haig and Weinberger, and Reagan's handlers opposed Haig's attempts to upstage the president in enunciating foreign policy. Like Carter, Reagan let the competition fester unresolved. Haig resigned.

Reagan weakened the role of the national security assistant and reigned over an NSC system run amok. For the first and only time, the president's national security assistant was denied direct access to the president. Reagan had six national security assistants in eight years. Still, NSC committees proliferated, and the staff grew. The president remained detached, and NSC staffers acted with sketchy guidance and minimum oversight. The Iran-Contra scandal—exchanging arms for the release of hostages—was the result. NSC staff engaged directly in policy implementation without the expertise resident in the departments and agencies and beyond congressional oversight. It brought the NSC to its lowest repute since inception.

Iran-Contra brought critical examination of Reagan's NSC system. The President's Special Review Board, commonly referred to as the Tower Commission, comprised John Tower, Edmund Muskie, and Brent Scowcroft.[10] The recommendations made remain salient today. A highly qualified national security executive, Frank Carlucci, implemented the recommendations. Colin Powell followed Carlucci as national security assistant. Together, they restored competence and collegiality. Reagan's detachment remained.

George H. W. Bush brought competence and departmental collegiality, and he produced the NSC organization that exists today. Colin Powell served as Chairman, Joint Chiefs of Staff. Dick Cheney and James Baker served as secretaries of defense and state, respectively. Brent Scowcroft served as the president's sole national security assistant throughout the administration and established a minimal public presence. Mutual respect, competency, and collegiality characterized the process. Bush, a president unusually well qualified in national security matters, capably steered the process and managed the personalities.

Clinton retained collegiality, kept his predecessor's NSC organization intact, and expanded the staff to record size. Clinton created the National Economic Council parallel to and modeled on the NSC. He also brought strong economic representation into the NSC system. Clinton's NSC was reactive. His second national security assistant, Sandy Berger, had greater public presence than his predecessor.

The younger Bush created a weak NSC, preferring a small group of like-minded advisors over rigorous analysis and vigorous debate. Interagency process in the NSC was overtaken by military process in the Pentagon. A highly qualified secretary of state, Colin Powell, did not share the dominant hard-line worldview and was marginalized. Vice President Cheney built a personal national security staff of unprecedented size and influence. He insinuated himself and his office into the NSC system in ways never before seen. Cheney, even more so than Kissinger, served as deputy president for national security. National Security Assistant Condoleezza Rice chose a low profile as did the articulate vice president, leaving a president who lacked the communication skills of Reagan or Clinton to attempt to explain U.S. policy to domestic and foreign audiences.

The NSC system was not instrumental in supporting presidential decision making or in policy formulation. The Bush 43 NSC organization was essentially that created by Bush 41 and retained by Clinton. The Bush 43 process, however, was quite different. The administration failed to use the NSC system effectively. Decisions were made in a closeted White House environment, with inadequate interagency participation, and policies failed painfully in implementation. Bush established a separate Homeland Security Council and staff in parallel with the NSC and NEC staffs.

Obama retained the NSC committee structure established by the elder Bush. The customary adjustments were made to the NSC staff organization to accommodate changing emphases. The administration quickly merged NSC and HSC staffs into a single National Security Staff.

Obama's decision-making style is more like Kennedy's and Clinton's. It includes intense, hours-long, substantive discussions with trusted advisors. The process included diverse views, debate, and collegiality. Secretary of State Hillary Clinton brought the Centrist Democrat's interventionism. Vice President Joe Biden brought caution born of the Vietnam era and a preference for discrete action over protracted conflict. Defense Secretary Robert Gates brought a preference for a strong military and some caution in its use. The process led to confident decision making but contained the potential to create a presidential bottleneck, and it did not thoroughly engage the expertise in the departments and agencies. Critics in both parties claimed that the administration did not adequately engage Congress, either.

For Consideration

All the agencies involved in assuring American national security— including the Defense Department, State Department, Justice Department, CIA, and USAID, for example—have long institutional histories. They have cultures derived from past successes and failures. They house specialized expertise found nowhere else. They naturally, and in some cases wisely, resist policy change imposed by new administrations.[11] Left alone, they conservatively follow their own trajectory. They represent continuity. If dramatic change is needed, only the president can institute that change. The NSC system is the president's principal instrument of control and change.

Alternatives for consideration are presented below. Some are oriented on improving the interagency process carried out by the coordinating committees of the NSC. Others return to the unification process begun after World War II centered in the departments and agencies of government that house the various instruments of national power.

Models and Competitions

Two distinct models exist for the national security system: the *presidential* and *secretarial* models.[12] The names reflect a presidential choice of who will be the chief enunciator of foreign policy—the president or the secretary of state. The role of the NSC system follows directly.

In the presidential model, the president reserves the role of foreign policy enunciator for him or herself. It naturally follows that foreign policy formulation resides in the White House and that responsibility falls to the president's national security assistant and NSC staff. To be effective, the NSC staff must be *activist*, aggressively advancing the president's policy agenda.

In the secretarial model, the president sets foreign policy objectives and priorities but delegates to the secretary of state the role of chief policy enunciator. Lead in foreign policy formulation naturally falls to the State Department. The national security assistant and NSC staff are not activist but must defer to the more conservative forces in State that place great value on continuity of foreign policy. The secretarial model is compatible with the American version of cabinet government.

A clear choice must be made and managed by the president to avoid dysfunction. Across administrations, competitions have often precluded collegiality. The most common competition is for the position of chief enunciator of foreign policy, and the president and secretary of state are the typical competitors. The competition between Reagan and Haig is a classic example. The president's national security assistants have on several occasions entered into the competition. Brzezinski and Vance offer the classic example of competition between the national security assistant and the secretary of state. In times of military conflict, the secretary of defense often adopts a high public profile, enunciating foreign policy instead of the secretary of state and president. McNamara and Rumsfeld are clear examples.

In an apparently unique case, a competition developed for the role of principal national security advisor to the president. During the Bush administration, Vice President Cheney and Defense Secretary Rumsfeld appear to have had greater influence with the president than the president's national security assistant, Condoleezza Rice.

A strong and visible national security assistant coupled with a strong NSC system shifts power to the president and the White House. The shift in power and influence comes at the expense of the State Department and its secretary. The result is a weak and demoralized State Department, an ineffective diplomatic instrument, and a bottleneck in the White House. One commentator concluded that with a strong national security assistant, the relationship between the White House, State, and Defense won't work well; but without a strong national security assistant, the relationship won't work at all.[13]

But "strong" is an imprecise characteristic. Kissinger was a strong national security assistant achieving dominance over the entire apparatus. Brzezinski was a strong assistant and entered into a competition with a strong secretary of state. Scowcroft was strong, maintained a low profile, and created the conditions for collegiality rather than competition.

It is not an accident that the pivotal point in the discussion above is who shall enunciate *foreign* policy. Nor is it inconsequential. National security policy is not equivalent to foreign policy. Nor is it the sum of foreign, military, and domestic policies. National security policy is the integration of relevant subsets of foreign, military, and domestic policies. The need to integrate across these policy domains reflects a flawed division of labor—there is no national security department.

Range and Authorities

The need for the NSC system is a direct result of the division of labor represented by the departments and agencies of government as directed in the National Security Act of 1947, as amended. No single department is responsible for national security policy formulation and implementation. State and Defense are the two leading contenders, but neither has the range of mission or authority over the other. During periods of great power conflict, the division of labor was reasonable. Coordination across departments and agencies was an adequate solution. The current environment—requiring the orchestration of all instruments of national power—exposes a deeply flawed division of labor and the organizations of government that it represents.

The question then becomes what, if anything, to do about it. The conservative course of action is to accept the inadequacies of the status quo and leave the system in place in anticipation of the next great power conflict. Another course of action, a continuation of *unification*, is to reorganize the appropriate instruments of power under one of the existing departments as was initially proposed after World War II. State and Defense are the most likely candidates. A third alternative is to create a superagency over the existing departments and agencies. The NSC is the likely starting point for a superagency. Rather than the current NSC approach—committees of representatives from the departments and agencies with no one in charge—the NSC would require directive authority over the subordinated departments and agencies. This, in turn, would require a large and capable professional staff.

The inadequacies of the current division of labor are made most conspicuous by national security strategies with a strong reliance on what the Clinton administration called nation building and the Bush administration called capacity building. It isn't at all clear that these missions have widespread public support. And the wisdom of the mission as a way to achieve national security ends is not yet clear. A massive reorganization of government without a sustainable political consensus is ill-advised.

Organization and Purpose

The National Security Act of 1947, as amended, does not specify in detail the organization and process of the NSC system. Presidents make a mix of demands on their NSC systems, but some exhibit specific tendencies. Some NSC staffs were activists; others were conservative. Some used the

NSC for long-range, strategic purposes; others used it in a reactive mode. Crisis response and decision making generally take place in the Oval Office or the West Wing's Situation Room rather than in the NSC.

The structure of the Bush 41, Clinton, Bush 43, and Obama administrations shows that organizational stability is possible. It also shows that organization does not determine outcomes. Personalities, not surprisingly, are stronger determinants of NSC performance than is organization. Particularly important is the complex personal interaction between the president, secretary of state, secretary of defense, and assistant for national security affairs. In one administration, the vice president weighed heavily in the calculation. But regardless of personalities, the purpose of NSC organization and staff work remains the same. Eisenhower is specific about the purpose of detailed, multilevel, interagency staff work in the NSC system:

> Its purpose is to simplify, clarify, expedite and coordinate; it is a bulwark against chaos, confusion, delay and failure. . . . Organization cannot make a successful leader out of a dunce, any more than it should make a decision for its chief. But it is effective in minimizing the chances of failure and in insuring that the right hand does, indeed, know what the left hand is doing.[14]

Eisenhower's NSC system included separate boards for policy formulation and for oversight of policy implementation. Kennedy and Johnson dropped the oversight function, incorrectly assuming that the departments and agencies would faithfully implement well-crafted policy approved by the president. Reagan's NSC ventured into policy implementation with disastrous consequences. Given the historical evidence, formulation of policy and oversight of policy implementation are necessary and sufficient functions of the NSC system. Implementation of policy should be left to the executive branch departments and agencies that have the expertise and statutory authorities and that are subject to congressional oversight.

The NSC system integrates the policies of the departments and agencies, or at least provides a forum for that integration. The departments and agencies house the instruments of power. The instruments must exist in the necessary proportion for orchestration to achieve the desired results. With the military as an exception, the NSC largely relies on the instruments as they exist. There is little evidence that the NSC has played a prominent role in assuring the necessary balance of instruments. In other words, its attention is focused on the *use* of the instruments of power, leaving the *production* of power to the departments and the associated congressional committees.

Personal Advice versus Process

By law, "The function of the Council shall be to advise the President with respect to the integration of domestic, foreign, and military policies relating to the national security." But advice about the activities and products of the NSC system must be distinguished from the personal advice presidents receive from NSC principals and other trusted advisors.

Some presidents preferred that their formal NSC meetings be attended only by the principals—the statutory members and advisors—while other presidents included principals and significant numbers of staff assistants in the formal setting. Presidents often looked beyond the NSC for advice. Many, perhaps all, sought candid advice in private Oval Office meetings. Johnson and Carter scheduled regular meetings with trusted advisors— Johnson over Thursday lunches and Carter over Friday breakfasts. The attendance list was largely the same as the NSC membership. They were, in essence, informal NSC meetings. But the distinction between formal and informal NSC meetings is of little consequence. The distinction that matters is whether the principals meet privately or accompanied by support staff.

Presidents understandably preferred the candid discussions that take place in private. Cabinet members tended to speak more freely in the informal, collegial environment. They were more likely to act as advisors and less as heads of departments and agencies. Leaks were less likely to occur than from meetings with staff in attendance. In all likelihood, presidents' decision making was better facilitated by private, informal meetings than by large, formal NSC meetings. There were negative consequences, too, of small, informal meetings. To prevent leaks, the agenda often went unannounced. Staff could not prepare their principals for the kind of fluid discussions presidents desired. Meetings without staff in attendance were weak in getting decision-making rationale back to the agencies for implementation, and they were weak in engaging the expertise resident deep in the agencies.

There are advantages and disadvantages to large, formal meetings versus small, informal meetings. Eisenhower's NSC meetings included staff support—back benchers. Observers claimed that members were better prepared when accompanied by staff, and the presence of staff meant that discussions were documented and carried back to the departments and agencies. But with staff in attendance, principals were more inclined to represent agency views and less inclined to give candid advice to the president. The larger the meeting, the more prone they were to leaks and the harder it was to identify the leak's source.

If presidential decision making is best supported in private meetings of NSC principals, then what is the purpose of formal NSC meetings with support staff in attendance? In the formal setting, discussion between the NSC principals takes place in front of staff. Staff members must engage their agencies to prepare their principals. Staff members hear the questions, the answers, and the positions of the other departments and agencies. The principal is free to engage in the discussion, and the staff is able to assist their principal upon return to their department or agency. With decisions made elsewhere, formal NSC meetings in front of a large audience may be mostly theater, but it is theater that successful executives have long used. The audience is better able to return to its home office and act in the president's stead.

It is tempting for presidents so inclined to use the NSC only as an advisory body and not engage the agencies more deeply in the process. The effect is to lose the considerable expertise resident in the agencies, to lose legislative oversight of the executive branch, and to lose objectivity.

Neither the large, formal meeting or the small, informal meeting should be chosen over the other. They can be complementary. The small, informal meeting may be best for advising the president for decision making. But the larger, formal meeting engages and energizes the interagency process in ways not possible in private settings.

Multiple Options

Presidents often prefer having multiple options. Outsiders criticized the Eisenhower process for producing homogenized, lowest-common-denominator solutions acceptable to all departments and agencies. But those critics confuse decision making made in the Oval Office with policy formulation that takes place through the NSC's interagency process.

There is more than one way to get multiple options. One way, the most likely way, is to solicit the views of the individual departments and agencies. Such solutions are likely to be based on a dominant role for the proposing department or agency and minor, supporting roles for the others. More desirable, and much harder to achieve, is to solicit multiple interagency solutions. Only the NSC system is positioned to produce multiple interagency options for presidential consideration. But that requires a large, sophisticated staff system found only in the departments and agencies. A third alternative is for a department with a strong staff—State or Defense—to develop the ability to deliver true interagency solutions.

Only the most sophisticated chief executive can benefit from the divergent views of competing cabinet members, and only the most sophisticated chief executive can manage strong, competing personalities. Strong NSC principals and collegiality—a matter of personality, not organization—appears to produce the best results but is not easy to realize. It is a responsibility that falls solely to the president.

Part 4

National Security Reform

10   Major Reform Proposals

This chapter introduces several prominent studies on national security for the twenty-first century. Of particular significance are issues of organizational design. In general, the studies are bipartisan even though some claim to be nonpartisan. They are staffed by senior personnel with lengthy service in the executive or legislative branch. Some have served as political appointees, and many hope for another appointment. Collectively they bring experience and expertise. The same individuals populate many of the studies. They are practitioners of the *art of the possible*; they often avoid the hotly contested issues to improve the political feasibility of their recommendations. And, too often, the contested issues are the ones that need examination. Edges can be rounded off and important issues glossed over.

The chapter begins by introducing three broad approaches to reform and identifies what appears to be the consensus starting point. The introduction is followed by reviews of notable reform efforts. The chapter concludes with a summary of common conclusions and recommendations.

Balancing and Orchestrating the Instruments

There have been radical swings in post–Cold War strategies, and there is no strategic stability on the horizon. The various agencies of government house the instruments of power that underwrite the chosen strategy. The uniformed military represents but one instrument of power. The military, as currently configured, is strained in the complex environment of the twenty-first century. It is tempting to conclude that the military should be transformed in response. But such a conclusion is premature.

The agencies of government, including Defense, cannot be redesigned for each incoming administration and its chosen strategy. Increasing the size of an organization takes several years; substantially changing the shape of an organization takes decades. An optimal solution for one strategy likely will fail catastrophically for another. The mechanisms of power must be designed to support a reasonable range of strategies. Suboptimal solutions are the only prudent choice.

Implementation of a nation-building capability remains an open issue. After determining the necessary balance of instruments, there are two questions to answer simultaneously. One question asks how the instruments of power will be distributed across the agencies of government. The other asks how those instruments will be orchestrated to achieve unity of effort toward national objectives.

Where Do the Instruments Lie? Transforming the military from a major-wars force to a small-wars force is one alternative requiring a radical transformation of the military away from its deeply engrained self-conception as a conventional war-fighting organization. This alternative simplifies the orchestration problem, as it would be handled in the existing chain of command that governs the use of military force from the president and secretary of defense to the combatant commander in the field. But the risk is that the transformed military will be unprepared for the next major war.

A second alternative is to create additional defense agencies to house the instruments of power necessary for nation building abroad. The Defense Department currently houses twenty defense agencies, including, for example, the Defense Intelligence Agency, National Security Agency, Defense Logistics Agency, and the Defense Information Systems Agency. More defense agencies could be added to complement the uniformed services. The uniformed military would be reconstituted and modernized for conventional combat operations and to provide security forces for the civilian defense agencies. This, too, has the benefit of simplifying the problem of orchestrating the instruments. Defense agencies can be established by executive order rather than legislation.

A third alternative is to leave the instruments distributed across the agencies of government, bring their respective capacities into balance, and turn attention to the problem of orchestration. The instruments of power are not neatly divided by agency. The White House and the State Department share the diplomatic instrument, and diplomacy is conducted to some extent by every government representative abroad. The Defense Department has a near-monopoly on the military instrument, but the Central Intelligence Agency (CIA) maintains its own paramilitary force, and a robust security force has grown in the private sector. The intelligence instrument is spread across almost all agencies of government including the CIA, State, and multiple defense agencies. The economic instrument is shared principally by Defense (military assistance) and the Agency for International Development (foreign aid), both nominally under State's guidance. The Justice, State, and Defense Departments share the law enforcement instrument. The information instrument is spread across government and is broken.

The reform studies share the third view. Leave the departments and agencies intact, rebalance the capabilities within them, and improve inter-agency processes.

Who Orchestrates the Instruments? Assuming that the instruments of power remain distributed across the agencies of government, orchestration remains a critical issue. One way to orchestrate is by assigning lead agency status, for example, to Defense or State. Another way is to give executive authority to the National Security Council.

Today, neither State nor Defense has the statutory authority to direct the efforts and resources of other agencies. Congress authorizes and appropriates to them separately. Prior to World War II, State had the capacity to conduct foreign affairs including direct access to the naval services. More recently, in the 1960s, State had the capacity to lead USAID and USIA. State's capacities have atrophied considerably.

The National Security Council (NSC) is an advisory body to the president. As such, it enjoys certain privileges to ensure that the president has unfettered access to advisors. Accordingly, the national security advisor is a presidential appointee not subject to Senate confirmation, and the Council and its staff are not subject to congressional oversight. Giving the Council executive powers likely would result in the loss of these privileges. It would certainly require major legislation and would be met with considerable resistance from cabinet-level secretaries, who would then report to a superagency interposed between them and the president.

Given this broad overview, we turn our attention to the relevant reform studies.

Hart-Rudman Commission

The U.S. Commission on National Security/21st Century, sometimes called the National Security Study Group (NSSG), is best known as the Hart-Rudman Commission. The Commission was chaired by two former senators, Gary Hart (D-CO) and Warren Rudman (R-NH). The Commission was established by the Clinton administration and delivered its report to the incoming Bush administration.[1] The report is not driven by the events of 9/11 that provided the advantage of hindsight to later studies, nor is it affected by the narrow focus on terrorism common to some studies following 9/11 or by the negativity often directed toward the Bush administration. Hart-Rudman was to be bold and consider the reforms necessary to adapt to the next twenty-five years and to lead to the biggest reform since the 1947 National Security Act.

Strategy. The Commission takes a broad view of national security strategy. It does not equate national security with "defense," and it rejects a sharp distinction between foreign and domestic security. Strategy is central to the Commission's thinking about both responding to dangers and seizing emerging opportunities. The Commission recommends using the president's national security strategy to allocate resources across government. The Commission recommends an interests-based strategy with interests at three levels: survival, critical, and significant. Interests are to be both protected and advanced. The recommended strategy has six objectives:

- Defend the United States against the dangers of a new era. Defending the homeland is *the* priority mission.
- Maintain America's social cohesion, economic competitiveness, technological ingenuity, and military strength. Included are improving education in science and mathematics and reducing dependence on foreign oil.
- Assist integration of key major powers, especially China, Russia, and India, into the mainstream of the emerging international system.

- Promote, with others, the dynamism of the new global economy and improve the effectiveness of international institutions and international law.
- Adapt U.S. alliances and other regional mechanisms to a new era in which America's partners seek greater autonomy and responsibility.
- Help the international community tame the disintegrative forces spawned by an era of change.[2]

The capabilities of government that were designed for the Cold War are poorly aligned with the needs of the twenty-first century. Strategy is used to guide the application of the instruments of power (the use of power), and strategy must be used to guide resource allocation across the instruments of power (the production of power). The president's national security strategy must be used to allocate resources to realign the instruments of power, and the president should submit an overall national security budget to Congress rather than submitting individual department and agency budgets. Congress should appropriate funds for a single integrated foreign operations budget for State to allocate across regions, functions, and agencies. The secretary of state should emphasize strategic planning, budgeting, and resource allocation.

Organizational Change. Prior to 9/11, the Commission concluded that "a direct attack against American citizens *on American soil* is likely over the next quarter century," and "our nation has no coherent or integrated governmental structures."[3]

At the time of the study, the Intelligence Community remained driven by military threats; attention to economic and political issues lagged. Congress should increase appropriations for expanded collection on economic and scientific issues with an increased emphasis on open sources. The director of central intelligence (DCI) should emphasize human source intelligence (HUMINT) capabilities appropriate for the new era. The NSC should set national intelligence priorities for the DCI in accordance with strategy.

Major issues needed attention at the Defense Department. First, the Department needed a reduction in staff by 10 to 15 percent across OSD, Joint Staff, military departments and services, and the combatant commands; a smaller staff would respond more quickly than the present large staff and ponderous staff procedures. The office of USD(Policy) needs reorganization to include abolishing ASD(SO/LIC). Recommendations for reform included streamlining weapon system acquisition regulations, revamping the antiquated personnel system, and shifting from Cold War conventional forces to more expeditionary forces for rapid deployment to austere environments. Infrastructure costs should be reduced by 20 to 25 percent, including increased outsourcing and privatization.

The Commission concluded that the NSC had become the principal *policy-making* body against long-standing warnings. To concentrate on its primary mission—*policy coordination* across departments and agencies—policy making lead should be returned to State. The National Economic Council should be abolished and its functions distributed to existing organizations. The treasury secretary should be made a statutory member of the NSC.

The State Department is a crippled institution. It lost the confidence of Congress, and decreases in appropriations followed, rendering the Department less capable still. State should be reorganized with a dominant regional focus to resolve the internal conflicts between regional and functional offices. USAID should be integrated into State. Greater emphasis should be given to the competence of ambassadors. Congress should increase appropriations to State consistent with strategy.

The Commission saw science and technology as an important underpinning of national security. Congress should double science and technology investment. The national laboratories, originally established to develop atomic energy, required significant reorganization and assignment of new missions driven by strategy. Science and mathematics education required a redoubling of efforts.

The NSSG made significant recommendations for human resource policy, including civil service, foreign service, and presidential appointees. The Commission recommended establishment of a National Security Service Corps. The Corps would comprise professional members of the various departments and agencies and give them broader, interdepartmental experience outside the confines of their parent organization.

The congressional committee and subcommittee structure remains a relic of the past. Congress should consider a complete review of its committee and subcommittee structure to better accomplish its constitutional responsibilities in the new era. There is no national security committee and no national security budget. Specifically, Congress should merge authorizing and appropriating functions. And Congress should establish a special body to deal with homeland security issues.

The Commission made defense of the homeland the highest priority and recommended the creation of a National Homeland Security Agency. Throughout the Cold War, the National Guard was organized, trained, and equipped as combat forces for overseas deployment. The Commission recommended that the National Guard be assigned homeland security as a primary mission. To facilitate bringing Defense Department resources into homeland security, the Commission recommended the new position of assistant secretary of defense for homeland security.

Legislation was introduced in the House March 2001 to combine the Federal Emergency Management Agency, Border Patrol, Customs, and other offices into a new agency. But no further legislative action was taken prior to 9/11. On 22 September 2001, President Bush announced an office of homeland security in the White House. On 11 October, a Senate bill was introduced to establish a department of homeland security. And legislation was signed into law on 25 November 2002.

Conclusion. The Hart-Rudman study was well received upon release, but not much came of it. Acting on the study's recommendations was not a priority of the new administration. The study demonstrates conclusively that dedicated, informed people could see the character of the changing geostrategic environment. What followed in history is evidence of how painfully slow it is to put good and necessary ideas into practice even after a shock like 9/11.

Without benefit of study, the Patriot Act was signed into law forty-five days after the attacks.

9/11 Commission

The roots of the 9/11 Commission are obvious. It was established in response to public pressure, particularly from the families of victims of the 9/11 attacks. The Commission was established by Congress and delivered its report on 22 July 2004.[4]

The strengths and weaknesses of the study are the same. The Commission had a sweeping mandate to examine all instruments of national power—diplomacy, intelligence, covert action, law enforcement, economic policy, foreign aid, public diplomacy, and homeland defense[5]—as well as commercial aviation, congressional oversight, etc. But the study was driven by a narrow focus on a specific militant Islamic organization—al-Qaeda and Associated Movements (AQAM)—and the terrorist acts it committed against the United States on 11 September 2001. The study does not address the traditional narrow meaning or the newer broader meaning of national security considered by other studies.

The report describes some of the symptoms and the shortcomings of the system in 2001, and it shows how the system was out of synch with the twenty-first-century terrorist threat. Some of the Commission's recommendations have been implemented, but many of its diagnoses remain relevant today. The report identifies the objectives of a strategy to counter the threat and recommends the changes in organization necessary to support the strategy.

The twentieth-century focus was on those states possessing industrial power. The twenty-first-century focus is on the underdeveloped world. According to the Commission, this is a time to reconsider strategy and governmental organization.

> This pattern has occurred before in American history. The United States faces a sudden crisis and summons a tremendous exertion of energy. Then, as that surge transforms the landscape, comes a time of reflection and reevaluation. Some programs and even agencies are discarded; others are reinvented or redesigned. Private firms and engaged citizens redefine their relationships with government, working through the processes of the American republic.

> Now [2004] is the time for that reflection and reevaluation. The United States should consider *what to do*—the shape and objectives of a strategy. Americans should also consider *how to do it*—organizing their government in a different way.[6]

The overarching finding of the 9/11 Commission is that terrorism had not been a high priority. The consequence was that the capabilities of government suited to dealing with terrorism were weak and were not aligned to achieve the necessary unity of effort. The Commission argued that ad hoc and incremental fixes were inadequate. Major governmental reform was necessary. A strategy for the future would require a *whole-of-government* approach to achieve unity of effort.

Strategy. The strategy proposed is not for the whole of national security strategy but for an important component, a subordinate strategy.[7] The strategy is threat-based, and the threat is posed by Islamist terrorism, especially AQAM. Those who hold to this fundamentalist ideology cannot be negotiated with. They must be killed or captured. But the strategy must be more comprehensive. The recommended political-military strategy rests on attacking terrorists and their organizations; preventing the continued growth of Islamist terrorism; and protecting against and preparing for terrorist attacks.

According to the Commission, the threat emanates not from U.S. policies but from the failure of governments in the Muslim world to modernize, including falling behind in political, economic, and military structures. Secular democracy with political and economic openness, religious tolerance, adherence to the rule of law, and extension of greater opportunities to women contribute to the long-term solution that can come only from inside the Muslim world, according to the Commission.

For U.S. strategy, "long-term success demands the use of all elements of national power: diplomacy, intelligence, covert action, law enforcement, economic policy, foreign aid, public diplomacy, and homeland defense. If we favor one tool while neglecting others, we leave ourselves vulnerable and weaken our national effort."[8] The threat is global, and it should be addressed by an international coalition. The Commission offers specific components of the strategy for denying sanctuary; engaging Muslim governments in Afghanistan, Pakistan, and Saudi Arabia; engaging in a contest of ideas to counter the extremist ideology; countering the proliferation of weapons of mass destruction; improving the ability to control travel and immigration with the assistance of information technology and information sharing; and greater investments in consequence management, also with an emphasis on information technology.

Diplomatic efforts failed to pressure Afghanistan and Pakistan to expel Osama bin Laden to a country where he could be brought to justice. Intelligence sharing with Saudi Arabia was disappointing to say the least. The Commission had several recommendations on what to do. Prominent among them was to deny sanctuary to AQAM. Denying sanctuary requires strengthening the government capabilities of Afghanistan and Pakistan, modernizing Muslim states to accept the rule of law and human rights, and pressing Saudi Arabia for intelligence cooperation befitting an ally.

Organizational Change. "As presently configured, the national security institutions of the U.S. government are still the institutions constructed to win the Cold War."[9] The overarching theme of the Commission's organizational reforms is achieving unity of effort from a diversity of instruments. Five major recommendations are offered:

- unify strategic intelligence and operational planning against Islamist terrorists across the foreign-domestic divide with a National Counterterrorism Center;
- unify the intelligence community with a new director of national intelligence;
- unify the many participants in the counterterrorism effort and their knowledge in a network-based information-sharing system that transcends traditional governmental boundaries;
- unify and strengthen congressional oversight to improve quality and accountability; and
- strengthen the FBI and homeland defenders.

The Intelligence Community (IC) comprises more than a dozen agencies spread across government. Intelligence agencies were divided by collection discipline. The CIA had primary responsibility for human source intelligence (HUMINT). The NSA had primary responsibility for signals intelligence (SIGINT), and the National Geospatial-Intelligence Agency (NGA) was responsible for image intelligence (IMINT). Separated by collection discipline, all source analysis was problematic.

The director of central intelligence (DCI), since 1947, had direct responsibilities for the Central Intelligence Agency (CIA) and had separate responsibilities for the overall Intelligence Community. The great majority of the Intelligence Community's budget was under the secretary of defense's authority. The NSA, NGA, and DIA are defense agencies and operate under the defense secretary's authorities. The priority was to military rather than national consumers. The IC's budget was appropriated to the defense secretary, who distributed it. The DCI had little or no true ability to realign the nation's intelligence system after decades of Cold War priorities and military focus.

The Commission recommended abolishing the DCI position. Responsibilities for managing the CIA would remain with the director of the Central Intelligence Agency (DCIA). Responsibilities for the broader Intelligence Community would be reassigned to the new director of national intelligence (DNI).

There were few credible military or paramilitary options offered after 9/11. The Defense Department remained oriented on countering traditional military threats and was not oriented on nontraditional threats like AQAM. The CIA's covert operations and proxy operations were inadequate. Specifically, the CIA's paramilitary capabilities were weak, and the Agency's language and human intelligence capabilities had not yet realigned from Cold War priorities. After establishing the DNI, the DCIA should concentrate on rebuilding analytic capability and transforming the clandestine service for the new era. The CIA should remain responsible for clandestine and covert operations, but responsibility for paramilitary operations should be transferred to DOD and specifically to the Special Operations Command.

The counterterrorism effort was weak and distributed across government. The CIA's Terrorist Threat Integration Center and Counterterrorist Center, as well as the growing counterterrorism capabilities of the Departments of Defense, Homeland Security, and Justice, consumed and competed for scarce resources and needed consolidation to achieve greater information sharing, effectiveness, and efficiency. The Commission recommended establishment of the National Counterterrorism Center (NCTC) to unify domestic and foreign intelligence operational planning, tasking of intelligence assets, and fusion of intelligence. The NCTC would neither make nor implement policy. It would assign lead agency within the IC for implementation. The NCTC was established by executive order in August 2004 and followed by codifying law later that year.

And, of course, information sharing across the departments and agencies was vastly inadequate and made it impossible to "connect the dots." Information technology—including identification cards, screening, and information sharing—required investment to achieve greater integration of the intelligence, law enforcement, and counterterrorism communities.

Airspace management was disjoint. The FAA and NORAD were looking outward for external threats. Borders were permeable. Immigration controls failed to deny entry and to expel those who overstayed their visas. Valuable information was not shared with law enforcement and intelligence communities. The post-9/11 establishment of the Department of Homeland Security (DHS) and the U.S. Northern Command (NORTHCOM) required reinforcement and continual reassessment. And greater resources should be devoted to emergency preparedness and consequence management.

The FBI's domestic capabilities were weak. The Bureau was oriented on after-the-fact prosecutorial investigations rather than on disruption and prevention of terrorist organizations and acts—it placed the criminal justice mission over the national security mission. The Bureau lacked the necessary intelligence collection and analysis capability and was hampered by real and perceived barriers to information sharing. The Commission recommended that domestic counterterrorist intelligence collection remain with the FBI and that the FBI should develop a true counterterrorist intelligence capability.

Like the executive branch, congressional responsibilities were also widely distributed. To unify and strengthen congressional oversight of intelligence and counterterrorism, the Commission recommended consolidating authorization and appropriation for intelligence and counterterrorism in a single committee. A similar committee solution was proposed for homeland security.

Conclusion. Although focused on a particular threat, the recommendations of the 9/11 Commission reiterate and reinforce the recommendations of Hart-Rudman. An isolated military instrument—organized, trained, and equipped to defeat an industrial-age military—with the mission to defend abroad is inadequate for the new era. The instruments of power are out of balance, the ability to orchestrate the instruments of power is of greater importance, and the mechanisms necessary to orchestrate the instruments spread across the departments and agencies are lacking. Government organizations and processes have not entered the information age.

Beyond Goldwater-Nichols

Goldwater-Nichols is the landmark legislation of 1986. Many consider it to have put the final touches on unification of the armed forces begun after World War II. A major reform like this can take ten to fifteen years to work its way through to completion. Unlike the other studies, Beyond Goldwater-Nichols (BG-N) is centered on the military instrument.

One way to look at the BG-N report is as a view from inside the DOD looking out at the whole of government. The stimulus for the study includes a great deal of frustration on the part of the uniformed military attempting to conduct operations that require all instruments of power. In fact, it's reasonable to say that BG-N takes the lessons learned within DOD and applies them to the whole of government. That is, lessons about getting the four uniformed services to work together under the rubric of *jointness* apply similarly to getting the various departments and agencies to work together under the rubric of *interagency*. While the military is supportive of the other departments and agencies, the other departments and agencies often resent having DOD solutions imposed on them.

At the end of the Cold War, *transformation* of the force became a central issue. The majority view was that the military needed to transform from the industrial-age force designed for great-power conflict to the information-age force designed for great-power conflict—the Revolution in Military Affairs. The minority view of transformation, however, was for transformation from a force designed for major wars (wars between major powers) to a force designed for small wars (wars involving lesser powers). After 9/11, those elements of the DOD legally responsible for the production of force failed and left transformation to field commanders who were legally responsible for the use of force in Iraq and Afghanistan— small wars requiring all instruments of power. The BG-N study was initiated in the context of failed transformation.

There are four phases to the BG-N study, each producing a report. The Phase I report focuses on the Pentagon but also addresses some whole-of-government issues.[10] The Phase II report focuses on the whole of government.[11] The Phase III report focuses on the Reserve Component of the military services.[12] The fourth phase is at a level of detail below our needs here.[13]

Strategy. Unlike the Hart-Rudman and the 9/11 studies, BG-N does not offer its own national security strategy. Instead, it assumes a continuation of high operational tempo and of complex contingency operations requiring extensive interagency coordination. The reason, perhaps, is that the military must execute whatever grand strategy a presidential administration might choose. The military is unlikely to tread on presidential prerogative by recommending a grand strategy. For this reason and others, this may be the weakest of the studies identified here, even though it is widely recognized.

Rather than an interests- or threat-based strategy, BG-N adopted a problem-centric approach. Problems included those of transformation and of efficiency. Problems are induced when tasking a system designed for the great power conflict of the twentieth century to undertake the missions of the twenty-first century. "Complex contingency operations" require unity of effort not just from the uniformed services but also from the entire national security apparatus. Study recommendations "aim to get the many disparate parts of the U.S. national security structure to row together, in both planning and execution."[14]

Organizational Changes. The study makes recommendations to achieve greater unity of effort, improve staff effectiveness and efficiency, build capacity in the civilian departments and agencies, and realign capabilities in the military's Reserve Component.

To improve unity of effort, a concept of operations should be developed for each interagency mission area, and a common terminology should be developed to facilitate communications. A training center for interagency and coalition operations should be established from Defense and State Department assets. Each department and agency divides the world into regional structures that make sense for their unique mission; aligning regional boundaries would facilitate interagency coordination. In some cases, capacity is lacking in the civilian departments and agencies. Needed is an Agency for Stability Operations and a Civilian Stability Operations Corps and Reserve capable of rapid deployment. USAID requires resources and support.

The Defense Department has a tremendous capacity for planning unmatched elsewhere in government. Each department and agency should establish its own planning office to develop its own plans and to participate in coordinating their plans with other departments and agencies. The NSC staff should be expanded to execute its lead role in integrating agency strategies and plans and to assure presidential intent by overseeing planning and execution of contingency operations. Furthermore, the Homeland Security Council should be disestablished and its functions integrated into the NSC.

Many of the study's recommendations were projections of successful processes associated with Goldwater-Nichols reforms imposed by legislation on the Department. Joint solutions across the four services were generalized onto interagency solutions across the several departments and agencies. The Quadrennial Defense Review aligning Defense capabilities with strategy should be generalized to a broader Quadrennial National Security Review to develop national security strategy and determine capabilities. The Defense Planning Guidance process integrating DOD programs should be generalized to a broader National Security Planning Guidance. The requirement for military officers to serve in approved joint assignments to compete for senior promotions should be generalized to require departmental civilians to serve in approved interagency assignments. Rather than forming an ad hoc joint task force headquarters as a crisis emerges, the combatant commands have established standing joint task force headquarters ready to respond immediately; the concept should be generalized to a standing interagency task force headquarters with civil-military staff ready for crisis response, including a rapidly deployable interagency crisis planning team.

The study recommended consolidation of Pentagon staffs. Large civilian staffs exist in the Office of the Secretary of Defense and in each of the three military departments. Large military staffs exist in the Joint Staff and in support of each of the four service chiefs. They are large, overlapping, and sometimes competing staffs that make Pentagon response slow and ponderous. The study recommends consolidating the separate staffs into a single staff reporting to the respective secretaries and service chiefs.

Congress should better define the role of the National Guard and Reserve in homeland defense and civil support to state and local authorities. The National Guard and Reserve went from a strategic reserve to operational reserve. The reserve component requires significantly greater appropriation, and the size of the force must grow. The study assumes that optempo will remain high and that, therefore, the use of the reserve component is not optional. The Reserve Component must stay multimission but should move away from conventional conflict and orient more on low-intensity conflict, stabilization operations, homeland defense, and civil support. Civil support should be a central mission of the National Guard.

The present weapon acquisition system was designed for a long-term technological competition between two major industrial powers. The system is not responsive to today's low-tech adversaries. The acquisition system must be more capable of rapidly acquiring and fielding military capabilities.

Congressional oversight of the Department has languished and needs rejuvenation. Moreover, Congress should review its committee and subcommittee structure to improve oversight and debate.

Conclusion. The BG-N study report was widely anticipated, but its effects have been modest. Some movement occurred within the Defense Department. But recommendations to expand the capacities of other departments and agencies met with less success. In some cases, the civilian departments and agencies were ill-suited to the tasks recommended for them. And in other cases, the affected departments and agencies were reluctant to change. Phase I was funded by a foundation grant and Phases II and III were funded by congressional appropriation. But the study's recommendations did not carry the gravitas of a presidential or congressional commission.

Project on National Security Reform

The Project on National Security Reform (PNSR) is the most recent study on reform.[15] The Project was led by James Locher III, principal architect of the Senate Armed Services Committee study that led to the Goldwater-Nichols legislation. It is oriented at the top and the totality of the national security system. A dominant issue is organizational design.

Originally initiated at the request of the CJCS, the nonpartisan project was formally commissioned by Congress in 2008.[16] The twenty-two members of the Project's Guiding Coalition affirmed "unanimously that the national security of the United States of America is fundamentally at risk." With more than three hundred members, the Project conducted thirty-seven major case studies and sixty-three smaller case studies. It was to be the "most far-reaching governmental design innovation in national security"[17] since 1947.

The national security system was designed in 1947 and driven by the lessons of World War II. It has been honed throughout the Cold War in response to the single and unambiguous threat posed by the Soviet Union. The threat and response were seen largely in military terms. The twenty-first century, in contrast, requires the ability to deal with highly differentiated threats spreading our attention and limited resources over a wide range of contingencies. Included in the list of challenges are rising state powers, rogue states, proliferation of WMD, transnational criminal organizations, and violent nonstate actors. Globalization brings with it widespread technology diffusion. Otherwise weak states and nonstates have access to a wide range of destructive technologies. Not all challenges to our security are through directed physical violence. A global financial crisis or a pandemic does not have a military solution. It is "impossible for any single nation to address on its own the full range of . . . security challenges."[18]

"Most challenges to the United States during the Cold War fell into the paths of well-honed departmental competencies."[19] A single-department response was adequate in many cases. In some cases, a sequential multidepartment response proved adequate, e.g., the application of military force followed by diplomatic resolution. But in cases like Vietnam, "when a contingency required not the sequential but the *simultaneous* integration"[20] of diplomatic, informational, military, and economic instruments, the process was cumbersome and the outcome costly.

Two approaches have been taken to improve interagency coordination. One approach was to designate a lead agency, but that quickly degenerates into sole agency. Another approach was to designate a lead individual, a *czar*, but the czar lacked authorities over the departments and agencies.

"The U.S. government has proved unable to integrate adequately the military and nonmilitary dimensions of a complex war on terror, or to effectively integrate hard and soft power" in Iraq and Afghanistan. The government has been "unable . . . to integrate properly the external and homeland dimensions of post-9/11 national security strategy, as the uneven performance of the federal government during and after Hurricane Katrina showed."[21] These complex contingencies require interagency coordination. This type of contingency is increasingly frequent, and is increasingly of paramount significance to American security.

"The system is grossly imbalanced" and remains organized hierarchically around traditional organizational disciplines.[22] The system supports strong departments and agencies with somewhat narrow core competencies. Each jealously guards its statutorily assigned "turf" and resists assignments outside its core. They grow more "ponderous and reactive."[23] Congress authorizes, appropriates resources, and effects oversight according to those core mandates. Shortchanged are the integrating mechanisms necessary to accomplish interagency missions. "Ossified and unable to adapt," the system can only handle those challenges that fall within the competence of a single agency.[24] Interagency coordination is left to the president. As the number and frequency of operations requiring interagency coordination increase, the president increasingly becomes a bottleneck. The Project concludes that the excessively hierarchical system cannot provide the unity of effort needed in the twenty-first century.

Unless organizational structures and processes are aligned with the needs of the twenty-first century, "we will pay increased costs in human lives, financial resources, and global influence from crises that could have been averted and nasty surprises that need never have happened. Important opportunities to promote a more benign international environment will go unexploited, probably even unnoticed."[25]

Strategy. The Project does not offer a national security strategy, but it does offer a broad definition of national security and offers three objectives of a strategy:

- To maintain security from aggression against the nation by means of a national capacity to shape the strategic environment; to anticipate and prevent threats; to respond to attacks by defeating enemies; to recover from the effects of attack; and to sustain the costs of defense
- To maintain security against massive societal disruption as a result of natural forces, including pandemics, natural disasters, and climate change
- To maintain security against the failure of major national infrastructure systems by means of building up and defending robust and

resilient capacities and investing in the ability to recover from damage done to them[26]

The operative definition of security must change from static to dynamic. Old processes, practices, and institutions must be discarded. There will be a greater number and variety of security challenges. Correspondingly, there must be an increased emphasis on foresight rather than reaction and a greater emphasis on understanding the nature of current challenges. All instruments of power, at home and abroad, must be mobilized rather than going it alone with an isolated military instrument. Responsiveness of the system can be achieved only if accountability is ensured. Relationships between the executive and legislative branches must be improved, and to enjoy the support of the American people, a consensus to commitment must be built. Setting an example through actions at home and abroad will produce hope for a world of freedom and prosperity.

The system is designed to provide resources to build capabilities, not to execute missions. As a result, there is no clear link between strategy and resources for interagency activities. Mission-essential capabilities that fall outside core mandates are not planned or trained for. Without a strategy, no one can say what policy tradeoffs are needed. We must rethink how we budget and manage scarce resources. Resource allocation drives strategy rather than strategy driving resource allocation. The inability to develop a coherent strategy leads to an inability to plan for contingencies. Without planning, the country can only react with the capabilities on hand.

Organizational Change. PNSR identifies missions that do not line up with departmental boundaries and argues that any organizational redesign must be *mission-oriented.*

Any large organization requires specialization. Organizational design involves "decomposition." That is, the business of government can be subdivided (decomposed) into the conduct of foreign relations, war fighting, raising revenue, etc. Each of these areas, in turn, is subdivided again, each subdivision with greater specialization. Government action, however, requires reassembling these pieces and orienting them coherently to accomplish a mission. But a hierarchy defined by discipline rather than by mission makes assemblage and coherent action difficult.

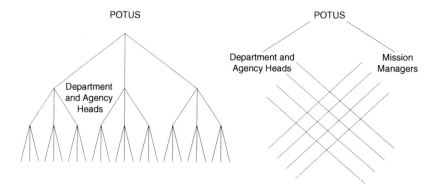

FIG. 13. Departmental hierarchy versus mission management

Imagine an upside-down branching tree structure with the president at the top and with branches drawn down to each of the department heads (see figure 13). Beneath each department secretary are branches drawn down to under secretaries, etc. In an ideal (and implausible) world, information flows up and down along the branches of the tree but never across. For communication to exist between offices of different departments low in the tree, information must flow up to the top and back down again, thereby engaging senior officials in decisions well below the level of their responsibilities, distracting them from their primary responsibilities, and inducing friction and degraded performance. The inevitable need to communicate (coordinate, collaborate) horizontally is evidence of a flawed decomposition. Flawed design is all that is possible. The object of real design is not to eliminate the frictional losses, but to reduce them to tolerable levels. Designing for interagency missions—for example, nation building—ostensibly will produce less friction.

Part of PNSR's argument is that the legacy hierarchical design was tolerable for the Cold War but is the source of insurmountable friction for the missions encountered in the twenty-first century. The increased need for interagency coordination falls solely to the president and has created a bottleneck in the White House. The design problem then is to relieve the bottleneck. The capacity of the president is limited to the capacities of a mere mortal. Expanding the processing capacity of the Executive Office of the President is one approach, but the capacity of the president remains the limit. Delegation to competent and accountable subordinates releases the president to focus on the biggest issues at the highest level.

Departments would survive with their core competencies intact, and the national security system would expand to embrace a wider array of existing departments. The State Department in particular requires considerable reform. Improving interagency cooperation manifests itself beginning in the White House and establishment of new organizational structures.

Addressing challenges must be as multidimensional as the challenges themselves. The national security system must be extended to include the Departments of Treasury, Justice, Agriculture, and Health and Human Services. The organizations not traditionally associated with national security should establish an assistant for national security affairs to participate in national security processes. The president should issue an executive order to define the broader national security system, and Congress should provide statutory expressions of national security roles for each department and agency.

The State Department needs not only rebuilding but transformation to improve international relations. The capacities of other departments and agencies that fall within State's core mandate should be transferred to State. The Department should reorganize along regional lines. The Project recommends a comprehensive revision of the Foreign Assistance Act of 1961.

Departments and agencies divide the globe into regions appropriate for their individual mandates. Because of the specialization of suborganizations, there are multiple regional decompositions in a single department or agency. The typical problems coordinating regional interagency response are compounded. State has no regional organization in the field. The Defense Department's regional combatant commands dominate regional responses, creating the perception and reality of a militarized foreign policy and sometimes breeding resentment abroad. PNSR recommends a unifying regionalization to give priority to the interagency response rather than to departmental responses.

The proposed design focusing on interagency missions begins at the top. In the White House, the National Security Council and Homeland Security Council should be merged, along with their staffs, into a

Presidential Security Council (PSC). The PSC includes new constructs to improve interagency response—interagency teams and interagency task forces—designed to reduce the presidential bottleneck. *Interagency Teams* are permanent, with full-time personnel, staffed and resourced to perform whole-of-government tasks that require an interagency approach beyond individual departmental capacities. To assure sustained stewardship of the foundations of national power, teams would be established for economic policy, energy security, health, and education systems. *Interagency Task Forces* would be established to handle crises as they emerge.

To make the mission-oriented system work, PNSR recommends establishment of a *director for national security* with strong statutory authorities. Whether or not this appointee would require Senate confirmation was left open. Providing unfettered advice to the president argues *against* Senate confirmation and congressional oversight. Exercising executive authorities argues *for* Senate confirmation and congressional accountability. Interagency Teams and Task Forces would also have directors—czars—with authorities and accountability.

In addition to changing structures, PNSR recommends changes to processes. It recommends that a National Security Strategy Review be required by statute at the beginning of each presidential term. Annual National Security Planning Guidance should be given to all departments and agencies setting priorities and assigning planning responsibilities. The president's budget submission to Congress should include a national security budget display that shows tradeoffs and linkages to the Strategy Review and Planning Guidance.

Information management techniques can and must be applied. PNSR recommends development of a collaborative information architecture to eliminate bureaucratic barriers, a single security classification system, and consolidated security clearance procedures. Organizations of the national security system should have chief knowledge officers to ensure proper sharing of knowledge and information.

For the legislative branch, the Project recommends establishing Select Committees on National Security in the Senate and the House of Representatives. Congressional rules need to be rewritten, especially those rules that impede the confirmation process as a new administration enters and the nation is at its most vulnerable. Similarly, the Project recommends consolidating authorization, appropriation, and oversight for the Department of Homeland Security.

Conclusion. After delivering its report, the Project turned its attention to drafting executive orders, amendments to Senate and House rules, and a new national security act. The Project continues to work with Congress and the executive to implement its recommendations. Energy for interagency reform in DC fell along with public support for the Iraq and Afghan wars.

Princeton Project on National Security

The Princeton Project is more oriented on a particular strategy than on organizational reform.[27] For this bipartisan effort, Anthony Lake and George Shultz served as honorary cochairs supported throughout by hundreds of partisans and nonpartisans. Funding was provided by a foundation grant. The Project was initiated in May 2004 and produced its final report in September 2006.

The Project concludes that the country lacks a single organizing principle for foreign policy. Antifascism served that purpose during World War II. Anti-Communism similarly served during the Cold War. As an organizing principle, antiterrorism falls far short of addressing the diverse challenges and opportunities of the twenty-first century. Project members hoped that the final report could serve today as did Kennan's "X" article *in Foreign Affairs*, establishing the logic of containment early in the Cold War.

Strategy. The Princeton Project "argues for an American grand strategy of forging a world of liberty under law by supporting popular, accountable, and rights-regarding governments; building a liberal international order; and updating rules on the use of force." Application of the strategy's principles "would strengthen the capacity of the United States to protect the American people and the American way of life for years to come."[28]

The Project takes a broad view of national security. The proposed strategy has three major objectives: (1) "*a secure homeland*, including protection against attacks on our people and infrastructure and against fatal epidemics; (2) *a healthy economy*, which is essential for our own prosperity and security; and (3) *a benign international environment*, grounded in security cooperation among nations and the spread of liberal democracy."[29]

In furtherance of the strategy, the U.S. response should employ hard power (the power to coerce) and soft power (the power to attract) and employ all instruments of power. Action should be interests-based rather than threat-based; the United States should engage the world based on common interests rather than by imposing its view of prioritized threats onto would-be allies. The vision should be based on hope rather than fear. Objectives should be pursued by building popular, accountable, and rights-regarding governments abroad and by connecting governments with their citizens through local, national, and regional networks including government and nongovernmental organizations.

The Project recommends rethinking the role of force. Rather than maintaining American military preponderance, the aim should be to maintain the military preponderance of liberal democracies. Preventive strikes against threatening terrorist capabilities may become a staple, but preventive wars against states should be rare and authorized by a legitimate international body. Deterrence should be expanded to hold the source of WMD materials accountable should a nonstate actor execute a nuclear terrorist attack. And the global nonproliferation regime needs to be reinvigorated to prevent the nexus of nuclear weapons and terrorists.

The Middle East will continue to figure prominently as a source of global conflict. The United States should lead in the pursuit of a two-state solution in Israel/Palestine. All actors in the Middle East should be engaged as long as they renounce terrorism. Iran must be prevented from acquiring nuclear weapons including, if necessary, a security guarantee. Assistance to Iraq should continue short of civil war. The European Union and Russian Federation should be engaged to assure regional stability.

The War on Terror needs to be reframed. Conceptualizing the conflict analogous to World War II or the Cold War gives greater prominence, credibility, and strength to AQAM. Allowing AQAM to dictate the agendas of the world's leading powers gives them strength and yields the initiative. The conflict should be reframed as a global insurgency with a criminal core. The response, then, is global counterinsurgency using law enforcement, intelligence, and surgical military tools such as special operations forces and strikes. But the ultimate solution lies in building liberty under law to reduce supporters and sympathizers.

Achieving oil independence is a major national security objective. Oil dependence transfers wealth to autocrats, degrades the environment, and contributes to climate change. To wean the country from oil and to fund energy alternatives, the Project proposes increasingly stringent fuel efficiency standards and a national gasoline tax that increases over the years.

The rising Asian powers constitute another major challenge. Rather than block the growth of China, the United States should influence and assist China in constructively integrating into the emerging international system. Rather than allowing a trans-Asia order to develop, the United States should attempt to develop a trans-Pacific order. An East Asian security system should build on the U.S.-Japan security system and include China, South Korea, and Russia. The United States should strengthen ties with India, recognizing that India's sustained economic growth balances China's influence in Asia.

Investments in domestic infrastructure are required. Public health, communications, and public education are all national security issues. Building public health systems at home and abroad should be a priority to protect against global pandemics like avian flu and AIDS.

Organizational Change. The goal is to build an international liberal order. The emphasis for organizational change is on international organizations. Internal organizational change requires some inference.

The United States pursuing its national interests unilaterally breeds "resentment, fear, and resistance," but the international institutions that the United States built after World War II are "broken" and in need of major reform. Needed UN reforms include expanding the Security Council with India, Japan, Brazil, Germany, and two unnamed African states as permanent members. Permanent membership would not include the veto power currently held by the original Permanent 5. Veto authority should be removed when considering Security Council resolutions authorizing actions in response to a crisis. All UN members must adopt the "responsibility to protect" their citizens against avoidable disasters and accept international intervention when they can't.

In addition to reforming the UN, the United States should create a Concert of Democracies with more stringent rules for admission. The Concert would institutionalize and ratify the "democratic peace." Existence of the

Concert would encourage the necessary UN reforms or serve as an alternative should UN reform fall short.

Building a liberal international order requires liberal international and liberal national institutions. The ability to build the capacities of foreign governments requires building and balancing the developmental capabilities of the U.S. government. Nation-building capacity plays prominently in this strategy.

Conclusion. This strategy achieves bipartisan support by combining the Democratic Party's established collective and cooperative security strategies and the Republican Party's new primacy strategy. Both are highly interventionist. Nation building is a prominent mission that requires the reorganizations of government advanced by other studies summarized in this chapter. It represents a new political consensus but is in stark contrast to the traditional Republican strategy, selective engagement, and the Libertarian branch of the Republican Party's strategy of homeland defense, or neo-isolationism.

Task Force on State Department Reform

The Council on Foreign Relations provides a study focused on the needed reforms for the twenty-first century State Department.[30] The nonpartisan study was chaired by Frank Carlucci and cosponsored by the Council on Foreign Relations and the Center for Strategic and International Studies. In one month's time, the task force reviewed and synthesized existing studies for recommendations and proposed a "resources for reform" plan of action that engaged Congress and the executive branch. Separate memoranda were provided for incoming President George W. Bush and Secretary of State Colin Powell.

"The Department of State suffers from long-term mismanagement, antiquated equipment, and dilapidated and insecure facilities."[31] The problem derives from estrangement of the State Department from Congress and the American public, from failures real and perceived, and from a preference for the military instrument over the diplomatic. All result in reduction of resources and support. Each reduction leads to even weaker performance. The downward spiral needs to be reversed, and the task force recommends a resources-for-reform exchange between the executive and legislative branches:

If this deterioration continues, our ability to use statecraft to avoid, manage, and resolve crises, and to deter aggression will decline, increasing the likelihood that America will have to use military force to protect our interests abroad. Renewal of American foreign policy making and implementing machinery is an urgent national security priority.[32]

An examination of recent studies reveals several common themes, but there was a small number of differences. There is no State Department regional organization with policy implementation responsibilities; implementation is on a country-by-country basis through the embassies. One study recommended a regional organization with implementation responsibilities. And there is discord over one critical issue. Some recommend that State should lead in foreign policy making and implementation, with the national security assistant leading in interagency policy coordination; others recommend that the national security assistant and staff should lead in foreign policy making.

Strategy. The task force study does not recommend a strategy. While the twenty-first century geostrategic environment and the U.S. response may exacerbate the problems associated with the State Department, the problems are the result of decades of decline.

Organizational Changes. The task force recommends consolidating the various departments' foreign services, including the Foreign Commercial Service and the Foreign Agricultural Service. It further recommends a single integrated foreign policy and national security budget. And it recommends reorganizing the current regional and functional bureaus with the regional bureaus dominating.

To a large extent, the morale of the State Department and the resources that flow to it derive from the stature of its secretary. The president should make clear in word and deed that the secretary of state is the principal spokesperson for U.S. foreign policy. The use of special presidential envoys undercuts the prestige and credibility of the secretary.

The ambassador is the president's direct emissary to sovereign states and heads the country team. The process of vetting ambassadorial nominees, political or professional, needs to be improved. Dozens of departments and agencies deploy personnel and resources around the world. The task force recommends a committee to rationalize and right size overseas posts. And ambassadors need stronger authorities to orchestrate the activities of all U.S. agencies under a unified foreign policy.

State's mission is to communicate with foreign governments. State's culture frowns on outreach both to Congress and to the American public. There is no natural domestic constituency for State. The Department must overcome that cultural characteristic and specifically develop better relations with its authorizing and appropriating committees in Congress.

Budgeting and policy need to be brought into alignment. The task force recommended that rather than piecemeal congressional appropriations, the president should submit an integrated foreign policy and national security budget that shows tradeoffs between instruments. The Department should have a consolidated foreign operations budget. The Department would have greater discretion over where resources are devoted and would require centralized planning, budgeting, and management.

The task force study concludes that "many Department of State facilities at home and abroad are shabby and insecure" and that "the communications and information management infrastructure is outdated."[33] In many cases, embassies lacked classified communications with the rest of government. Embassies lacked even email capabilities. In light of the terrorist attacks on U.S. embassies in East Africa, overseas facilities needed to be made secure, and the embassies needed to be brought into the information age with modern communications and information technology.

The president and the secretary should work to enhance interagency coordination. USAID should be fully integrated with the Department. And the Department should expand its engagement of the private sector, including commercial and nongovernmental organizations.

Dysfunctional human resources policies have generated serious workforce shortfalls, the study asserts. At the time of the study, archaic hiring processes accompanied by the departure of experienced officers left the Department with a shortfall of 15 percent in Foreign Service Officers.[34]

While there is a broad consensus on the needed reforms, the task force understood that Congress would need to be convinced that reform would follow from additional resources. The president should "declare reform of the Department of State to be a national security priority."[35] The secretary should look for opportunities to effect improvements immediately. The president and secretary should engage congressional committees directly to achieve further reforms.

Conclusion. The State Department that Colin Powell inherited from Secretary of State Madeleine Albright was "in a state of serious disrepair."[36] It would improve under Powell but return to decline under Secretary of State Condoleezza Rice. Powell's professional career as a senior military officer developed leadership and executive skills suited to his position as chief executive officer of the Department, and he had considerable credibility when approaching Congress for resources. A largely academic career allows considerable opportunity to study international relations and foreign policy, but it does not develop leadership or executive skills. The State Department remains in a state of serious disrepair.

Building National Security Professionals

A recurring theme in reform studies is building national security professionals to populate interagency organizations like the NSC that orchestrate the policies of the various departments and agencies. The problem is often compared to that of building commanders and staffs for the joint military organizations charged with integrating the plans and actions of the four uniformed services.

The NSC began as a weak, distrusted institution but grew to become a principal tool of the president. In the early days, the NSC staff was populated by experienced career bureaucrats who often brought the biases of their department of origin. But they were quickly augmented or replaced by political appointees owing loyalty only to the president. Politicization of the NSC staff extended rather than diminished the president's power.

Politicization of the NSC staff has other consequences. Many witnesses to the Tower Commission identified lack of continuity in the NSC staff as problematic:

One problem affecting the NSC staff is lack of institutional memory. This results from the understandable desire of a President to replace the staff in order to be sure it is responsive to him. Departments provide continuity that can help the Council, but the council as an institution also needs some means to assure adequate records and memory.[37]

Individual competence is a key factor in improving national performance with respect to national security. Yet no clear path exists for professional development and no institution exists to house and manage professional development. Career progression must be crafted to produce competent national security professionals. Periodic education and rotating assignments in the various national security departments and agencies as one advances in the profession are important parts of career progression.

The current process is largely conducted within the context of political party and presidential administrations. If a party is out of power for eight or twelve years, its corps of national security experts are not gaining experience. Instead, they often find employment in industry, ideologically aligned think tanks, as lobbyists, or at universities. Too great a reliance on political appointees greatly degrades competence within and continuity across administrations. A greater reliance on nonpartisan professionals enables continuity but potentially weakens presidential initiative. There are at least three approaches to professional development: lead agency, superagency, and academy.

Lead-Agency Approach. One approach is to designate a department as lead agency for national security. To that department falls the responsibility for coordinating the actions of the others. National security professionals would anchor their careers in one department or another, seek alternative temporary assignments from there, and return to their parent department for advancement.

Superagency Approach. A second approach is to establish a new department or agency that serves as the national security professional's home institution. If the superagency spanned all instruments of power, career progression could be managed internally. If not, alternative assignments could be sought outside the new institution, and the professional would return to the parent institution for advancement.

Academy Approach. A third approach is something like a government-run national security academy, which would attract the "best and brightest"—the most promising national security professionals. After initial entry (perhaps through civil service), their career progression would be managed as in other agencies. Career progression would include two- to three-year stints each in four or five different existing government agencies and Congress as a professional committee (nonpartisan) staffer. The individuals would return to the academy periodically for special career development, mentoring, education, research, and training, as needed. However, the academy's only function would be to train this pool of professionals. It would be strictly nonpartisan. The president would then have a ready-made pool of national security professionals who understand a range of government instruments to call upon for senior national security positions and for national emergencies or for special cases like the rebuilding of Iraq.

The Intergovernmental Personnel Act (IPA) is an existing mechanism that could be exploited. Today, civil servants can participate and be put into two- or three-year assignments elsewhere in government and then return to their home organization. The process is analogous to joint assignments in the military, but the process is purely voluntary (it is mandatory in the military for senior positions). As a government agency, the academy could be the place into which people were hired; they would repeatedly use the IPA mechanism to gain assignments in other agencies and then return home to the academy.

The academy could also be implemented as a Federally Funded Research and Development Center (FFRDC), like Rand, the Institute for Defense Analyses, and the Center for Naval Analyses. The legislation and federal regulations for FFRDCs already exist. FFRDC employees are already authorized to participate in the IPA program. Professionals not assigned to a department or agency would be resident at the Center doing independent and objective studies and analyses exclusively for the NSC, State, and the CIA, none of which currently has an FFRDC for studies and analyses.

Comparison of Approaches. The lead-agency and superagency approaches would certainly produce resistance from the existing agencies. Lead agency would be contested by the agencies not selected and would certainly produce a long-term bias in career progression toward the designated lead. The superagency approach likely would be resisted by all existing agencies, which would see the superagency as a barrier between themselves and the president. Both of these approaches would require significant legislation, superagency more so than lead agency. Establishing the civil service positions and building the work force would take considerable time.

The academy approach could be politically and bureaucratically easier than establishing a new agency. Chartering a new center to be the academy would be the path of least resistance. Employees of the FFRDCs are hired and fired under private sector rather than civil service rules. What is required is an FFRDC charter and congressional appropriation. The academy would serve as the institution for career progression that is currently lacking. The academy approach also preserves options; it can be an incremental step toward either lead agency or superagency.

Other Common Issues

A consensus begins to build within a policy community on problems and solutions. Often, a single study has little effect. Multiple studies that independently arrive at similar conclusions suffer a similar fate. A high-profile failure, unfortunately, is sometimes required to get the attention of decision makers or to provide the political capital necessary to impose change. At that point, the body of studies provides a reservoir of well-reasoned and vetted ideas. The presence of such a consensus is called "ripeness."

Problems achieving unity of command over military forces in World War II led to postwar legislation that unified the military departments under the secretary of defense and the Defense Department. But unity of command issues persisted. When evidence accumulated on the inadequacy of last-minute integration of the separate uniformed services, Goldwater-Nichols legislation was passed in 1986. When evidence accumulated on the inadequacy of last-minute integration of the special operations forces of the separate services, Nunn-Cohen legislation was passed in 1987.

Today, there is mounting evidence of the inadequacy of last-minute integration of the separate agencies of government. The legislative attention paid to the military instrument has not been matched by attention to integrating the capabilities of the other departments and agencies. Legislation on the order of the National Security Act of 1947 is necessary to improve interagency operations. Unity of command may be beyond reach in the near term, and unity of effort may be a more realistic goal.

Evidence of problematic interagency response exists in foreign and domestic domains. Some explicitly reject the arbitrary distinction between the internal and external spheres, but the distinction is far from arbitrary.

Solutions to the problem of achieving national security objectives in the domestic sphere are constrained by the American version of federalism established in the Constitution. Achieving national security objectives externally do not have those constraints. But the distinction between internal and external leaves the nation's borders somewhere in between.

The country has always been subjected to national disasters, including floods, hurricanes, earthquakes, tornadoes, and droughts. Managing the consequences can be handled in most cases by state and local authorities bolstered by federal support in extreme cases. Establishing the Department of Homeland Security (DHS) was a strong step in the right direction. But it is entirely unreasonable to expect this new department to deliver excellence in the near term. If unification of the armed forces under the Department of Defense is any guide, it will take decades of attention to get it right and considerable sustained effort to keep it right. The same capacities used to respond to natural disasters will be brought to bear in a man-made disaster such as a large-scale terrorist attack or an offshore oil spill.

Establishment of DHS was an important step in bringing the instruments of national power to bear on matters of internal security, including the law enforcement agencies' ability to prevent terrorist attacks and the ability to manage the consequences of natural and man-made disasters. Without considerable modifications to the Constitution, state and local governments will carry the primary burden of providing consequence management. Police, fire, and emergency medical services will respond first, stay throughout, and remain after a disaster. Local hospitals will carry the load. Federal actors can only support and bring additional resources when state and local capacities are exceeded.

Unity of command affected by the federal government is not an option. State and local authorities will *command*, and federal authorities will *support*. Unity of effort is the only viable approach.

The maritime states of New England once had their own coastal navies for protection. Later, coastal artillery was a prominent branch of the federal army. The Spanish-American War of 1898 was a tipping point, after which the United States increasingly pursued a *defend forward* posture. Wars would be fought abroad. It has been a very long time since the U.S. military defended the nation's borders. Illegal immigration, illicit drug trafficking, and the potential for smuggling weapons of mass destruction across borders convince some that defending U.S. borders is a priority military matter.

More to the subject of this text are the problems of overseas operations. There is overwhelming evidence of imbalanced instruments and an inability to orchestrate the instruments. In addition, there is a strong consensus among those who make and those who implement national security policy about the need and nature of reform. The studies reviewed above are voluminous and include long lists of specific recommendations.

It is safe to say, at a high level, the consensus includes the following conclusions and recommendations:

- Whole-of-government solutions are required.
- Interagency processes must be improved to achieve unity of effort.
- The instruments of power are out of balance.
- The State Department is in need of serious rehabilitation.
- Professionalism in the national security workforce is problematic.
- Information sharing across bureaucratic boundaries is thwarted.
- Major reform is necessary.

The necessary reforms require sustained effort at all levels, and the desired results will take years if not decades to achieve. The decision to undertake a reform of this magnitude cannot be taken lightly.

For Consideration

Issues needing resolution exist at multiple levels. Some issues will defy resolution until a new strategic consensus is reached in Washington. Regional issues abound, and coordination issues extend deep into the countries and provinces where the United States conducts operations.

The national security apparatus was designed for and remains suited to maintaining peace between great powers and, if necessary, transitioning to war between great powers. It is suited to the serial application of instruments and unsuited to the simultaneous application of instruments requiring the capabilities of several departments and agencies. Simultaneous application of instruments requires integration by the president.

Strategic Consensus. In Washington, a new post–Cold War consensus is lacking. There is no consensus on the meaning of national security. That is, there is no consensus on the nature of the geostrategic environment and the principal threats and opportunities. Are security threats something that can be addressed by tough-minded diplomats and backed by a prescient intelligence community and powerful military, or are they a wide range of real problems without military solutions? Lacking a shared conception of the strategic environment, there can be no consensus on a security strategy. And without strategic consensus, there can be no consensus on the capabilities that must be made available for later application or on the ways of organizing and applying existing means to achieve the ends of strategy.

Diffuse Focus. Much depends on the missions the president decides to pursue. If the president assigns a mission that can be accomplished by a single department or agency—for example, war or diplomacy—then the current organization of government is appropriate, and delegation rather than orchestration is sufficient. If, however, the president assigns a mission that requires the simultaneous application of the core competencies of more than one agency, then the responsibility for orchestration falls solely to the president.

There is no national security department. When orchestration is necessary, the NSC is the president's primary mechanism for orchestrating the instruments of power. Statutorily, it is an advisory body to the president and thus escapes congressional oversight. But because it does far more than advise the president on policy integration, the NSC approaches being an executive agency without congressional oversight. And a bottleneck is created at the presidential level.

There is no national security committee in either house of Congress, nor is there a national security budget. The congressional responsibilities for authorization, appropriation, and oversight are divided along lines similar to those in the executive branch, holdovers from the Cold War era. Briefly, the House Armed Services Committee was renamed the House National Security Committee, reflecting the notion that national security was a military problem with a military solution. The name change was short-lived.[38]

Regionalization. Regionalization remains problematic. The various departments and agencies of the executive branch subdivide the world into regions consistent with their specific mission. If the president assigns a mission to a single department or agency, then each department and agency should regionalize according to its own jurisdiction. If, however, the missions assigned by the president do not lie solely within the core competency of a single agency, then agencies must coordinate their actions, and their divergent regionalization becomes problematic. The more agencies involved, the larger the problem. Regionally oriented congressional subcommittees provide yet another regionalization. Given this, formulating, implementing, and overseeing coherent regional policies is nearly impossible.

The uniformed military updates its regionalization periodically by producing the Unified Command Plan (UCP). The UCP provides the basis for the regional combatant commands and defines their boundaries. These commands have great organizational capacities. No other agency of government has any regional organization that comes close in capacity, influence, or prestige. The militarization of foreign policy is the unintended (or intended) consequence.

Mission. For decades, the ambassador, through the country team, guided the application of the capabilities housed in the Agency for International Development, Agriculture Department, Commerce Department, and others in a slow, deliberate process of state building and economic development abroad. Since the end of the Cold War, the United States is more aggressively pursuing nation building led by military forces that were designed for major war and supported by civilian agencies that were understaffed and underfunded. Presidential policies for nation building were put in place *after* initiating action.

11   Strategy First

There appears to be a consensus among those who make and implement America's national security policy. Policy makers from left and right recommend assertive strategies that promote democracy and free markets abroad. The recommended strategies require nation building in the failed and failing states that may harbor our enemies. Those who implement policy have served under highly interventionist post–Cold War administrations and have witnessed firsthand the problems associated with nation building, including instruments out of balance and the inability to orchestrate those instruments. The nation-building mission is the strongest determinant requiring reform of the national security apparatus.

A third group apart from policy makers and policy implementers, strategists appear to be forming a different consensus, or at least a challenge to the makers of policy. Strategists do not assume unlimited *means*. Nor do they assume that nation building is an effective *way* to apply resources in furtherance of security *ends*. Strategy guides resource allocation and resource application. And strategy is a choice.

Redefining National Security for the Twenty-First Century

There appears to be agreement on the need to redefine national security for the twenty-first century. The meaning of national security has been redefined at least twice in the post–Cold War era. International economics was added to the list of national security issues in the 1970s. A profound redefinition was sought as the Soviet Union disintegrated. And another redefinition followed the attacks of September 2001.

When national security is narrowly defined, strategies guide the use of military power. When national security is more broadly defined, strategies guide the application of all instruments of power. For some, not all, environmental degradation, pandemics and HIV/AIDS, transnational crime and terrorism are all threats to national security, and they are without military solution. Without agreeing on what constitutes national security, it is impossible to agree on a national security strategy.

Dissolution of the Soviet Union: From Military to Nonmilitary Threats

The disintegration of the Soviet Union left a vacuum in U.S. national security thinking. Some from the realist camp quietly filled the vacuum with China and continued standard operating procedures with little disruption. Others from the realist side sought to bring military forces home to organize, train, and equip for major combat operations, most likely over major-power competition for resources in the Middle East and Africa.

A large group from the liberal and internationalist schools proposed filling the vacuum by elevating a long list of issues traditionally considered important foreign or domestic policy issues.[1] Revolutions in information and communications technology increased the porosity of international borders. The flows of financial capital further eroded state sovereignty. Population growth makes extreme demands on the environment and causes international migrations from economic, political, and environmental pressures. The inequalities between the haves and the have-nots are growing. In addition to these, transnational criminal organizations and infectious diseases were recognized as threats to national security. Internationalist approaches would be required.

These might traditionally be considered important issues to pursue as matters of foreign or domestic policy. Not all foreign policy issues are matters of national security unless we choose to define them as such. Shifting an issue into the national security realm increases its urgency, moves it from a department secretary's desk to the president's, and attracts increased resources. The nontraditional issues fill the vacuum left by the withdrawal of the Soviet Union from the world stage. These are not military problems with military solutions. The national security apparatus would need to be redefined and the military reorganized to support rather than lead.

Many issues compete for resources, including dollars, congressional attention, and presidential energy. Pursuing activities without international support erodes U.S. influence, and being on the right side of an alliance structure is a product of actions taken over time. Achieving a greater degree of energy independence would allow greater freedom of action and strengthen the economy. Building and rebuilding domestic infrastructure would help improve economic competitiveness. Controlling borders would contribute to societal stability and address a variety of transnational threats, including terrorism and drug trafficking. The wisdom of reorganizing government to do nation building abroad must be evaluated in the context of these other demands for resources.

Attacks of September 2001: From State to Nonstate Threats

Post-9/11, national security was redefined again. This time, terrorism was identified as the primary threat to national security. During the twentieth century, the priority threat came from industrial-age major powers; in the twenty-first century, the threat comes from nonstate transnational actors. But even nonstate actors must operate from a state, and the ungoverned space, the failing or failed state, becomes the problem. Nation building immediately follows as the solution. The question becomes, Does nation building, and a strategy relying on it, constitute the best use of scarce resources in the pursuit of American national security?

The national security system was designed for interstate warfare, specifically for war between major industrial powers with equal access to populations, technology, and resources—major wars. Post–Cold War conflicts have increasingly been about intrastate warfare involving governments that are either failed or failing—small wars. Governments are either incapable of providing security to their populations from internal forces, or they deliberately exploit all or portions of their populations. Some of these states are considered to constitute a threat to U.S. national security, for example, Afghanistan, Pakistan, Somalia, and other African states.

Current Status

Seeing the threat as a failed state is a state-centric problem definition, and nation building is a state-centric solution. All the while, the true threat is a nonstate actor: al-Qaeda and associated movements (AQAM). Globalization continues to erode the preeminence of the state. The possibility of pandemics, challenges to and by the environment, and transnational crime did not diminish after 9/11. The country still lacks a stable consensus on the meaning of national security and lacks a sustainable national security strategy. Whatever the definition of national security, it is much larger than the very real threat posed by militant Islamists.

The very powerful forces of modernization, globalization, and nationalism are all at work. Modernization marches ineluctably forward. Some claim that the rate of change is accelerating. Fundamentalists, whether religious or secular, will resist, sometimes violently. Globalization may or may not be an unstoppable force. Even if it is, it will likely suffer temporary setbacks. Nationalism is not dead and can be in opposition to the forces of globalization. Nationalism exerts its influence abroad when weak nations demand the right of self-determination and territorial sovereignty. In the United States, domestic nationalism resists globalization by asserting the need to control its borders, by pursuing energy independence, and by returning jobs outsourced to the rest of the world.

The United States can either exert itself over others by pursuing dominion and pay the costs of overcoming the forces of foreign nationalism, or it can marshal the power of foreign nationalism by pursuing policies aligned with shared interests. The United States can choose to lead with the power of ideas, what Carr called the power over opinion. These are choices.

An offensive realist would predict that the end of the superpower competition would lead to an expansion of U.S. interests, "that states expand in the absence of countervailing power; unbalanced power will act without moderation, and states not subject to external restraint tend to observe few limits on their behavior."[2] The United States will expand its interests and actions until credibly opposed or until it exhausts itself. For entirely different reasons, the political Left and Right rise to the prediction.

The checks and balances no longer apply. Congress no longer checks the president, and, as Enlightenment thinking predicts, an executive unchecked by the people's branch is prone to war. The only check is presidential self-discipline, and that, expressed in grand strategy, was not apparent until the Obama administration. Neither party represents fiscal conservatism, rhetorical claims to the contrary. Neither party represents a restrictive use of force. It is possible that one or both parties may fragment, allowing for a realignment of the many political factions and producing a party representing mainstream America that favors a strong military but one prepared to fight America's wars rather than fighting others' wars as global cop.

Repeatedly since 2010 Secretary of Defense Robert Gates and Chairman, Joint Chiefs of Staff Admiral Michael Mullen identified the national debt as the greatest threat to national security.

Strategy First

No resolution to the issue of twenty-first-century grand strategy appears on the horizon. As the wars in Iraq and Afghanistan draw down, the United States still must decide what role it will play in the international system of states. There appears to be a backlash and withdrawal from the beyond-primacy strategy of the post-9/11 Bush-Cheney administration. But it is unlikely that the pendulum will swing all the way to homeland defense, although political forces are building in that direction.

Operations in Afghanistan and Iraq offer clear evidence to consider. First, the capacities present in the U.S. military virtually guarantee the defeat of an opposing state's military. Second, building the institutions of democratic government in a failed state is a long, difficult process with little to suggest that optimism about the outcome is warranted. Third, attempting to build governments in only two countries simultaneously strained the resources of the last remaining superpower. Engaging the resources of the other major powers would expand the numbers somewhat, but there are many countries to build. This cannot be the basis of a sustainable strategy to achieve American national security, but that may not stop presidents from trying.

There is convincing evidence that the U.S. government is hard pressed to meet its objectives in a timely and predictable manner. Because of the prominent role played by the military in these operations, it is tempting to conclude that the military instrument is out of alignment with the needs of the twenty-first century and to recommend realignment within the uniformed services. But the symptoms of the misalignment of the military force structure are a direct product of the demonstrably unsustainable national security strategies of post–Cold War administrations. A restructuring of the force is ill-advised without a thoughtful examination of U.S. grand strategy.

There are some things common to all available strategies. All strategies call for maintaining a strong second-strike nuclear capability, although there is debate on how large the nuclear force need be. And there is general agreement on the need for missile defense, although the costs are extraordinarily high and the technology not yet mature. All strategies require paying the bill incurred by three post–Cold War presidents who used force extensively while force levels fell and modernization accounts were raided to pay for accumulating operations.

If the country pursues any of the heavy-use strategies—collective, cooperative, primacy—the ability to build government institutions in the Third World will be required. That, in turn, requires the ability to bring all instruments of power to bear. The pieces of the reconnaissance strike complex are distributed around the globe in small-wars roles. Under the heaviest of the heavy-use strategies, the reconnaissance strike complex must be reconstituted and modernized; a separate and true small-wars capability must be built. These simultaneous objectives are not achievable in the near term due to the delay between funding and fielding of capability.

If the country pursues one of the more restrictive, light-use strategies—homeland defense, selective engagement—the ability to build government institutions in the Third World is not called for. At most, a modest part of the military focused on small wars would be sufficient, for example, the Marine Corps and special operations forces. The reconnaissance strike complex must be reconstituted and modernized, and significant parts of it held in the reserve component. In addition to the nuclear strike capability, long-range precision strike with conventional weapons would be a principal military mission, including the ability to conduct attacks with land- and sea-based aircraft and cruise missiles. And parts of the Army, Marine Corps, and special operations forces should be focused on in-and-out strike operations rather than on sustained operations, such as major combat, occupation, and nation building.

Strategy is a linkage of ends, ways, and means. Although national security is much larger than thwarting attacks from AQAM, the threat remains real and significant. High on the list of *ends* are reducing the risk and severity of attacks on the United States. Preventing our enemies from acquiring weapons of mass destruction, denying sanctuary to those who would do us harm, and disrupting plots all contribute to reducing those risks.

There are a variety of *ways* to reduce the risks. Preventing the spread of WMD can be pursued by international nonproliferation regimes, economic sanctions and rewards, strikes and raids, or any combination. Denying sanctuary to those who would do us harm can be accomplished by the slow, deliberate state-building efforts typified by USAID; by the more aggressive and costly nation building led by the military in the hope of achieving results more quickly; or by diplomacy backed by strikes and raids, or any combination of these. Disrupting plots is accomplished by intelligence and law enforcement, including international cooperation. Strikes and raids can take away capability before it is used.

Means are finite whether they are measured in dollars, troop levels, or the capabilities of the departments and agencies. If a change in capability is needed, it will take years to translate dollars into capabilities. Nation building, strikes and raids, law enforcement, intelligence, and diplomacy are all valuable capabilities, but the solution lies in finding the right mix of capabilities. And the right mix can only be determined with reference to a strategy.

Not all strategies rely on nation building or small wars. Not all strategies accept the U.S. role as global policeman or social engineer. Nation building applies the most pressure for reform. Some strategies lean strongly toward military-led nation building; others lean strongly toward strikes and raids, law enforcement, and intelligence. Strategy is a choice.

In choosing between alternative strategies, each should be evaluated on whether it depletes, maintains, or enhances the instruments of power upon which U.S. national security rests. In Edward Carr's conception, those instruments are economic power, military power, and the power over opinion.

Economic Power. The United States possessed the dominant economy after World War II. The consolidating economies of the European Union and the impressive growth of China and India indicate relative decline of the U.S. economy. In the production of military force, the U.S. expenditure on military capability is far out of proportion to that of its competitors. In the use of military force, both parties are heavily interventionist. The production and use of force and the borrow-and-spend practices of both parties are the strongest contributor to the massive national debt. The recent performance of the U.S. economy during the

"Great Recession" leads many abroad to question the United States as an authority when advancing economic policy.

Military Power. The heavy expenditure on the production of military force supports a military force very capable of military victory. The United States remains the dominant nuclear power and the dominant conventional military power. The United States now also has the largest and most experienced military force for low-intensity conflict, small wars, peacekeeping, and nation building. But military power rests on economic power and the power over opinion.

Power over Opinion. The power over opinion is the forgotten instrument. It was replaced by the information instrument under the assumption that the power over opinion—at home and abroad—is a matter of what we say rather than of what we do. If we truly had power over opinion abroad, then other major powers would join in pursuit of our initiatives. But our traditional allies have drastically reduced expenditures on their militaries, and they have declined participation in important U.S. initiatives, most noteworthy, the 2003 invasion of Iraq. If we truly had power over domestic opinion, then the American public would support U.S. actions by increasingly joining in government service and supporting higher taxes to support U.S. policies. None of these are apparent. The power over opinion, more than through promulgating information, is built by setting a good example through supportable action.

Restructuring the National Security System for the Twenty-First Century

Expanding the capacities of government requires public support and leadership. Support comes in the form of votes, tax dollars, and personal commitment. Both parties are highly interventionist, and neither party offers a more restrictive and sustainable use of force. Both parties wage wars with deficit spending rather than raising taxes to pay as they go. And an increasing proportion of the public must enter public service in the organizations, requiring long, arduous tours in austere Third World environments: the military, the civilian defense agencies, and the civilian departments. The requisite leadership and public support do not appear to be forthcoming.

Are U.S. military forces aligned with the needs of the twenty-first century? Is the larger, overarching national security apparatus aligned with those needs? The answer to the first question must wait on an answer to the second, and neither question can be answered without reference to a national security strategy, which has been anything but consistent since the end of the Cold War. Depending on the chosen strategy, military force structure is about right or it is wildly out of alignment. The instruments of power appear to be out of balance regardless of the chosen strategy, but determining a reasonable balance requires reference to strategy. The various national security strategies make different demands on the national security system. Absent a stable consensus on national security strategy, or range of strategies, a significant reorganization of the national security system seems ill-advised.

NOTES

INTRODUCTION

1. United States Marine Corps, *Small Wars Manual*, I-1.
2. United States Marine Corps, *Small Wars Manual*, I-1, I-33, II-2, I-18, II-2, I-12, I-32.
3. Poole and Rosenthal, *Congress: A Political-Economic History of Roll Call Voting*.
4. Friedman, *Essays in Positive Economics*, 315.

1. A PRIMER ON SECURITY CONCEPTS

1. Waltz, *Man, the State and War*.
2. Moseley, "Just War Theory."
3. See, for example, Holcomb and Ribbing, "War Has Changed. The Laws of War Must, Too."
4. Augustine, *The Political Writings of Saint Augustine*, 162–83. For commentary, see Dean, *The Political Writings and Social Ideas of Saint Thomas Aquinas*, 134–71.
5. Howard, *The Invention of Peace*, 9.
6. Walzer, "The Triumph of Just War Theory—and the Dangers of Success."
7. Grotius, *On the Laws of War and Peace*, 5–58.
8. Vattel, *The Law of Nations*, 469–649.
9. Walzer, *Just and Unjust Wars*, 72.
10. Wallis, *God's Politics*, 113.
11. Schelling's *Arms and Influence* is the seminal work in this area, complemented by Art, "To What Ends Military Power?" Mearsheimer, *Conventional Deterrence*, elaborates on deterrence theory; and Cimbala, *Coercive Military Strategy*, does the same for the coercive use of military force.
12. Schelling, *Arms and Influence*, 71, 72, 4.
13. Watson, "Reagan's Raiders," 26; for the policy implications of the raid on Libya, see Rubner, "Antiterrorism and the Withering of the 1973 War Powers Resolution."

14. Levy, "Declining Power." This article was selected both because of its accurate expression of the concepts and because it predates the 9/11 attacks and the apparent deliberate misuse of the terms afterward.
15. Levy, "Declining Power," 90.
16. Quoted in Walzer, *Just and Unjust Wars*, 74. See also Akerman, "But What's the Legal Case for Preemption?," B2.
17. Levy, "Declining Power," 87, 91.
18. Levy, "Misperceptions and the Causes of War." See also Levy, "Declining Power."
19. Friedman, "You Gotta Have Friends."
20. Bishara, "The Political Repercussions of the Israeli Raid on the Iraqi Nuclear Reactor"; Ramberg, "Attacks on Nuclear Reactors."
21. Lobel and Ratner, "Bypassing the Security Council."
22. Carr, *International Relations*, 1–21.
23. Carr, *International Relations*, 21.
24. Carr, *International Relations*, 92.
25. Carr, *International Relations*, 8.
26. Carr, *International Relations*, 10.
27. Mearsheimer, "The False Promise of International Institutions"; Glaser, "Realists as Optimists"; Wohlforth, "Realism and the End of the Cold War"; Keohane and Martin, "The Promise of Institutionalist Theory"; Kupchan and Kupchan, "The Promise of Collective Security"; Ruggie, "The False Premise of Realism"; Wendt, "Constructing International Politics"; Mearsheimer, "A Realist Reply." Mearsheimer's article in volume 19 of *International Security* generated most of the rebuttal in volume 20, and the interested reader may wish to begin there.
28. Herz, "Power Politics and World Organization."
29. Mill, *Considerations on Representative Government*, 382.
30. Carr, *International Relations*, 161.
31. Carr, *International Relations*, 153.
32. Carr, *International Relations*, 153.
33. Thucydides, *The Peloponnesian War*.
34. Sun Tzu, *The Art of War*.
35. Kautilya, *Arathashastra*.
36. Machiavelli, *The Prince*.
37. Hobbes, *Leviathan*.
38. Von Clausewitz, *On War*.
39. Morgenthau, *Politics among Nations*.
40. Morgenthau, "Six Principles of Political Realism," in *International Politics*, ed. Art and Jervis, 16, 18.
41. Mearsheimer, "False Promise," 10.
42. Bull, *The Anarchical Society*.

43. Monten, "The Roots of the Bush Doctrine."

44. Emeric Vattel, qtd. in Wright, *A Study of War*, 119–20.

45. Wright, *A Study of War*, 63.

46. Kennedy, *The Rise and Fall of the Great Powers*.

47. Hume, "Of the Balance of Power," provides an early and classically British articulation. Vagts and Vagts, "The Balance of Power in International Law," provides a historical development from the perspective of international law. Gulick, *Europe's Classic Balance of Power*, is perhaps the best and most thorough articulation of balance of power theory.

48. Mearsheimer, *The Tragedy of Great Power Politics*, 29.

49. Doyle, "Kant, Liberal Legacies, and Foreign Affairs," 114–16.

50. Mearsheimer, "False Promise," 28–30.

51. Ninkovich, *The Wilsonian Century*.

52. Ricardo, *Principles of Political Economy and Taxation*, 262–72.

53. Russett, *Grasping the Democratic Peace*; Layne, "Kant or Cant?"

54. Carr, *International Relations*, 114.

55. Smith, *Wealth of Nations*.

56. Mill, *Principles of Political Economy* II, bk., 5, chap. xi, qtd. in Carr, *International Relations*, 45.

57. Carr, *International Relations*, 46.

58. Carr, *International Relations*, 47.

59. Carr, *International Relations*, 115.

60. Williams, *The Tragedy of American Diplomacy*; Chomsky, *Hegemony or Survival*.

61. Kant, *Perpetual Peace*. See also Kant, *Universal History with a Cosmopolitan Aim*.

62. Kant, *Perpetual Peace*, 4.

63. Kant, *Perpetual Peace*, 5.

64. Kant, *Perpetual Peace*, 11–12.

65. Small and Singer, "The War-Proneness of Democratic Regimes, 1816–1865," 67–68.

2. WAR AND AMERICAN DEMOCRACY

1. Monten, "Roots of the Bush Doctrine."

2. Ruggie, "American Exceptionalism, Exemptionalism, and Global Governance."

3. John Winthrop is commonly associated with the "city on the hill" reference. Winthrop, a Puritan, referenced Matt. 5:14–15 in a 1630 sermon written while he was en route to the New World. What would become the Massachusetts Bay Colony would be a godly utopia and the envy of oppressed people everywhere. Winthrop preferred a mixed aristocracy to "mere democracy." The Colony

was a theocratic state intolerant of religious diversity. Baptists, Catholics, and Jews were hanged in the town square.

4. Monten, "Roots of the Bush Doctrine," 145.
5. Tocqueville, *Democracy in America*.
6. Fitzpatrick, *Writings of George Washington*, 256.
7. Kissinger, *Does America Need a Foreign Policy?*, 237–51.
8. Kissinger, *Does America Need a Foreign Policy?*, 237–38.
9. Kissinger, *Does America Need a Foreign Policy?*, 245.
10. Kissinger, *Does America Need a Foreign Policy?*, 238–39.
11. Woodrow W. Wilson, *War Messages*, 2 April 1917, qtd. in Kissinger, *Does America Need a Foreign Policy?*, 243.
12. Kissinger, *Does America Need a Foreign Policy?*, 242–46.
13. Howard, *Invention of Peace*, 28.
14. Monaghan, *John Jay*, 323.
15. Doyle, "Kant, Liberal Legacies, and Foreign Affairs," 114–26.
16. Snow, *National Security for a New Era*, 41–43.
17. Vaughn, "Transparency—The Mechanisms: Open Government and Accountability," 19.
18. Adorno, Frenkel-Brunswick, Levinson, and Sanford, *The Authoritarian Personality*; Altemeyer, "Highly Dominating, Highly Authoritarian Personalities," 421–47.
19. Sageman, *Understanding Terror Networks*, 152–58.
20. Duckitt, "Authoritarianism and Group Identification," 70–71.
21. See www.newamericancentury.org.
22. Kristol also established *The Public Interest*, a quarterly, in 1965. Its last issue was published in 2005, and its obituary was written by Charles Krauthammer in the *Washington Post* on 29 April.
23. Neuhaus, *The Catholic Moment*.
24. "The End of Democracy?," 18.
25. Novak, *The Spirit of Democratic Capitalism* and *Toward a Theology of the Corporation*. See also George Weigel, *Catholicism and the Renewal of American Democracy*.
26. Linker, *The Theocons*.
27. *New York Times*, "A Guide to the 2005 Republican Herd."
28. www.eagleforum.org.
29. Wagner, *The New Temperance*, 4, 18.
30. Rushdoony, *The Roots of Reconstruction*; and *The Institutions of Biblical Law*.
31. See also Olasky, *Renewing American Compassion*.
32. Goldberg, *Kingdom Coming*, 111.
33. Goodstein, "The Nation."
34. Green, "American Religious Landscapes and Political Attitudes."

35. See, for example, Christian Churches Together, www.christianchurchestogether. org and www.sojo.net. See also Meyers, *Why the Christian Right Is Wrong.*
36. Gould, *Grand Old Party*; and Witcover, *Party of the People.*
37. Von Drehle, "Origins of the Species," *Washington Post*, W12.
38. Washington, Farewell Address.
39. Adams, Letter to Jonathan Jackson, 511.
40. Madison, *Federalist* No. 10, 79.
41. Roosevelt, Theodore. Address before the Convention of the National Progressive Party in Chicago, 6 August 1912.
42. Von Drehle, "Origins of the Species," *Washington Post*, W12.
43. Fiorina, *Culture War?* The back cover of Fiorina's book shows a shaded map that better characterizes the electorate than does the simplistic red-blue depiction.
44. Fiorina, *Culture War?*, 227–28.
45. Fiorina, *Culture War?*, 81–82.

3. WAR POWERS
1. There is a rich literature on the topic of presidential war powers. The long-running classic is Corwin, *The President: Office and Powers* and its successor editions. The Nixon-era classic is Schlesinger, *The Imperial Presidency.* The Clinton-era and present-day authority is Fisher, *Presidential War Power.* Two new entries on the Bush era are Schwarz and Huq, *Unchecked and Unbalanced: Presidential Power in a Time of Terror*; and Crenson and Ginsberg, *Presidential Power: Unchecked and Unbalanced.* Neustadt, *Presidential Power and the Modern Presidents* deals with the officeholder's leadership rather than the office's legal authorities.
2. Crenson and Ginsberg, *Presidential Power*, 215–79.
3. "The War Power," 194.
4. "The War Power," 194.
5. Crenson and Ginsberg, *Presidential Power*, 217.
6. Schlesinger, *Imperial Presidency*, 3.
7. Schlesinger, *Imperial Presidency*, x.
8. Jay, *Federalist Paper*, No. 64; Hamilton, *Federalist Paper*, No. 75.
9. Crenson and Ginsberg, *Presidential Power*, 354.
10. Schlesinger, *Imperial Presidency*, 3.
11. Hamilton, *Federalist Paper*, No. 74.
12. Schlesinger, *Imperial Presidency*, xxvii.
13. James Madison to Thomas Jefferson, 2 April 1797, in *Madison: Writings*, ed. Rakove, 586.
14. Hamilton, *Federalist Paper*, No. 69.
15. Madison, *Federalist Paper*, No. 51.

16. Schlesinger, *Imperial Presidency*, 22.

17. Crenson and Ginsberg, *Presidential Power*, 324.

18. Schlesinger, *Imperial Presidency*, 21.

19. Elsea and Grimmett, *Declarations of War and Authorizations for the Use of Force*.

20. Schlesinger, *Imperial Presidency*, xv.

21. Qtd. in Crenson and Ginsberg, *Presidential Power*, 326.

22. Schlesinger, *Imperial Presidency*, xvi.

23. Banks and Straussman, "A New Imperial Presidency?"; Schlesinger, "Back to the Imperial Presidency," new introduction to the 2004 edition of *The Imperial Presidency*, ix–xxiv.

24. Corwin, *The President*, 171. The reference to the 1940 edition is Schlesinger, *The Imperial Presidency*, 501n6 and 502n15.

25. Levy, *Original Intent and the Framers' Constitution*.

26. Yoo, *The Powers of War and Peace*. See also the Heritage Foundation, *The Heritage Guide to the Constitution*. A foreword claims to employ the doctrine of original intent.

27. Mervin, "Demise of the War Clause," 770. See also Adler, "The Clinton Theory of the War Power"; and Adler, "Virtues of the War Clause."

28. Hess, "Presidents and the Congressional War Resolutions of 1991 and 2002," 94.

29. Crenson and Ginsberg, *Presidential Power*, 318–23.

30. Qtd. in Schlesinger, *Imperial Presidency*, 444.

31. Corwin, *Presidential Powers*, 216.

32. See reclama attached to Banks and Straussman, "A New Imperial Presidency?," 567. Levitan, "The Foreign Relations Power," 493.

33. *California Law Review* qtd. in Schlesinger, *Imperial Presidency*, 103.

34. Schlesinger, *Imperial Presidency*, 145.

35. Nichols, *Genius of Impeachment*.

36. Nichols, *Genius of Impeachment*, 7.

37. Qtd. in Schlesinger, *Imperial Presidency*, xvi.

38. Representative Robert McClory (R-IL), qtd. in Nichols, *Genius of Impeachment*, 97.

39. Nichols, *Genius of Impeachment*, 23–44.

40. Nichols, *Genius of Impeachment*, 30, 36, 42.

41. Nichols, *Genius of Impeachment*, 31–32.

42. Nichols, *Genius of Impeachment*, 144.

43. Schlesinger, *Imperial Presidency*, xviii.

44. Nichols, *Genius of Impeachment*, 124–28.

45. Hallett, *The Lost Art of Declaring War*, 109.

46. The United States separately declared war against Germany and Austria-Hungary in the First World War and with Japan, Germany, Italy, Bulgaria, Hungary, and Rumania in the Second World War.

47. Public Law 93-52, Sec. 108.

48. Hoxie, *Command Decision*, 89–94.

49. Hoxie, *Command Decision*, 75–78.

50. Hoxie, *Command Decision*, 17.

51. Hoxie, *Command Decision*, 20–21.

52. Kyle, *Suez*, 527–28.

53. The Senate voted 58–41 in favor of air and missile strikes on 23 March 1999. The House voted a 213–213 tie on 28 April 1999.

54. Adler, "The Clinton Theory of the War Power," 156.

55. The interested reader should acquire Congressional Research Service (hereafter CRS), *The War Powers Resolution: After Thirty-Three Years*. In addition to a thorough discussion of events since enactment, its appendices include the full text of the Resolution, all instances reported under the Resolution, and instances formally reported. See also CRS *War Powers Resolution: Presidential Compliance*; and CRS, *Declarations of War and Authorizations for the Use of Military Force*. Each is updated periodically. One reliable source is www.fas.org/man/crs/natsec.

56. Richard Nixon, "Veto of the War Powers Resolution."

57. CRS, *War Powers Resolution: Presidential Compliance*, 15.

58. Hendrickson, "War Powers."

59. Hendrickson, "War Powers," 246.

60. CRS, *Congressional Use of Funding Cutoffs since 1970*.

61. CRS, *The War Powers Resolution: After Thirty-Three Years*, 51–55.

62. Adler, "Virtues of the War Clause," 780.

63. Hendrickson, "War Powers," 254; Schlesinger, *Imperial Presidency*, xviii.

64. Schlesinger, *Imperial Presidency*, 434–35.

65. Fisher and Adler, *WPR Goodbye*, 18.

66. Nichols, *Genius of Impeachment*, 81.

67. Mervin, "Demise of the War Clause."

68. Adler, "Virtues of the War Clause," 782.

69. Schlesinger, *Imperial Presidency*, xxvii.

70. Crenson and Ginsberg, *Presidential Power*, 368.

71. Crenson and Ginsberg, *Presidential Power*, 278.

72. Hendrickson, "War Powers."

73. Nichols, *Genius of Impeachment*, 139.

74. Crenson and Ginsberg, *Presidential Power*, 279.

75. Schlesinger, *Imperial Presidency*, xxv, 501n2.

4. GRAND STRATEGY

1. Freeman, *Arts of Power: Statecraft and Diplomacy*, 71.

2. Nitze, "Atoms, Strategy and Policy." Nitze proposed the distinction between declaratory and employment ("action") policy. Donald Snow and others later

inserted force development and deployment policy between these two policy levels.

3. Press, *Calculating Credibility*.
4. Press, *Calculating Credibility*, 10.
5. Cambone, *New Structure*, 8–31.
6. Cambone, *New Structure*, viii.
7. Freeman, *Arts of Power*, 9–14. Freeman lists supreme interest, vital interests, strategic interests, tactical interests, and national concerns.
8. One prominent attempt categorized national interests as vital, extremely important, important, and less important (Commission on America's National Interests, *America's National Interests*).
9. Freeman, *Arts of Power*, 10.
10. *Oeuvres* XXVIII, 16.
11. Cambone, *New Structure*, viii.
12. Freeman, *Arts of Power*, 12.
13. Ikenberry and Slaughter, codirectors, "Forging a World of Liberty under Law."
14. Freeman, *Arts of Power*, xx, 129.
15. Freeman, *Arts of Power*, 34.
16. Fontana, "State and Society," 28.
17. Worley, *Shaping U.S. Forces*.

5. COLD WAR STRATEGIES

1. The principal source for review is Gaddis, *Strategies of Containment*.
2. Gaddis, *Strategies of Containment*, 346.
3. Long telegram of February 1946 while Ambassador Averill Harriman was away.
4. X [Kennan], "The Sources of Soviet Conduct." Kennan wrote the *Foreign Affairs* article in December 1946 in response to a question from Secretary of Defense Forrestal while Kennan was deputy commandant at the National War College and following three tours of duty in Stalin's Russia.
5. Gaddis, *Strategies of Containment*, 99.
6. Gaddis, *Strategies of Containment*, 59, 60.
7. Gaddis, *Strategies of Containment*, 72–74.
8. Gaddis, *Strategies of Containment*, 71.
9. Gaddis, *Strategies of Containment*, 84.
10. NSC-68: "United States Objectives and Programs for National Security: A Report to the President Pursuant to the President's Directive of January 31, 1950." 14 April 1950.
11. Gaddis, *Strategies of Containment*, 91.
12. Gaddis, *Strategies of Containment*, 93.
13. Gaddis, *Strategies of Containment*, 101.
14. Gaddis, *Strategies of Containment*, 126.

15. NSC-20/4 "U.S. Objectives with Respect to the USSR to Counter Soviet Threats to U.S. Security," *Foreign Relations of the United States* 1, pt. 2 (1948): 663–69.

16. NSC-1/1, presented 14 November 1947 and signed 24 November. The intervention in Italian elections included laundered money, direct funding of the Catholic Democratic Party, and a propaganda campaign against the Communist Party (Christopher Andrew, *For the President's Eyes Only: Secret Intelligence and the American Presidency from Washington to Bush* [New York: Harper-Collins, 1995], 171–74).

17. Arab League Declaration on the Invasion of Palestine, www.jewishvirtual library.org/jsource/History/arab_invasion.html.

18. *Naval War College Review* 27 (May–June 1975): 51–108. Also in U.S. Department of State, *Foreign Relations of the United States* 1 (1950).

19. Hoxie, *Command Decision*, 94.

20. Eisenhower, *Waging Peace*, 11.

21. Gaddis, *Strategies of Containment*, 135.

22. The Central Treaty Organization (CENTO), earlier the Middle East Treaty Organization (METO) or the Baghdad Pact, was created in 1955 and dissolved in 1979. The Southeast Asia Treaty Organization (SEATO), or the Manila Pact, was signed 8 September 1954, formally established in February 1955, and dissolved on 30 June 1977.

23. Gaddis, *Strategies of Containment*, 130.

24. Dwight Eisenhower, news conference given on 7 April 1954, *Public Papers of the Presidents, 1954*, 382.

25. Ruehsen, "Operation 'Ajax' Revisited"; Zahrani, "The Coup That Changed the Middle East." See also www.gwu.edu/~nsarchiv/NSAEBB/NSAEBB28/.

26. Nikita Khrushchev, "On the Personality Cult and Its Consequences," speech given to the Twentieth Party Congress, 25 February 1956. The speech was disseminated publicly beginning 5 March.

27. Some Western texts do not include the Suez Crisis as one of the wars comprising the larger Arab-Israeli Conflict.

28. Kyle, *Suez*.

29. Kunz, *The Economic Diplomacy of the Suez Crisis*.

30. See, for example, www.eisenhowermemorial.org/stories/.

31. Andrew, *President's Eyes Only*, 206. See also www.gwu.edu/~nsarchiv/NSAEBB /NSAEBB4/.

32. Dwight D. Eisenhower, "The Chance for Peace," speech given to the American Society of Newspaper Editors, 16 April 1953.

33. The "Alliance for Progress" address was given to members of Congress and Latin American diplomats.

34. Karnow, *Vietnam, A History*, 513–54.

35. Johnson, *The Vantage Point*, 389–92, 406–7.

36. Leonid Brezhnev to the Fifth Congress of the Polish United Workers' Party, 13 November 1968. The Doctrine was previously articulated by S. Kovalo in Pravda on 26 September 1968 (Kovaleo, "Sovereignty and the International Obligations of Socialist Countries").

37. Initially announced on 25 July 1969 during a press conference in Guam and reinforced in "Address to the Nation on the War in Vietnam" on 3 November 1969.

38. Quoted from the transcript of Henry Kissinger's meeting with Zhou Enlai, 20 June 1972. Source: The National Security Archive; George Washington University: "Memorandum of Conversation with Zhou Enlai, June 20, 1972," 27–37. Date and time: Tuesday, 20 June 1972, 2:05–6:05 p.m. Place: Great Hall of the People, Peking.

39. Flynn, *The Draft*, 265.

40. Flynn, *The Draft*, 268.

41. Crenson and Ginsberg, *Presidential Power*, 265.

42. Davis, "The Angola Decision of 1975."

43. Address at the commencement exercises of Notre Dame University on 22 May 1977.

44. Gaddis, *Strategies of Containment*, 347.

45. Gaddis, *Strategies of Containment*, 346–47.

46. Gaddis, *Strategies of Containment*, 352.

47. Stockwell, "Why I'm Leaving the CIA"; and Stockwell, *In Search of Enemies*. Stockwell was a Marine Corps officer who also served as a paramilitary officer with the CIA.

48. Televised speech given on 15 July 1979 and later called "The Crisis of Confidence" speech.

49. *Le Nouvel Observateur* (Paris), "Les Revelations d'UN Ancien Conseiller de Carter: 'Oui, la CIA est entrée en Afghanistan avant les Russes.'" 15–21 January 1998. For a translation, see www.globalresearch.ca/articles/BRZ110A.html.

50. State of the Union Address given 23 January 1980. See also Gaddis, *Strategies of Containment*, 345–46.

51. Garthoff, *Great Transition*, 33.

52. Kirkpatrick, "Dictatorships and Double Standards."

53. Krauthammer, "The Reagan Doctrine."

54. Bodenheimer and Gould, *Rollback!: Right-Wing Power in U.S. Foreign Policy*.

55. Weinberger, "The Uses of Military Power," speech at National Press Club, Washington DC, 28 November 1984.

56. Cannon, *Role of a Lifetime*, 337.

57. Cannon, "What Happened to Reagan the Gunslinger? Now His Problem Is Convincing Skeptics He Isn't a Pussycat," *Washington Post*, 7 July 1985, B-1.

58. Crocker, "Strategy for Change"; and "Southern Africa: Eight Years Later."

59. Cannon, *Role of a Lifetime*, 608.

60. Garthoff, *Great Transition*, 11.

61. Terrill, "Placing the Libya Breakthrough in Perspective."

62. Speech delivered to the American Committee on East-West Accord (Washington DC: 17 May 1983). See Kennan, *At a Century's Ending*, 82, 114–15, 124.

63. Hugh Downs in an ABC Radio commentary, 18 March 1991.

64. Pat Buchanan announced that Reagan "won the Cold War" at the Republican National Convention on 17 August 1992.

65. The Organization of African Unity was established on 25 May 1963, disbanded on 9 July 2002, and replaced by the African Union. The Union would oppose colonialism, support independent African states, press for majority rule in countries like Angola and South Africa, and remain neutral in world affairs to avoid further external domination.

66. Kennan, *At a Century's Ending*, 186.

67. For a rational assessment, see Knopf, "Did Reagan Win the Cold War?"

6. POST–COLD WAR STRATEGIES

1. Posen and Ross, "Competing Visions."

2. Odom, *America's Military Revolution*; Jervis, "International Primacy," 292.

3. Posen and Ross, "Competing Visions," 33–34.

4. Posen and Ross, "Competing Visions," 42–43.

5. Posen and Ross, "Competing Visions," 39–40.

6. Posen and Ross, "Competing Visions," 41.

7. Posen and Ross, "Competing Visions," 35.

8. Posen and Ross, "Competing Visions," 43.

9. Buchanan, *A Republic, Not an Empire*.

10. Posen and Ross, "Competing Visions," 9, 12.

11. Posen and Ross, "Competing Visions," 13–14.

12. Posen and Ross, "Competing Visions," 16.

13. Posen and Ross, "Competing Visions," 29.

14. Carter and Perry, *Preventive Defense*; and Carter, Perry, and Steinbruner, *Cooperative Security* well represent cooperative security.

15. Carter, Perry, and Steinbruner, *Cooperative Security*, 7.

16. Posen and Ross, "Competing Visions," 25–27.

17. Carter, Perry, and Steinbruner, *Cooperative Security*, 11.

18. Carter, Perry, and Steinbruner, *Cooperative Security*, 7. See also Carter and Perry, *Preventive Defense*.

19. Posen and Ross, "Competing Visions," 30–31.

20. Art, *A Grand Strategy for America*; Clarke and Clad, *After the Crusade*.

21. Posen and Ross, "Competing Visions," 17–19.

22. Posen and Ross, "Competing Visions," 20.

23. Posen and Ross, "Competing Visions," 18.

24. Posen and Ross, "Competing Visions," 20–23.

25. Layne, "From Preponderance to Offshore Balancing"; Layne, "Rethinking American Grand Strategy."

26. Data from http://siadapp.dmdc.osd.mil/personnel/MILITARY/miltop.htm.

27. Aubin, "Stumbling toward Transformation."

28. Powell, *National Military Strategy of the United States*. Includes Base Force data.

29. Tyler, "U.S. Strategy Plan Calls for Insuring No Rivals Develop."

30. G. H. W. Bush, *National Security Strategy of the United States* (1991).

31. Kissinger, *Does America Need a Foreign Policy?*, 29, 41–42.

32. Posen and Ross, "Competing Visions," 44–51.

33. Clinton, *A National Security Strategy of Engagement and Enlargement* (1994); *A National Security Strategy of Engagement and Enlargement* (1995); *A National Security Strategy of Engagement and Enlargement* (1996); *A National Security Strategy for a New Century* (1997); *A National Security Strategy for a New Century* (1998); *A National Security Strategy for a New Century* (1999); *A National Security Strategy for a Global Age* (2000).

34. Weiner and Perlez, "Crisis in the Balkans."

35. Carter and Perry, "If Necessary, Strike and Destroy."

36. Personal communication with Wesley Clark on 8 January 2006.

37. Burk, "Public Support for Peacekeeping in Lebanon and Somalia."

38. Apple, "A Domestic Sort with Global Worries."

39. Rice, "Campaign 2000."

40. Rice, "Campaign 2000," 61.

41. Rice, "Campaign 2000," 52–54.

42. G. W. Bush, *National Security Strategy* (2002).

43. Rice, "Campaign 2000," 49.

44. G. W. Bush, *National Security Strategy* (2002), 5–6.

45. G. W. Bush, *National Security Strategy* (2002), 6.

46. G. W. Bush, *National Security Strategy* (2006).

47. Suskind, *The One Percent Doctrine*, 2.

48. Public Law 107–243.

49. Hirsh, "Bush and the World," 24–25.

50. Altman and Haass, "American Profligacy and American Power."

51. Difo, "Ordinary Measures, Extraordinary Results."

52. See, for example, *Foreign Affairs* 90, no. 3 (May/June 2011).

53. Bronner, "As Biden Visits, Israel Unveils Plans for New Settlements," A4.

54. Atwan, *The Secret History of Al-Qaeda*, 221.

55. *Al-Islah* (London), 2 September 1996, 1–12.

56. [Scheuer], *Imperial Hubris*, 241.

57. Atwan, *The Secret History of Al Qaeda*, 287.

58. Worley, "From Concept to Policy."
59. Beutel and Ahmad, "Examining Bin Laden's Statements."
60. Personal communication with Dana Priest, 28 April 2006; Priest, *The Mission*.
61. Caudle, "National Security Strategies."
62. Gelb, "GDP Now Matters More Than Force," 35.
63. Gelb, "GDP Now Matters More Than Force," 41.

7. INSTRUMENTS OF POWER

1. Carr, *International Relations*, 1–21.
2. Carr, *International Relations*, 108.
3. DOD Dictionary of Military and Associated Terms: "All of the means available to the government in its pursuit of national objectives. They are expressed as diplomatic, economic, informational and military," www.dtic.mil/doctrine /jel/doddict/index.html.
4. G. W. Bush, *National Security Strategy* (2006).
5. National Defense University, *Strategic Assessment 1996*.
6. Freeman, *Arts of Power*, 40.
7. Armitage and Nye, "Implementing Smart Power."
8. Armitage and Nye, "Implementing Smart Power." Hillary Clinton referred to smart power during her 13 January 2009 Senate confirmation hearings for the position of secretary of state.
9. Donnelly, "Battle Brewing over Five-Sided Diplomacy."
10. Pincus, "Taking Defense's Hand out of State's Pocket."
11. Easterly, *White Man's Burden*.
12. Worley, *Shaping U.S. Forces*, 177–80.
13. General Accounting Office, "Foreign Aid: Police Training and Assistance."
14. Foreign Assistance Act of 1961.
15. Foreign Assistance Act of 1973 (P.L. 93-184, sec. 2, 87 stat. 714, 716); and Foreign Assistance Act of 1974 (P.L. 93-559, sec. 30(a), 88 stat. 1795, 1804).
16. The Foreign Intelligence Surveillance Act of 1978.
17. Course 2 Directive, AY 99, "War, National Policy and Strength" (Carlisle Barracks, Pa. U.S. Army War College, Department of National Security and Strategy), 35.
18. Altman and Haass, "American Power and Profligacy."
19. Altman and Haass, "American Power and Profligacy," 33.
20. Altman and Haass, "American Power and Prolifigacy," 32.
21. Altman and Haass, "American Power and Prolifigacy," 34.
22. Powell, *My American Journey*, 576.

1. Positions are listed in the *United States Government Policy and Supporting Positions* ("Plum Book"), 2008 ed., updated every four years (www.gpoaccess.gov /plumbook/).

2. White House, Fact Sheet on Foreign Affairs Reorganization, 30 December 1998, www.fas.org/news/usa/1998/12/98123003_tlt.html.

3. State Department Office of the Historian, www.state.gov/r/pa/ho/pubs/c6059 .htm.

4. The Fulbright Act of 1946 is an important piece of legislation for exchange programs. The 1961 Mutual Education and Cultural Exchange Act expanded and consolidated exchange programs.

5. Smith-Mundt Act of 1948.

6. The Arms Control and Disarmament Act of 1961.

7. Blechman and Nolan, "Reorganizing for More Effective Arms Negotiation," 1164, qtd. in Dixon, *National Security Policy Formulation*, 44–45.

8. *Washington Post*, March 2006.

9. Gelb, "Why Not the State Department?," 29, qtd. in Dixon, *National Security Policy Formulation*, 45.

10. The secretary was first authorized a deputy in 1919 with the title of under secretary of state.

11. Political-geographic divisions were established in 1909. The position of deputy under secretary for political affairs was established in 1949 and was elevated to under secretary in 1959.

12. Section 161(b) of the Foreign Relations Authorization Act for Fiscal Years 1994 and 1995 (P.L. 103-236; 108 Stat. 402).

13. P.L. 103-236 [H.R. 2333].

14. P.L. 105-277 [H.R. 4328].

15. White House, *National Strategy for Combating Terrorism*, September 2006, www.whitehouse.gov/nsc/nsct/2006.

16. www.state.gov/s/ct/about/index.htm.

17. *Government Executive*, 1 January 2006.

18. Enthoven and Smith, *How Much Is Enough?*

19. CENTCOM's major war plan was to counter a Soviet invasion through the Caucuses Mountains into Iran to seize Iranian oil fields by entering Iran through the Zagros Mountains in the south, largely supported by the Eighteenth Airborne Corps.

20. The National Commission on Terrorist Attacks upon the United States (the 9/11 Commission). The Intelligence Reform and Terrorism Prevention Act of 2004, P.L. 108-458 (Intelligence Reform Act).

21. Dixon, *National Security Policy Formulation*, 123.

22. Jones, "Will Reform Change Congress?," 247–60, qtd. in Dixon, 123.

23. The Patriot Act is formally known as Uniting and Strengthening America by Providing Appropriate Tools Required to Intercept and Obstruct Terrorism.
24. The 9/11 Commission is formally known as the National Commission on Terrorist Attacks Upon the United States.
25. http://oversight.house.gov and http://hsgac.senate.gov.
26. http://foreign.senate.gov and http://internationalrelations.house.gov.
27. http://armed-services.senate.gov and http://armedservices.house.gov.
28. http://hsgac.senate.gov and http://homeland.house.gov.
29. http://intelligence.senate.gov and http://intelligence.house.gov.
30. http://appropriations.senate.gov and http://appropriations.house.gov.
31. Priest, *The Mission.*
32. "An Interview with Vice President and Director of Foreign Policy Studies of the Brookings Institution, Carlos Pasqual," 83.

9. NATIONAL SECURITY COUNCIL

1. U.S. Congress, Senate, Committee on Naval Affairs, *Report to HON James Forrestal, Secretary of the Navy on Unification of the War and Navy Departments and Postwar Organization for National Security, 22 October 1945,* 79th Cong., 1st sess., 1945. This report is often referred to as the Eberstadt Report, or the Eberstadt Unification Report, of September 1945.
2. Often referred to as the Collins Plan or Marshall-Collins Plan. *Hearings on Department of Armed Forces* (S. 84), Committee on Military Affairs, Senate, 79th Cong., 1st sess., October–December, 1945.
3. Inderfurth and Johnson, *Fateful Decisions,* 342.
4. GAO/NSIAD-89-31, *National Security: The Use of Presidential Directives to Make and Implement U.S. Policy,* December 1988.
5. Inderfurth and Johnson, *Fateful Decisions,* 131–215.
6. Data from Kennedy to Clinton was reported in Ivo H. Daalder and I. M. Destler, *A NSC for a New Administration.* Policy Brief No. 68 (Washington DC: Brookings Institution, November 2000), also reported in Inderfurth and Johnson, *Fateful Decisions,* 132. Ivo Daalder generously provided updated information from Kennedy to Bush. Data from Truman and Eisenhower administrations are from the respective presidential libraries. Numbers for the Obama administration are from CQ Press.
7. Daadler and Destler, Policy Briefing.
8. History of the National Security Council, 1947–1997,www.whitehouse.gov/nsc/history.html.
9. Falk, "The National Security Council under Truman, Eisenhower, and Kennedy." This article provides a superb summary of the Council's formative years.
10. Tower Commission, *Tower Commission Report.*
11. Tower Commission, *Tower Commission Report,* 30.

12. Inderfurth and Johnson, *Fateful Decisions*, 158–61.

13. Leslie Gelb defined the "iron laws governing relations between the White House, Defense Department, and State Department, qtd. in Inderfurth and Johnson, *Fateful Decisions*, 337.

14. Inderfurth and Johnson, *Fateful Decisions*, 29.

10. MAJOR REFORM PROPOSALS

1. U.S. Commission on National Security/21st Century, *Roadmap for National Security*.

2. U.S. Commission on National Security/21st Century, *Road Map for National Security*, 5–6.

3. U.S. Commission on National Security/21st Century, *Roadmap for National Security*, viii.

4. National Commission on Terrorist Attacks upon the United States, *Final Report of the National Commission on Terrorist Attacks* (henceforth "9/11 Commission").

5. 9/11 Commission, *9/11 Commission Report*, 363–64.

6. 9/11 Commission, *9/11 Commission Report*, 361.

7. 9/11 Commission, *9/11 Commission Report*, 361–98.

8. 9/11 Commission, *9/11 Commission Report*, 363–64.

9. 9/11 Commission, *9/11 Commission Report*, 399–428.

10. Murdock et al., *Beyond Goldwater-Nichols* (2004).

11. Murdock et al., *Beyond Goldwater-Nichols* (2005).

12. Wormuth et al., *Beyond Goldwater-Nichols* (2006).

13. The products of the multiphase study are available from the Center for Strategic and International Studies at http://csis.org/program/beyond-goldwater-nichols.

14. Murdock et al., "Beyond Goldwater-Nichols (2005)," 6.

15. Reports of the group are available from www.pnsr.org and www.old.pnsr.org.

16. National Defense Authorization Act FY 2008, §1049 (Public Law 110-181).

17. Project on National Security Reform, *Forging a New Shield*, i.

18. Project on National Security Reform, *Forging a New Shield*, iv.

19. Project on National Security Reform, *Forging a New Shield*, ii.

20. Project on National Security Reform, *Forging a New Shield*, ii.

21. Project on National Security Reform, *Forging a New Shield*, ii–iii.

22. Project on National Security Reform, *Forging a New Shield*, ii–vi.

23. Project on National Security Reform, *Forging a New Shield*, ii.

24. Project on National Security Reform, *Forging a New Shield*, viii.

25. Project on National Security Reform, *Forging a New Shield*, iv.

26. Project on National Security Reform, *Forging a New Shield*, v.

27. Ikenberry and Slaughter, codirectors, *Forging a World of Liberty under Law*.

28. Ikenberry and Slaughter, *Forging a World of Liberty under Law*, 3.

29. Ikenberry and Slaughter, *Forging a World of Liberty under Law*, 6.

30. Carlucci, *State Department Reform*.

31. Carlucci, *State Department Reform*, 1.

32. Carlucci, *State Department Reform*, 2.

33. Carlucci, *State Department Reform*, 8.

34. Carlucci, *State Department Reform*, 8, 10.

35. Carlucci, *State Department Reform*, 3.

36. Carlucci, *State Department Reform*, 1, 5.

37. Tower Commission, *Tower Commission Report*.

38. The committee was known as the House Committee on Armed Services since 2 January 1947. It was renamed the House Committee on National Security during the 104th and 105th Congress (H. Res. 5, 4 January 1995). Its original name was restored in the 106th Congress (H. Res. 5, 6 January 1999).

11. STRATEGY FIRST

1. Mathews, "Redefining Security."

2. Monten, "Roots of the Bush Doctrine," 117.

BIBLIOGRAPHY

Adams, John and Charles Francis Adams. "Letter to Jonathan Jackson, 2 October 1780" in *The Works of John Adams*, 9, 511.

Adler, David Gray. "The Clinton Theory of the War Power." *Presidential Studies Quarterly* 30, no. 1 (March 2000): 155–68.

———. "Virtues of the War Clause." *Presidential Studies Quarterly* 30, no. 4 (December 2000): 777–82.

Adorno, Theodor, Else Frenkel-Brunswick, Daniel J. Levinson, and R. Nevitt Sanford. *The Authoritarian Personality*. New York: Harper & Brothers, 1950.

Akerman, Bruce. "But What's the Legal Case for Preemption?" *Washington Post*, 18 August 2002, final edition, sec. "Outlook," B2.

Altemeyer, Bob. "Highly Dominating, Highly Authoritarian Personalities." *Journal of Social Psychology* 144, no. 4 (August 2004): 421–47.

Altman, Roger C., and Richard N. Haass. "American Power and Profligacy: The Consequences of Fiscal Irresponsibility." *Foreign Affairs* 89, no. 6 (November/December 2010): 25–34.

Andrew, Christopher. *For the President's Eyes Only: Secret Intelligence and the American Presidency from Washington to Bush*. New York: HarperCollins, 1995.

Apple, R. W., Jr. "A Domestic Sort with Global Worries." *New York Times*, 25 August 1999, late edition–final, A1.

Armitage, Richard L., and Joseph S. Nye Jr. "Implementing Smart Power: Setting an Agenda for National Security Reform." Statement before the Senate Foreign Relations Committee, 24 April 2008.

Art, Robert J. "Defensible Defense: America's Grand Strategy after the Cold War." *International Security* 15, no. 4 (Spring 1991): 5–53.

———. *A Grand Strategy for America*. Ithaca NY: Cornell University Press, 2003.

———. "To What Ends Military Power?" *International Security* 4 (Spring 1980): 4–35.

Art, Robert J., and Robert Jervis, eds. *International Politics: Enduring Concepts and Contemporary Issues*. 10th ed. New York: Pearson Education, 2011.

Atwan, Abdel Bari. *The Secret History of Al-Qaeda*. Berkeley: University of California Press, 2006.

Aubin, Stephen P. "Stumbling toward Transformation: How the Services Stack Up." *Strategic Review* 5 (Spring 2000): 39–47.

Augustine. *The Political Writings of Saint Augustine*. Edited by Henry Paolicci. Chicago: Henry Regnery, 1962.

Banks, William C., and Jeffrey D. Straussman. "A New Imperial Presidency? Insights from U.S. Involvement in Bosnia." *Political Science Quarterly* 114 (Summer 1999): 195–217.

Beutel, Alejandro J., and Imad-ad-Dean Ahmad. "Examining Bin Laden's Statements: A Quantitative Content Analysis from 1996 to 2011." Bethesda MD: Minaret of Freedom Institute. 30 September 2011. www.minaret.org/ubl.pdf.

Bishara, Ghassan. "The Political Repercussions of the Israeli Raid on the Iraqi Nuclear Reactor." *Journal of Palestine Studies* 11, no. 3 (Spring 1982): 58–76.

Blechman, Barry M., and Janne E. Nolan. "Reorganizing for More Effective Arms Negotiation." *Foreign Affairs* (Summer 1983): 1164.

Bronner, Ethan. "As Biden Visits, Israel Unveils Plans for New Settlements," *New York Times*, 10 March 2010, A4.

Brzezinski, Zbigniew. *The Choice: Global Domination or Global Leadership*. New York: Basic, 2004.

Buchanan, Patrick J. *A Republic, Not an Empire: Reclaiming America's Destiny*. Washington DC: Regnery, 1999.

———. *Suicide of a Superpower: Will America Survive to 2025?* New York: St. Martin's, 2011.

Bull, Hedley. *The Anarchical Society*. New York: Columbia University Press, 1977.

Burk, James. "Public Support for Peacekeeping in Lebanon and Somalia: Assessing the Casualties Hypothesis." *Political Science Quarterly* 114, no. 1 (1999): 53–78.

Bush, George H. W. *National Security Strategy of the United States of America*. Washington DC: The White House, August 1991.

Bush, George W. *The National Security Strategy of the United States of America*. Washington DC: The White House, September 2002.

———. *The National Security Strategy of the United States of America*. Washington DC: The White House, March 2006.

Califano, Joseph Jr. "The Case against an All-Volunteer Army, *Washington Post*. 21 February 1971.

Cambone, Stephen A. *A New Structure for National Security Policy Planning*. Washington DC: CSIS Press, 1998.

Cannon, Lou. *President Reagan: The Role of a Lifetime*. New York: Simon & Schuster, 1991.

Cannon, Lou. "What Happened to Reagan the Gunslinger? Now His Problem Is Convincing Skeptics He Isn't a Pussycat." *Washington Post*, 7 July 1985, b-1.

Carlucci, Frank C. *State Department Reform*. New York: Council on Foreign Relations Press, 2001. www.cfr.org/content/publications/attachments/state_department.pdf.

Carr, Edward Hallett. *The Twenty-Years' Crisis 1919–1939: Introduction to the Study of International Relations*. New York: HarperCollins, 1964.

Carter, Ashton B., and William J. Perry. "If Necessary, Strike and Destroy: North Korea Cannot Be Allowed to Test This Missile." *Washington Post*, 22 June 2006; A 29.

——. *Preventive Defense: A New Security Strategy for America*. Washington DC: Brookings Institution Press, 1999.

Carter, Ashton B., William J. Perry, and John D. Steinbruner. *A New Concept of Cooperative Security*. Washington DC: Brookings Institution Press, 1992.

Caudle, Sharon, L. "National Security Strategies: Security from What, for Whom, and by What Means." *Berkeley Electronic Press* 6, no. 1 (2009).

Cimbala, Stephen. *Coercive Military Strategy*. College Station: Texas A & M University Press, 1998.

Clarke, Jonathan, and James Clad. *After the Crusade: American Foreign Policy for the Post-Superpower Age*. Lanham MD: Madison Books, 1995.

Clausewitz, Carl von. *On War*. Edited by Michael Howard and Peter Paret. Princeton NJ: Princeton University Press, 1976.

Clinton, William J. *A National Security Strategy for a Global Age*. Washington DC: The White House, 2000.

——. *A National Security Strategy for a New Century*. Washington DC: The White House, 1997.

——. *A National Security Strategy for a New Century*. Washington DC: The White House, 1998.

——. *A National Security Strategy for a New Century*. Washington DC: The White House, 1999.

——. *A National Security Strategy of Engagement and Enlargement*. Washington DC: The White House, 1994.

——. *A National Security Strategy of Engagement and Enlargement*. Washington DC: The White House, 1995.

——. *A National Security Strategy of Engagement and Enlargement*. Washington DC: The White House, 1996.

Commission on America's National Interests. *America's National Interests*. Washington DC: Commission on America's National Interests, 1996. www.nixoncenter.org/publications/monographs/nationalinterests.pdf.

Congressional Research Service (CRS). *Congressional Use of Funding Cutoffs since 1970 Involving U.S. Military Forces and Overseas Deployments*, RS20775. Washington DC: CRS, 10 January 2001.

——. *Declarations of War and Authorizations for the Use of Military Force: Historical Background and Legal Implications*, RL31133. Washington DC: CRS, 2006.

———. *The War Powers Resolution: After Thirty-Three Years*, RL32267. Washington DC: CRS, 2007.

———. *War Powers Resolution: Presidential Compliance*, RL33532. Washington DC: CRS, 2007.

Corwin, Edward S. *The President: Office and Powers*. New York: New York University Press, 1940.

Crenson, Matthew A., and Benjamin Ginsberg. *Presidential Power: Unchecked and Unbalanced*. New York: Norton, 2007.

Crocker, Chester A. "Southern Africa: Eight Years Later." *Foreign Affairs* 68, no. 4 (Fall 1980): 144–64.

———. "Strategy for Change." *Foreign Affairs* 59, no. 2 (Winter 1980): 323–51.

Davis, Nathaniel. "The Angola Decision of 1975." *Foreign Affairs* 57, no. 1 (Fall 1978): 109–24.

Dean, Herbert A. *The Political Writings and Social Ideas of Saint Thomas Aquinas*. New York: Columbia University Press, 1963.

DeYoung, Karen, and Steven Mufson. "A Leaner and Less Visible NSC; Reorganization Will Emphasize Defense, Global Economics." *Washington Post*, 10 February 2001, A1.

Difo, Germain. "Ordinary Measures, Extraordinary Results: An Assessment of Foiled Plots since 9/11." Washington DC: American Security Project, May 2010. www.AmericanSecurityProject.org.

Dixon, James H. *National Security Policy Formulation: Institutions, Processes, and Issues*. Lanham MD: University Press of America, 1984.

Donnelly, John M. "Battle Brewing over Five-Sided Diplomacy." *CQ Weekly* (11 June 2007): 1727.

Doyle, Michael W. "Kant, Liberal Legacies, and Foreign Affairs." In *International Politics: Enduring Concepts and Contemporary*, edited by Robert J. Art and Robert Jervis, 10th ed., 114–26. Boston: Longman, 2011.

Drehle, David Von. "Origins of the Species; Up from the Ooze, into the Mud—a Brief History of the American Political Evolution." *Washington Post*, 25 July 2004, W12.

Duckitt, John. "Authoritarianism and Group Identification: A New View of an Old Construct." *Political Psychology* 10, no. 1 (March 1989): 63–84.

Easterly, William. *The White Man's Burden: Why the West's Efforts to Aid the Rest Have Done So Much Ill and So Little Good*. New York: Penguin, 2006.

Eisenhower, Dwight D. *Waging Peace: The White House Years 1956–1961*. Garden City NY: Doubleday, 1965.

Elsea, Jennifer K., and Richard F. Grimmett. *Declarations of War and Authorizations for the Use of Force: Historical Background and Legal Implications*, RL31133. Washington DC: Congressional Research Service, 2006.

"The End of Democracy? The Judicial Usurpation of Politics." *First Things* 67 (November 1996): 18–20.

Enthoven, Alain C., and K. Wayne Smith. *How Much Is Enough? Shaping the Defense Program, 1961–1969.* New York: Harper & Row, 1971.

Falk, Stanley L. "The National Security Council under Truman, Eisenhower, and Kennedy." *Political Science Quarterly* 79 (September 1964): 403–34.

Fallows, James. "The Fifty-First State." *Atlantic Monthly*, November 2002, 53–64.

Fiorina, Morris P. *Culture War? The Myth of a Polarized America.* Boston: Longman, 2011.

Fisher, Louis. *Presidential War Power.* Lawrence: University Press of Kansas, 1995.

Fisher, Louis and David Gray Adler, "The War Powers Resolution: Time to Say Goodbye." *Political Science Quarterly* 113 no. 1 (1998): 1–20.

Fitzpatrick, John, ed. "Washington to Henry Laurens, November 14, 1778." In *The Writings of George Washington* 13. Washington DC: United States Printing Office, 1931–44.

Flynn, George Q. *The Draft, 1940–1973.* Lawrence: University Press of Kansas, 1993.

Fontana, Benedetto. "State and Society: The Concept of Hegemony in Gramsci." In *Hegemony and Power: Consensus and Coercion in Contemporary Politics*, edited by Mark Haugaard and Howard H. Lentner, 23–44. Lanham MD: Lexington Books, 2006.

Frederick the Great. *Oeuvres de Frédéric le Grand.* 30 vols. Edited by Johann D. E. Preuss et al. Berlin, 1846–57.

Freeman, Charles "Chas" W., Jr. *Arts of Power: Statecraft and Diplomacy.* Washington DC: United States Institute of Peace Press, 1997.

Friedman, Milton. *Essays in Positive Economics.* Chicago: University of Chicago Press, 1953.

Friedman, Thomas L. "You Gotta Have Friends." *New York Times*, 29 September 2002, late edition–final, sec. 4, p. 13.

Gaddis, John Lewis. *Strategies of Containment: A Critical Appraisal of Postwar American National Security Policy.* New York: Oxford University Press, 1982.

Garthoff, Raymond L. *The Great Transition: American-Soviet Relations and the End of the Cold War.* Washington DC: Brookings Institution, 1994.

Gelb, Leslie H. "GDP Now Matters More Than Force: A U.S. Foreign Policy for the Age of Economic Power." *Foreign Affairs* 89, no. 6 (November/December 2010): 35–43.

———. "Why Not the State Department?" *Washington Quarterly*, Special Supplement (Autumn 1980): 25–40.

General Accounting Office. "Foreign Aid: Police Training and Assistance," GAO/ NSIAD-92-118, March 1992.

Gladney, Dru. "Xinjiang: China's Future West Bank?" *Current History* 101, no. 656 (September 2002): 268.

Glaser, Charles L. "Realists as Optimists: Cooperation as Self-Help." *International Security* 19, no. 3 (Winter 1994–95): 50–90.

Goldberg, Michelle. *Kingdom Coming: The Rise of Christian Nationalism*. New York: Norton, 2006.

Goodstein, Laurie. "The Nation: The 'Hypermodern' Foe; How the Evangelicals and Catholics Joined Forces." *New York Times*, 30 May 2004. http://www.nytimes.com/2004/05/30/weekinreview/the-nation-the-hypermodern-foe-how-the-evangelicals-and-catholics-joined-forces.html.

Gould, Louis L. *Grand Old Party: A History of the Republican Party*. New York: Random House, 2003.

Government Accountability Office. *National Security: The Use of Presidential Directives to Make and Implement U.S. Policy*, GAO/NSAID-89-31. Washington DC: GAO, December 1988.

Green, John. "American Religious Landscapes and Political Attitudes." Pew Forum for Religion and Public Policy. http://pewforum.org/publications/surveys/green-full.pdf.

Grotius, Hugo. *On the Laws of War and Peace*. Originally published in 1625. http://socserv2.socsci.mcmaster.ca/econ/ugcm/3ll3/grotius/Law2.pdf.

Gulick, Eduard Vose. *Europe's Classic Balance of Power: A Case History of the Theory and Practice of One of the Great Concepts of European Statecraft*. New York: Norton, 1967.

Hallett, Brien. *The Lost Art of Declaring War*. Chicago: University of Illinois Press, 1998.

Hamilton, Alexander, James Madison, and John Jay. *The Federalist Papers*. New York: Nal Penguin, 1961.

Hendrickson, Ryan C. "War Powers, Bosnia, and the 104th Congress." *Political Science Quarterly* 113, no. 2 (1998): 241–58.

Heritage Foundation. *The Heritage Guide to the Constitution*. Washington DC: Regnery, 2005.

Herz, John H. "Power Politics and World Organization." *American Political Science Review* 36, no. 6 (December 1942): 1039–52.

Hess, Gary R. *Presidential Decisions for War: Korea, Vietnam, and the Persian Gulf*. Baltimore: Johns Hopkins University Press, 2001.

———. "Presidents and the Congressional War Resolutions of 1991 and 2002." *Political Science Quarterly* (Spring 2006): 93–118.

Hirsh, Michael. "Bush and the World." *Foreign Affairs* 81, no. 5 (September/October 2002): 18–43.

Hobbes, Thomas. *Leviathan*. New York: Barnes & Noble, 2004.

Holcomb, Scott, and Mark Ribbing. "War Has Changed. The Laws of War Must, Too. The Geneva Conventions Are Outdated for Today's War on Terror. The

U.S. Should Lead a Call to Modernize Them." *Christian Science Monitor*, 16 November 2006. http://www.csmonitor.com/2006/1116/p09s01-coop.html.

Howard, Michael. *The Invention of Peace*. New Haven CT: Yale University Press. 2000.

Hoxie, R. Gordon. *Command Decision and the Presidency: A Study of National Security Policy and Organization*. New York: Reader's Digest Press, 1977.

Hume, David. "Of the Balance of Power." In *Political Writings*, edited by Stuart D. Warner and Donald W. Livingston, 135–42. Indianapolis: Hackett, 1994.

Ikenberry, G. John, and Anne-Marie Slaughter, codirectors. "Forging a World of Liberty under Law: U.S. National Security in the 21st Century." Princeton NJ: Princeton Project on National Security, 2006.

Inderfurth, Karl F., and Loch K. Johnson. *Fateful Decisions: Inside the National Security Council*. New York: Oxford University Press, 2004.

"An Interview with Vice President and Director of Foreign Policy Studies of the Brookings Institution, Carlos Pasqual." *Joint Forces Quarterly* (Summer 2006): 80–85.

Jervis, Robert. "International Primacy: Is the Game Worth the Candle?" *International Security* 17, no. 4 (Spring 1993): 52–67.

Johnson, James Turner. *Just War Tradition and the Restraint of War: A Moral and Historical Inquiry*. Princeton NJ: Princeton University Press, 1981.

Johnson, Lyndon B. *The Vantage Point*. New York: Holt, Rinehart, & Winston, 1971.

Jones, Charles O. *Will Reform Change Congress?* Edited by B. Oppenheimer and L. Dodd. New York: Praeger, 1977.

Kant, Immanuel. *Perpetual Peace: A Philosophical Essay*. Edited by A. Robert Caponigri. Translated by M. Campbell Smith. New York: Liberal Arts Press, 1948.

———. *Universal History with a Cosmopolitan Aim*. 1784.

Karnow, Stanley. *Vietnam, A History*. New York: Viking Press, 1983.

Kautilya (Chanakya Vishnu Gupta). *Arathashastra*. Translated by R. Shamasastry. India: Penguin, 1992.

Kelsay, John, and James Turner Johnson, eds. *Just War and Jihad: Historical and Theoretical Perspectives on War and Peace in Western and Islamic Traditions*. Westport CT: Greenwood, 1991.

Kennan, George F. *At A Century's Ending: Reflections 1982–1995*. New York, Norton, 1996.

[———, writing as "X"]. "The Sources of Soviet Conduct." *Foreign Affairs* 25, no. 4 (July 1947): 566–82.

Kennedy, Paul. *The Rise and Fall of the Great Powers*. New York: Vintage, 1989.

Keohane, Robert O., and Lisa L. Martin. "The Promise of Institutionalist Theory." *International Security* 20, no. 1 (Summer 1995): 39–51.

Kirkpatrick, Jeane. "Dictatorships and Double Standards." *Commentary* 68, no. 5 (1979): 34–45.

Kissinger, Henry. *Does America Need a Foreign Policy? Toward a Diplomacy for the 21st Century.* New York: Simon & Schuster, 2001.

Knopf, Jeffrey W. "Did Reagan Win the Cold War?" *Strategic Insights.*" August 2004. https://www.hsdl.org/?view&did=444565.

Kovaleo, S. "Sovereignty and the International Obligations of Socialist Countries." *Pravda*, 26 September 1968.

Krauthammer, Charles. "The Reagan Doctrine." *Time*, 1 April 1985. www.time.com /time/magazine/article/0,9171,964873-1,00.html.

Kristol, Irving. *Neo-conservatism: The Autobiography of an Idea.* New York: Free Press, 1995.

Kunz, Diane. *The Economic Diplomacy of the Suez Crisis.* Chapel Hill: University of North Carolina Press, 1991.

Kupchan, Charles A., and Clifford A. Kupchan. "The Promise of Collective Security." *International Security* 20, no. 1 (Summer 1995): 52–61.

Kyle, Keith. *Suez.* New York: St. Martin's Press, 1991.

Layne, Christopher. "From Preponderance to Offshore Balancing: America's Future Grand Strategy," *International Security* 22, no. 1 (Summer 1997): 86–124.

———."Kant or Cant? The Myth of the Democratic Peace." *International Security* 19, no. 2 (Autumn 1994): 5–49.

———. "Rethinking American Grand Strategy: Hegemony or Balance of Power in the Twenty-First Century?" *World Policy Journal* (Summer 1995): 8–28.

Le Nouvel Observateur (Paris). 15 January–21 January 1998.

Levitan, D. M. "The Foreign Relations Power: An Analysis of Mr. Justice Sutherland's Theory." *Yale Law Journal* 55, no. 3 (April 1946): 467–97.

Levy, Jack S. "Declining Power and the Preventive Motivation for War." *World Politics* 40, no. 1 (October 1987): 82–107.

———. "Misperceptions and the Causes of War: Theoretical Linkages and Analytical Problems." *World Politics* 36, no. 1 (October 1983): 76–99.

Linker, Damon. *The Theocons: Secular America under Siege.* New York: Doubleday, 2006.

Lobel, Jules, and Michel Ratner. "Bypassing the Security Council: Ambiguous Authorizations to Use Force, Cease-Fires and the Iraqi Inspection Regime." *American Journal of International Law* 93, no. 1 (January 1999): 124–54.

Machiavelli, Niccolò. *The Prince.* New York: Cambridge University Press, 1988.

Madison, James. *James Madison: Writings.* Edited by Jack N. Rakove. New York: Library of America, 1999.

Mansfield, Edward D., and Jack Snyder. "Democratization and the Danger of War." *International Security* 20, no. 1 (Summer 1995): 5–38.

Mathews, Jessica Tuchman. "Redefining Security." *Foreign Affairs* 68, no. 2 (Spring 1989): 162–77.

Mearsheimer, John J. *Conventional Deterrence.* Ithaca NY: Cornell University Press, 1983.

———. "The False Promise of International Institutions," *International Security* 19, no. 3 (Winter 1994–95): 5–49.

———. "A Realist Reply." *International Security* 20, no. 1 (Summer 1995): 82–93.

———. *The Tragedy of Great Power Politics.* New York: Norton, 2001.

Mervin, David. "Demise of the War Clause." *Presidential Studies Quarterly* 30, no. 4 (December 2000): 770–76.

Meyers, Robin. *Why the Christian Right Is Wrong: A Minister's Manifesto for Taking Back Your Faith, Your Flag, Your Future.* San Francisco: Wiley, 2006.

Mill, John Stewart. *Considerations on Representative Government, in John Stuart Mill.* In *Three Essays.* Oxford: Oxford University Press, 1975.

———. *Principles of Political Economy* II. Book 5.

Monaghan, Frank. *John Jay: Defender of Liberty.* Indianapolis: Bobbs-Merrill, 1935.

Monten, Jonathan. "The Roots of the Bush Doctrine: Power, Nationalism, and Democracy Promotion in U.S. Strategy." *International Security* (Spring 2005): 112–56.

Morgenthau, Hans Joachim. *Politics among Nations: The Struggle for Power and Peace.* New York: Knopf, 1948.

Moseley, Alexander. "Just War Theory." In *The Internet Encyclopedia of Philosophy.* www.iep.utm.edu/j/justwar.htm.

Murdock, Clark A., et al. *Beyond Goldwater-Nichols: Defense Reform for a New Strategic Era.* Washington DC: CSIS Press, 2004.

———. *Beyond Goldwater-Nichols: U.S. Government and Defense Reform for a New Strategic Era.* Washington DC: CSIS Press, 2005.

National Commission on Terrorist Attacks upon the United States. *Final Report of the National Commission on Terrorist Attacks upon the United States.* Washington DC: GPO, 22 July 2004. www.gpoaccess.gov/911/index.html and http://govinfo.library.unt.edu/911/report/index.htm.

National Defense University, Institute for National Strategic Studies. *Strategic Assessment 1996: Instruments of U.S. Power.* Washington DC: GPO, 1996.

Neuhaus, Richard John. *The Catholic Moment: The Paradox of the Church in the Postmodern World.* New York: Harper & Row, 1987.

New York Times. "A Guide to the 2005 Republican Herd." 5 April 2005. http://www.nytimes.com/interactive/2005/04/02/sunday-review/a-guide-to-the-republican-herd.html?ref=sunday-review&_r=0.

———. *The Naked Public Square: Religion and Democracy in America.* Grand Rapids MI: Eerdmans, 1984.

———. *Presidential Power and the Modern Presidents: The Politics of Leadership from Roosevelt to Reagan.* New York: Simon & Schuster, 1991.

Nichols, John. *The Genius of Impeachment: The Founders' Cure for Royalism*. New York: New Press, 2006.

Ninkovich, Frank. *The Wilsonian Century: U.S. Foreign Policy since 1900*. Chicago: University of Chicago Press, 1999.

Nitze, Paul H. "Atoms, Strategy and Policy." *Foreign Affairs* 34, no. 2 (January 1956): 187–98.

Nixon, Richard. "Veto of the War Powers Resolution." 24 October 1973.

Novak, Michael. *The Spirit of Democratic Capitalism*. New York: Simon & Schuster, 1982.

———. *Toward a Theology of the Corporation*. Washington DC: American Enterprise Institute, 1981.

Odom, William E. *America's Military Revolution: Strategy and Structure after the Cold War*. Washington DC: American University Press, 1993.

Olasky, Marvin. *Compassionate Conservatism: What It Is, What It Does, and How It Can Transform America*. New York: Free Press, 2000.

———. *Renewing American Compassion*. New York: Free Press, 1996.

Pasztor, Andy. *When the Pentagon Was for Sale: Inside America's Biggest Defense Scandal*. New York: Scribner, 1995.

Peters, Katherine McIntire. "Redefining National Security Building Stability." *Government Executive*, 1 January 2006.

Pillar, Paul R. "Informed Decisions: Process before Policy." www.americansecurity project.org/issues/iraq_lessons_learned.

Pincus, Walter. "Taking Defense's Hand out of State's Pocket." *Washington Post*, 9 July 2007, 13.

Poole, Keith, and Howard Rosenthal. *Congress: A Political-Economic History of Roll Call Voting*. New York: Oxford University Press, 2000.

Posen, Barry R., and Andrew L. Ross. "Competing Visions for U.S. Grand Strategy." *International Security* 21, no. 3 (Winter 1996/1997): 5–53.

Powell, Colin L. *My American Journey*. New York: Random House, 1995.

———. *National Military Strategy of the United States*. Washington DC: Joint Chiefs of Staff, January 1992.

Press, Daryl G. *Calculating Credibility: How Leaders Assess Military Threats*. Ithaca NY: Cornell University Press, 2005.

Priest, Dana. *The Mission: Waging War and Keeping Peace with America's Military*. New York: Norton, 2003.

Project on National Security Reform. *Forging a New Shield*. Arlington VA, November 2008.

Rakove, Jack N., ed. *James Madison: Writings*. New York: Library of America, 1999.

Ricardo, David. *On the Principles of Political Economy and Taxation*. London: John Murray, 1817.

Rice, Condoleezza. "Campaign 2000: Promoting the National Interest." *Foreign Affairs* 79, no. 1 (January/February 2000): 45–62.

Roosevelt, Theodore. Address before the Convention of the National Progressive Party in Chicago, 6 August 1912.

Ruehsen, Moyara de Moraes. "Operation 'Ajax' Revisited: Iran, 1953." *Middle Eastern Studies* 29, no. 3 (July 1993): 467–86.

Ruggie, John Gerard. "American Exceptionalism, Exemptionalism, and Global Governance." In *American Exceptionalism and Human Rights*, edited by Michael Ignatieff, 304–37. Princeton NJ: Princeton University Press, 2005.

———. "The False Premise of Realism," *International Security* 20, no. 1 (Summer 1995): 62–70.

Rushdoony, Rousas John. *The Institutions of Biblical Law*. Phillipsburg NJ: Presbyterian and Reformed Publishing, 1973.

———. *The Roots of Reconstruction*. Vallecito CA: Ross House, 1991.

Russett, Bruce. *Grasping the Democratic Peace: Principles for a Post–Cold War World*. Princeton NJ: Princeton University Press, 1993.

Sageman, Marc. *Understanding Terror Networks*. Philadelphia: University of Pennsylvania Press, 2004.

Schelling, Thomas C. *Arms and Influence*. New Haven CT: Yale University Press, 1966.

[Scheuer, Michael]. Imperial *Hubris: Why the West Is Losing the War on Terror*. Washington DC: Brassey's, 2004.

Schlesinger, Arthur M., Jr. *The Imperial Presidency*. New York: Houghton Mifflin, 1973.

Schwarz, Frederick A. O., and Aziz Z. Huq. *Unchecked and Unbalanced: Presidential Power in a Time of Terror*. New York: New Press, 2007.

Small, Melvin, and J. David Singer. "The War-Proneness of Democratic Regimes, 1816–1865." *Jerusalem Journal of International Relations* 1, no. 4 (Summer 1976): 50–69.

Smith, Adam. *An Inquiry into the Nature and Causes of the Wealth of Nations*. New York: Oxford University Press, 2008.

Snow, Donald M. *National Security for a New Era: Globalization and Geopolitics after Iraq*. 3rd ed. New York: Pearson Longman, 2008.

Stockwell, John. *In Search of Enemies: A CIA Story*. New York: Norton, 1978.

———. "Why I'm Leaving the CIA." *Washington Post*, 10 April 1977.

Study Group on a New Israeli Strategy toward 2000. "A Clean Break: A New Strategy for Securing the Realm." Jerusalem and Washington: The Institute for Advanced and Political Studies, June 1996. www.iasps.org/strat1.htm.

Sun Tzu. *The Art of War*. Philadelphia: Running Press, 2003.

Suskind, Ron. *The One Percent Doctrine*. New York: Simon and Schuster, 2006.

Taylor, Maxwell D. *The Uncertain Trumpet*. New York: Harper & Brothers, 1959.

Terrill, W. Andrew. "Placing the Libya Breakthrough in Perspective." *In the National Interest*, 4 February 2004. http://nationalinterest.org/article/placing-the-libya-breakthrough-in-perspective-2557.

Thucydides. *The Peloponnesian War: The Complete Hobbes Translation*. Translated by Thomas Hobbes. Chicago: University of Chicago Press, 1989.

Tocqueville, Alexis de. *Democracy in America*. New York: Knopf, 1994.

Tower Commission (President's Special Review Board). *Tower Commission Report*. New York: Bantam/Time, 1987.

Tyler, Patrick E. "U.S. Strategy Plan Calls for Insuring No Rivals Develop: A One-Superpower World: Pentagon's Document Outlines Ways to Thwart Challenges to Primacy of America." Special to the *New York Times*, 8 March 1992, sec. 1, pt. 1, p. 14.

United States Marine Corps. *Small Wars Manual*. Washington DC: GPO, 1940.

U.S. Commission on National Security/21st Century. *Roadmap for National Security: Imperative for Change*. Arlington VA: U.S. Commission on National Security/21st Century.

———. *Seeking a National Strategy: A Concert for Preserving Security and Promoting Freedom*. Arlington VA: U.S. Commission on National Security/21st Century, 15 April 2000.

Vagts, Alfred, and Detlev F. Vagts. "The Balance of Power in International Law: A History of an Idea." *American Journal of International Law* 73, no. 5 (October 1979): 555–80.

Vattel, Emerich de. *The Law of Nations*. Originally published in 1758. http://lf-oll.s3.amazonaws.com/titles/2246/Vattel_1519_LFeBk.pdf.

Vaughn, Robert G. "Transparency—The Mechanisms: Open Government and Accountability." *Issues of Democracy* (electronic journal of the U.S. Department of State) 5, no. 2 (August 2000).

Vidal, Gore. *Perpetual War for Perpetual Peace: How We Got to Be So Hated*. New York: Nation Books, 2002.

Wallis, Jim. *God's Politics: Why the Right Gets It Wrong and the Left Doesn't Get It*. New York: HarperCollins, 2005.

Waltz, Kenneth N. *Man, the State and War*. New York: Columbia University Press, 1954.

Walzer, Michael. *Just and Unjust Wars: A Moral Argument with Historical Illustrations*. New York: HarperCollins, 1977.

———. "The Triumph of Just War Theory—and the Dangers of Success—International Justice, War Crimes, and Terrorism: The U.S. Record." *Social Research* 69 (Winter 2002): 925–44.

"The War Power." *Congressional Quarterly's Guide to Congress*. 4th ed. Washington DC: Congressional Quarterly, Inc., 1991.

Washington, George. Farewell Address, 19 September 1796.

Watson, Russell. "Reagan's Raiders." *Newsweek*, 28 April 1986, U.S. ed., 26.

Weigel, George. *Catholicism and the Renewal of American Democracy*. Mahwah NJ: Paulist Press, 1989.

Weinberger, Caspar. "The Uses of Military Power." National Press Club, Washington DC: 28 November 1984.

Weiner, Tim, and Jane Perlez. "Crisis in the Balkans: How Clinton Approved the Strikes on Capital." *New York Times*, 4 April 1999, late edition–final, sec. 1, p. 1.

Wendt, Alexander. "Constructing International Politics." *International Security* 20, no. 1 (Summer 1995): 71–81.

The White House. *National Strategy for Combating Terrorism*. September 2006.

Williams, William Appleman. *The Tragedy of American Diplomacy*. London: Norton, 1972.

Wohlforth, William C. "Realism and the End of the Cold War." *International Security* 19, no. 3 (Winter 1994–95): 91–129.

Worley, D. Robert. "From Concept to Policy: Evolution of Thinking on the War against Terrorism 2002–2004." *Small Wars Journal* 6, no. 12 (December 2010).

———. *Shaping U.S. Military Forces: Revolution or Relevance in a Post–Cold War World*. Westport CT: Praeger Security International, 2006.

Wormuth, Christine E., et al. *Beyond Goldwater-Nichols: The Future of the National Guard and Reserve*. Washington DC: CSIS Press, 2006.

Wright, Quincy. *A Study of War: An Analysis of the Causes, Nature, and Control of War*. Abridged ed. Chicago: University of Chicago Press, 1964.

X [George F. Kennan]. "The Sources of Soviet Conduct." *Foreign Affairs* 25, no. 4 (July 1947): 566–82.

Yoo, John. *The Powers of War and Peace: The Constitution and Foreign Affairs after 9/11*. Chicago: University of Chicago Press, 2005.

Zahrani, Mostafa T. "The Coup That Changed the Middle East: Mossadeq v. the CIA in Retrospect." *World Policy Journal* 189, no. 2 (Summer 2002): 93–99.

INDEX

Abrams, Elliot, 164
Acheson, Dean, 118, 121
Adams, John, 36, 53
Adams, John Quincy, 35
Adler, David, 83
Afghanistan: Bush 41, 194; Bush 43,
    205; Carter, 156–57, 158; Obama,
    209, 212; Reagan, 165, 168, 169
Afghan War: Civil (1989–92), 194;
    Soviet (1979–89), 156, 158, 160, 165,
    168; U.S.-led (2001–14), 205, 209
Africa: Bush 43, 208; Carter, 152
air strikes, 74, 77, 135, 169
Albright, Madeleine, 244, 257, 355
al-Fatah, 137
Allende, Salvador, 134, 148
Alliance for Progress, 132, 172
all volunteer force, 146
al-Qaeda: Afghanistan, 205; as
    non-state, 8, 29; attack on USS *Cole*,
    200; attacks of 9/11, 204–5; East
    Africa embassy bombings, 286;
    strategy to 2020, 175, 213–16; U.S.
    counter strategy, 216–17; World Trade
    Center bombing, 286; Yemen, 209
al-Qaeda and associated movements,
    217; 9/11 Commission, 333–38; FBI,
    287; Obama, 208; reform, 350; in
    strategy, 365, 368

Altman, Roger, 242
Amin, Idi, 152
Angola: Bush 41, 193; Carter, 153;
    Clinton, 198–99; Nixon-Ford,
    148–50; Reagan, 165–66
Aquinas, Thomas, 5
Arab-Israeli War: 1st (1948), 118; 2nd
    (1956), 126; 3rd (1967), 10, 138–39,
    155; 4th (1973), xxvi, 147–48, 276;
    5th (1982–84), 161–63; War of
    Attrition, 139, 146–47
Aramas Castillo, Carlos, 121
Aristide, Jean-Betrand, 197
arms control: Bush 41, 192; Bush
    43, 204; Johnson, 133; Nixon,
    147; Obama, 209; Reagan, 167
Arms Control and Disarmament
    Agency, 253–54, 259
Army of the Republic of Vietnam,
    135, 144
Asia Pacific, 101, 212, 351
Augustine, 5
Austin, Warren, 117
authoritarianism, 42–44, 160,
    173
axis of evil, 202

Bachman, Michelle, 210
Baker, James A., III, 193, 315

balance of power, 111; Clinton, 196;
defined, 18; Hamilton, 35; in
international law, 23; Kennan,
110–12; Nitze, 112–14, 124; Nixon,
150; Reagan, 159; realism, 23;
security dilemma, 14, 21; selective
engagement, 172, 179, 186
balancing power, 19, 188; Nixon-Ford,
142; offshore balancing strategy,
187–8. *See also* defensive power;
offensive power; preponderant
power
Balaquer, Joaquin, 134
Bao Dai, 128
Base Force, 190–91, 201
Bas v. Tingy, 63
Batista, Fulgencio, 121, 129
Bay of Pigs, 133, 140
Begin, Menachem, 153, 162
Bennett, William, 47
Berger, Samuel Richard "Sandy," 201,
204, 315
Berlin Airlift, 115, 118
Berlin Crisis, 115, 118
Beyond Goldwater-Nichols (bg-n),
339–42
Biden, Joe, 210
bin Laden, Osama: Bush 43, 200,
204–5; declaration of war, 214;
Obama, 209; Reagan, 162
Black, Hugo, 69
Blechman, Barry, 253
Bohlen, Charles "Chip," 122, 127
Bolton, John, 207, 254
bomber gap, 130, 159
Bosch, Juan, 134
Bosnia and Herzegovina: Clinton, 80
Bottom-Up Review, 201
Bowie, Robert, 126–27
Brandeis, Louis D., 84

Brezhnev Doctrine: Carter, 158;
Johnson, 133, 140; Kennan, 170, 174;
Nixon-Ford, 142; Reagan, 167
Brezhnev, Leonid, 133, 139, 140, 147,
168
Brzezinski, Zbignew: Africa, 153; and
Vance, 152, 314, 318; arms control,
253; national security assistant, 310,
314, 318; strategy, 153, 155
Buchanan, Pat, 51
Bull, Hedley, 17
Bundy, McGeorge, 310
burden sharing, 102, 191, 210, 212
Bush, George H. W.: end of Cold War,
174; Libya, 169; National Security
Council, 310–11, 315, 316, 320;
Panama, 158; strategy, 90, 190–95,
218; war powers, 71
Bush, George W.: capacity building,
217, 246, 319; Homeland Security
Council, 333; Libya, 169; National
Security Council, 315, 316; strategy,
90, 95, 202–8, 218, 367

calibration, 114, 131
Califano, Joseph, 146
Cambodia: Civil War (1967–75), 135;
Johnson, 135, 136; Nixon, 73,
144, 151
Camp David Accords, 153, 158
capacity building, 204, 246, 319.
See also nation building
Carlucci, Frank C., 315, 352
Carr, Edward: instruments of power,
225–27, 241–43, 244; realism and
idealism, 12–23, 40
Carter, Jimmy: Afghanistan, 165;
arms control, 253; China, 143;
Iranian Hostage Crisis, 164;
National Security Council, 314, 321;

reform, 246, 252; strategy, 90, 95, 151–58, 172

Carter Doctrine, 157, 159, 276

Castro, Fidel: Eisenhower, 129; Kennedy, 131, 133; Truman, 121

Caucuses, 206

Caudle, Sharon, 219, 220

censure, 69–71. *See also* impeachment

Central Intelligence Agency: established, 284, 301; role in Intelligence Community, 231, 336–7. *See also* covert operations; paramilitary forces

Chamoun, Camille, 127

Cheney, Richard "Dick": National Security Council, 315, 316, 318; secretary of defense, 191, 315

Chiang Kai-shek, 120, 129, 176

Chile: Kennedy, 134; Nixon-Ford, 148

China: Carter, 143; Eisenhower, 11, 66, 129; Nixon, 143, 150, 175; in strategy, 180, 351; Truman, 120, 123, 135

Chomsky, Noam, 25

Christian Reconstructionism, 47

Christian Revisionism, 47

Christopher, Warren, 155, 257

Clark, Wesley, 197

Clark Amendment, 149, 153, 165

Clarke, Richard, 204, 217

Clifford, Clark, 137

Clinton, Hillary, 50

Clinton, William J., 50, 66, 246, 253; International Criminal Court, 34; Libya, 169; nation building, 217, 246, 319; National Security Council, 315, 316; strategy, 95, 195–202, 218

coercion, 8. *See also* compellence; deterrence

collective security strategy: Bush 41, 191, 194; critique, 183, 184, 188, 189; defined, xxiii, 179, 182–84

Collins, J. Lawton, 299

compellence, 8. *See also* coercion; deterrence

consensus to commitment, 82, 90, 345; Bush 41, 195, 218; Bush 43, 91, 218; defined, 176–77; Johnson, 91, 141, 171, 177; Roosevelt, 91, 176; Truman, 91, 122, 176; Washington, 177

conservatism, 37–42, 45–50, 51

constructive ambiguity, 92, 124

containment strategy: Kennan, 110–12; Nitze, 112–14

Contract with America, 80, 249

Contras, 71, 160, 164

cooperative security strategy: Bush 43, 203; Clinton, 196, 197; critique, 188–89, 352; defined, xxiii, 184–85

Cooperative Threat Reduction, 192, 197

Coors, Joseph, 52

Corwin, Edward S., 66, 68

cost-imposing strategy, 107, 170, 171, 175, 213

covert operations, 149, 337; Carter, 153; Eisenhower, 125, 127, 130; Kennedy, 132, 133, 134; Nixon, 148–50; Reagan, 164, 165; Truman, 117, 121

credibility gap, 137, 151

Crocker, Chester, 165

Cuba: Eisenhower, 129; Kennedy, 133; Truman, 121

Cuban Missile Crisis, 133

current calculus theory, 93

Czechoslovakia: Johnson, 139

Darwin, Charles, 25

Davis, Nathaniel, 149

Dèby, Idriss, 161

declaratory policy, 108, 238; Bush 41, 194; Bush 43, 261; Carter, 157; Clinton, 196; defined, 92, 93; Kennedy-Johnson, 140; Obama, 212; Reagan, 159, 164, 168; Truman, 122

defense. *See* global defense; perimeter defense; strongpoint defense

Defense Planning Guidance, 191, 341

Defense Security Cooperation Agency, 233, 250

defensive power, 19, 188. *See also* balancing power; offensive power; preponderant power

defensive war, 12

de Gaulle, Charles, 135, 138

democracy theory, 38

democratic peace theory, 20, 38, 50, 85, 351; defined, 26–29

Department of Defense, 266–82

Department of Defense Reorganization Act of 1958, 303

Department of Energy, 254

Department of Homeland Security, 52, 237–38, 254, 333; reform, 338, 349, 359

Department of Justice, 237, 241, 254, 285

Department of State, 255–66, 292; diplomacy, 238–41; reform, 252, 253, 332, 347, 352–55; role of, 233, 241, 250, 251

Departments, Military, 268–69, 299–300

deployment policy, 180, 189; Bush 41, 191, 193, 195; Carter, 157; defined, 92, 93; Obama, 212; Truman, 112, 117

détente: Carter, 151; defined, 142; Nixon, 143, 150; Reagan, 159

deterrence, 8, 9, 74, 160; extended, 188, 243. *See also* security guarantee

developmental instrument, 352; defined, 234–35

development policy, 103, 106, 172, 189; Bush 41, 189–90, 195; Bush 43, 190; Carter, 158, 189; Clinton, 189, 201; defined, xxii, 92, 93, 105–7; Eisenhower, 124; Kennedy-Johnson, 131; Nixon-Ford, 189; Obama, 190, 212; Reagan, 159, 168, 169, 172, 189; reform, 282; Truman, 119

Dien Bien Phu, 128, 136

DIME, xxiv, 225–26

diplomatic instrument, 226, 238–41; Clinton, 197; defined, 238–41; Eisenhower, 124; Obama, 209; reform, 352

doctrines. *See* Brezhnev Doctrine; Carter Doctrine; Dulles Dictum; Eisenhower Doctrine; Johnson Doctrine; Kennedy Doctrine; Khrushchev Thaw; Kirkpatrick Doctrine; Manifest Destiny; Monroe Doctrine; Powell Doctrine; Reagan Corollary; Reagan Doctrine; Roosevelt Corollary; Sinatra Doctrine; Truman Doctrine; Weinberger Doctrine

Dole, Robert, 80

Dominican Crisis, 134

dominionism, 48

domino theory, 116, 124, 173

Dubček, Alexander, 139

Dulles, Allen W., 121

Dulles, John Foster, 124, 257

Dulles Dictum, 124, 172

Duong Van Minh, 135, 176

East-West debate, xxii, 118, 132, 151

Eberstadt, Ferdinand, 299

economic instrument: Clinton, 197; defined, 232–34; Eisenhower, 124, 126; Nixon, 143; Obama, 209 economic power: Bush 41, 195; Bush 43, 207–8; Clinton, 202; defined, 226; evaluated, 242, 369; reform, 220

economic theories, xxv–xxvii, 23–26

Eisenhower, Dwight David, 76, 133; National Security Council, 313, 320; preventive war, 11; reform, 245, 272; strategy, 90, 123–30; war powers, 66

Eisenhower Doctrine, 76, 126, 127, 172

Ellsberg, Daniel, 144

El Salvador, 166

employment policy, 108, 172, 187, 189–90; Bush 41, 192, 194, 195; Bush 43, 190, 204; Carter, 158; Clinton, 190, 196, 197, 201; defined, 92, 93, 105, 106; Obama, 212; Reagan, 164, 168, 172; reform, 282; Truman, 122

end strength, 104, 189, 191, 201

exceptionalism, 33, 34; defined, 32. *See also* exemplarism; exemptionalism; vindicationism

exemplarism, 33, 34, 98; defined, 31, 32. *See also* exceptionalism; exemptionalism; vindicationism

exemptionalism, 34. *See also* exceptionalism; exemplarism; vindicationism

Falwell, Jerry, 48, 49

financial instrument, defined, 235–36

Fiorina, Morris, 54–56

flexible response, 114, 131, 140

Ford, Gerald, 79, 305, 314; strategy, 142–51

Forestall, James, 119, 299, 300

freedoms: negative, 39; positive, 39

Frei, Eduardo, 134

Friedman, Milton, xxvi, 146

Gaddis, John Lewis, 109, 150, 152, 158

Gates, Robert, 280, 310

Gates, Thomas, 146

Gaza, 139

Gelb, Leslie, 220, 257

Gemayel, Bachir, 162

General Offensive, 136

General Uprising, 136, 214

genocide, 34, 97, 197, 198, 230

Gingrich, Newton "Newt," 80, 210, 246, 249

global defense, 132. *See also* perimeter defense; strongpoint defense

Golan Heights, 137–39

Goldwater-Nichols DOD Reorganization Act of 1986, 289, 303, 339, 358

Gorbachev, Mikhail, 168, 173, 174, 192

Gore, Al, 50

Grand March, 214, 215

grand strategy. *See* national security strategy

Great Betrayal, 215

Greek Civil War (1946–49), 116

Grenada, 163, 168

Grotius, Hugo, 5

Gulf of Tonkin Resolution, 73, 135, 144

Gulf War (1990–91), 183, 192, 193, 194, 195

Haass, Richard, 242

Habrè, Hissène, 161

Haig, Alexander M., Jr., 257, 314, 317

Haiti: Bush 41, 194, 195; Clinton, 80, 197

Hamilton, Alexander, 35–36, 54, 60, 62

hard power, 91, 227, 350

harmony of interests, 24, 25

Hart-Rudman Commission, 330–33

hegemony, 19; global, 142, 179; regional, 101, 157, 174, 179, 182

Hezbollah: Bush 43, 206; Clinton, 201; Reagan, 162, 166

Hobbes, Thomas, 16
Ho Chi Minh, 116, 128, 176
hollow force, 190
Holocaust, 44, 45, 198
homeland defense strategy, 35, 191;
    critique, 188–89, 352; defined, xxiii,
    179, 181–82
Homeland Security Council, 311, 316,
    341; reform, 347
Hoover, Herbert, 123, 245
Hoover, J. Edgar, 285
Hoover Commission, 245, 251
Howard, Michael, 5
Hume, David, 18, 35
Humphrey, Hubert, 76
Hussein, Saddam, 156, 161

idealism, defined, 12–16, 19–23, 23
imminent threat, 10, 11
impeachment, 58, 69–71, 314. See also
    censure
incrementalism, 37
individualism, 42, 43
indivisibility of peace, 30, 191;
    defined, 15
Indochina: Eisenhower, 128, 129;
    Truman, 116, 128
Indochina War: First (1946–54), 116;
    Second (1955–75), 134. See also
    Vietnam War
informational instrument: Carter,
    252; defined, 229–30; Eisenhower,
    251; Ford, 252; Obama, 209; Reagan,
    252; Rumsfeld, 294; Truman, 119,
    251; world wars, 251
institutionalism, 21; in international
    law, 23
instruments of political power
    (Carr's) 225, 242–43, 369. See also
    economic power; military power;
    power over opinion

instruments of power, 93, 327–29, 339;
    defined, 225–44; orchestrating, 293,
    294, 295, 328–29, 361; in policy, 292;
    reform, 338, 350; in strategy, 91, 100,
    180, 182. See also developmental
    instrument; diplomatic instrument;
    economic instrument; financial
    instrument; informational
    instrument; intelligence
    instrument; law enforcement
    instrument; military instrument
instruments of power by
    administration: Bush 41, 195; Bush
    43, 207, 265; Clinton, 202; Obama, 213
intelligence instrument, 231–32;
    Rumsfeld, 294; Truman, 120
internationalism: defined, 21;
    Eisenhower-Taft, 123; in strategy,
    181, 185, 196, 203
invisible hand, 24
Iran, 121; Bush 41, 209; Clinton, 201,
    209; Eisenhower, 125; Obama, 209;
    Truman, 121
Iran-Contra, 164, 168, 306, 315
Iranian Hostage Crisis, 155, 161
Iranian Revolution, 154, 155, 156, 160
Iran-Iraq War (1979–88): Carter,
    155–56; Reagan, 161, 164
Iraq: Clinton, 201; Reagan, 206. See
    also Gulf War (1990–91); Iran-Iraq
    War (1979–88)
Iraq War (2003–11), 84, 205–6, 209, 215
Israel, birth of, 117
Israel-U.S. relations, 173; Bush 41, 193;
    Carter, 153; Clinton, 199–200;
    Kennedy-Johnson, 141; Obama,
    210–11

Jackson, Andrew, 35, 36–37, 71
Jackson, Henry M., 46, 130
Jackson, Robert H., 68–69

Jay, John, 39
Johnson, Lyndon Baines: National
    Security Council, 313, 321; strategy,
    90, 130–41
Johnson Doctrine, 134
Jordan River resource competition,
    125, 137
just war theory, 4–7, 46

Kagan, Robert, 45
Kant, Immanuel, 15, 26–29, 32
Kautilya, 16
Kennan, George: Eisenhower, 124;
    end of Cold War, 173–74; strategy,
    110–12, 112–14, 172; Truman, 115, 119
Kennedy, John Fitzgerald, 130;
    National Security Council, 313, 316;
    strategy, 90, 130–41
Kennedy, Paul, 214, 243
Kennedy Doctrine, 132, 172
Kenya, Clinton, 196
Kerry, John, 50
Keynesian economics, xxv–xxvi, 109,
    114, 152
Key West Agreement, 302
Khartoum Resolution, 138
Khomeini, Ayatollah Ruhollah, 155
Khrushchev, Nikita, 125, 134, 174
Khrushchev Thaw, 126, 130, 133, 140
Kirkpatrick, Jeanne, 160
Kirkpatrick Doctrine, 160, 173
Kissinger, Henry: national security
    assistant, 257, 310, 314, 316, 318;
    strategy, 142–51
Koch, Charles, 52
Korean War: Eisenhower, 130;
    Truman, 113, 120, 122; war
    initiation, 75–76
Kosovo: Clinton, 77, 196, 197; war
    powers, 77
Krauthammer, Charles, 45

Kristol, Irving, 45, 46
Kristol, William, 45, 46

Lake, W. Anthony, 349
Laos: Kennedy-Johnson, 134, 135;
    Nixon, 74, 144
law enforcement instrument, defined,
    236–38
law of unintended consequences, 37
Lay, James, 310
Layne, Christopher, 187–88
Leahy, William D., 299
Lebanon: Bush 43, 206; Eisenhower,
    76, 127; Reagan, 161–62, 164, 168
Lebanon Hostage Crisis, 164
Levy, Leonard, 67
Libby, I. Lewis "Scooter," 191
liberalism: defined, 19–22, 23, 37–53;
    economic, xxv, 23; institutional,
    22; interdependence, 22; in
    international law, 23; republican,
    22; sociological, 22
libertarianism, xxvi, 52, 181
Libya: Nixon-Ford, 148; Obama, 209;
    Reagan, 9, 161, 166–67, 169
Lieberman, Joe, 50
Lincoln, Abraham, 65
Little v. Barreme, 64
Locke, John, 65
Lodge, Henry Cabot, 123

Machiavelli, Niccolo, 16
Madison, James, 33, 53, 60, 67
Madrid Conference, 193, 199
major non-NATO ally, 192, 197
major war: defined, xx–xxi;
    development policy, xxiii, 267, 279,
    339, 362; employment policy, 365; in
    strategy, 184, 185, 186
Manifest Destiny, 33, 179
Mao Zedong, 120, 143, 176

Marshall, George C., 117, 239; China, 120; secretary of defense, 120; secretary of state, 115, 117, 257, 266

Marshall, John, 63, 68

Marshall Plan, 76, 112, 249

Marx, Karl, 25

massive retaliation, 124, 131

McCain, John, 77, 80, 162, 168, 210

McCarthy, Eugene, 123

McCarthyism, 120, 128

McNamara, Robert Strange: attack on uss *Liberty*, 139; development policy, 131; Gulf of Tonkin Incident, 135; mutual assured destruction, 133; National Security Council, 318; resignation, 137; Success Offensive, 136

Mearsheimer, John, 17–20

mechanisms of power, introduced, xxiii–xxiv; U.S. Agency for International Development, 250; Defense Security Cooperation Agency, 250; U.S. Information Agency, 251–53; Arms Control and Disarmament Agency, 253–54; Department of State, 255–66; Department of Defense, 266–82; Combatant Commands, 276–81; Intelligence Community, 283–87

Mervin, David, 67, 83

Mexican-American War, 72

MIDLIFE, xxiv, 226

military instrument, 172, 297; Bush 43, 204; defined, 227–29; Eisenhower, 126; Kennedy, 140–41; Obama, 209; reform, 339, 352, 367; Truman, 113, 114

military power: Bush 41, 195; Bush 43, 207; Clinton, 202; defined, 226; evaluated, 370

Mill, John Stuart, 14, 24

missile gap, 130, 151, 159

Monroe Doctrine, 140, 179, 194

Morgenthau, Hans, 16

Mossadegh, Mohammed, 121, 125

mujahideen: Carter, 156, 157; Reagan, 160, 165, 169, 173

Muskie, Edmund, 315

mutual assured destruction, 131

Nasser, Gamal Abdul, 126, 127, 137, 138

National Economic Council, 311, 315, 332

national military strategy, 190, 194, 195

National Security Act Amendments of 1949, 302

National Security Act of 1947: Central Intelligence Agency, 249, 284; Defense Department, 267, 268; introduced, 245; Joint Chiefs of Staff, 249; legislation, 298–303; National Security Council, 292, 319

National Security Council, 296–324; Central Intelligence Agency, 283; Defense Department, 270, 271, 295; functions, 304–5; national security assistants, 309–11; organization, 305–8; process, 308–9; reform, 347; role of, 248, 292; staff, 311–12; State Department, 241, 256, 266, 289, 293; U.S. Information Agency, 251, 252

national security strategy, reform, 220, 330–31, 340–41, 349

national security strategy, meaning of: defined, 89–90; evaluated, 90–91, 171; expressed, 91–94; formulated, xx, 95–101, 221

national security strategy, post-Cold War. *See* collective security strategy; cooperative security strategy; homeland defense strategy; offshore balancing

strategy; primacy strategy;
selective engagement strategy
national security strategy by
administration: Bush 41, 190–95;
Bush 43, 202–8; Carter, 151–58;
Clinton, 195–202; Eisenhower,
123–30; Kennedy-Johnson, 131–41;
Nixon-Ford, 142–51; Reagan, 159–70;
Obama, 208–13; Truman, 115–23
nation building, 236, 246; Bush 43,
202, 203, 217, 265; Clinton, 197, 204,
217, 319; Kennedy-Johnson, 135;
mechanisms, 236, 279, 282, 292;
Obama, 209, 212; reform, 328, 363,
365, 368, 369; in strategy, 216, 246.
See also capacity building
Netanyahu, Benjamin, 200
Neuhaus, Richard John, 46–47
New Right, 47, 52, 160, 190
New START, 209
Ngo Dinh Diem, 128–29, 135, 176
Nguyen Khanh, 135
Nguyen Van Thieu, 135, 144–45, 150
Nicaragua: Carter, 157, 158; Reagan, 164
9/11 Commission, 333–38
Ninkovich, Frank, 21
Nitze, Paul: Kennedy, 131; primacy
strategy, 180; Reagan, 159; strategy,
112–14; Truman, 115, 119, 122
Nixon, Richard Milhous: abuses,
69, 70, 71; China, 91, 143, 174;
liberalism, 52; National Security
Council, 314; strategy, 90, 142–51,
169; war powers, 66, 73, 78
noninterference: Bush 43, 203;
Clinton, 196; defined, 15;
Eisenhower-Taft, 123; Kant, 27, 32;
realism, 17; in strategy, 30, 96, 97
Noriega, Manuel, 164, 192
North Korea: Clinton, 197; Truman,
75, 135

North-South debate, xxii, 118, 132
North Vietnamese Army, 150
Novak, Michael, 46
Nunn, Sam, 50
Nunn-Cohen Amendment, 289, 358

Obama, Barack H.: National Security
Council, 311, 316; strategy, 90,
208–12, 218, 366
offensive power, 19. *See also*
balancing power; defensive
power; preponderant power
offset strategy, 107, 170
offshore balancing strategy: critique,
189; defined, 187–88
Ogaden War, 153
"one China policy," 143
Oslo Accords, 200
overstretch, 18, 181

Pakistan: Carter, 156; Eisenhower, 129;
Reagan, 165
Palestinian Liberation Front, 167, 217
Palestinian Liberation Organization,
137, 162
Panama: Bush 41, 192–93, 194, 195;
Carter, 157, 158; Reagan, 164
Pan-Arabism, 127
Panetta, Leon, 211
paramilitary forces, 205, 206, 209,
329, 337
Paris Peace Accords, 144, 146, 150
parties, political, 53–56
Pascual, Carlos, 265, 295
past actions theory, 93
Patriot Act, 289, 333
Perez, Shimon, 200
perimeter defense, 113, 124, 132, 172.
See also global defense; strongpoint
defense
Perry, William, 197

Persian Gulf: Bush 41, 158, 193; Carter, 156–57, 158, 276; Nixon, 142; Reagan, 157, 159, 276

Pinochet, Augusto, 148

Plato, 19

plausible deniability, 117, 133

Podhoretz, Norman, 45–46

Point Four Program, 118, 172

Poland, Reagan, 167, 168

Polk, James, 71

Popular Front for the Liberation of Palestine, 217

Powell, Colin: chairman, Joint Chiefs of Staff, 190–91, 194, 195, 315; national security assistant, 315; secretary of state, 257, 265, 315, 355

Powell Doctrine, 163, 195

power. *See* balancing power; defensive power; hard power; offensive power; preponderant power; smart power; soft power

power over opinion: and soft power, 227; Bush 41, 195; Bush 43, 207, 208; Clinton, 202; defined, 226; evaluated, 230, 235, 242, 370; Obama, 209, 213

Powers, Francis Gary, 129, 272

pragmatism, 49, 52

preemptive strike, 11

preemptive war, 138; Clinton, 197; defined, 9, 10

preponderant power, 19, 187–88, 243; Nixon-Ford, 142; in strategy, 179, 180, 185; Truman, 119, 122. *See also* balancing power; defensive power; offensive power

Press, Daryl, 94

preventive war: and just war, 6; Clinton, 197; cooperative security strategy, 185, 189; defined, 9–10; Eisenhower, 11; Kant, 26; neocons,

45; Nitze, 119; primacy strategy, 189; reform, 350; Truman, 10

primacy strategy: Bush 41, 191, 194; Bush 43, 202–3, 367; Clinton, 196; critique, 188–89, 352; defined, xxiii, 179–81

Princeton Project on National Security, 349–52

principles of international relations. *See* indivisibility of peace; noninterference; security dilemma; self-determination; territorial sovereignty; universalism

Project for the New American Century, 46

Project on National Security Reform, 342–49

Project Solarium, 123

Rabin, Yitzhak, 193, 200

rationalism, 20, 38

Reagan, Ronald, 159–70, 173; abuses, 71; Afghanistan, 165; Libya, 169; National Security Council, 314–15, 317; strategy, 90, 172

Reagan Corollary, 159

Reagan Doctrine, 160

realism: balancing, 19; defensive, 19, 179, 181, 186; defined, 12–16, 16–19, 20, 23; in international law, 23; offensive, 19, 186, 188, 243, 366; in strategy, 96

reconnaissance strike complex, 183, 201, 368

reforms. *See* 9/11 Commission; Beyond Goldwater-Nichols; Contract with America; Goldwater-Nichols DOD Reorganization Act of 1986; Hart-Rudman Commission; Hoover Commission; National Security Act of 1947; Princeton Project on National Security;

Project on National Security Reform; Reinventing Government; Task Force on State Department Reform

Reinventing Government, 249

Ricardo, David, 22, 25

Rice, Condoleezza: national security assistant, 316, 318; secretary of state, 207, 257, 355; strategy, 202–3

Robertson, Marion G., 48, 49

Rogers, William, 146, 257, 314

rollback: Eisenhower, 123, 127; Kennedy, 132; Nitze, 110, 114; Reagan, 159–60; Truman, 119, 122

Roosevelt, Franklin, 65, 299–300

Roosevelt, Theodore, 54, 82, 240, 285

Roosevelt Corollary, 140

Rumsfeld, Donald: Afghanistan, 205; development policy, 280; employment policy, 280–81; Iraq, 206; National Security Council, 318; Reagan, 161; reform, 265, 271, 294

Rushdoony, Rousas, 47, 48

Rusk, Dean, 257

Russell, Bertrand, 14

Russia, 122

Rwanda, Clinton, 197

Sandinistas, 157, 160, 164

Savimbi, Jonas, 173, 198

Schelling, Thomas, 8

Scheurer, Michael, 217

Schlafly, Phyllis, 47

Schlesinger, Arthur, 66, 155

Scowcroft, Brent, 310, 315, 318

Scowcroft Commission, 168

security dilemma: balance of power, 18; defined, 14; institutionalism, 21

security guarantee, 102, 103, 188; Eastern Europe, 202; Iran, 350; Israel, 193

selective engagement strategy: Bush 41, 190, 194–95; Bush 43, 202–3; Clinton, 196; critique, 189, 352; defined, xxiii, 179, 185–87

self-determination, 127, 168; defined, 14, 32; in strategy, 96, 97, 98

Serbia, 77

Shamir, Yitzhak, 193

Shultz, George, 165

Sinai, 138–39

Sinatra Doctrine, 168

Situation Room, 320

Six-Day War. *See* Arab-Israeli War: 3rd (1967)

small war: defined, xix–xxi; development policy, xxiii, 228, 269, 339, 362, 368; employment policy, xxvii, 236, 269, 365; in strategy, 369

smart power, 227

Smith, Adam, 24

Smith, Walter Bedell "Beetle," 121

soft power, xxiv, 227, 343, 350

Somalia: Bush 41, 194, 195; Carter, 153; Clinton, 80, 198; Obama, 209

Somoza Debayle, Anastasio, 121, 157

Southeast Asia, 73, 78, 135, 143, 173

South Korea, 92

Southwest Asia, Clinton, 201

Soviet Union, dissolution of, 173–74, 197, 364

Spanish-American War, 72, 235

Stalin, Joseph, 123, 125, 174

Stockwell, John, 149, 153

Strategic Defense Initiative, 160–61, 167

Strategic Offensive Reductions Treaty, 204

strategy, containment. *See* containment strategy; offset strategy

strategy, national security, by administration. *See* national security strategy by administration

strategy, post-9/11: al-Qaeda
strategy to 2020, 215–16; U.S.
counterterrorism strategy, 216–17
Strauss, Leo, 45
strongpoint defense, 111, 113, 172. *See also* global defense; perimeter
defense
Success Offensive, 136
Suez Crisis, 124, 126, 138
Sun Tzu, 16
Sutherland, George, 68

Taft, Robert A., 123, 285
Talbot v. Seeman, 63
Tanzania, under Clinton, 196
Task Force on State Department
Reform, 352–55
Taylor, Maxwell, 131
Taymiyya, Ibn, 214
territorial sovereignty: defined, 15;
realism, 17, 18; in strategy, 30, 96,
97, 194; vindicationism, 32
terrorism: al-Qaeda, 213–15, 334;
Bush 43, 204, 205; Clinton, 200;
mechanisms, 254, 262, 264, 280,
286; Obama, 209; Reagan, 159,
166–67, 168; in strategy, 175, 221
Tet Offensive, 136, 144
Thatcher, Margaret, 163, 168, 173
theories. *See* current calculus theory;
democracy theory; democratic
peace theory; domino theory; just
war theory; past actions theory
Thucydides, 16, 17, 32
Thurman, Strom, 54
Tito, Marshal, 174
totalitarianism: defined, 42–43;
Kirkpatrick, 160, 173; Truman,
112, 174
Tower, John, 315
Tower Commission, 306, 315, 355

Trujillo Molina, Rafael Leonidas,
134
Truman, Harry S: Korea, 75; National
Security Council, 297, 300, 313;
preventive war, 10; reform, 245;
strategy, 90, 115–23; war powers,
66, 69, 76
Truman Doctrine, 116, 172
Tyler, John, 71

Ukraine, Obama, 211
undifferentiated interests, 174
undifferentiated threat, 90
universalism: defined, 14; in
international law, 23; in strategy,
30, 97
universal monarchy, 18, 32
U.S. Agency for International
Development, 234, 237, 250
uses of force, 8–9, 71–78
U.S. Information Agency, 230, 249,
251–53
uss *Cole*, 200, 214, 287
uss *Liberty*, 139
uss *Maddox*, 73
U.S. v. Belmont, 68–69
U.S. v. Curtiss-Wright, 68–69
U.S. v. Pink, 68

Vance, Cyrus: Africa, 153; and
Brzezinski, 152, 314, 318; arms
control, 253; strategy, 155
Vatell, Emer de, 5
Vidal, Gore, 29
Viet Minh, 116
Vietnam: Nixon, 143; in strategy, 180
Vietnam War: Ford, 150; Johnson,
314; just war, 7; Kennedy-Johnson,
73, 135–37, 140, 171; Nixon, 142,
143–46, 151; Nixon-Ford, 150; war
powers, 73

vindicationism, 33, 34, 98, 180; defined, 32. *See also* exceptionalism; exemplarism; exemptionalism

von Bismarck, Otto, 16

von Clausewitz, Carl, 16

Von Drehle, David, 54

Vo Nguyen Giap, 116

Wallace, George, 54

Wallis, Jim, 7, 50

Waltz, Kenneth, 3

Walzer, Michael, 5

war: general, 63, 119, 123; imperfect, 63; limited, 63; perfect, 63; total, 7, 21, 25. *See also* major war; small war

war, causes of, 3–4

war, initiation, 9–12

war initiation. *See* defensive war; preemptive war; preventive war; war of aggression; war of choice; war of discretion

war of aggression, 12

war of choice, 12

war of discretion, 12

War Powers Resolution, 59, 78–84

Washington, George, 33, 53, 58, 65

weapons of mass destruction: Bush 41, 191, 192; Bush 43, 203; cooperative

security strategy, 184, 185; deterrence, 180; homeland defense strategy, 181; mechanisms, 240, 273; prevention, 9, 11; selective engagement strategy, 185. *See also* arms control

Weigel, George, 46

Weinberger, Casper "Cap," 163, 314

Weinberger Doctrine, 163

West Bank, 125, 137, 138–39

Westmoreland, William Childs, 136–37

Weyrich, Paul, 52

Wilson, Woodrow, 14, 16, 21, 34, 35

Wolfowitz, Paul, 191

year of maximum danger, 119

Yemen: attack on the uss *Cole*, 287; drone attacks in, 209

Yom Kippur War. *See* Arab-Israeli War: 4th (1973)

Yoo, John, 67

Youngstown Sheet & Tube Co. v. Sawyer, 69, 76

Yugoslavia: Clinton, 77, 197; Truman, 174

Zhou Enlai, 143, 145

Zia-al-Huq, Muhammed, 156, 165

OTHER WORKS BY D. ROBERT WORLEY

Shaping U.S. Military Forces: Revolution or Relevance in a Post–Cold War World

.

CPSIA information can be obtained at www.ICGtesting.com
Printed in the USA
LVOW07s0802280216

476983LV00001B/11/P